THE NANTUCKET WEATHER BOOK

THE
NANTUCKET
WEATHER BOOK

David M. Ludlum

Historic Nantucket Press
Nantucket, Massachusetts

To
Rita Manion Ludlum
My constant companion in research and in life

LIBRARY OF CONGRESS CATALOGING IN PUBLICATION DATA

LUDLUM, DAVID McWILLIAMS, 1910-
THE NANTUCKET WEATHER BOOK
1. NANTUCKET-CLIMATE. I. TITLE.

ISBN-0-9607340-4-X

PRINTED IN BOSTON BY THE NIMROD PRESS
EDITED BY LESLEY FARLOW
DESIGNED BY BRUCE COURSON

Contents

Foreword

The Sea! The Sea!   What with seas and storms, Nantucket has almost been washed away! During the past month Boreas has raged so horribly around us that the tides have been higher than at any time within the period of fifty years. Consequently great inroads have been made upon our sand bank in different parts of the island, though, fortunately, what is taken from one part of it is only carried to another. However, at Siasconset, such was the run upon the bank there, that it has become necessary to remove the houses which stood upon it to a greater distance from the margin; and that interesting hamlet has now lost forever that very spot no doubt faithfully chronicled in the memory of many a loving pair, where their first vows of affection were to each other plighted! Mr. Franklin Folger, it is said, was carried down the avalanche, and was, with much difficulty, rescued from his perilous situation. A passage has been cut through Brant Point and Smith's Point, where the stump of a very large tree was laid bare, having probably been imbedded there for many years. What will become of us?

Nantucket Inquirer, January 17, 1840.

Acknowledgments

In its final form, a book is a cooperative composition in the true sense of the phrase. Though the original inspiration resides in and the initial perspiration is expended by one person, the work ultimately is the product of many minds and efforts. When the author delivers his manuscript to the publisher, he is immediately elevated from the presidency of the project to serving an advisory capacity as chairman of the board. Though he may be consulted frequently on major matters, the decisions are now made by others who coordinate the activities of a variety of workers, from copy editors to salespeople. The final product is a composite of efforts, and I wish to acknowledge the assistance of the following in particular:

Lesley Farlow of New York City and Nantucket for skillful and pleasant editorial acumen.

Edouard Stackpole, Louise Hussey, and Peter MacGlashan of the Nantucket Historical Association for research assistance.

John Welch and Bruce Courson of the Nantucket Historical Association for editorial guidance.

Bruce Courson and Lucy Bixby for design and production.

Barbara Andrews and staff of the Nantucket Atheneum for facilitating research in microfilm files.

Drs. Emilia Belserene, M. Jane Stroup, and Dorritt Hoffleit of the Maria Mitchell Association for guidance in astronomical matters.

The late Eric Sloane once my associate in *Weatherwise* magazine, for the reproduction of four weather murals which appeared long ago in the *Amateur Weatherman's Almanac*

Merle Orleans, Charles Sayle, and Tom Giffin of the *Inquirer and Mirror* for their instructive weekly comments on current weather.

The Astronomical Data Service of Colorado Springs, CO for solar calculations of Nantucket.

The staff of the Firestone Library of Princeton University for making available much background historical material.

James and Curtis Clark of Princeton and Siasconset for comfortable shelter when on the Island.

Rita M. Ludlum for many eye-weary hours of researching Nantucket history in the microfilm files of the *Inquirer and Mirror*.

The Katherine Ann Ludlum Fund, a memorial to our daughter, for facilitating the publication of this book.

All the Nantucket weathermen of the past whose daily devotion to duty provided the basic material for the Island's weather drama.

David M. Ludlum
Princeton, New Jersey
January 22, 1986

Part One:
A Nantucket Weather and Sky Almanac

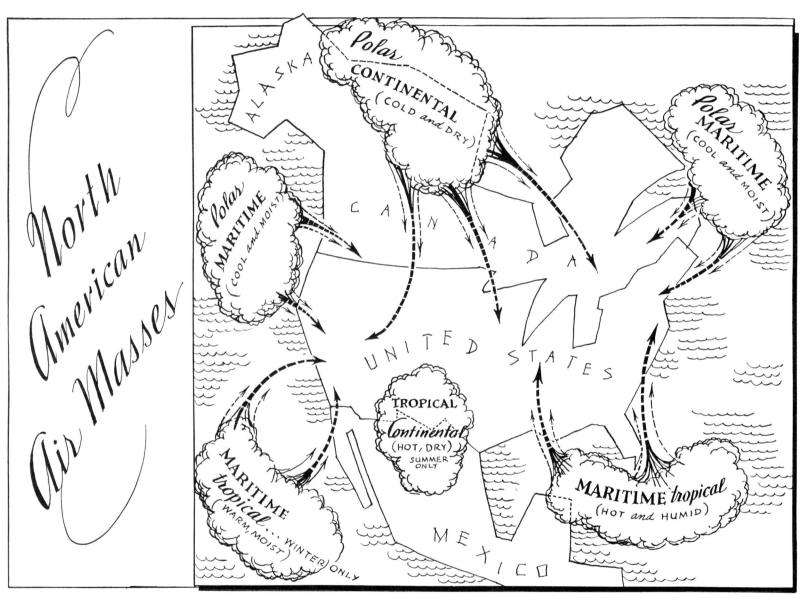

North American Air Masses

Polar CONTINENTAL (COLD and DRY)

Polar MARITIME (COOL and MOIST)

Polar MARITIME (COOL and MOIST)

TROPICAL Continental (HOT, DRY) SUMMER ONLY

MARITIME tropical (WARM, MOIST) WINTER ONLY

MARITIME tropical (HOT and HUMID)

ALASKA

CANADA

UNITED STATES

MEXICO

Air masses are constituent parts of the atmosphere whose compositions differ according to the region of their origin. When a large body of air remains over a portion of the ocean or land for several days, it acquires the weather characteristics of that region and at different levels aloft becomes homogeneous. Air masses are set in motion by the dynamics of air flow around the globe. They carry the weather of the source region to lands several thousand miles distant, though in modified form.

Illustration by Eric Sloane.

THE ATMOSPHERIC GEOGRAPHY OF NANTUCKET

If a Martian landed on Federal Street and asked for information about Nantucket's weather, he might be directed either to the nearby Atheneum or to the library of the Nantucket Historical Association to read this book. Upon finishing his perusal, he might conclude that the island was a very stormy and inclement place indeed, with terrific hurricanes, mighty snowstorms, severe cold waves, ice embargoes, dank fogginess, and much minor meteorological unpleasantness.

A local resident, however, would inform him that these are the exceptions and that Nantucket enjoys many pleasant days in every season. In fact, the long-term record shows that the sun shines about 66 percent of the time year-round, and in September the figure rises to 86 percent of the possible hours. Rain falls on only 32 percent of the 365 days, and in September it drops to only 10 percent. The wind averages 13.2 miles per hour, which insures a freshness to the atmosphere. Air pollution and smog from the mainland are at a minimum. Snow does fall but melts quickly. Hurricanes strike from decade to decade, but the topography of the island lessens their damaging effect. Tornadoes are only a very minor threat. Ocean breezes temper heat waves. The number of people who choose to spend their vacations on the island from Easter through Christmas vouches for the general affability of the climate.

Insularity—a single word describes the principal factor controlling the behavior of the atmosphere over Nantucket. Water, water everywhere—it lies in all directions, and this is what makes the island's climate unique. Nantucketers are always talking about their daily weather and boast of its difference from that experienced on the "continent" only thirty miles distant. Airstreams—cold and warm, wet and dry—coming from distant regions with different characteristics receive a final conditioning of their elements over the local waters surrounding the island's approximately forty-five square miles. Ever since the end of the Ice Age some 12,000 years ago, the shifting winds, unceasing waves, and changing weather patterns have been transforming the topography of the sandy island outpost and have directly influenced the daily activities of the residents.

Nantucket's daily weather results from the struggle of four directional forces for control of the air space over the island. Clashes take place overhead between airstreams coming from the continent and from the ocean, as well as from the polar regions to the north and tropical regions to the south.

Once part of the terminal moraine of the great North American glacier, Nantucket now occupies an eastern extension of the North American landmass. To the west along the 41° parallel lie about three thousand miles of dry land extending all the way to the Pacific Ocean, and to the east about three thousand miles across the Atlantic Ocean lie Spain and Portugal. In the other dimension, Nantucket, sitting astride the 70°W meridian, is located some 1500 miles north of the point where the Tropic of Cancer passes through the southern Bahama Islands, and some 1700 miles south of the point where the Arctic Circle crosses Baffin Island.

From the quadrant of the compass extending west through north, airstreams have only a short trajectory over Nantucket Sound; nevertheless, the overwater passage has an effect on the thermal and moisture content of the wind-borne air moving off the continent. From the other three quadrants of the compass rose—north through east to south and around to west—the airstreams arrive after passages of varying length over the ocean surfaces of greatly differing temperature conditions. Airstreams arriving from the northeast, for example, must travel over the cold Labrador current. When coming from the east, they must pass over the more temperate North Atlantic Ocean, from the southeast and south, over the warm waters of the Gulf Stream, and from the southwest, over the hot, humid surface of the Gulf of Mexico.

In addition to Nantucket's fixed position about halfway between the equator and the north pole, another factor of prime importance in determining the nature of Nantucket's climate is the changing altitude of the sun. It varies at noontime throughout the year from only 26°17′ above the southern horizon at the winter solstice to a high of 73°26′ at the summer solstice. This results in a ratio of 1 to 4.5 in the receipt of solar energy between the low point in the month of December to the high point in the month of June. As a result of the thermal lag in the seasons, largely induced by the action of the ocean in giving up its heat and cooling more slowly than land surfaces, the extremes in mean temperature on Nantucket do not occur until early February (31°) and until late July (69°). The absolute extremes in temperature also follow this pattern with the coldest ever registered coming on February 5 and the warmest on August 2.

Nantucket's location enables it to serve as a strategic vantage point for checking the progress of coastal storms as they move northeast along the Atlantic seaboard. Their strength and direction of movement can be measured, yielding vital information for coastal dwellers and marine interests. In addition, the dynamics of airstreams sweeping off the continent can be assessed from the island in order to determine their influence on trans-Atlantic maritime and air travel. Accordingly, a government weather observation station with cable connections to the continent was established on Nantucket in 1886. The one hundred years of daily records now collected affords an insight into the weather regime of this unique location and an opportunity to determine the normals and extremes of the island's weather.

The General Circulation of the Atmosphere over Nantucket

The dominant feature of the atmospheric circulation over North America is a vast circumpolar movement of air whirling in broad streams from west to east over the middle latitudes of the globe. This has traditionally been known as the "prevailing westerlies," but meteorologists now prefer the designation of "westerly airstream." Migrating north and south with the seasons and waxing and waning periodically in strength, it controls most of the atmospheric traffic during the year from the Arctic Circle to the tropical seas bordering southern United States.

The westerly airstream is made up of contributions from many different source regions. As the waves in its flow undulate across ocean and continent, they entrain reservoirs of air resident along its borders, both to the north and to the south. For awhile these injections of homogeneous air dominate a particular section of the flow until later a mixing with air from other source regions alters its original characteristics of temperature and moisture content.

The air content of these reservoirs is known as an airmass and consists of a large expanse of the atmosphere possessing generally similar qualities of heat, moisture, and stability. They have been likened to atmospheric oceans. At equal elevations above the surface of the earth are found nearly identical temperatures, humidities, and cloud conditions throughout the airmass. Over certain regions of our hemisphere, such as the frozen tundras of northern Canada, the vast stretches of the Atlantic and Pacific oceans, and the tropical waters of the Gulf of Mexico and Caribbean Sea, the air tends to stagnate for days at a time. Like giant air conditioners, the surfaces of these regions impart their native characteristics of temperature and humidity to the air above and airmasses of generally uniform conditions are created. The source region can usually be identified on a weather map by the persistence of a high pressure area or anticyclone for several days in a row.

While resting for many days in the source regions undisturbed, the lower layers of the air continue to acquire more of the general properties of heat and moisture of the land or water surface beneath and tend to become homogeneous in lateral extent. This conditioning process continues until the dynamics of the atmospheric circulation, the ebb and flow of pressure areas, causes the airmass to be set in motion and become an airstream entering the general westerly flow.

During its journey the characteristics of an airstream may undergo modification either from the type of terrain over which it is passing—land or water, snow-covered or bare, hilly or flat—or from the contact and mixing with other airstreams from different source regions. If the trajectory from its source to Nantucket is relatively short and the terrain fairly uniform, the airstream will arrive with most of its native properties remaining; if coming from a long distance and traveling over diverse country, it will be modified considerably. The origin of an airstream and the history of its journey are important factors in determining the type of weather Nantucket will experience.

The Jet Stream

The most spectacular aspect of the westerly airstream is exhibited in narrow zones of maximum speed, aptly called jet streams. They may be likened to swift currents in the middle of a river racing through a more placid, slower flow. The principal jet stream circles the greater part of the Northern Hemisphere in a mean position between $30°$N and $40°$N. On occasion it may stray a considerable distance north or south of its normal position and exhibit an undulating motion with large surges northward and dips southward in its fast travel over continent and ocean. The greatest development of the jet stream occurs above 25,000 feet where speeds are normally in the 80 to 100 miles per hour range, but can reach as high as 200 miles per hour or more.

The jet stream is a thermal product deriving its great dynamic energy from the temperature difference between warm air rising northward out of the tropics and cold air descending southward from the polar regions. The clash of contrasting airstreams is what gives the jet stream its tremendous energy. The importance of the jet is its role in generating cyclonic storm systems directly under its flow and guiding them in their subsequent move around the global weather map. Storms usually generate to the north of the core of the jet and are steered eastward in accord with its ever-varying flow.

Travelling Cyclones and Anticyclones

The most striking feature of the daily surface weather map is the succession of high pressure and low pressure areas moving alternately in a steady procession across the continent. These are designated anticyclones and cyclones by the meteorologist; winds in an anticyclone circulate in a clockwise direction, and in a cyclone in the opposite counterclockwise direction. In more popular terms, they are called "highs" and "lows," in reference to the relative height of the barometer at their centers. Though varying greatly in surface configurations, the migrating systems usually have centers enclosed by contours representing lines of equal barometric pressure, called isobars.

Anticyclones and cyclones extend upward to considerable heights. On charts of upper-air flow they appear as ridges of high pressure and troughs of low pressure. Sometimes they have distinct centers aloft surrounded by closed isobars and their own circulation imbedded in the upper-air flow; other times their isobars are open-ended, being appendages of more permanent pressure systems to the north for low pressure troughs and to the south for high pressure ridges.

Anticyclonic and cyclonic circulatory systems are essentially eddies of various sizes imbedded in the general circumpolar whirl moving from west to east around the globe.

Migrating anticyclones may be as large as 1500 miles across and extend vertically to four or five miles. Cyclones, on the other hand, tend to be somewhat smaller in lateral breadth, some 500 to 800 miles being an average; but if well-developed, a cyclonic circulation may extend vertically to the tropopause, the boundary between the lower atmosphere where the weather takes place and the stratosphere where iso-thermal conditions prevail, usually found at an altitude of six to eight miles in the temperate zones.

Cyclones and anticyclones differ in the dynamics of their internal circulations. The winds moving around a cyclonic center tend to converge toward a central core, circling in a counterclockwise direction, always moving inward and crowding air particles together. The only outlet is upwards. The rising air cools as it ascends and eventually reaches its dew point when moisture condenses into solid droplets to form clouds. Overcast, wet weather usually ensues, and a storm system may develop.

Anticyclones, on the other hand, exhibit a clockwise circulation with air particles descending and spreading out in a diverging pattern. The descending air column is warmed dynamically in this process and its dew point lowered. This enables the air to hold additional moisture in the invisible, gaseous state and to inhibit the formation of cloud and precipitation. Dry, fair weather usually accompanies.

Cold Fronts

Since the cold front generates the most spectacular action in a cyclonic storm, it is the feature of the weather map that must be kept under constant watch by the forecaster in order to time the coming weather sequences. The arrival of a cold front in an area not only causes turbulent conditions, but also introduces a complete change of airmass and brings different temperature and humidity conditions. The cold front's passage signals

the concluding phase of cyclonic control and the introduction of anticyclonic dominance over the local weather.

The cold front is the leading edge of a cool or cold airmass that is actively on the move. The front's dynamic energy is furnished by the dense cold air of a high pressure system, usually consisting of fresh polar air from central Canada or, less frequently, of North Pacific air greatly modified by its transcontinental journey.

The approach of a cold front is often hard to discern since it may be imbedded in an extensive cloud sheet in which precipitation is occurring. Winds from a southerly quadrant

with warming usually precede a cold front and their speed increases with the nearing of the front. A distinct shift of wind direction occurs with the cold front passage and the barometer rises rather abruptly.

No two cold fronts have the same structures or behave in the same manner. Some are fast-moving; others are sluggish and may even become stationary. Some may slope steeply to considerable heights; others are shallow with gradual slopes. The characteristics of an individual cold front may vary from day to day, and even from hour to hour. Their different structures produce different types of weather.

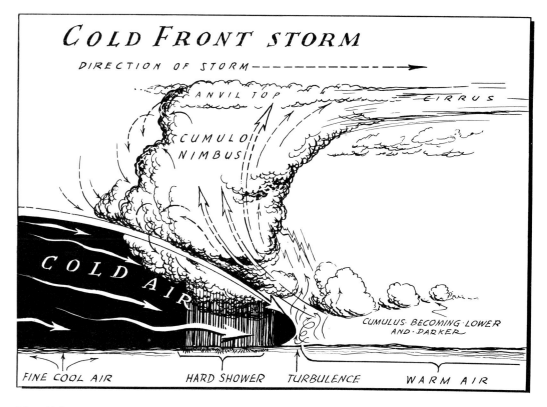

The cold front is the leading edge of a polar air mass that is actively on the move. The air behind the front is usually from Canada or the North Pacific Ocean. The advancing cold air displaces either tropical air or old, *modified polar air. Turbulence, rain or snow showers, and sharp drops in temperature usually announce the arrival of a cold front.*

Illustration by Eric Sloane.

Warm Fronts

The approach of a warm front is a more subtle performance, with weather changes coming more gradually than with a bustling cold front. A warm front heralds the end of settled, anticyclonic conditions, and the beginning of a period of cyclonic activity with cloudiness and precipitation prevailing. The forecaster must take heed when a warm front is charted to the south or southwest of his area, for change is in the offing.

A warm front is the leading edge of an advancing mass of warm air that is displacing a cooler or colder airmass. Since warm air is lighter than cold air, it tends to glide up over the wedge of cold air hugging the surface. While the upper strata of the warm air speed ahead two or three hundred miles, the main body of the warm air continues to advance along the surface at a much slower pace.

The first sign of an approaching warm front appears on the southwest to northwest horizon in the form of cirrus cloud streamers at elevations of five or six miles or more. These climb to the zenith and in a couple of hours may cover the entire sky. The frozen ice crystals aloft that compose cirrus clouds indicate the arrival of moist air overhead.

Sometimes they cause interesting solar or lunar haloes. The cloud sheet gradually thickens and lowers, and clouds at middle levels appear in a few hours, and then at low levels with the initiation of precipitation.

With the approach of a warm front, winds tend to shift from an easterly direction, to southeast and south. The barometer drops gradually until the passage of the surface front and then may remain steady or become unsteady with small rises and falls.

Warm fronts are the principal rain producers for the New England coastal region during the colder months of the year. They form an integral part of a coastal storm moving from the southwest and draw on the moisture of the North Atlantic to give the region an occasional dousing of an inch or more of rain. Since their behavior does not always follow the textbook description, timing the onset and judging the amount of precipitation are quite difficult.

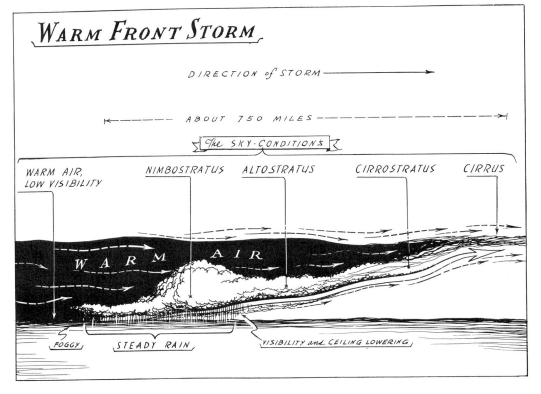

A warm front is the leading edge of a forward-moving warm air mass that is displacing a cooler air mass. Usually of tropical origin, the warm air glides up over the polar air at the surface. The wedge of warm air aloft often extends two to three hundred miles. This causes extensive cloudiness and steady precipitation to fall over a wide area.
Illustration by Eric Sloane.

Storm Generation Regions

In three broad regions of North America contrasting airmasses meet regularly and frequently generate storms. The Gulf of Alaska is the home of the semi-permanent Aleutian low pressure area, where cold airstreams from Siberia, Alaska, and Canada mingle with warm air flowing northward from the vast Pacific high pressure area. The Gulf of Alaska has been called the "greatest storm factory of the world" where cyclonic activity is most frequent and extremely vigorous. Storm systems generating in the Gulf of Alaska regularly batter the Pacific coasts of Canada and the United States from October to April. Cyclogenesis is the meteorologist's word for storm formation.

The second region, an extension of the Aleutian low pressure area, runs eastward through British Columbia and southeast along the crest of the Rocky Mountains into the United States. It marks the meeting place of cold, dry air from central Canada and mild, moist air from the Pacific Ocean. New storm circulations may form at any place along this extensive frontal zone, or weakened disturbances from the Pacific Ocean, having survived a passage over the Pacific mountains and the Intermountain region, may regenerate into active storm systems. Eastern Alberta in the north, and eastern Colorado in the south, in the lee of the Rocky Mountains, are the sites of most frequent cyclogenesis in the colder months of the year.

A third storm-generating region extends in a sweeping arc from northwest Texas, southeast across the central Gulf of Mexico to north Florida, and then northeast to the Atlantic waters off Georgia and the Carolinas. Tropical air originating over the Gulf of Mexico, the Caribbean Sea, and the tropical North Atlantic often lies poised here ready to challenge the southward-moving outbreaks of polar air; in the process, cyclonic storms are born along the meeting places of these contrasting airmasses. In the colder months of the year, the Gulf of Mexico and the coastal waters off Florida, Georgia, and the Carolinas are important breeding areas for Nantucket storms. Within the space of forty-eight hours, a cyclonic center may form here and race northeast along the coast and burst onto the latitude of Nantucket!

Storm Tracks

From the three main regions of cyclogenesis, storm centers tend to follow well-defined channels on their way to affect Nantucket's weather. The chart on page 6 marks their average paths. Except for storms in tropical latitudes during the summer months, all have an eastward component, and most in their latter stages exhibit a northeasterly trend. Occupying a geographic position near the northeast extremity of the country, Nantucket seems to serve as a storm mecca, drawing a majority of the country's disturbances toward its shores.

The storm track followed most frequently at all seasons leads from the Canadian Northwest in a southeasterly direction to a position near the Great Lakes and then heads northeast to follow the St. Lawrence stormway over the Atlantic Provinces of Canada to the Atlantic Ocean. Storm centers that follow this track are called Alberta lows since they first appear on weather maps in that prairie province in the lee of the Rocky Mountains. They may be regenerations of Pacific Ocean storms which have lost their organization in passing over the high British Columbia mountains, or they may be new disturbances formed by the clashing of maritime and continental airstreams over the Great Divide.

In summer, Alberta lows take a more northerly track across southern Hudson Bay and eastward across Labrador, but often their trailing fronts reach well into the United States and influence New England weather conditions. In wintertime, the storm centers dip well to the southeast and cross the lower Great Lakes, their low-pressure troughs reaching southward to the Gulf of Mexico. Nantucket usually experiences the influence of Alberta lows as they follow either route. Since storm centers are usually fast movers, the precipitation periods are generally brief and may occur only as the cold front passes. At this time, southerly winds on the island shift rather abruptly into the northwest and cold airstreams arrive on the scene.

Another source region, active at all seasons except summer, lies on the western Great Plains in the lee of the Rocky Mountains. Storm centers that organize in this region usually form in eastern Colorado and hence are known as Colorado lows. These may be storms from the Pacific Ocean that have become disorganized in passing over the mountains and high plateaus, and then regenerate under the favorable circumstances found east of the Rockies. They may also be new centers generated from atmospheric impulses in the upper air which cause surface airstreams of different characteristics to clash and to institute cyclonic circulations. Colorado lows usually track to the northeast toward the Great Lakes and often develop intense cyclonic centers, drawing tropical air from the Gulf of Mexico ahead of them and arctic air from Canada into the rear of the circulation.

Under favorable circumstances when the storm is over Lake Erie and Lake Ontario, a secondary center may develop over Virginia, the Carolinas, or the offshore waters near Cape Hatteras. The new and often more vigorous center moves northeast with a warm front extending over the Atlantic Ocean to the east. As the front approaches Nantucket, the clouds thicken and a canopy of moderate to heavy rain arrives, with a good probability of snow in winter. With the arrival of the cold front from the west, intense showers of brief duration may occur, followed by rapid clearing.

Storm centers generating in the third region of cyclogenesis are known as Texas or West Gulf lows, according to their place of origin. Fresh polar air and mature tropical air often clash in this region and result in the speedy formation of active storm centers, especially in winter and early spring. The resultant action centers drive northeast to New England, hugging either slope of the Appalachian Mountains. If the disturbance remains west of the crest of the mountains, it will pass over Lakes Erie and Ontario and down the St. Lawrence stormway. This gives Nantucket a storm period of several hours. If the track lies to the east of the Appalachians, the center may pass over coastal New England or the immediate offshore waters, producing a variety of precipitation, usually of moderate to heavy intensity. The exact path determines whether Nantucket will get rain or snow, or a combination of both.

The eastern extension of the southern storm-generating region lies over the eastern Gulf of Mexico and the waters off the southeast coast from northern Florida to the Carolinas. In winter especially, new storms may form in the southern end of a long north-south trough of low pressure over the relatively warm waters of the region. These quickly intensify with swiftly falling pressure

Storm centers are born in areas where air masses of different types come into energetic contact. This usually takes place along the polar front marking the meeting place of polar and tropical air. Several areas in North America serve as places where air masses regularly meet and storm systems generate. In accordance with the season of the year, the storm centers generally follow regular tracks from west to east across the country. Illustration by Eric Sloane.

at the center and rapidly increasing wind circulation. They usually track close to, but east of, Cape Hatteras and head northeast in the direction of the offshore waters of Cape Cod and the Islands. They are known as coastal storms and may be northeasters or southeasters according to the path they take with respect to the Nantucket observer.

A cyclonic disturbance passing over or near Nantucket may entrain several airstreams successively into its circulatory system. A storm approaching from the southwest may first induce a northeast flow of cool, damp air. If the center passes to the west of Nantucket over southeast New England, it will cause a "warming storm" on the island. Winds veering to southeast and south will draw in air that has been warmed over the Gulf Stream. As the center approaches the latitude of Nantucket, winds will veer farther into the southwest and bring even warmer tropical air to the scene. If the barometric gradient across the storm's low pressure trough is steep, winds may increase to fresh or strong or even to gale force as a southwester rages.

After the storm center has moved on to the north, a cold front from the west or northwest usually sweeps across the island with the winds normally making an abrupt shift to west or northwest. This introduces airstreams from the continent which are much colder and drier and produce rapidly clearing conditions. If the high pressure area following the storm trough is of some magnitude, the wind may mount to gale force and a northwester will prevail. In winter, snow showers may occur following the passage of the cold front as the interaction of the cold air and the warmer waters of the Sound cause a sea-effect snowstorm, usually of brief duration.

After this type of storm, mariners say the wind has "boxed the compass," all four quadrants of the compass having contributed an ingredient to Nantucket's weather mix.

If the storm center passes to the east of the island, it brings a "cooling storm." A southeast wind often prevails on the backside of an eastward-moving high pressure area off

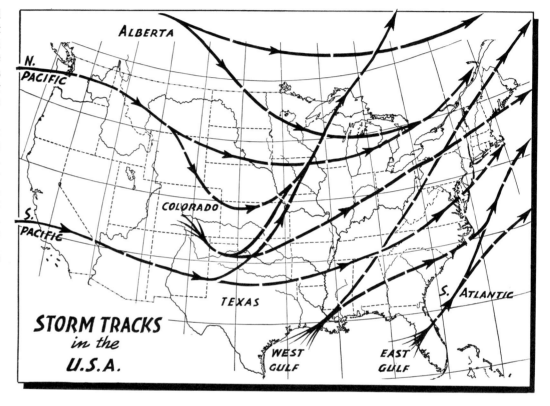

the New England coast, but with the approach of a storm center from the south or southwest, the wind will back to the east, bringing moderately cool air from south of Newfoundland. As it shifts farther into the northeast, it will tap the cold air conditioned over the Labrador Current off Nova Scotia and Maine. When the center reaches the latitude of Nantucket, the winds will continue to back to north and eventually to northwest, ushering to the scene cold, dry air from the tundras of central Canada. During winter, though precipitation may start as rain or wet snow under an easterly flow, it will usually change to dry snow as the wind backs to the northeast. All of Nantucket's heaviest snowstorms have occurred with northeast to north winds prevailing during the hours of greatest accumulation. A dry snow prevails under these conditions rather than a wet snow when the wind is easterly. During

northeasters, and sometimes in southeasters, winds reach gale and whole gale force.

There is an old saying on the athletic field that "it ain't over until it's over." This applies to Nantucket's weather as well. Seasoned mariners know that a hurricane is only half over when the calm eye of the storm arrives since the wind will shortly shift and blow as hard from the opposite direction as it did before the lull. Coastal storms passing Nantucket often act in much the same way. The northwest winds following a storm center may be as strong as the easterly winds preceding it. Furthermore, the storm center may stall to the north in the Gulf of Maine or between Nova Scotia and Newfoundland, deepen its barometric center, and increase its intensity. Then the winds may blow harder than before and continue for many hours after the storm has seemingly passed the latitude of Nantucket. This is the backlash of a storm.

Extremes of Weather Elements on Nantucket, compared with Boston, Massachusetts, New England, United States, North America and the World.

Precipitation in inches

Greatest in 24 hours:

Nantucket	6.53	1967, May 25–26
Boston	8.40	1955, Aug. 18–19
Westfield, MA	18.15	1955, Aug. 18–19
New England	18.15	1955, Aug. 18–19
Alvin, TX	43.00	1979, July 25–26
North America	43.00	1979, July 25–26
Cilaos La Reunion, Indian Ocean	73.62	1952, Mar. 15–16

Greatest in one month:

Nantucket	12.92	1946, Aug.
Boston	17.05	1955, Aug.
Westfield, MA	26.85	1955, Aug.
New England	26.85	1955, Aug.
Helen Mine, CA	71.54	1909, Jan.
Swanson Bay, B.C.	88.01	1917, Nov.
Kukui, Maui, HI	107.00	1942, Mar.
Cherrapungi, India	366.14	1861, July

Greatest in one year:

Nantucket	60.39	1958
Boston	65.62	1955
Westfield, MA	70.33	1955
New England	70.33	1955
Wynochee Oxbow, WA	184.56	1931
McLeod Harbor, AK	332.29	1976
Kukui, Maui, HI	578.00	1950
Cherrapungi, India	905.00	1861
Cherrapungi, India	1042.00	1860–1861 season

Least in one year:

Nantucket	25.31	1965
Boston	23.71	1965
Chatham Light, MA	21.76	1965
New England	21.76	1965
Death Valley, CA	0.00	1929
Bagdad, CA	0.00	Oct. 3, 1912 to Nov. 8, 1914 (767 days)
North America	0.00	Oct. 3, 1912 to Nov. 8, 1914
Arica, Chile	0.00	Oct. 1903 to Dec. 1917 (171 months)

Temperature in Fahrenheit

Maximum:

Nantucket	100°	1975, Aug. 2
Boston	104°	1911, July 4
New Bedford & Chester, MA	107°	1975, Aug. 2
New England	107°	1975, Aug. 2
Death Valley, CA	134°	1913, July 10
North America	134°	1913, July 10
El Azizia, Libya	136°	1922, Sept. 13

Minimum:

Nantucket	−6.2°	1918, Feb. 5
Boston	−18°	1934, Feb. 9
Chester, MA	−35°	1981, Jan. 12
Bloomfield, VT	−50°	1933, Dec. 30
Rogers Pass, MT	−69.7°	1954, Jan. 20
Prospect Creek, AK	−79.8°	1971, Jan. 23
Snag, Yukon Territory	−81.0°	1947, Feb. 3
Northice, Greenland	−87.0°	1954, Jan. 9
Vostok, Antarctica, U.S.S.R.	−128.6°	1983, July 21

Atmospheric Pressure in inches

Highest:

Nantucket	31.02	1949, Dec. 25
Boston	31.08	1981, Feb. 13
Northfield, VT	31.14	1920, Jan. 31
Miles City, MT	31.42	1983, Dec. 24
Northway, AK	31.44	1980, Dec. 31
Mayo, Yukon Territory	31.53	1974, Jan. 1
Agata, Siberia	32.00	1968, Dec. 31

Lowest:

Nantucket	28.11	1954, Sept. 11
Boston	28.45	1932, Mar. 7
Chatham, MA*	28.05	1954, Sept. 11
Hartford, CT	28.04	1938, Sept. 21
Long Key, FL	26.35	1935, Sept. 2
North America	26.35	1935, Sept. 2
Typhoon Tip, near 17°N,138°W, Pacific Ocean	25.69	1979, Oct. 12

* Readings of 27.77 inches were reported at Woods Hole and 28.02 inches at Edgartown on Sept. 11, 1954, but not verified officially.

A CALENDAR OF WEATHER EVENTS

January

1

1782 Seven drowned while crossing the bar in a whaleboat on "a cold and windy day."

1890 Record high barometer of 30.99″, not exceeded until Christmas Day in 1949 when it reached 31.02″.

1918 Coldest New Year's Day at 5° during extreme cold wave beginning December 20; minimum below freezing every day to February 12; maximum below freezing December 29 to January 6.

2

1904 Heavy snowstorm ended in blizzard conditions; 14.6″ of snow fell in a little over 24 hours on 2d and 3d; wind gusted to 53 miles per hour; "It is a long time since Nantucket has been visited by a blizzard of the magnitude of that of Sunday."

3

1904 Severe cold wave following blizzard dropped temperature to 2° on 2d, and to 7° on each of 3d and 4th.

1947 Panamanian freighter *Kotor* ran aground east of Madaket Coast Guard station in fog; hauled off later by cutters.

4

1922 Fishing boat *Doris* ashore along Madaket channel in fog, became a total loss.

5

1832 First ship broke through long ice embargo resulting from the coldest December of record; New Bedford averaged 10.9 degrees below normal for December 1831.

1905 Cold wave caused extremely frigid day with minimum of 1° and maximum of 14° accompanied by strong winds.

6

1856 Heavy snowstorm, "a regular smotherer ... such a violent gale has not been experienced in years . . . streets almost impassable."

1929 Temperature soared to 58°, then a record high for January.

7

1977 Coastal storm dropped 2.16″ of rain on Nantucket, while Boston had 13.8″ of snow.

8

1835 End of "Cold Week" with temperature continuously below freezing; harbor frozen solid.

1883 "One of the severest tempests and snowstorms in years"; high tide encircled Brant Point causing much damage.

1958 Northwester set new January wind record of 59 mi/h.

9

1881 Heavy snowstorm; South Shoals lightship broke loose and drifted for eleven days; huge snowdrifts on land; high tide submerged wharves.

1884 Surf described in press as "terrific ... producing more serious results than any rage for years"; Surfside bluffs cut down considerably.

10

1886 "The Blizzard of '86" raged along the New England shore; "such a chronicle of wrecks we have never before been called on to chronicle"; three-masted schooner *T.B.*

Witherspoon came ashore on the south side during night.

11

1882 Three-day storm raged, causing damage along wharves.

1932 North wind at 55 mi/h; after an unusual shift to southwest, it increased to 60 mi/h; heavy rain; barometer 28.98″.

12

1891 Big coastal storm caused huge waves which threw up and twisted railroad tracks on the south shore.

13

1914 Cold wave dropped temperature to −1° just before midnight, remained at that figure for two hours, then rose, so that both the 13th and 14th had a minimum of −1°.

1915 Severe storm with 1.66″ rain and wind gusting to 89 mi/h; wharves submerged, water rising nearly to Water Street; Muskeget Island inundated.

1925 Submarine S-19 grounded in northeast blizzard about one-half mile offshore; crew rescued; boat pulled off six weeks later.

1964 Fourth heaviest snowstorm of record with 19.2″, of which 17.8″ fell within 24 hours.

14

1905 Severe northeaster with winds reaching 67 mi/h, attended by 0.84″ precipitation.

1932 64° maximum, highest ever in January by six degrees.

15

1831 "The Great Snowstorm" with east-northeast gale and high tide; 36″ at New

All quotations unless otherwise specified are from the *Nantucket Inquirer* or *Inquirer and Mirror.* All temperature information comes from records compiled between October 18, 1886 and March 31, 1982. Records have not been compiled since then. Temperatures are in degrees Fahrenheit. Wind speeds prior to 1928 are corrected to the current three-cup anemometer standard Mi/h = miles per hour. Symbol ″ = inches. Symbol + = also on earlier dates. All dates prior to 1752 corrected to New Style.

Bedford and Sandwich on Cape Cod; "very deep" on Nantucket, but no actual measurement.

1910   "One of the worst snowstorms in the memory of the present generation" dropped 17″; northeast gales for 40 hours peaked at 54 mi/h; barometer dropped to 29.31″.

1957   Cold morning: Nantucket 6°, Edgartown 0°, East Wareham –13°.

1980   Heavy rainstorm dropped 2.22″.

16

1957   Snowstorm followed quickly on cold wave with 5.9″ falling.

17

1867   Famous Northeast storm of '67 hit New England; high wind in morning, lull in afternoon; in evening "a tremendous gale"; no steamer service on 16th or 17th.

18

1810   Schooner *Lucy* driven seaward from Vineyard Sound and never heard from again, a victim of "Cold Friday" gale.

1857   Famous cold storm of '57; 8° in morning, followed by violent snowstorm; no snow measurement, but 1.70″ precipitation fell; gales caused much damage, including some at observatory.

19

1901   Cold wave dropped temperature to 3° on 19th, to 2° on 20th.

1961   Kennedy Inaugural Snowstorm began; dropped 16.0″ to rank as sixth worst; temperature ranged from 32° to 12° at end.

20

1892   Three-masted schooner *H.P. Kirkham* wrecked on Rose and Crown shoal off Great Point.

1900   Temperature soared to 57° to break the existing January record.

21

1857   *S.S. New York*, westbound from Europe, ran out of fuel and anchored off Siasconset; 115 tons of coal were hauled from town over snow-cleared road; ship proceeded to New York.

22

1888   Thermometer dropped to –2°, introducing coldest part of cold month.

1918   Ice boating and skating ended on harbor ice after 21 days of freezing conditions, an unusually long period.

1935   "One of the worst winter storms"; 11.2″ fell and remained on ground for many days; wind peaked at 55 mi/h.

23

1857   Cold Friday II, "said to be the coldest ever known"; William Mitchell's thermometer at –6.5°, but others reported as low as –11°, or equal to Obed Macy's figure in February 1815.

1970   Official thermometer at Airport dropped to –1°, the most recent below-zero reading in weather service records.

24

1882   Thermometer reported at –6° in press, "the coldest in 20 years."

1888   Weather bureau thermometer dropped to –3.5°, long an official minimum record for Nantucket.

1908   "The worst storm in the history of the station (since 1886)"; wind steady at 64 mi/h with gusts to 83 mi/h; 1.08″ precipitation; tide 7 feet above mean low water; great erosion.

25

1921   Temperature dropped to 2°, but rose to 19° in afternoon.

1928   Wind hit a steady 54 mi/h during a southwest gale.

26

1905   "Great Nantucket Blizzard" on 25–26th; total snowfall 21.4″, with 17.8″

within 24 hours; wind peaked at 70 mi/h; temperature hovered around 26° during heavy snow period.

27

1889   Ship *Antoine* came ashore on Tuckernuck; crew of 17 and three passengers rescued.

1933   Longest easterly blow in weather bureau history raged from 26th to 29th; at gale force for 79 hours; averaged 40.8 mi/h on 26th and 33.0 mi/h on 27th.

28

1852   Ice embargo of two weeks' duration ended with arrival of steamer.

29

1844   A famous cold week; Cunarder *Britannia* frozen at dock in Boston Harbor; path had to be cut through ice for seven miles to open water so ship could sail.

1908   Schooner *Frederika Schepp* went ashore on north side of Coatue.

1973   High winds gusting to 80 mi/h; house under construction blown down; airplane flipped over, pilot injured.

30

1857   Longest ice embargo of 31 days; no communication with mainland except by outside route with sloop from Siasconset to Chatham on Cape Cod.

1939   Heavy three-day rainstorm: 2.32 inches fell on 30th with storm total of 2.87″.

31

1815   Cold wave sent mercury down to −11°, lowest ever known on Nantucket, according to Obed Macy (1835).

1898   Great storm began: rain on Nantucket, very heavy snow over southeast New England; "most severe known here for many years . . . minor damage but considerable in the aggregate"; peak wind 56 mi/h; lowest barometer 28.63″.

1905   Cold ending of January, 24° max. and 10° min., stood in contrast to warm ending of January 1904, 30° max. and 25° min.; both were very cold months in the aggregate.

February

1

1826   Mercury at −1° at sunrise, coldest since 1815; ice seen in all directions.

1918   *Crossrip* lightship carried away by ice; last seen from Great Point on 5th; crew of eight disappeared.

2

Ground Hog Day on mainland, Quahog Day on Island; warmest ever 54° in 1976; coldest 0° in 1961.

1970   Heavy rainstorm with 1.81″.

3

1857   "We are no longer 'Know Nothing';" schooner *Pizarro* from Hyannis broke ice blockade of 30 days' duration.

1961   Third major snowstorm of 1960–61 season; 14.4″ fell, mixed with rain; wind hit 43 mi/h; temperature rose to 36°, ending string of 16 days continuously below freezing.

4

1926   Storm with gales of 69 mi/h drove South Shoals lightship and Pollock Rip lightship from stations.

5

1918   Thermometer fell to −6.2°, lowest ever in weather bureau history; wind during night at 46 mi/h produced windchill of −65°; daytime maximum of 4° produced mean of −1.1°; Nantucket's bitterest day.

6

1855   Severe cold wave, 4° on island, but extreme cold on mainland.

1918   End of coldest wave ever known; 2° in the morning, rose to 32°.

7

1861   Spectacular temperature drop of 48 degrees from noon on 7th to −6.5° on morning of 8th; some thermometers went to −10°; arctic sea smoke (steam fog) covered Nantucket Sound; rose to only 1° at 2:00 p.m. for coldest day in early period; barometer rose over a full inch to 30.48″.

1875   Temperature reported at −8° in press during severely cold month.

8

1855   Big snowstorm; 18″ fell, increasing snow depth to 24″; called "worst in 30 years."

9

1908   Cold wave of four days' duration; mercury at 3°.

1934   Record cold day of 20th century at coastal cities on mainland; 4° on Island, −12° at Hyannis, −18° at Boston.

10

1881   *Island Home* released from ice after 13 days of imprisonment.

11

1899   Great Arctic Outbreak of '99 drove mercury down to 2°; minimums during four-day period below 10° on each day.

1973   Snowstorm dropped 6.1″, temperature ranged from 28° to 18°.

12

1885   Six vessels caught in ice, driven to and fro until grounding on Muskeget flats on 15th.

1899   Great Eastern Blizzard followed Great Arctic Outbreak; 13.6″ of new snow fell on 12th and 13th, increasing depth to 21.9″, the greatest in weather bureau records.

13

1851   Highest barometer of pre-weather bureau period; William Mitchell reported 31.03", not equaled since.

1914   Thermometer fell to –4°, matching coldest previously recorded by weather bureau.

14

1940   St. Valentine's Day Blizzard; severe northeaster dropped barometer to 28.66"; 51 mi/h northeast gale drove snow, sleet, and rain; only 4.1" snow accumulation on ground, but total precipitation had water equivalent of 1.71"; temperature range from 35° to 31°.

15

1943   Fast-moving cold wave plummeted mercury to –5°, the second lowest reading in weather bureau records; maximum only 11°.

16

1930   Snowstorm of 9.3" on local election day; roads blocked so voters walked to town; no milk delivery from Hummock Pond Road.

1958   Snowstorm dropped 9.9" on 16th and 17th; barometer fell to 28.69"; wind peaked at 50 mi/h from east; center of storm passed over island.

17

1896   Temperature went down to –1°, rose to 15°, for coldest day in a cold and stormy month.

1952   Two-Tanker Gale of '52; gale force winds prevailed for two days; sank *Pendleton* and *Fort Mercer* off Cape Cod; peak wind on island 51 mi/h; barometer sank to 28.79"; heavy rain of 1.83" fell, then 4.9" of snow.

18

1893   Snowstorm, called heaviest of winter, deposited 10".

1958   Northwest wind drove mercury to 5° after storm.

19

1852   Great aurora, "one of the most magnificent displays," among many appearances of northern lights this winter.

1898   Ship *Asia* struck on Round Shoals in a "furious northeaster."

20

1934   Great snowstorm raged during coldest month in recent history; wind attained 56 mi/h from southwest following passage of deep barometric center at 28.81"; 7.8" snow fell on island.

21

1930   Maximum reached 60°, highest ever in February.

1952   Snowstorm of 10.1" was second big snow in four days.

22

1802   Famous snowstorm and gale was described by Kezia Fanning in diary; three large Indiamen, outward-bound from Salem, lost off Cape Cod.

1829   "Worst snowstorm since 1806," according to *Inquirer*; barometer fell to 28.54"; harbor filled with ice.

23

1723   Greatest tide in colonial times occurred at Boston, high stage not approached until December 1786 when Nantucket had record high tide also.

24

1862   Great storm on Georges Bank sank 13 fishing schooners; on Nantucket, "some buildings were blown down, 'Walks' (Widows' Walks) from the tops of houses were carried away, chimnies blew off, and trees of large size prostrated."

25

1934   Second severe snowstorm in five days; windy ending for record cold month.

26

1923   *S. S. Sankaty* released after eight-day imprisonment by ice.

1979   Heavy rain of 2.06" carried off much snow and ice.

27

1902   Mercury sank to 0°, latest date for such in record books.

1952   The Cape Cod and Outer Islands Blizzard of '52; wind steady at 61 mi/h, gusts to 72 mi/h; 21.4" of snow fell from 27th to 29th; barometer down to 29.09"; temperature ranged from 36° to 27°.

28

1875   *Island Home*, breaking through the ice, arrived with 18 overdue mails, the largest number at one time since 1857.

1969   Nantucket received only 3.0" of snow during great four-day storm which gave Fall River 22.2" and Boston 26.3".

29

1836   First sloop sailed from harbor ending 30-day ice embargo.

1964   Leap Day Snowstorm; 6.8" falling on top of 4.8", increased depth to 11.6" on ground.

March

1

1914   Great First-of-March Gale; barometer dropped to near-record 28.50"; wind hit extreme speed of 91 mi/h from east; rainfall 1.05"; temperature ranged from 49° to 38°.

Snow is an uninvited visitor to Siasconset in winter.

Photograph courtesy of H. Flint Ranney.

2

1833   Severe night, very cold and windy; similar to Cold Friday.

1907   Revenue cutter *Dexter* broke through ice to inner harbor and opened navigation.

3

1868   Cold March; temperature down to 8°; island "completely ice-bound without a drop of water to be seen on north side."

1836   Sloop *Barclay* arrived after an ice embargo of 30 days' duration.

4

1916   Blizzard dropped 12.9" of snow within 15 hours; wind hit 67 mi/h; severely cold March followed with temperature averaging 6.3 degrees below normal.

5

1833   Temperature dropped to 8° during record cold early March.

1920   Heavy rainstorm precipitated 2.70" on 5th and storm total of 3.44" on 5th and 6th; great snow and sleet storm raged on mainland.

1960   Nantucket's greatest snowfall ended mixed with rain; a total of 31.3" snow fell, but melting kept the maximum on the ground at one time to 19.0"; total rain and snow amounted to 3.85" precipitation; wind attained 59 mi/h.

6

1811   Brig *Ocean* of Nantucket, inbound from Rio de Janeiro, grounded on Great Point in "a heavy NE gale and smothering snowstorm"; went ashore back of Coatue.

1962   Great Atlantic Storm and Tide of March '62; raged for three days from 5th to 7th; 50 mi/h from northeast; each successive high tide compounded erosion of beaches.

7

1932   Coastal storm with very deep barometric center; record 28.35" set on Nantucket; 47 mi/h from the northeast; only minor damage on the island.

8

1953   Record heavy rainstorm for March: 1.15" on 7th, 2.21" on 8th, for total of 3.36".

9

1774   Windstorm, suspected tornado, crossed island, blew down structures and demolished the harbor lighthouse.

1887   Bark *W. F. Marshall* struck on beach near Mioxes Pond in fog; crew rescued.

10

1855   Great snowstorm with 24" falling on

9th and 10th; 3.83″ total precipitation; "there cannot be much less than three feet" on ground; storm so great Atheneum did not open.

11

1924   Six-masted schooner *Wyoming*, 330 ft. long, 3370 tons, lost in Sound during blizzard; wreckage along north shore; crew of 13 drowned.

12

1888   Great Blizzard of '88 began; rain and howling gale struck Nantucket while mainland was buried in record deep snowfall.

13

1968   Heavy rainstorm: 1.35″ on 12th, 1.88″ on 13th, total 3.23″.

14

1888   Light snow, 1.3″, fell on Nantucket as the Blizzard of 1888 ended; telegraph lines were blown down, cutting off communication to mainland.

15

1843   Severe coastal storm on 15–16th, center passed over island; wind shifted from NNE to SSW; barometer 28.96″.

16

1870   Southerly storm washed away Humane Society's lifesaving house at Smith's Point.

17

1956   Famous St. Patrick's Day Storm; very heavy snow at Boston; Nantucket's 8.6″ snowfall was reduced by heavy rain at end of storm; highest tide in 25 years covered Washington Street with two feet of water.

18

1899   Heavy rainstorm dropped 3.32″ on 18th and 19th; fell on existing deep snowcover, causing extremely sloppy traveling conditions.

19

1956   Second heavy snowstorm, 11.2″, within three days; raised snow depth only one inch due to constant melting.

20

1957   Moist snowstorm accumulated to 11.7″ on 20th and 21st, though water equivalent of 2.38″ precipitation fell.

21

1874   Very low tide reported, supposedly lowest of record; only four feet of water at Steamboat Wharf.

1921   Record warm day on mainland, Boston 83°, but Nantucket only 55°.

22

1973   Late-season snowstorm dropped 6.2″ on 22d and 23d.

23

1898   Barkentine *Culloon* ran ashore at Nobadeer in dense fog, towed off three days later.

1933   Heavy, wet snowstorm of 13.1″ fell within 24 hours; clung to telephone and power lines; "most damaging to wires since April 1917."

24

1806   Sloop *Julian* cast ashore on Great Point "in heavy gale of wind accompanied by snow."

25

1909   Severe easterly storm; wind to 55 mi/h from northeast; barometer 29.03″; 1.19″ precipitation; temperature ranged from 48° to 33°.

26

1921   Maximum of 65°, warmest ever for so early in season; highest during very warm March, which averaged 6.7 degrees above normal.

27

1933   Heavy, moist snowfall accumulated to a thickness of 1.5 inches on trees and wires.

1957   Heavy northeast snowstorm turned to rain; winds mounted to 40 mi/h.

28

1843   Second big storm of stormy month which was coldest March of pre-weather bureau record; southeast gales raged; barometer dropped to 29.12″.

1969   Great aurora; "most brilliant since 1941."

29

1907   Maximum of 68°, warmest ever on island in March, during two-day heat wave; 62° on 30th.

1923   Minimum of 8° set late-season record; third lowest reading ever in March.

1984   Great Point Lighthouse Storm; severe northeaster with winds at Chatham peaking at 60 mi/h and barometer at Nantucket Airport dropping to 28.82″; structure erected in 1818 finally undermined by advancing sea and destroyed.

30

1823   Famous End-of-March Storm; "accompanied by severe gale from eastward with rain, snow, hail, thunder and lightning"; temperature hovered near 34°.

31

1879   Eleven schooners grounded "in violent storm of wind and rain."

1959   Heavy rainstorm of 2.54″ fell in 24 hours.

April

1

1879   Deep low pressure off coast caused severe gales and heavy rain of 1.15″; followed by intervals of hail, then sleet, and then snow.

1923   Record late-season cold wave set April minimum mark of 15°; maximum that day only 28°.

1983   Snow fell most of the day, heavy at times; only about ¾″ accumulated as most melted. Temperature ranged from 33° to 31°.

2

1958   High winds gusting to 82 mi/h with snow and sleet through the day; surging tide did minor damage along waterfront.

3

1915   Coastal storm on Easter Sunday; some snow fell; barometer dropped to 29.28″; wind peaked at 61 mi/h.

4

1907   Heavy storm produced only 1.0″ snow on Nantucket, but Hyannis had 9.0″, and Boston 16.0″.

1954   Minimum of 20°, the coldest ever so late in the spring.

1955   Heavy snowfall of 8.0″ set April record for 24 hours; melted down to 4.0″ at the end.

5

1874   First of series of cold April storms which brought bad weather on every weekend of notoriously cold month.

6

1983   Snowstorm with very high winds; peaked at 83 mi/h from northwest; barometer down to 28.70″; schools let out at 1:00 p.m.; town meeting postponed; many power outages.

7

1953   Record April rainfall of 4.48″ in 24 hours, and storm total of 4.59″ on 7th and 8th.

8

1929   Early heat wave on mainland; Boston at 84°, but Nantucket only 68°.

1950   "Worst April storm in 77 years"; snow fell to depth of 4.0″; wind at 54 mi/h from northeast; 18 fishermen lost off Cape Cod.

9

1938   Heavy rainstorm totaled 2.81″.

10

1917   "Sleighing on the 10th of April!"; heavy snowstorm dumped 11.6″ which melted down to 5.0″ in afternoon; 1.16″ water equivalent precipitation; many electric cables broken; temperature ranged from 41° to 25°.

11

1955   Thermometer soared to 69° for early-season record high.

12

1841   "Our whole town is one vast theatre of slush and slop"; slush half-a-leg deep after heavy wet snow in famous mid-April snowstorm; no boat service.

13

1875   New Bedford had 12″ of wet snow, but Nantucket escaped with only wind and rain.

1959   Snowfall of 1.5″ melted quickly.

14

1945   Maximum of 71° was highest ever so early in the season.

1953   Snow caused postponement of Red Sox opening game of season, but Nantucket had only rain.

15

1854   Great April Snowstorm; from 3:00 a.m. to mid-afternoon; "we should judge more than eighteen inches fell"; some localities on mainland reported 24″.

16

1851   The Lighthouse Storm; Minot Light off Cohasset destroyed by huge waves, two keepers lost; on Nantucket, "one of the heaviest and long continued gales"; tide highest in 12 years, but little damage on island.

17

1854   Second major storm in three days brought gales and snow that turned into a drizzle as temperature rose.

18

1976   Maximum of 76° on Easter Sunday; Boston had 94° during unusual heat wave.

19

1933   Persistent northeaster with winds to 43 mi/h and 0.64″ of rain from 17th to 19th.

20

1897   Minimum at 26°, set record for coldest ever so late in the season.

1915   Maximum at 74° set new record for warmest so early in the season.

1941   Record heat on mainland: 95° in New Hampshire, Boston 89°, but Nantucket reached only 62°.

21

1957 "Beautiful, although windy on Easter Day"; Nantucket maximum at 64°, but Boston reached 88° in early-season heat surge.

1967 Minimum at 30°, reading tied in 1969.

22

1874 "Winter is hardly over yet. On Tuesday evening (22d), we had a smart little fall of snow, which, indeed, was much needed — to keep the early peas warm in the ground."

23

1893 Norwegian bark *Mentor* struck on Old South Shoal and was abandoned with all sails set; ship refloated itself and was discovered ten miles south of island; two salvage crews boarded and shared prize money.

24

1967 Light snowfall of 0.8″ with temperature ranging from 45° down to 32° that day.

25

1909 Snow flurries occurred during the day.

1961 Temperature rose to 73°.

26

1809 Cold snowstorm, according to Kezia Fanning's diary.

27

1717 Captain Bellamy lost along with pirate ship *Whidah* off Nauset Beach on Cape Cod; 144 fellow pirates also drowned, only two saved.

28

1948 Temperature sank to 29°, a record low for so late in the season.

29

1967 Great storm raged, wind averaging 43.9 mi/h for 24 hours, with a one-minute speed recorded at 63 mi/h; structural damage on Nantucket; 1.73″ rain fell.

30

1874 "Smart snow squall about 9:00 a.m., ice formed night before," concluded record cold and snowy April.

1942 Temperature soared to 79° for April maximum record; never as warm again in any year until May 2, 1931.

May

1

1876 "Ice seen in streets on Nantucket"; snow fell at New Bedford.

1917 34° set a May minimum record for town station.

1947 Heavy rainstorm of 3.07″ fell in 24 hours.

2

1861 "Winter made a flying visit, bringing as companions a cold east wind and a heavy snowstorm"; no details given in *Inquirer*.

1914 Killing frost occurred with temperature of 35° on 1st and 41° on 2d.

1967 Freezing at Airport, but rose to 56° maximum that day.

3

1876 "It snowed through the evening of the 3d. Chalk it down on the stable floor."

4

1946 Two cold days for May: 48° max., 32° min. on 3d; 52° max., 31° min. on 4th.

1947 During the first four days of May, 4.84″ of rain fell.

5

1906 Record maximum of 67° is lowest for any date in May.

6

1871 Heavy storm of 1.82″ rain, according to Charles Coleman records.

1920 Killing frost, with 35° in town; max. on 5th only 44°.

1930 Temperature soared to 77° on 6th and to 76° on 7th.

7

1967 Freeze at Airport after 48° max. on 6th.

8

1803 Famous May snowstorm from Indiana to Massachusetts; Philadelphia, New York, and Boston had about 6.0″; presumably some on Nantucket.

9

1917 "First May snowstorm of [weather bureau] record . . . fell thick and fast before dawn"; then changed to rain; *Inquirer* reported 2.8″ in morning, but most had melted when weather bureau made daily measurement at 8:00 p.m.

10

1945 May storm spread snow over interior of New England; Nantucket barometer dropped to 29.19″, and 0.83″ of rain fell.

1977 May storm along New England coast; gale force winds and extremely high tides on Nantucket; no boat to mainland on 9th and only one on 10th; temperature ranged only two degrees from 40° to 42°.

11

1907 Cold day: max. 47°, min. 40°.

12

1882 "A bleak northeaster" raged on 12–13th.

1970 Two-day heat wave; thermometer peaked at 84° after reaching 79° on 11th.

13

1975 Heavy rainstorm of 1.41"; an additional 0.17" fell on 14th.

14

1834 Famous mid-May snowstorm over interior of New England; temperature on Nantucket dropped to 38° on 14th and 35° on 15th, but no snow fell.

15

1938 May storm; barometer at 29.20"; gales mounted to 42 mi/h; 1.43" rainfall; only minor damage.

16

1954 Heavy rainstorm over southeast New England; Boston had 5.74" in 24 hours, but Nantucket had only 1.95".

1974 Temperature mounted to 80° in one-day heat wave.

17

1957 Mercury dropped to 30° for lowest ever in May; 37° on 16th and 18th.

18

1892 Great aurora over New England; "a beautiful display of northern lights on Wednesday evening."

19

1780 Famous Dark Day during Revolution; candles needed between 2:00 p.m. and 5:00 p.m. as soot from forest fires filtered out sunlight; all foliage took on a brassy hue; cleared up at night.

1966 Heavy rainstorm dropped 2.74", along with 0.15" on 20th.

20

1840 Comet observed in the northeast sky, probably one of Galle's.

21

1842 "Extraordinary solar phenomena" of multiple halos observed at Boston; no mention of it on Nantucket.

22

1842 Climax of three-day cool spell with minimums of 36°, 35°, and 36° from 20th to 22d.

23

1941 Temperature rose to 82° in one-day heat wave.

24

1888 Heavy rainstorm, 2.78" fell in 24 hours on 24th and 25th.

25

1902 In thick weather, five-masted schooner *Arthur Seitz* and four-masted *Frank A. Palmer* stranded on Skiff Island about 5 miles southwest of Muskeget; *Palmer* later refloated, but *Seitz* became a total wreck.

26

1967 Most intense rainfall in all Nantucket records occurred while great May storm raged over all of New England; 6.48" fell in 24 hours, total of 7.08" fell from 24th to 26th setting single-storm record.

27

1961 Heavy rain storm of 2.55" on 27th, additional 0.10" on 26th and 0.11" on 28th.

28

1890 Late-season killing frost occurred on island, though official thermometer in town dropped only to 43°.

29

1890 Record high May wind registered, 47 mi/h from northeast.

1900 Ice formed in early morning; 34° at weather bureau.

1931 Warm ending of May; mercury above 70° for four days; peak of 81° on 29th.

30

1970 Thermometer dropped to 35° at Airport, coldest ever observed so late in season.

31

1858 "White frost on the morning of the 31st," Mitchell records.

1859 Highest May temperature ever recorded, 86°, marked the beginning of a three-day heat wave.

June

1

1812 Apple trees at New Haven blossomed later than ever observed in long record running from 1794 to the present; presumably Nantucket had as backward a spring.

1943 June minimum record of 43° was set at Boston, but at Nantucket thermometers dropped to only 49°.

2

1838 Fire burned about 25 buildings in center of town; wind from south fanned flames.

1895 Thermometer climbed to 89° for an early season record.

The Old Mill in full summer regalia.
Collection of the Nantucket
Historical Association.

Island and Massachusetts; heavy rain and thermometer at 55°.

1947 Coldest ever in June, 39° at Airport maximum of 60°.

6

1925 Early-season heat wave set daily records from 5th to 7th with readings of 83°, 87°, 82°; Boston's mercury hit 100° on 6th.

7

1816 "Remarkably cold for season — a good fire is comfortable"; famous "Year without a Summer" began with freezing weather.

8

1816 Again very cold, "ice on the water pail."

9

1874 "Terrible Tempest ... most severe for over thirty years"; lightning shattered flagstaff on Ocean View House, Orange St.

1953 Heavy thunderstorm occurred on evening of the day when the Worcester Tornado killed 90 people; only 0.13″ rain fell on Nantucket.

10

1774 Schooner *Lowden* struck on Great Rip; quarterdeck swept away; 13 of crew gained wreckage and paddled ashore; their cries were heard that night in Siasconset and rescue effected; "but for the fine weather they must have inevitably perished."

11

1825 Temperature soared to 92°, warmest ever known so early in the season; record hot summer followed.

1881 "Boisterous storm ... unusual for June" heavy rain.

12

1973 Heat wave on mainland: Boston 96°,

3

1959 Heavy rainstorm dropped 3.00″ on 2d and 3d during northeaster in which winds hit 32 mi/h.

4

1903 Smoke and sooty particles from forest fires in Maine caused dark days from 3rd to 7th giving a brassy tinge to sky and outdoor objects.

1967 Thermometer at 40° for second coldest June reading; temperatures in the 40s every night for first six days of June.

5

1825 Early-season hurricane moved from Florida along the Atlantic seaboard causing extensive damage to shipping; Nantucket had northeast gales shifting to southwest, indicating center passed inland over Rhode

New Bedford 94°, but Nantucket had maximum of only 72°.

13
1968 Big storm dropped 2.30″ rain.

14
1780 Seven-week drought alleviated by rainfall; "as dry as ever known at this season."

1966 Tropical storm Alma dissipated over Massachusetts Bay; dropped only 0.22″ on Nantucket.

15
1917 Heavy storm produced 2.61″ in three-day rain from 15th to 17th.

16
1956 One-day heat wave with mercury rising to 87°.

17
1965 First tropical storm of season passed about 200 miles to southeast; only a trace of rain fell.

1929 84° marked start of three-day heat wave; mercury reached 87° on 18th.

18
1875 June storm with northeast gale; 1.33″ fell.

1891 43, coolest ever in June in town records.

1893 Tropical storm passed to southeast; wind from southeast at 29 mi/h; 0.64″ rain.

19
1905 Heavy rain fell, measuring 3.74″ on 19th; light rain for five days afterward.

1934 Hurricane which had lost its tropical structure moved to the northwest over Buzzards Bay; 0.93″ rain fell on island.

20
1945 Tropical storm, well to northwest over central New England, precipitated only 0.24″ on Nantucket.

20
1967 Very intense rainfall; 0.84″ in one hour; 1.86″ in three hours; 2.68″ in 24 hours; 3.33″ storm total from 19th to 21st; not a tropical storm.

21
1923 90°, earliest date with reading in 90s during the weather bureau period in either town or airport records; only 68° maximum next afternoon.

22
1947 43°, coldest for so late in the season at the Airport.

23
1814 Violent gale from northwest; "so cold that aged people in passing about wore mittens. The inhabitants in general made fires in their houses." Obed Macy.

24
1936 June storm; northeast gales from 3:29 a.m. to 6:43 p.m.; not a tropical storm; average wind speed over 24 hours, 32.3 mi/h; peak 58 mi/h; 1.82 inches rain; temperature ranged from 58° to 54°.

25
1884 Easterly storm brought "a charming rain" to end drought; 2.75″ fell on 25th and 26th.

26
1977 Heavy rain 2.50".

1981 Heavy rain 2.03".

27
1945 Severe thunderstorm attending tropical storm; wind 55 mi/h from mortheast; barometer 29.43″; heavy rainfall of 4.61″ on 26th and 27th.

28
1978 Mercury rose to 90° in one-day heat wave, the highest on that date in New England, though equaled by New Haven, Providence, and Taunton.

29
1933 Boston temperature hit high of 99°, but Nantucket recorded only 81°.

30
1959 Maximum of 88°, the third highest ever in June; maximums were only 64° on 29th and 65° on July 1.

July

1
1964 92° equalled July record on Nantucket; Martha's Vineyard reached 95°, Boston 97°.

2
1891 48° at weather bureau, lowest ever in July for town location.

1905 Severe rainstorm dropped 3.04″ in 24 hours, 1.06″ on 2d and 1.98″ on 3d.

1932 Low barometer of 29.25″ set July record for period 1886 to 1946.

3
1911 Boston's worst heat wave began with maximum of 102°, Nantucket reached only 75° that day.

4
1911 Boston's hottest day ever at 104°; Nantucket only 77°.

1919 Nantucket heat wave: 92° on 4th and 5th, highest since 1886; not equaled until 1964.

1933 Fourth of July northeaster raged for 25 hours; wind speed of 62 mi/h recorded at 4:50 p.m.; high tides; 0.78″ rain fell; barometer at 29.62″.

1978 Wettest Fourth of July, 4.37″ of rain deluged island.

5

1881 Cold, frost at New Bedford.

1911 Boston's minimum of 77° equaled Nantucket's maximum.

6

1930 Brief deluge: 0.40″ in 5 minutes, 0.57″ in 10 minutes; 1.13″ total.

1971 Ex-hurricane Arlene, born off the Carolinas, passed about 150 miles south of the island; only a trace of rain fell on Nantucket.

7

1892 Highest July barometer reading, 30.52″, recorded between 1886 and 1946.

1969 Cool day: 50° minimum, 69° maximum.

8

1915 Nantucket escaped with only .09″ rainfall as deluges up to 4.00″ swept other parts of New England.

9

1953 Short heavy shower: 0.42″ in 5 minutes, 0.52″ in 15 minutes.

1962 Short heavy shower: 0.28″ in 5 minutes, 0.65 in 15 minutes.

10

1967 Notably cool season with summer maximum only 82° on 10th.

11

1914 *George P. Hudson,* 5-masted schooner, run into by collier *Middlesex* off Great Round Shoal in fog; nine of crew survived.

1959 Ex-hurricane Cindy passed over island; winds at 34 mi/h from south; 0.38″ on 10th, 0.22″ on 11th; no damage.

12

1888 Severe thunderstorms swept Massachusetts as deep cyclonic center crossed state from west to east; snow fell on northern mountains.

13

1846 Great Fire started about 11:00 p.m.

14

1918 Schooner *Evelyn M. Thompson* wrecked on Low Beach; crew of 19 reached shore safely; vessel was a total loss.

15

1935 Heavy rainstorm on 15–16th, 3.69″ fell in 24 hours, 3.75″ total; not a tropical storm.

16

1946 Mid-month cool wave; 49° on 15th, 47° on 16th (record low for July) 48° on 17th, 52° on 18th; month averaged 2.1 degrees below normal.

17

1902 Schooner *M. J. Soley,* from Nova Scotia to Providence, stranded on Great Point during heavy blow; hauled off next day.

18

1969 One-day heat wave, maximum 90°; only 78° maximum on 17th and 19th.

19

1850 First of Triple Tropical Storms of '50

brought "copious showers of rain, which the thirsty earth drank up with relish."

20

1907 Quick deluge: 0.26″ in 5 minutes, 0.39″ in 10 minutes, 0.57″ in 15 minutes.

21

1916 Tropical storm made landfall on Martha's Vineyard; Nantucket barometer read 29.48″; wind at 38 mi/h from southwest; rainfall of 0.39″.

22

1926 Boston heat wave at 103°; Nantucket only 86°.

23

1905 Easterly storm with gales at 38 mi/h; only 0.23″ rain.

1963 Waterspouts seen between Cape Cod and Nantucket in Sound; total number unknown.

24

1952 July heat wave: 83° on 22d, 89° on 23d, 88° on 24th; month averaged 3.2° above normal.

25

1961 Heavy rainstorm of great intensity: 1.14″ in 30 minutes, 2.03″ in 60 minutes; 2.65″ of rain was storm total; not a tropical storm.

26

1946 Midsummer cool wave: 53° minimum on 26th and 27th.

27

1925 Lightning struck several homes in Siasconset, tore up fairways on golf course.

28

1911 Schooner *Nakomis* lost on fishing grounds during severe northeast storm; wind from northeast at 42 mi/h; 2.12″ rain; crew of eight escaped in two dories; one capsized drowning all, others rescued by fishing smack.

1953 Severe hailstorm struck Islands; on Martha's Vineyard, "a greenhouse was smashed, windows in many residences shattered, parked cars suffered roof and window damage, gardens, lawns and foliage hard hit."

29

1949 Heat wave: 90° on 29th; maximum stayed above 83° during last four days of month.

1958 Deluge: 0.39″ in 5 minutes, 0.72″ in 10 minutes, 1.24″ in 20 minutes, 2.19″ in two hours.

30

1916 Yellow day throughout New England climaxed a very rainy, cloudy month; Nantucket had only four clear days, 16 days of measurable rain and three days with traces of rain.

1960 Tropical storm Brenda moved northeast on New York City –Hartford, CT – Concord, NH line; Nantucket winds rose to 42 mi/h from south; tides 3 to 5 feet above normal.

31

1917 Thermometer rose to 90° in town for the first time since weather bureau records began in 1886.

August

1

1908 Hurricane passed about 100 miles offshore; 1.23″ rain.

2

1867 Strong hurricane not far offshore; barque *Oak Ridge* passed through center, sank in high cross seas; South Shoals lightship broke loose; "truly disastrous" to shipping.

1975 Nantucket's only century mark; maximum 88°, 100°, and 97° on 1st, 2d, and 3d; New Bedford hit record 107°.

3

1968 Rainstorm dropped 2.13″ adding to very wet, gloomy summer.

4

1944 Tropical storm passed about 75 miles to southeast, but no rain fell on island.

5

1915 Tropical storm moved northeast on Hartford–Boston line; Nantucket barometer read 29.69″; wind at 34 mi/h; rainfall of 1.03″.

1930 Thermometer at 90°, hottest ever in town in August since 1887.

1955 Hot day: Boston 100°, Nantucket 88°.

1958 Very cool summer; reading of 78° was highest all season, a record low maximum for an entire summer.

6

1971 Tropical storm Beth tracked about 125 miles to southeast; caused only 0.36″ rain.

7

1835 Severe northeast storm prevented any ship arrivals; "a chilling storm of rain and wind ... greatcoats and hearths are indispensable"; New Bedford had 2.50″ rain.

1946 Heavy rainstorm dropped 3.67″ in 24 hours on 6th and 7th.

1956 Coastal storm passed southeast causing strong winds, heavy rains, and rough seas; winds to 47 mi/h; 3.37″ rain; boats damaged and sunk.

8

1949 Heat wave: Boston recorded 95°, 99°, 101° from 8th to 10th, but Nantucket reached only 85°, 83°, 92°; other maximums were: Hyannis 99°, Sandwich 100°, Edgartown 98°.

9

1976 Hurricane Belle threatened trouble when located 100 miles south of Long Island, but lost energy over cool water; caused 15-foot breakers on Nobadeer beach; gusts to 60 mi/h, but no rain fell.

10

1917 Weak tropical storm dissipated off Cape Cod; 1.03″ rain.

11

1944 Heat wave from 11th to 17th, "perhaps the longest of record of sustained heat in New England"; Boston had 97° or above for seven days; Nantucket below 82° on the same days.

12

1778 Naval battle between French and British in Rhode Island Sound prevented by arrival of strong hurricane; ships severely damaged and scattered; extensive wind damage to corn crop on Vineyard and presumably on Nantucket.

13

1638 A hurricane, one of the Triple Storms of 1638, caused double tide and rise of 15 feet at Boston.

14

1889 Deluge of 5.73″ in 24 hours set record for 24-hour rainfall until the big rain in 1967; streets ran with water, basements flooded.

15

1953 Hurricane Barbara threatened island; but passed about 100 miles to southeast; caused 2.00″ rain on 14th.

16

1870 Waterspout reported off Barnstable on Cape Cod.

17

1830 Hurricane off Nantucket Shoals, "one of the severest gales experienced in a long time"; barometer read 29.66″; high winds around midnight.

1944 Thunderstorms ended long heat wave on mainland; Boston had 1.05″ of rain, Nantucket only 0.14″.

18

1879 "August Gale of '79" crossed from Buzzards Bay to Cape Cod Bay, center over Woods Hole; "assumed great violence" on Cape Cod, but "not damaging" on Nantucket.

19

1896 Large waterspout formed in Nantucket Sound off Cottage City (now Oak Bluffs) on Martha's Vineyard; described by a Nantucketer.

1955 Ex-hurricane Diane centered at 7:00 a.m. between Martha's Vineyard and Nantucket; lowest barometer reading 29.54″; wind at 38 mi/h from northwest; Nantucket had only 2.50″ of rain, but Boston measured 12.47″ for all-time record one-day rainfall.

1968 Minimum of 46° was second lowest ever in August.

20

1843 Waterspout off Nantucket "dissailed" a ship.

1856 Strong southeast gales hit island as tropical storm crossed Rhode Island and southeastern Massachusetts.

1950 Hurricane Able moved to about 75 miles southeast of Nantucket; wind at 37 mi/h from north; 0.81″ rain; little damage.

21

1893 Tropical storm caused waves to cover and dislodge railroad tracks on South Shore; "stood them on end like a snow fence"; engine *Dionis* stranded at Siasconset.

22

1887 Ex-hurricane well to southeast.

1888 Ex-hurricane well to north.

23

1873 Grand Banks Hurricane, the severest known on the Newfoundland fishing grounds; 1,123 vessels wrecked, many from Cape Cod and the Islands.

24

1806 Severe hurricane attended by heavy rains; northeast gales; an empty barrel on Martha's Vineyard filled with 30″ rain water; ship *Olive* drifted over Nantucket bar, bilged and sank.

25

1635 Great Colonial Hurricane crossed from Narragansett Bay to Massachusetts Bay; extreme tides; great forest destruction.

1885 Schooner *Oregon*, loaded with granite, struck on Great Point Rip in rough seas; beached at Wauwinet to prevent foundering.

26

1924 Large hurricane passed very near; barometer 28.71″; wind at 62 mi/h from northeast; 2.07″ rain.

27

1948 Late-season heat wave: 92° on 26th and 91° on 27th; Boston recorded temperature of 99° and 100°.

28

1883 "Heaviest surf at south shore known for years"; caused further erosion.

1958 Hurricane Daisy passed about 65 miles to southeast; raised gale of 42 mi/h; 3.20″ rain.

30

1839 Strong hurricane; "we have not had so severe a gale for many years"; three schooners and one brig grounded.

31

1954 Hurricane Carol moved inland over eastern Connecticut; raised 72 mi/h winds from southeast; highest blow did not coincide with high tide.

1965 Temperature dropped to 39°, a full 10 degrees lower than any previous August reading; had been at 42° the night before.

September

1

1940 Hurricane developed directly south of Nantucket in the Bahamas on August 30; center passed about 40 miles to southeast early on morning of the 2d; wind clocked at 57 mi/h at 3:00 a.m. with peak gust at 65 mi/h; total rainfall 2.51″; only slight damage.

2

1952 Ex-hurricane Able passed to northwest over central New England; only 0.02″ rainfall.

1953 Peak of 10-day heat wave on mainland: 101° at Hartford, 100° at Boston, 81° at Nantucket.

3

1821 Strong hurricane passed over western Connecticut; only a "gale" occurred on Nantucket, with no damage reported; one shipwreck on north shore.

1850 Heavy rain of 4.05″ fell between 9:00 a.m. and 2:00 p.m.

1931 Thermometer climbed to 88°, hottest ever in September.

1972 Tropical storm Carrie struck on Labor Day weekend disrupting all transportation schedules; 4.09″ rain on island; Edgartown reported 7.06″, and East Wareham 8.89″.

4

1873 Long drought ended with rainfall of 1.62″; only 2.94″ fell from May 12 to September 4.

1973 Climax of eight-day heat wave: Boston and Hartford 94°, Nantucket 80°.

5

1965 47°, cool wave of six days' duration with readings in high 40s.

6

1881 Famous Yellow Day; similar to but not as intense as Dark Day in 1780; "all pervaded with a yellowish tinge"; caused by Michigan and Ontario forest fires.

7

1850 "Line Gale" occurred; "was more violent than for several years"; wind shifting from southeast to southwest caused some damage to wharves and shipping.

1953 Tropical storm Carol passed about 50 miles to east; wind hit 54 mi/h on island; rainfall 1.77″.

8

1869 September Gale of '69; "a severe gale veering from southeast to southwest" as center moved inland over Rhode Island; little damage and no wrecks in vicinity.

1932 Tropical storm passed offshore; northeast gales at 56 mi/h; caused destructive erosion at south end where sea broke into ponds.

1934 The *Morro Castle* Storm crossed central Long Island, and on Nantucket caused strong winds but little rain; storm named for the fire and destruction of cruise ship *Morro Castle* off New Jersey coast.

9

1821 Severe lightning storm on Nantucket, hit houses and stunned boy; occurred on same day as the famous New Hampshire Whirlwind.

1896 Severe tropical storm; wind 50 mi/h from east on 9th, 55 mi/h from south on 10th; barometer at center, 29.36″; surf broke into ponds at flood tide.

1949 Pleasure cruiser *Constance* sank on Tuckernuck Shoal, nine of eleven on board drowned.

1969 Hurricane Gerda passed well to southeast, but close enough to drop 5.05″ of rain on Nantucket within 24 hours.

10

1854 "Easterly storm with thunder"; wind first at north-northeast, then east; barometer 29.78″; 6.06″ rain fell, a 19th-century record. brig *Calcutta* on beam-ends on Nantucket shoals.

1889 Hurricane turned southwest off Long Island; caused great surf on Nantucket; seas broke into Hummock and Miacomet ponds; highest wind was 34 mi/h from east.

11

1821 Lightning hit house and North Congregational Meetinghouse.

1954 Hurricane Edna passed over Martha's Vineyard and Nantucket Sound; Nantucket barometer at 28.18″, lowest ever recorded on island; wind steady from southeast at 73 mi/h at 1:04 p.m., gusting to 90 mi/h; at gale force for nine hours; averaged 57 mi/h from noon to 1:00 p.m.

12

1882 Hurricane passed close to the southeast; "small gale brought much needed showers"; 1.15″ rain fell.

1950 Hurricane Dog caused two-day storm; passed about 150 miles to the southeast; wind peaked at 72 mi/h on Nantucket; 4.43″ rain fell; many small boat losses.

1960 Hurricane Donna moved inland over Long Island on northeast track; steady 56 mi/h from south, gusts to 73 mi/h; "a severe lashing but light damage"; Madaket roads washed out.

13

1838 Tropical storm with wind shifting from south-southeast to west-southwest; "amounted to something like a tornado"; much minor wind damage.

14

1944 Great Atlantic Hurricane; center moved from Narragansett Bay to South Shore of Boston Harbor; Nantucket's lowest barometer reading was 29.04″; steady wind at 54 mi/h, peak gust at 79 mi/h; much damage to trees, roofs, and small buildings; Vineyard Lightship foundered, crew of 12 lost.

15

1904 Tropical storm moved over Cape Cod; lowest barometer reading on Nantucket was 29.44″; wind hit 58 mi/h from south; only 0.01″ rain.

1938 Deluge of 4.05″ fell during preliminary wet period preceding the New England hurricane of 1938.

16

1858 "Line Gale"; "a terrible gale prostrating chimnies and fences throughout town"; wind south by east to south-southwest; barometer 29.42″.

1900   Heavy rain of 2.42″ broke drought, said to be the worst since 1825.

17

1876   "Equinoctial Storm"; moved over central New England; high surf broke into ponds, but little other damage on island.

1933   Strong hurricane moved over Virginia; barometer on Nantucket fell to 29.15″; wind steady at 54 mi/h northeast, gusts to 75 mi/h; 5.58″ of rain fell in five days.

18

1917   "Worst September Gale of record"; or since 1887; steady wind speed at 67 mi/h for five minutes, gusts to 80 mi/h; low tide, minor damage.

1941   Aurora borealis: "One of the most glorious ever witnessed."

19

1876   "Severe white frost occurred last Tuesday [19th]." *Island Review.*

1928   Tropical storm moved near island; wind at 48 mi/h from northeast; heavy rain of 2.06″ fell.

1936   Hurricane moved offshore; barometer at 29.27″; wind at 58 mi/h very heavy rain: 7.79″ at Provincetown; 3.24″ at Nantucket.

20

1770   Stiles's Hurricane caused highest tide at Newport since 1723; no report from Nantucket; storm named for its historian, Reverend Ezra Stiles of Newport.

21

1938   New England Hurricane moved across Long Island and on mainland near Milford, CT, west of New Haven; Nantucket escaped worst; winds only 52 mi/h but 0.04″ of rain fell; considerable erosion on south shore and at Madaket.

22

1961   Hurricane Esther approached within 100 miles of Nantucket, then performed a large loop to south, returned on 25th as heavy rainstorm, but produced little wind.

23

1815   The Great September Gale; crossed eastern Long Island and into Connecticut near Saybrook; "the gale was not severe here," wrote William Mitchell.

1891   Old bathhouse and railroad depot at Surfside blown down by gale.

24

1963   Three-day cold spell inland; on Nantucket temperature dropped to 40° on 24th, 43° on 25th.

25

1858   "A very heavy and unseasonable frost occurred here on Saturday night [25th] and which we are afraid has been disastrous for the cranberry crop."

1888   Calm center of ex-hurricane passed over island, providing a lull of 30 minutes of sunshine; barometer reading 29.08″; wind at 50 mi/h from northeast preceding the eye.

1961   Ex-hurricane Esther returned from south; heavy rain of 1.60″; considerable erosion, Smith's Point became Esther Island.

26

1950   Blue Sun and Moon; smoke aloft from forest fires in Alberta filtered out other colors causing strange sky effect for almost a week.

27

1717   Hurricane: "The Lord sent a great rain and horrible wind; whereby much hurt was done, both on the water and on the land." Reverend Samuel Phillips of Boston.

28

1958   Heavy rainstorm, 3.39″ on 27th and 28th.

29

1908   Brilliant aurora borealis: "greenish in color with streamers changing to pink at times. The arch was high as the pole star."

1947   Temperature dropped to 35° at Airport, lowest ever recorded in September.

30

1676   Ephraim Howe with family and friends were blown off Cape Cod in a small boat by storm; finally landed on small island off Nova Scotia; rescued six months later by passing fishing boat; his two sons and two others died of starvation before the rescue.

1881   Temperature of 41° was lowest ever recorded in September in town records.

October

1

1822   Fishing boat from Nantucket upset on Chatham bar; crew rescued the next day.

1894   Northeast gale caused tremendous surf; a large section of the railroad tracks near Nobadeer buried in sand.

2

1927   Hottest October ever experienced on mainland New England: Hartford 84°, Nantucket 77°.

3

1841   "The Memorable October Gale of '41"; wind began at 8:00 a.m. on 3d and reached its height from 2:00 to 6:00 a.m. on 4th, terminating at 8:00 a.m.; 190 vessels wrecked on New England coasts; generally regarded as Nantucket's worst hurricane experience.

1961   Heavy rain; 2.49" fell in 12 hours; 3.08" storm total from 2d to 4th.

4

1869   "Saxby's Gale"; dangerous hurricane passed very near island; wind shifted from southeast to southwest; lowest barometer 28.70"; named for British naval officer who predicted it eleven months before.

5

1877   Hurricane on northeast track passed just southeast; "a heavy storm of rain, high winds blew it along the streets in wild tumult."

1881   Severe two-day gale; six schooners grounded nearby; occasional snow mixed with rain, 36° at 7:00 a.m.

6

1849   East and northeast storm "blew with great violence, but caused little damage"; described by Henry Thoreau in his travel book *Cape Cod*.

7

1962   Heavy rainstorm of 2.41".

1984   Killing frost with temperature of 29° put end to growing season and heightened fall foliage coloring.

8

1825   Smoky skies on 7th and 8th from forest fires in Maine.

9

1804   The Snow Hurricane passed northeast over Connecticut and Massachusetts; snow in northern New England, rain in south; schooner *Republican* aground on shoal outside Great Point, captain and his wife swam ashore.

10

1925   Snow flurries during the day, the earliest snow ever reported by the weather bureau from 1886 to present.

11

1836   Tropical storm with wind shifting from northeast to east to southeast; heavy rain; temperature dropped to 43°.

12

1846   "The southeast gale was very severe, the worst since 1841"; large vigorous hurricane moved north over central Pennsylvania following a track identical to that of Hazel in 1954.

1878   Major hurricane moved just offshore; "not since the October Gale of 1841 has anything occurred here to equal it"; 10 schooners grounded in vicinity; steamer *Island Home* damaged.

13

1896   Dry northeaster blew from hurricane well offshore; very high tides caused extensive shore damage and erosion.

14

1891   Tropical storm raged from 11th to 14th; winds attained 51 mi/h; rainfall 1.97".

15

1875   Hurricane center passed over Nantucket; "a severe blow but comparatively little damage."

1876   "We had all sorts of weather from brief sunshine to a hard snowstorm"; second earliest snowfall of record; *Island Home* took five hours and twenty minutes for run to Woods Hole.

16

1900   Four schooners lost on Nantucket in a "raging tempest, wind 43 miles per hour but

seemed more."

17

1868   "A sudden and very heavy gale from the north"; four schooners and one small vessel wrecked; "it is not often that we had so many disasters in a single gale."

1929   "Heavy, moist snow" fell with temperature at 40°; no accumulation.

18

1886   U.S. Army Signal Service established a first-class weather station on Nantucket and began series of extensive observations which continued to 1970; FAA at Airport continued limited program.

1965   Temperature at 29°, then record cold for so early in season and equal to lowest ever before in October.

19

1923   Tropical storm passed over island; wind at 38 mi/h from northeast; 0.17" rain; barometer 29.52".

20

1770   Late-season hurricane did extensive damage along New England coast; Boston barometer sank to 28.96".

1961   Hurricane Gerda, well offshore, caused gales for five days; many boat trips cancelled; airlift to Hyannis arranged for passengers.

21

1899   Snow flurries during the day.

1944   Second hurricane of season threatened, but storm became extratropical, losing strength before passing over island; winds only 36 mi/h; rainfall 1.49"; barometer 29.37".

22

1878   Hurricane brought severe southeaster followed by a westerly blow; no steamer from mainland this day.

Schooner Henry F. Kreger *struck on Little Round Shoal off Great Point during a northeast gale on October 26, 1921. The hulk soon broke up and the stern grounded at Gideon's Valley east of Cisco.* Photograph courtesy of Charles F. Sayle.

1948   Temperature fell to 29°, equal to lowest ever in October.

23

1761   Strong hurricane blew down steeple on Trinity Church at Newport, RI.

24

1948   Very heavy rain of 3.21″; "it was blowing 25 to 35 miles an hour and some snow mixed in with the rain."

25

1962   Snow flurries on 25th, followed by ice pellets on 26th.

26

1800   Brant Point lighthouse blown down in gale.

1921   Four-masted schooner *Henry F. Kreger* grounded on Little Round Shoal.

27

1859   One-inch snowfall, "giving our island a decidedly whitish appearance;" only measurable October snowfall of record until 1925.

1869   "Snow driving all day from clouds, ice formed."

1963   Late-season heat wave; Boston registered 80°, 84°, and 85° from 25th to 27th, while Nantucket had 68°, 61°, and 68°.

28

1879   Tropical storm moved across Rhode Island with little local effect.

1934   Snow flurries during the day.

29

1963   Long-lived Hurricane Ginny passed about 140 miles southeast of Nantucket, causing "high winds and heavy rain but little damage"; 75 mi/h gusts; 2.25″ rainfall; huge waves hit beaches.

30

1925   An early wintry day: 32° with 0.2″ snowfall.

1928   Temperature 30°, lowest ever in town for October.

31

1829   Severe gale: "a heavy storm, a higher tide than has been known for many years, trees down"; probably a late-season hurricane.

1925   Cold day throughout New England with a hard freeze inland; Nantucket had a maximum of 41° and a minimum of 36°.

November

1

1716   Dark Day in New England caused by smoke from forest fires on mainland; conditions described by Reverend Cotton Mather in letter to the Royal Society of London.

1956   Temperature at 69°, highest ever in November on Nantucket.

2

1743   Ben Franklin's Hurricane: the Philadelphian surmised that this and other coastal storms moved from southwest to northeast, despite contrary winds, since hurricane clouds prevented his viewing of an evening eclipse of the moon; but his brother at Boston saw the lunar phenomenon before the storm clouds arrived.

1861   Hurricane moving near coast caused high water; "the tide rose to a great height" on Nantucket; at Wareham the greatest damage in years occurred; new moon came on November 2.

3

1778   *H. M. S. Somerset*, 64 guns, wrecked near Truro in storm; crew of 480 taken prisoner and marched to Boston.

1879   Whirlwind crossed Nantucket harbor, "causing considerable commotion in the waters and upsetting a boat."

1966   Excessive rainfall of 4.93" in 24 hours, storm total 5.24", the greatest rainstorm since August 1889.

4

1727   Smoky day in New England from forest fires in West.

5

1894   Election Day Snowstorm of '94 on the mainland interfered with voter turnout; only rain fell on Nantucket.

6

1953   Severe coastal storm with high winds and heavy rain; 98 mi/h gusts at Block Island; Nantucket recorded 56 mi/h wind speed sustained for one minute.

7

1904   Unseasonably cold day; temperature ranged from 37° to 33°.

1938   Maximum of 68°, warmest ever so late in the fall season.

8

1947   Southeaster caused more erosion at west end near Smith's Point; one residence and six bath houses washed away.

9

1819   Widespread dark day over New England, caused by forest fires in Adirondack Mountains in New York.

10

1908   Driving windstorm closed opening to the sea at the Haulover, which had been employed as a short cut from harbor to fishing grounds since a severe storm in December 1896 cut through the sand spit just north of Wauwinet.

1948   Newspaper plane fogged out after 135 days of uninterrupted service.

11

1835   Great southwest blow put eight vessels ashore on Cape Cod; Nantucket barometer fell to 28.90"; wind shifted from south-southeast to southwest and then to northwest.

12

1947   Coastal storm did extensive damage; winds up to 58 mi/h from northwest; center passed well west of island; 1.26" rain.

13

1833   "The night the stars fell"; a celebrated shower of Leonid meteors.

1859   Brig *Harvard*, Philadelphia to Boston, hove down off South Shoals; six saved in boat, picked up and carried to New York, but captain, his wife, and three other men perished.

14

1904   Great November storm; barometer dropped to 28.69" on Nantucket; wind 47 mi/h northeast; rainfall 1.09".

15

1972   Large storm dropped 2.61" of rain; heavy snow fell over northern New England on 14th and 15th.

16

1875   Coastal storm; high tide; temperature at 23°.

17

1873   Storm dropped barometer to low reading of 28.30", the second lowest ever reported on island; "very heavy surf" caused extreme erosion.

1911   Schooner *Charles H. Woolston* wrecked on Great Point; crew rescued by Coskata lifesavers.

1924   Temperature at 17°, lowest ever so early in the cold season.

18

1930   Very heavy rainstorm of 3.58" on the 17th and 18th.

19

1620   *Mayflower* experienced difficulty in navigating Pollock Rip off Monomoy Point and Great Point on account of adverse winds and tides; ship returned north to Provincetown instead of continuing south to original destination in the lands of the Virginia Company, thus changing the course of American history.

1876   Severe, prolonged storm from 18th to 22d; high tide undermined part of Steamboat Wharf.

20

1846   First of three successive gales within a week; others on 22d and 25th.

21

1798   Famous Long Storm raged from 18th to 22d; many wrecks on Cape Cod; very deep snows fell along coast on mainland.

1962   Very heavy rainstorm of 3.11″ in 24 hours on 21st and 22d.

22

1828   Southwester with heavy rain; barometer at 29.14″.

1831   Severe gales caused damage to property and shipping when the wind shifted from east-northeast to east-southeast as storm center passed to the west.

23

1892   Latest date in the year for first killing frost to occur in record from 1886 to 1930.

1931   Late-season heat wave from 21st to 25th: 65°, 63°, 66°, and 59° on Nantucket; Boston reached a peak of 77°.

24

1901   Severe coastal storm known as "Marconi Storm" because high winds blew down new wireless antenna at South Wellfleet on Cape Cod; Nantucket barometer at 29.13″; wind reached 53 mi/h from east.

25

1783   Dutch frigate *Erfprins*, 54 guns, foundered about 24 miles east of Nantucket with loss of 303 men; probably New England's greatest sea tragedy.

1846   Severe storm dropped barometer to 29.62″, the lowest in 10 years; tide rose 6.7 feet above normal level.

1950   The Great Easterly Gale of 1950 raged on mainland; Nantucket escaped the worst due to its distance from the center over Pennsylvania; wind 47 mi/h; rainfall 2.33″ on 25th and 26th.

26

1885   Severe storm coincided with the astronomical high tide; called "a northeast screamer" by local editor.

1888   Late-season hurricane passed about 50 miles east of Nantucket; waves driven up to gates of Surfside Hotel, higher than August 1883; wind only 30 mi/h.

27

1898   The Portland Storm reached height on island about 1:00 to 2:00 a.m.; winds rose to 55 mi/h; lull about noon, then storm renewed; schooner *Luther Eldredge* drove on submerged wharf and sank; passenger ship *Portland* lost off Cape Cod with all 192 persons aboard.

1904   Heaviest early-season snowfall of 8.1″, a record for November.

28

1878   High winds and waves; "surf broke across beaches into caves, spray at Siasconset went over the first row of houses."

29

1901   Temperature dropped to 15°, lowest ever recorded in November in weather bureau records.

1921   Severe icestorm raged for four days on mainland; Nantucket escaped with 2.54″ of rain; temperature ranged from 45° to 40°.

1945   Severest November storm since 1898; sustained winds at 42 mi/h with gusts to 56 mi/h; barometer at 29.13″; 2.06″ rainfall; waterfront took a beating; streets near harbor flooded.

1963   Storm center passed northwest over western New England, but raised winds of 65 mi/h on Nantucket on 30th; 1.02″ rain; extensive damage along New England south coast.

30

1842   Severe gale; barometer dropped to 29.11″; wind east-northeast and east; temperature rose to 40°.

1872   Bitterly cold ending of cold November: 7° in morning and evening.

December

1

1927   Maximum of 61°, warmest ever in December on Nantucket.

2

1942   Severe storm passed northward over interior of New England; Nantucket barometer dropped to 28.67″; 0.82″ rain fell; highest wind at 38 mi/h from southwest.

3

1878   Severe storm raged over Islands and Cape Cod; Woods Hole recorded wind at 64 mi/h.

1896   "A very brilliant aurora"; three arches between 40° and horizon.

1890   Maximum and minimum temperatures for month occurred on same day, the 3d: maximum 47°, minimum 3°.

4

1786   First of the Triple Snows of December 1786 on 4th and 5th; "Wind extreme. Tides as high as ever known. Snowed very fast all day," wrote Kezia

Fanning in her diary; extensive high water damage around harbor; Smith's Point broken through by high seas.

5

1915   Six-masted schooner *Alice M. Lawrence,* 305 feet long, 3132 tons, struck submerged wreck and became a total loss; it was "the largest vessel ever wrecked in the vicinity."

6

1830   Severe storm, "the fury of the invisible element was unexampled"; barometer dropped to 28.85″; tide said to have been higher than any since December 1786.

1983   High winds from southeast to southwest; Wauwinet reported gusts to 80 mi/h; many phone and power outages occurred.

7

1945   Boston suburbs deluged with 6.59″ in 24 hours, but Nantucket received only 1.29″.

8

1786   Second of Triple Storms of December 1786 brought more snow.

1902   Record early-season cold: minimum 1° and maximum only 10°.

9

1885   Schooner *Austen Locke* ran ashore near Miacomet; crew rescued by breeches buoy.

1978   Heavy rainstorm brought 2.02″.

10

1786   Third of Triple Storms of December '86 raised snow depth at Kingston on Plymouth Bay to 48″; no report on depth from Nantucket.

1905   Gale of 64 mi/h from north sank South Shoals lightship.

11

1883   Crimson glow for an hour after sunset "had appearance of distant fire"; caused by volcanic dust carried around the world from eruption of Krakatoa in East Indies; brilliant coloring of skies before sunrise and after sunset continued for over a month.

12

1883   Extremely low tide; steamer grounded in harbor.

1911   Temperature at 60°, latest date ever for reading in the 60s.

1960   The Pre-Winter Storm of '60; snowfall of 15.7″; average hourly wind 35.8 mi/h, gusts to 51 mi/h; barometer dropped to 28.86″; blizzard conditions prevailed at the end of the storm.

13

1875   Heavy rainstorm dropped 2.61″.

14

1677   Plymouth: "Before day and till sometime in the night was here such a dreadful storme, as hath not bin knowne these 28 years, viz. Jan. 13 [23] 1649." Reverend John Cotton.

15

1839   First of Triple Storms of December '39; easterly gale prevailed; barometer dropped to 28.96″; rain on island, but heavy snow inland.

16

1835   New England's bitterest daylight; steady drop from 5° at sunrise to –6° at 6:00 p.m.; northwest gale prevailed all day; two women froze to their death in their home on the island.

1896   Severe storm with steady wind at 49 mi/h and gusting to 80 mi/h; average 38 mi/h for 24 hours; wires blown down outside town.

1960   Heavy rainstorm of 2.10″ washed away most of the big snow on 12th.

17

1831   Thermometer read 8° at sunrise, the lowest temperature during the coldest December ever known; harbor froze early and continued frozen solid well into January 1832.

1896   Heavy storm continued; made breach in South Beach at the Haulover north of Wauwinet; channel remained open for 12 years until closed by storm.

18

1620   Pilgrim exploring party, searching for a permanent homesite, first visited Plymouth during a wild wind and sleet storm.

1919   Temperature at 3° during early cold wave; at 6° on 19th.

19

1909   Six-masted schooner *Mertie B. Crowley* stranded on Tuckernuck Shoal; refloated, but grounded again near Martha's Vineyard and became a total loss.

20

1942   Record early cold wave dropped thermometer to –3°; minimum readings from 16th to 22d were: 12°, 3°, 20°, 4°, –3°, 4°, 9°; maximum during this period reached only 20° on 20th.

21

1901   Five days of intermittent snowfall left 15.0″ on ground.

1921   Warm autumn; first freeze did not occur until very late; temperature at 59° on solstice was warmest ever so late in season.

22

1884 Three-masted schooner *Warren Sawyer* ran aground at Surfside; more than 1000 bales of cotton salvaged; ship broke up in storm on January 6, 1885.

1952 Heavy rainstorm of 2.82″ on 22d and 23d.

23

1839 Second of Triple Storms of December '39; heavy snow fell over Middle Atlantic region, but only about 6.0″ along New England shore; high winds prevailed as storm center passed well to east.

1883 Home thermometers fell to 0° at localities across island.

24

1811 Severe cold storm raged along southern New England coast and on Long Island with heavy snow and near zero temperatures; many ships wrecked on windward shores and several crews frozen to death on beaches.

1865 Ice-encrusted vessel *Haynes* from Santo Domingo wrecked on island.

1966 Donner and Blitzen Storm over southern New England; snow fell amid thunder and lightning; Nantucket had only 0.3″ and missed white Christmas.

25

1876 Good sleighing on Main Street on Christmas.

1878 Sleighing once more, but not again on Christmas Day until 1912.

1885 "The Christmas Gale of '85" arose in morning and raged through the following day; northeast flow caused waves to break over wharves, damaging ships and installations; great erosion at Sesachacha and Quidnet; no steamer until 28th.

1889 Temperature at 53°, for warmest Christmas Day; tied in 1979.

1949 All-time high pressure in weather bureau record, 31.02″, but not accompanied by cold or wind as is usual with very high pressure.

1963 White Christmas with 4.0″ snow remaining on ground from storms on the 18–19th and 23d–24th.

1980 Coldest Christmas Day ever; thermometer fell from 36° just after midnight to 1° by 11:59 p.m. Christmas night.

26

1778 The Magie Storm (called Hessian Storm at Newport); small ship with militia aboard under command of Captain Magie lost near Cape Cod in blizzard conditions; all drowned.

1872 The Day after Christmas Storm of '72; after a cold wave, "a tremendous storm" broke on Nantucket; island both snowbound and icebound.

1909 Three-masted schooner *Belle Holiday* grounded on Coatue flats in great storm, but hauled off later; "Nantucket escaped the blizzard but experienced a phenomenal high tide."

1969 Extreme heavy rainstorm of 4.25″, would have amounted to over 40″ of snow if colder; temperature that day ranged 33° to 54°.

27

1904 Heavy snowfall of 11.6″ in 24 hours; temperature fell from 48° to 8° during northwest gale.

1930 Wind peaked at 62 mi/h from northwest following coastal storm.

28

1839 Third of Triple Storms of '39; "one of the most violent within the recollection of the oldest inhabitant"; barometer dropped to 28.80″; wind mainly southeast; Nantucket lay on opposite side of storm center from Boston.

1866 Cross Rip lightship broke from moorings in westerly gale and drifted; crew picked up by passing ship and taken to New Orleans, LA; returned home after being listed as missing for four weeks.

29

1853 "One of the most violent storms which has occurred here since the great October gale in '41"; wet snow accompanied hurricane-force winds.

1933 Harbor covered with ice for the first time since 1923; severe cold wave dropped mercury to −3°; minimum on 30th at 2°.

1959 High tides at new moon; streets along waterfront flooded by sea water backing up through drains.

30

1917 Most prolonged severe cold in Nantucket history ended year and extended into January; minimums of 8°, 8°, and 11° on 29th, 30th, and 31st; harbor icebound.

31

1895 Very warm ending of year: 55° on 30th, 57° on 31st.

1962 Northerly gale created coldest New Year's Eve ever; drove the thermometer down to −3°; severest windchill ever known on island; maximum during day only 14°.

METEOROLOGICA MISCELLANEA
Events, Extremes, and Experiences

Eighteenth Century

Cast Ashore, Then Frozen, December 1771

December 6th, English sloop *Paoli*, Delap, of and for Halifax, N.S., from Philadelphia, was cast ashore on Great Point during a violent gale and snow storm. All on board succeeded in getting ashore, but Captain Delap and the mate, Mr. Otis, both natives of Barnstable, perished on the point. Two of the sailors attempted to walk to town and perished on Coatue point. Two others and a boy named John Weiderhold succeeded in reaching a barn at Squam, and placed the boy between them, covered themselves with hay and kept from freezing. The vessel was discovered from town next day, high and dry on the beach. Had they remained on board all would have been saved.

Arthur H. Gardner,
Wrecks Around Nantucket, 1915.

"A Most Violent Gust of Wind," 1774

We hear from Nantucket that on Wednesday the 9th of March Instant (1774) at about 8 o'clock in the Morning, they had a most violent Gust of Wind that perhaps was ever known there, but it lasted only about a Minute. It seemed to come in a narrow Vein, and in its progress blew down and totally destroyed the Light-House on that Island, besides several Shops, Barns, etc. Had the Gust continued fifteen Minutes it is thought it would not have left more than half the Buildings standing, in the Course that it passed. But we don't hear of any Persons receiving much hurt, nor much Damage done,

Bark W. H. Marshall *came ashore near head of Mioxes Pond in a thick fog on March 9, 1877. Salvage was attempted, but gales on July 1–2* caused her to heel over and the ship *became a total wreck.* Collection of the Nantucket Historical Association.

except the loss of the Light-House which in every respect is considerable.

The Massachusetts Gazette and the Boston Post-Boy and Advertiser, March 12, 1774.

"A Violent Stormy Day," February 1778

Saturday Feb. 7   A violent stormy day   a higher tide than has been known for a number of years   stove boats   drove water fences away   hurt mill   storm commenced on Friday snowed very hard Sat.

Kezia Fanning diary
Nantucket Historical Association library.

The Wonderful Dark Day, 1780

Almost, if not altogether alone, as the most mysterious and as yet unexplained phenomenon of its kind, in nature's diversified range of events, during the last century (1776–1876), stands the *Dark Day of May Nineteenth, 1780*,—a most unaccountable darkening of the whole visible heavens and atmosphere in New England,—which brought intense alarm to multitudes of minds, as well as dismay to the brute creation, the fowls fleeing, bewildered, to their roosts, and the birds to their nests, and the cattle returning to their stalls. Indeed, thousands of the good people that day became fully convinced that the end of all things terrestrial had come; many gave up, for the time, their secular pursuits, and betook themselves to religious devotions; while many others regarded the darkness as not only a token of God's indignation against the various iniquities and abominations of the age, but also as an omen of some future destruction that might overwhelm the land—as in the case of the countries mentioned in biblical history,—unless speedy repentance and reformation took place.

Richard M. Devens,
Our First Century, 1880.

"A Day Which I Never Saw the Like Before"

On the 19th of the 5th month, 1780, the morning opened with thunder and lightning with the wind SSW. The sun shined out about 8 o'clock in the morning. About 9 o'clock it began to rain small showers and continued to about 10 o'clock. Then the rain ceased and the clouds seemed to be gathering together in great thickness and about ½ after ten there seemed to be a darkness gradually appear and by eleven it was quite discovered to be something uncommon, and by 12 o'clock it was so dark that we could not see to dine, but were forced to have candles lit, as in the evening when the moon shone out not very bright. So the darkness continued for about two hours with but little alternation from 12 to 2 o'clock.

At length the darkness began gradually to go off, but left a heavy yellow which was all the time, insomuch that silver buckles looked

exactly like gold in our shoes. That yellow looks continued until about ½ after 3, when it went off pretty suddenly and left the looks of Nature much as usual, but in evening the wind had got to north, or eastward of it, when it smelled of sulphur or something like being to the leeward of a swamp that had been burning or a chimney that has been on fire. A darkness came on in the evening, insomuch that we could not see any odds when our eyes were shut fast or when they were opened, notwithstanding, that the moon was at its full. The darkness continued until after 12 o'clock at night and then went off.

It was to the astonishment of all and terror of, I believe, almost every person. For my part, I was not without thought that the last day was come. No one who did not see it can imagine how gloomy it looked.

I leave this a memorandum for future generations to see how it was at this time so that if the like was ever to be again they may know it was no more than has been before.

S. (Sylvanus) Hussey,
reprinted in *Inquirer and Mirror*,
August 5, 1916.

Friday, May 19   rainy after the morn   no rain in afternoon   very uncommon weather   clouds very yellow   exceeding dark in the house so that many people were obliged to light candles   it was so for about 3 hours from 2 to 5   but little wind S.W.

Kezia Fanning diary.

The Dark Day of May 1780 achieved fame during the crisis period of the American Revolution. Many thought it was sent by God as a warning against the warlike spirit prevailing among Christians and the general moral iniquities of the time. It was observed in the morning on the Vermont-New York border, during the noon hour across most of southern New England, and in the afternoon on Cape Cod and the Islands. The cause was smoke and partially incombustible debris from forest fires.

Lightning Strikes, July 1780

Saturday   July 29   the thunder struck the W. End of Eben Calif's House   broke the chimney and shattered the wall inside & shingles outside very much.

Kezia Fanning diary.

Looming on May Day, 1781

Tuesday May 1 — Land loomed so over Cape Cod that we could see the trees & vessels along the shore   old town was to be seen very plain   it loomed near 2 hours.

Kezia Fanning diary.

Looming, an atmospheric phenomenon whereby objects normally below the horizon become visible, is caused by a density decrease in the atmosphere with increase of elevation. A warm layer aloft is superimposed on a cool layer at the surface, resulting in the bending downward of light rays originating below the horizon.

Loss of a Boat's Crew on Nantucket Bar, January 1782

This melancholy event happened on the 1st of the 1st month, 1782. Captain Robert Barker, commander of a brig lying without the bar of the harbor, bound to Virginia, on the morning of the above-mentioned day, invited a number of his intimate friends to spend a day on board with him. Seven in number, accepting his invitation, left the wharf with him in a whale boat. The weather was cold, and the wind blowing strong from the N.W. caused a heavy sea on the bar. These circumstances occasioned some anxiety for their safety. Every movement of the boat was carefully watched by the friends of those on board her. The company pursued their course with safety, until they attempted to cross the bar; then the boat was seen to upset. The distance from the shore being about two miles, every motion was observed. Some of the company were not seen after the accident, others clung to the boat awhile, but were soon, one by one washed off to a watery grave. As soon as it was discovered that the boat had upset, two boats went to their relief. It was hoped that those in peril would be able to cling to their boat, until they had drifted across the bar. But this hope was fallacious.

The bodies of most of those who perished were found in the following spring. We shall introduce, hereafter among some specimens of our island poetry, an elegy written on this mournful occasion. [An Elegy on the Sudden and Awful Death of Seven Men Who were Drowned on the Nantucket Bar, 1st of 1st Month, 1782].

Obed Macy,
History of Nantucket, 1835.

"The Sudden Change,"1782

Sun Jan 13   Just at day blew extreme hard at E. for several minutes & instantly as quick as thought from blowing it was an entire calm   never before knew such a sudden alternation   Had been windy all night but was calm all day after the sudden change.

Kezia Fanning diary.

Severe Drought, 1800

Friday August 30   Shower last eve   Been the driest season most ever was known.

Kezia Fanning diary.

Wind Downs Brant Point Lighthouse, 1800

The Washington *Daily Intelligencer* carried the following dispatch in the issue of November 28, 1800:   "On Sunday evening the 26th October the Light-House on Brant Point (Nantucket) was blown down."

Nineteenth Century

High Winds, April 1807

Sun Apr 5   Such winds as have blown for past week have not been known for 30 years.
Kezia Fanning diary.

A very severe storm with barometer readings at 28.75 inches at New Haven, cut across southern New England March 31 to April 1, known as the All Fools' Day storm. First, southeast gales must have lashed Nantucket, then the backlash of northwest gales swept the island.

The Cold June Gale, 1814

Obed Macy made note of an unseasonable cool episode during the cold years from 1811 to 1817:

On the 23d of 6 month there was a violent gale of wind from the N.W. and the weather, at the same time, so cold that aged people, in passing about, wore mittens. The inhabitants in general made fires in their houses. The season had before been dry which caused the wind to have such an effect on the fields of corn as to injure much of it in some places where it was most exposed; but afterwards it pretty generally recovered its growth and yielded a tolerably good crop.

The Year Without a Summer, 1816

The diary notes of Mrs. Kezia Fanning give us an indication of conditions on Nantucket for the unusual season:
June 7—   Remarkable cold for the

season—a good winter fire is very comfortable.
June 8—   Very cold.
June 15—   Remarkable cold weather for the season. Ice was on water pail in the morn this week. Vegetation almost destroyed.
June 16—   Very cold morning. Fire as comfortable as in winter.

Though no actual thermometer readings on the island have been uncovered, the freezing of water would indicate a figure below 32°F. The lowest official thermometer readings for the modern period from 1886 to 1985 in June was 35°F in 1976 at the Airport.

Thomas Rodman's record at New Bedford gave a good indication of the departures from normal for the region during this summer, in degrees Fahrenheit: May –2.8, June –5.1, July –5.8, August –2.1, September –3.4, and October + 0.2,

June, July, and August also ran below normal in inches of precipitation: June –0.79 (75 percent of normal), July –2.19 (32 percent), and August –2.77 (35 percent). A tropical storm moving up the Atlantic seaboard in the middle of September broke the drought and boosted the month's total to 6.05 inches (172 percent). New Bedford measured 3.02 inches on the 12th to 14th.

On June 10, 1816, the *Nantucket Gazette* mentioned "the gale of Friday last [7th] when the brig *Greyhound* of Hartford struck on Swan Island shoals. It had not bilged, and would probably be got off." This was the cold front gale of northwest winds that introduced the Canadian airstreams producing the remarkably cool period in early June.

The Sabbath Thunderstorm, September 1821

Thunder Storm. On Sabbath morning, this Island was visited by one of the severest Thunder Storms, perhaps ever known in this place. It commenced raining in torrents, early in the morning, and continued, three or four hours, attended with very heavy thunder and sharp lightning. A dwelling house at the north part of Town was struck by lightning and a young person within the house, sitting near a bed, was knocked down, and remained senseless for some time. We understand it struck in several other places on the Island without doing any material injury. The lightning rod attached to the North Congregational Meeting House, was struck, and the ground at the bottom considerably thrown up.

Nantucket Inquirer,
September 13, 1821.

Candlemas Day, 1824

Today being Candlemas, and not very stormy, according to ancient tradition, the most severe portion of winter is to come. The old Ladies will therefore refrain from frying dough-nuts.

Nantucket Inquirer,
February 2, 1824.

Thermal Humor in 1825

The following item appeared in the *Nantucket Inquirer* on June 6, 1825:
Thermometrical Observations. A gentleman perceiving a man swolling liquor from a thermometer, inquired of a bystander the reason for such a strange proceeding, to which he replied, "Oh, he is getting intoxicated by degrees."

Smoky Sky, October 1825

For two days past our atmosphere has been filled with a dense and disagreeable vapour, supposed to have been driven by the East winds from the neighborhood of the late fires in the forests of Maine.

Nantucket Inquirer,
October 10, 1825.

Walter Folger, Jr., whose weather records appeared in the Nantucket Inquirer *during the 1820s and 1830s, was also a maker and repairer of astronomical and navigational instruments. He designed this attractive compass rose to show direction to 32 points as well as degrees of azimuth.* Collection of the Nantucket Historical Association.

The Year Without a Winter, 1828

For these six years [1823 to 1829] there is no record. It is during this interval that I am inclined to place a snowless term of years referred to in family reminiscences as the time when snowstorms were supposed to have permanently gone out of fashion and people talked of selling their sleighs.

Ellen Larned diary,
Brooklyn, Connecticut.

The editor of the *Inquirer* took notice of the mild weather of early winter in December 1827 and January 1828: "After five or six weeks of very moderate winter weather, occasionally tinctured with the mildness of May, a sudden change took place on Monday Last [Jan. 23]." Though the temperature dipped to 10°F on the island, the cold did not last, and February showed an even greater departure from normal than the preceding months.

According to Walter Folger's temperature record, January averaged a +3.7 degrees departure from normal, and February an amazing +7.5 degrees Fahrenheit. His record for December 1827 has not been preserved.

These figures were backed up by the New Bedford record of Samuel Rodman. His departures from normal for the three winter months were: +2.9, +5.9, and +8.8 degrees. March, too, was also above normal at +3.0 degrees Fahrenheit.

An Old-fashioned Snowstorm, January 1836

January 8   Snow now about 2 feet deep
January 9   Snowed all day 2 feet deep this morning
January 10   First day. So snowy and windy, thought it not prudent to attempt going to meeting   Snow all day. Nathan thinks about 3 feet deep this evening, in some places very great drifts, continuous snowing with wind.

Thomas Burns Marriett diary,
Nantucket Historical Association library.

An Ice Embargo Incident, 1837

An old diary bears the following comments on the winter siege in 1837:

The harbor was closed for seven weeks, in the year 1837. No mail left the island during that time. One or two mails from the continent were landed at Great Point, and brought to town. There was some trouble apprehended to our ships at sea. I do not know the cause. Some negotiations going on between France and our country, or some other country, made the people very anxious to hear from abroad. It was very near the close of General Jackson's second term as President. When at last communication was opened, the mails arrived before noon. They caused great rejoicing. The bells were rung, flags raised, and all spoke of eagerness of the "good news." I was then assistant in the boy's department of the Coffin school. Hon. William H. Wood, late Judge of Probate of Plymouth County, was the principal. The boys brought to school in the afternoon little paper flags, with "Peace" written on them, which they stuck in their desks. They were so wild with excitement that Mr. Wood judiciously gave them a half holiday. I remember the date, as it was the last year of my teaching. It was this year that Lake Michigan was frozen over.

Quoted in Harry B. Turner,
*The Story of
the Island Steamer* Nantucket, 1910.

"A Scene of Awful Grandeur," Hurricane Surf, September 1838

The Storm at Nantucket—On Thursday (the 13th) we were visited with a storm of rain and wind; the latter of which, increasing by degrees at length amounted to something very like a tornado. Many objects exposed to its force, in and out of town, were prostrated—as fences, barn roofs, terraces, &c. Trees, corn and other plants were uptorn, or bowed to earth; and much mischief of various sorts, is said to have ensued.

The ocean on the southern and eastern borders of the island presented an awfully magnificent spectacle lashed by the gale into uncontrollable fury, it seemed disposed to pour its vengeance upon terra firma which actually trembled beneath the weight of its wrath. Nothing but mountains of foaming liquid, in the most tumultuous agitation, could be seen for miles: the spray breaking from their summits, the columns of vapor from the crater of a volcano—the surf, as it curved from the height of thirty or forty feet, and broke upon the echoing strand with incessant thunderings—altogether presented a scene of awful grandeur inconceivable but by actual observers; and many persons left town for the purpose of witnessing its tremendous sublimity. It may be said to have formed a multiplied picture, immeasurably enlarged, of the great cataract of the Lakes—the Fall of Niagara.

Nantucket Inquirer,
September 22, 1838.

Salt Spray from the August Hurricane, 1839

The severe storm of the 30th and 31st August seemed to operate on most of the plants in our vicinity, withering and killing the foliage which generally soon dropped off, leaving limbs and trunks in a great measure denuded. Succeeded by new dress.

Nantucket Inquirer,
October 19, 1839.

The same phenomenon occurred during the Great September Gale of 1815 when the spray was carried forty miles into the mainland.

St. Elmo's Fire on April Fools' Day, 1840

Two sloops: Lightning which played about the mast and rigging, and fell as it were as balls of fire on the decks. Similar extraordinary phenomena were observed by persons who watched the church steeple and other elevated points. Luminous globuls were distinctly seen to touch the tips of the two principal spires, and thence roll down and burst upon the roofs of the main building below. Part of a boy's kite, which had lodged on the upper portion of one of the steeples, was ignited and consumed.

Nantucket Inquirer,
April 7, 1840.

St. Elmo's Fire is a corona discharge, luminous and often audible, that is intermediate in nature between a momentary spark discharge and a continuous point discharge. It occurs from the peak of objects, especially pointed ones, when the electric field strength near their surfaces attains a value near 1000 volts per centimeter. It is seen during stormy weather emanating from the yards and masts of ships at sea.

The name was given to the phenomenon by sailors who regarded it as a visitation of their patron saint, Elmo (Eramus). An appearance of St. Elmo's fire was regarded as a good omen, for it tends to occur in the latter phases of a violent thunderstorm when most of the surface wind and wave disturbance is over.

The *Joseph Starbuck* Storm, 1842

One of the most costly shipwrecks in all Nantucket history occurred on November 27, 1842, when the new ship *Joseph Starbuck*, while in the midst of fitting out for a second trip to the Orient, broke its tow to Edgartown and struck on the eastern extremity of the Bar.

The weather records of Walter Folger indicate the passage of a strong cold front during the midday hours of November 27. His barometer dropped 0.19 inch from 7:00 a.m. to 29.44 inches and rose 0.21 inch by 9:00 p.m. The wind in the morning came out of the west-southwest, at noon from the west, and by evening from the west-northwest. Indications are that a strong low pressure system crossed central or northern New England during the day. Rain fell at noon at the time of the frontal passage, but the other

observations were fair. The temperature dropped from a morning 44° to an evening 28°F.

Another severe storm followed on November 30 and December 1 with the barometer dropping from a high of 30.27 inches on the morning of the 30th to a low of 29.19 inches at noon of the 1st. The windshift was from east, to southwest, to west-northwest, indicating another cyclonic storm passage to the north.

The "Smotherer" Snowstorm, January 5–6, 1856

The Churches remained closed, men went unshaved, the only branch of business pursued as usual was 'courting.' No storm ever yet been known sufficiently severe to interfere with that interesting pursuit.

Nantucket Inquirer,
January 9, 1856.

The Cold Wave of January 1857

January 22, 1857. Hard winters are becoming the order of things. Winter before last was hard, last winter was harder, and this surpasses all winters known before.

We have been frozen into our island now since the 6th. No one cared much about it for the first two or three days; the sleighing was good, and all the world were trying out their horses on Main street—the race-course of the world. Day after day passed, and the thermometer sank to a lower point, and the winds rose to a higher and sleighing became uncomfortable; and even the dullest man longs for the cheer of a newspaper. The 'Nantucket Inquirer' came out for a while, but at length it had nothing to tell and nothing to inquire about, and so kept its peace . . . .

Last night the weather was so mild that a plan was made for cutting out the steamboat; all the Irishmen in town were ordered to be

on the harbor with axes, shovels, and saws at seven this morning. The poor fellows were exulting in the prospect of a job, but they are sadly balked, for this morning at seven a hard storm was raging—snow and a good northwest wind . . . .

January 23. Foreseeing that the thermometer would show a very low point last night, we sat up until near midnight, when it stood one and one-half below zero. The stars shone brightly, and the wind blew freshly from west-north-west.

This morning the wind is the same, and the mercury stood at six and one-half below zero at seven o'clock, and now at ten A.M. is not above zero. The Coffin School dismissed its scholars. Miss F. suffered much from exposure on her way to school . . . .

There are seven hundred barrels of flour in town; it is admitted that fresh meat is getting scarce; the streets are almost impassable from the snow-drifts . . . .

The last snow drifted so that the sleighing was difficult, and at present the storm is so smothering that few are out. A. has been to school every day, and I have not failed to go out into the air once a day to take a short walk.

January 24. We left the mercury one below zero when we went to bed last night, and it was at zero when we rose this morning. But it rises rapidly, and now, at eleven A.M., it is as high as fifteen. The weather is still and beautiful . . . .

We hear of no suffering in town for fuel or provisions, and I think we could stand a three months' seige without much inconvenience as far as physicals are concerned.

January 26. The ice continues, and the cold. The weather is beautiful, and with the thermometer at fourteen I swept with the telescope an hour and a half last night comfortably . . . .

January 29. We have had now two days of warm weather, but there is no hope of getting our steamboat off . . . .

It was worth the trouble of a ride to 'Sconset to see the masses of snow on the road. The road had been cleared for the coal-carts, and we drove through a narrow path, cut in deep snow banks far above our heads, sometimes for the length of three or four sleighs, and there was much waiting on this account. Then, too, the road was much gullied, and we rocked in the sleigh as we would on shipboard, with the bounding over hillocks of snow and ice.

Now, all is changed: the roads are slushy, and the water stands in deep pools all over the streets. There is a dense fog, very little wind, and that from the east. The thermometer above thirty-six.

Mails arrived February 3 . . . OUR STEAMBOAT LEFT February 5.

Maria Mitchell diary.

Walking on the Sea, January 1857

I will state that there are two men on this island who walked around the South Shoal lightship (at that time anchored about twenty miles off the east-southeastern shore of the island), the ice being 12 inches thick. The bark "Modena," of Boston, was in the ice forty miles south of the lightship, and a short time afterward she drifted near the lightship, received letters, and delivered them to Boston.

On the 7th of January 1857, the lanterns of the lightship froze to the masts and it took application of pickle to get them down to the deck. The mercury was at zero.

"One Who Was There,"
Nantucket Inquirer and Mirror,
January 6, 1934.

A Winter Incident During the Hard Winter of 1856–57

On the afternoon of January 21, steamer *New York,* from Glasglow, anchored off Squam Head and set signals for assistance. A whale-boat was sent out to her from shore and

it was found that the steamer's supply of coal had nearly given out, owing to an unusually long and stormy passage across the ocean. The whale-boat brought ashore news from the mainland which had been received in Europe before the departure of the steamer for America, and it was the first information from the outside world that Nantucketers had received since January 5. The *New York* remained off Quidnet until the following Saturday, but as no favorable opportunity had been presented for putting coal aboard up to that time, she was taken around off 'Sconset in the afternoon.

Ice, however, formed in between the vessel and the shore and it was not until Tuesday that another attempt was made to board her. The following day a large gang of men and teams were put at work transporting coal from town to the beach at 'Sconset, and it was estimated that at least 1,000 tons of snow had to be removed from the roads in order to allow the coal teams to pass. Coal was placed in bags and carried out to the steamer in boats—a total of 115 tons being placed on board, which amount was sufficient for the steamer to reach New York. Three boats, containing twenty men and five tons of coal, drifted with the tide nearly three miles from the ship, and it was only by great exertion that the men reached shore, where the boats were towed back to the starting point with horses.
Nantucket Inquirer,
January 30, 1857.

Cross Rip Lightship Adrift, 1866

December 28th, the Cross Rip lightship, manned by a Nantucket crew, in charge of the mate, Charles M. Thomas, (the captain and watch being ashore on liberty) broke her moorings during a heavy westerly gale and drove out to sea. No tidings were heard of her for six weeks and all hands had been given up as lost when a letter was received from New Orleans announcing the arrival of the

crew there the last of January on ship *Henry L. Richardson,* from Thomaston, ME, which had sighted the lightship December 29th in a sinking condition, with signals of distress flying, and taken off the crew.

Gardner,
Wrecks Around Nantucket, 1915.

Good Visibility, 1868

March 10, 1868—South shoals lightship seen and smoke of engine at Hyannis.

Inquirer and Mirror,
March 14, 1868.

The *Nantucket Inquirer,* founded in 1821, and the *Nantucket Mirror,* founded in 1845, merged and the *Inquirer and Mirror* first issued on April 1, 1865. Publication of the latter is now in the 166th volume (1986).

Drought in Summer 1873

From May 12 to September 4, only 2.94 inches of rain fell over the 114 days. The heaviest fall during this period was 0.70 inches on July 17–18. The drought was alleviated by a storm of 1.62 inches on September 4.

Record of Charles Coleman quoted in
Inquirer and Mirror,
October 1, 1938.

Exceptional Visibility, April 1875

The weather was very pleasant, and the air so clear last Sunday [April 11], that the South-shoals Light-ship was distinctly visible from south tower in the afternoon; as were churches on the Cape. At the same time one hundred vessels were in sight of the sound.

Inquirer and Mirror,
April 17, 1875.

British bark Minmaneuth *came ashore at south end of island near Miacomet Pond in a thick fog on July 30, 1873. After discharging 1000 of 4000 bags of Brazilian coffee, she was gotten off three days later. Meantime, she became a mecca for sightseers.* Collection of the Nantucket Historical Association.

Good Old-fashioned Winters, 1875

The freeze-up has set our elderly friends to gossiping about the 'good old-fashioned winters.' When our harbor was covered with sleighs and other teams, when lighters discharged their cargoes of oil on the ice and rolled it ashore, and all that sort of thing. Is it really true that our winters as a rule, are milder than those of the older time? We know that the remark is often made; but who can demonstrate it by any figures? And if it be really true, who can give a philosophical reason for it? It would be as difficult to do this, perhaps, as it is to predict in any particular case, whether a coming winter is to be a mild or a severe one; a matter concerning which all calculations and signs appear to fail.

Inquirer and Mirror,
January 30, 1875.

Candlemas Day, 1876

Last Wednesday was Candlemas day. The 'old folks' were wont to remark that
"If Candlemas day be fair and bright,
Winter will take another flight
If Candlemas bring snow or rain,
Winter has gone, not to come again."
But Wednesday was rather a conundrum, for it brought all three. What view do you take of it?

Inquirer and Mirror,
February 5, 1876.

Sleighing on Main Street, Christmas 1876

Shortly after noon the sleighs began to increase in number, and Main Street presented an extremely lively appearance. Everything with runners was brought into active service. Owners of fast teams put in an appearance, and there were some fine sports. These trials of speed drew together a large concourse of spectators who thronged the street on either side, and became more or less demonstrative as the race grew exciting or became devoid of fun.

The cold weather of Sunday [Dec. 24] tended to increase the quality of the sleighing and Monday morning the crisp surface caused a calm smile to o'erspread the countenance of the owners of teams, who (it being Christmas day) could afford to give their time to the sport. The streets were dotted with sleighs, and the merry jingling of the bells added to the general good cheer of Christmas day . . . .

We have had the longest period of sleighing known here for many years.

Inquirer and Mirror,
December 30, 1876.

Squally Weather in the Sound, 1877

The squall of wind Tuesday afternoon was as sudden and fierce as that of a colliky baby . . . Squall of wind Tuesday at Great Point.

Inquirer and Mirror,
October 20, 1877.

The *Monthly Weather Review* (Washington) reported a waterspout near Nantucket on this date.

A Harbor Whirlwind, 1879

A Whirlwind—By the sudden change of wind on Monday last [3d], a whirlwind was formed which swept across the harbor causing considerable commotion in the water, and nearly upsetting the boat of Mr. Alexander B. Dunham which happened to be in its course.

Inquirer and Mirror,
November 8, 1879.

Ice Blockade, 1881

During a protracted ice blockade from the last of January to the middle of February, steamer *Island Home,* an English steamship and eight sailing vessels were imprisoned in the ice at the north of the island for many days, and several were driven ashore on Great Point by one tide, to be floated off by the next. Two of the number, however, left their bones on our shores. The *Island Home,* in attempting to force her way through the ice to this port on the 29th of January, became hemmed in by heavy ice floes just back of the bar and was unable to advance or return until the 10th of February. Meantime the ice became so compact that men and teams passed to and fro between the shore and steamer and five head of cattle on board were driven ashore on the ice. The steamer was coaled from shore and on the 10th of February the ice had softened sufficently to enable her to force her way through open water and return to Woods Hole. As the ice softened and broke up, the English steamship and five of the imprisoned vessels worked clear.

Gardner,
Wrecks Around Nantucket, 1915.

The Ice Scene, February 1881

From the tower the view is sublime. At the north of us an immense ice pack extends as far as the eye can reach, even with the aid of the most powerful glass. The angular edges of huge pieces of ice point upward in every conceivable direction from the cold, cheerless field, while on shoal ground huge piles of ice have been thrown up by the action of the currents and sparkle brightly in the sunlight. These towering barriers change with each succeeding tide, and thus the scene in their particular locality is an ever-shifting one. The monotony of the frozen surface on Wednesday morning [Feb. 2] was broken by the numerous sailing craft that have been caught and held fast,—eleven of them in number,—which lay scattered between Great Point and Muskeget. Eight of these (including the steamer) came within range of the naked eye while two of the others were partially hidden from view by Tuckernuck Island . . . .

A wide ice-belt encircles us on the outer shores, depriving residents of the east end of the island of their usual fine water prospect, and extending far to the south and west. The fall of snow of Tuesday [Feb. 1] was sufficient to complete the desolate scene. This is, as nearly as pen will describe, the picture which met our gaze from the tower.

Inquirer and Mirror,
February 5, 1881.

The Yellow Day, September 1881

The sun was obscured, and early in the afternoon [6th] it was found necessary to light the gas in shops and stores, the air at the time being pervaded with a yellowish light, in which the flames of the gas took on a white gleam. The grass and foliage generally assumed a livid green tinge. As the hour of sunset arrived, the glow faded, and by 11 p.m., the moon was shining with her usual brilliancy.

Inquirer and Mirror,
September 10, 1881.

Dark days have occurred in North America since the years of earliest settlement. The most famous was on May 19, 1780, when the New England sky was darkened all day and candles were needed to carry on the day's business. The dark pall also covered Nantucket as described earlier in this chapter.

The first reports of the Yellow Day in September 1881 came from Albany, New York, in the afternoon. Cambridge, Massachusetts, experienced its darkest hours in the early morning, as did Nantucket. Widespread fires in Michigan and Ontario were ascertained to be the source of the obscuring layer of smoke and minute arboreal debris aloft.

A Terrible Experience, February 1882

The steamer *Island Home,* which plies between Nantucket and Woods Hole, had a terrible experience during Saturday night's storm. As the boat did not arrive at Nantucket on Saturday it was generally believed that Captain Manter had not started from Woods Hole. There were a few, however, who held an opposite view, and anxiously awaited the breaking of day and a cessation of the snow, that they might scan the northern shores of the island and ascertain what the fate of the *Island Home* had been . . . .

Captain [Nathan H.] Manter, on being interviewed, told the story of his tussle with the waves as follows:

We were detained at Woods Hole until nearly half-past one waiting for the other boat, and then put out. When nearly up to Cape Poge we had fine snow, but the weather was moderate, and the wind E.N.E., and I did not anticipate anything serious. We made all our buoys, but after leaving Tuckernuck Shoal buoy the snow increased, and we were unable to see ten feet ahead. Ran out our time to the bar, but could not see the buoy; then tracked the bar to the eastward about twenty minutes, but still no buoy; came about and ran twenty minutes to the westward with like result, and as night was coming on and the wind increased to a strong breeze, decided to anchor, putting out the small anchor with fifteen fathoms chain, but found we were dragging, and increased the chain to forty fathoms. The night was terrible, and we were finally obliged to put out our large anchor.

At five o'clock Sunday morning the wind blew the strongest, and as I made my way along the upper deck, it seemed as if the hurricane deck must blow off. We ripped open sacks of grain to get the bags to wrap about the hawser to prevent its chafing. The boat rode like a duck, though, and when it lighted up toward morning, made land close to us, which we took to be the Cliff, until, later on we found we were close upon Tuckernuck, and could see the hotel. I realized the precarious situation, and when the tide had fallen and we began to strike bottom, knew that something must be done, and that quickly, and decided to beach her on the island. Buoyed the large anchor and slipped the cable, then cut the hawser, when the wind favored and headed us so we could run for the bar. Our cook knows every inch of the ground up that way, and he brought her through the slues among the Swile islands into five fathoms of water, when we put for the bar.

The seas were terrific, and swept clean across the bow, running aft, and Mr. Bucknam, the engineer, was at times almost ankle deep in water in his engine room. The old boat rolled fearfully, and when we reached the outer bar, lying in the trough of the sea, a wave towering above the hurricane deck struck her as she rose upon it, knocking that hole in the side, and sweeping through to the outer saloon. I wouldn't have given two cents at the time for the boat and all on board, but we have passed safely through it, with all hands safe, but slight damage to the boat, and with anchors gone, which can be recovered. It was as much worse than being in the ice as you can imagine, and was one of the wildest times I have known in my many years' life on the ocean. The wheel rope broke once, but we managed with some difficulty to get it repaired.

Inquirer and Mirror,
February 11, 1882.

The Summer Drought, 1882

The three summer months of June, July, and August brought only 3.97 inches of rain, according to figures in the *Inquirer and Mirror*. This amounted to 44 percent of the normal. The three months in the New Bedford record matched this with only 41 percent.

No August storm appeared and the month had only two days of rain, the 11th and the 16th, amounting to 0.75 inch. During the summer, Wannacomet Pond lowered its level by 22 inches. The drought was finally broken in September by a tropical storm which dropped 1.15 inches on the 11th and the 12th. September received additional rainfall for a month's total of 6.26 inches, or 178 percent of normal.

Krakatoa's Red Sunsets, Autumn 1883

December 1—Phenomenon—Crimson glow one hour after sunset on November 27 and 28 had every appearance of a distant fire. December 8—Lasted one hour after sunset. December 15—The crimson glow in the west after sunset is still a daily object of interest.

Inquirer and Mirror,
December 1883.

The volcanic island of Krakatoa in Sunda Strait, between Java and Sumatra, Indonesia, exploded on August 26, 1883. The noise was heard 3000 miles away and the tidal wave reached South America and Hawaii. An estimated five cubic miles of rock fragments were thrown into the air, forming a great dust cloud which traveled around the world several times. In late 1883 it moved into the Northern Hemisphere and resulted in brilliant sunrises and sunsets in November and December, and to a lesser degree for the next two years.

The Wreck of the *T.B. Witherspoon,* January 10, 1886

On Sunday the three-masted schooner 'T.B. Witherspoon,' of Rockport, Me., Capt. Alfred H. Anderson, bound from Surinam to Boston, with a cargo of molasses, sugar, cocoa, pickled limes and spices, came a shore at the south side of the island near the head of Little Mioxes Pond, in a driving snow storm about 5 o'clock in the morning. They had experienced heavy weather accompanied by thick snow squalls coming on to the coast and had been unable to get an observation for several days.

Shortly before they struck, they sighted Sankaty light between the snow squalls, which they mistook for Montauk and shaped their course accordingly until they brought up in the breakers. Despite the severe cold, the mercury standing at 16 degrees, hundreds of citizens hastened to the shore as soon as news of the disaster reached town, and remained on the beach throughout the day, powerless to render assistance, while the crew slowly perished before their eyes in the rigging or fell into the sea and were drowned.

Lines were shot over the vessel by the Surfside life-saving crew, but the men on board were frozen and powerless to haul off the hawser attached. A fearful sea was raging, which rendered it impossible to launch a boat. Nevertheless, in the face of almost certain death, a life-raft was launched and nine men, Charles E. Smalley, Joseph M. Folger, Jr., Benjamin Beekman, Charles W. Cash, John P. Taber, William Morris, Horace Orpin, Benjamin Fisher, and Everett Coggin, attempted to haul off by a small line which had been shot over the vessel.

Gardner,
Wrecks Around Nantucket, 1915.

Fun on the Harbor Ice, 1888

Curiosity is often expressed by the casual visitor to Nantucket as to what the natives find to do with themselves in the winter, yet during those two weeks [January 1888] there was a genuine carnival on the harbor. Sleighing parties drove over its surface with absolute security, iceboats darted hither and thither, merry skaters flitted to and fro, eel fishermen drew wiggling treasures from the bottom of the sea, and altogther the harbor presented an animated panorama. Mechanics also found more or less profitable employment.

Letter from Nantucket
to a Philadelphia paper,
Nantucket Historical Association library.

Ice Blockade, January 1888

We are frozen in. And we use the first person plural pronoun in this case not in the editorial sense exclusively, but collectively as to include every man, woman and child and every living, moving creature and every creeping thing and every animate and inanimate object which has an abiding place on that portion of the earth between the eastern shores of Great Point and the Southeast Quarter and the farthermost end of Smith's Point on the west. In fact, the island of Nantucket stands solitary and alone in the midst of the Atlantic ocean, with the continent of America anchored to it by a one-inch iron cable, while away to the northward and westward, as far as the eye can reach; stretches a boundless, unbroken field of ice; but we have no fears for the safety of the continent so long as the cable holds, though we pity the inhabitants in their loneliness, shut off from their intercourse with this outside world.

Nantucket Journal,
January 26, 1888.

Temperatures on the island on Sunday morning ranged from 0° to −6°, officially −3.5°F at the weather bureau.

The last iceboating took place on solid harbor ice in early February 1982. January had averaged 6.7 degrees below normal along coastal New England. Photograph courtesy of H. Flint Ranney.

The Non-Blizzard of '88 over Nantucket

During the greater part of Monday [March 12], a cold southeast rainstorm accompanied by high wind which increased during the afternoon to a hurricane, the wind blowing for some time at the rate of 60 mph [47 mph corrected]. As the night came on the gale gradually subsided, and late in the morning [13th] had died away to a dead calm. The storm signals meanwhile announced an impending northwester, but the weather vanes stubbornly persisted in pointing southward. At 1 a.m. [14th] the wind was again blowing with a fury that equaled if not exceeded the gale of the afternoon, when morning dawned the wind had subsided somewhat, though occasional flurries of snow were driven about in blinding clouds during the day. The mercury meanwhile had dropped to 19 deg. during the night, but ranged somewhat higher during the day. Through it all the wind remained at the south, a remarkable incident as was universally conceded. During Tuesday night [13th–14th] and the early part of yesterday, there were occasional flurries of snow, but at the time of our going to press the weather had softened materially. The steamer left here yesterday morning [14th] for the first time since Saturday [10th].

Arthur Gardner,
Nantucket Journal.

Whirlwind at Siasconset, 1889

Whirlwind—A veritable whirlwind passed over Sconset Monday [5th] scattering clothes-line, hangings, light material and weak fences in brief order. The storm began at 11 in the forenoon with a pouring rain and the wind south; at quarter to 12 it was East; at half past 12 North, and at one was due West. Thus the wind completely boxed the compass in just 2 hours.

Inquirer and Mirror,
August 10, 1889.

The Great Street Flood, August 1889

"Damp" "Quite Moist" "A trifle wet"—Such expressions as these were what greeted the *Inquirer and Mirror* representative Wednesday afternoon [Aug. 14], as he strolled about town to note the effects of the remarkably heavy rainfall of the day.

It was indeed damp. No such fall of water in so short a time was ever before recorded here, the total amount registered at the Signal station being 5.53 inches. Of this amount, five inches fell in three hours, and during that time the streets bore the appearance of veritable rivers. It was a wild rush of the falling waters for an outlet to the sea, which created considerable damage to the thoroughfares in different sections of the town.

The day opened with a light southeasterly wind, and during the forenoon there were several heavy showers, with some thunder and lightning. The breeze freshed shortly before noon, and by 1 p.m. was blowing a stiff gale, which the torrent that darkened the sky was pouring forth and was without a parallel. The gutters were babbling brooks, and the streets were impossible to all save the rubber-clad pedestrian.

Inquirer and Mirror,
August 17, 1889.

Thunderstorm "of Immense Proportions," February 1891

Saturday last [Feb. 28] early in the evening drizzling rain, occasional flashes of lightning. About 11 p.m. wind swung to SW . . . Rain, snow, and hail fell in blinding sheets . . . thunder storm of immense proportions burst. Storm lasted about an hour . . . "the little" end of a very severe storm over Bristol, Barnstable, and Dukes counties.

Inquirer and Mirror,
March 7, 1891.

Lament for a Favorite Locomotive, 1893

The locomotive *Dionis* was a favorite of the riders of the Nantucket Rail Road. A tropical storm, which moved over the Middle Atlantic States and into New England on August 29, caused a very high tide and rough surf that destroyed part off the road bed of the rail road. This caused an accident which derailed the *Dionis* and almost caused her to run into the sea.

LAMENT FOR A FAVORITE LOCOMOTIVE.

Air: "The Harp That Once Through Tara's Halls"—

O, where is dear Dionis now
　And all her festive train?
The headlight on her iron brow
　We seek, alas, in vain!
In rows the silent sleepers lie,
　No warning toot they hear,
Nor tremble, as she rushes by,
　The hills of Nobadeer.

To " 'Sconset" her beloved mate,
　She loaned a rib or two,
A valve, a piston and a grate,
　Which left her feeling blue.
Old " 'Sconset" hobbled out one morn,
　And never home came he;
Said poor Dionis, lone and lorn,
　"Life hath no charms for me."

Next morning like a lightning flash
　She scuttled out of town;
At Nobadeer with one fell splash
　She to the deep went down.
They said she only sought to cool
　The fever in her blood,
And mistook for a wayside pool
　The ocean's raging flood.

Those dulcet strains we loved to hear
　Along the Goose-pond shore
Are silent now—alas, we fear
　Forever—evermore!
Oh, cruel irony of fate
　That such a road may rust,
And all the frogs may hibernate
　Beneath the drifted dust!

O, flagman by the Goose-pond shore
　Your banner waves in vain;
For you shall greet O, nevermore,
　Dionis and her train!
Be yours a heartfelt sympathy
　For strangers at our gate
Who in the station mournfully
　With season tickets wait!

And when the doughty William D.
　Says "Go-o-o and see the surf!"
A mighty host will eagerly
　Go tramping o'er the turf.
And as with disappointed glare
　They find it simmered down,
O, fancy them with injured air
　Come trudging back to town.

Still oft on moonlit summer night
　May dreamers hear again
Dionis, as in spectral flight
　She scuttles o'er the plain.
From lonely hills of Nobadeer
　Reverberate once more
Those witching strains we loved to hear
　Along the Goose-pond shore.

Nantucket Sound off Oak Bluffs was the scene of New England's most spectacular waterspout on August 19, 1896. Photographic analysis determined that the spout lay 5.75 miles offshore, the column was 3600 feet high and 144 feet wide in the middle. Photograph by J. N. Chamberlain; courtesy of the Dukes County Historical Society, Edgartown.

"A Wonderful Mirage," December 1895

A wonderful mirage occurred last Saturday [December 21]. The entire Cape shore from Monomoy along nearly to Falmouth and the eastern end of Martha's Vineyard were so very distinct to the naked eye as to appear not more than 10 miles away. Vessels in the Sound appeared to be bottom side up. The aspect from the Cape was the same, our island seeming to be close at hand.

Inquirer and Mirror,
December 28, 1895.

"A Huge Black Tongue," The Waterspout in Nantucket Sound, August 1896

Thousands of summer residents of Martha's Vineyard, Nantucket, and adjacent Massachusetts coast were treated to a spectacle of remarkable grandeur one day in August last. Guests at the hotels and occupants of cottages at the various resorts were just rising from dinner when the cry was raised, "A waterspout, a waterspout!" The scene presented to view was such as not one in a thousand had ever witnessed before or would ever see again.

A large mass of heavy black cloud hung high above the ocean between Nantucket and Cape Cod. Suddenly it was seen to project a circular column of its own dense vapor perpendicularly downward, rapidly but not precipitantly, until sea and cloud were connected by a cylinder one or two hundred feet in diameter, straight as a pine tree, and at least a mile high. It was a waterspout indeed, and of most unusual proportion and indescribable beauty.

The sea was perfectly calm, the air almost motionless, the sun shining brightly, light summer clouds hanging here and there over the deep blue sky; and in strange contrast with all the rest, was this lofty mass of black vapor with its absolutely perpendicular support. To add to the weird effect occasional livid streaks of forked lightning shot athwart the black monster cloud above. The column was only slightly funnel-shaped just where it joined the cloud, and was of equal diameter the remainder of its length. At its base the sea was lashed into a mass of white foam and spray that mounted upward as high as the masts of a large schooner.

Reverend Crandall J. North,
Christian Advocate,
September 1896.

August 19, 1896. — Clear weather all day, except in the afternoon, when light rain began at 2:40 P.M. and ended at 4:00 P.M. Total amount 0.03 inch. Cooler, with rising barometer. Mr. Wagner went to Cottage City in the morning to check up; from there he observed a big waterspout that formed in Nantucket Sound. An ordinary thundershower was passing across the sound at 12:40 P.M., a huge black tongue shot down from the alto-cumulus cloud that floated a half-mile high at the northern edge of the shower, and after rising and falling a number of times, finally joined a shorter tongue that seemed to leap out of the water to meet it. Twice the column parted for a moment, but joined again instantly. There was no apparent motion of the waterspout forward, and the phenomenon lasted for half an hour. It was pronounced by many sea captains who witnessed it the finest waterspout they had ever seen. No damage was done by the spout, but a small catboat which arrived at night [here] reported being becalmed near the spout, the crew badly scared.

Extract from the Daily Journal of the U.S. Weather Bureau Station, Nantucket, MA, Max Wagner, Observer.

The dimensions of the waterspout were calculated by Professor Frank H. Bigelow of the United States Weather Bureau by subjecting several photographs of the spout to mathematical calculations. He employed the known distances between telegraph poles that appeared in the photographs and their distances from the camera in his survey. The results were published in *Monthly Weather Review,* July 1906.

Diameter of spout at the water	240 feet
Diameter of foot of cascade	720
Height of cascade	420
Diameter of vortex at tube in middle	144
Diameter of tube at face of cloud	840
Approximate length of tube	3600
Approximate height of top of cloud	16000
Average forward speed of spout	1.1 mi/h

The Haulover Opening, December 1896

The narrow band of sand dunes separating the Head of the Harbor and the Atlantic Ocean just north of Wauwinet hold a special place in the economic and physiographic history of Nantucket. Sometime in the early nineteenth century, certainly before 1846 when it appeared on a survey map of the coastline, fishermen from the town cut an opening through the dunes so that they could drag their boats from the harbor over the sand and launch them into the ocean, enabling them to reach the rich fishing grounds to the south of the island without making the long voyage around Great Point to the north.

This route served for over a half century until December 1896, when almost miraculously, the sea opened a channel through the sand following a path known as the Haulover. It soon widened and attained a depth of eight feet so that small boats could pass through, eliminating the laborious task of dragging the boats over the sand. During

the next years the opening widened to a quarter of a mile, but it showed a constant tendency to migrate northward after 1902 and almost attained the northern reach of the Head of the Harbor by 1908. Then came a storm in November 1908 which finished the job that nature was doing, by closing the opening permanently. Though there have been temporary break-throughs in this vicinity in recent years, no lasting channel has been cut through the dunes by the sea.

Tornado During Severe Coastal Storm, 1898

About noon [on Nov. 26] a small cyclone struck the barn of Capt. Samuel Harris, at Polpis, lifting the roof bodily from the plates and carrying it some distance, then dashing it to the earth with a violence which shivered it to splinters.

Nantucket Journal,
November 29, 1898.

The Drought of Summer 1900

The drought started in March and continued through the end of the year. During the ten-month period, only 23.16 inches were measured against a normal of 35.80 inches, or a 65 percent amount.

According to the *Inquirer and Mirror,* rain fell "in copious volume" on September 16, breaking a drought which the oldest inhabitants on the island claimed had not been equaled since 1825. The 2.42 inches resulted from a cyclonic storm; no tropical storm was in the vicinity on that date.

The Marconi Storm, November 1901

The chief feature of the month was the storm of the 24th and 25th, which caused

general precipitation, mostly as rain, and high winds of hurricane force along the coast. This disturbance was of southern origin, and swept the entire Atlantic coast. It was destructive to shipping and to property along the coast, but fortunately there was little, if any, loss of life.

New England climatologist.

The principal damage occurred at Wellfleet on Cape Cod where the newly erected radio antenna poles employed in pioneer trans-Atlantic wireless communication were blown down.

On Nantucket the wind mounted to 53 miles per hour. The barometer sank to 29.13 inches on the 25th. Only 0.36 inch of rain fell during the three-day storm.

From U.S. Weather Bureau records.

"The Particularly Disagreeable" First Week of June 1903

The last substantial rain of spring fell on Nantucket on April 15 with 0.71 inch. The remainder of April measured only 0.15 inch additional. For the first 28 days of May only 0.05 inch wetted the rain gauge. Then a substantial fall of 0.88 inch came on the 29–30th. May had a total amount of 0.93 inch. The first 11 days of June were rainless until 0.66 inch fell on the 12–13th. In all of June, only 1.10 inches were received. The summer months of July, August, and September also were very dry, having 1.81, 2.69, and 1.37 inches, respectively, for a three-month total of only 5.87 inches, or 58 percent of normal. October ran just about normal with 3.33 inches.

Smoke from forest fires in Maine and New Brunswick partially obscured the sun on Nantucket during the first week of June. It was first noticed on the 3d, increased in intensity on the 5–6th, and disappeared on the 7th. The *Inquirer and Mirror* called it. "particularly disagreeable." Maine endured a month-long drought during May, not sharing in the moderately heavy rains which fell over southern New England on the 30th.

From U.S. Weather Bureau records.

The Line Gale, 1904

Mr. Grimes, down at the weather bureau station, has been repeatedly asked what has become of the "line gale." Now Mr. Grimes is a scientifically educated weather sharp, and claims there is no such thing as a "line gale," and if you will call upon him, he will give you his reasons, which seem good and sufficient.

"The long period free from wind disturbance is unusual at this time of year," he said Wednesday morning to our inquiry; "but you may expect a change very quickly now." And it was not fifteen minutes after he made this prophecy when the telegraph announced an approaching southeaster. The sky became overcast, and a storm of some energy resulted.

"I am not much of a believer in signs, as applicable to weather," said he in response to an inquiry of what conditions led him to prophesy an approaching storm, "but you may set it down that a very heavy dew or white frost precipitation here in October will almost invariably be followed by a southeaster, and we had the first frost of the season last night."

His interlocutor asked if he had ever noted that between the first and fifteenth days of October we usually had the greatest wind velocities of the month. He had not, but produced his record. . . .

It will be difficult to convince many there is no such thing as a "line gale," but Mr. Grimes seems to feel sure of his position in the matter, and his convincing statements, backed by scientific data, will make one who attempts to prove otherwise feel like thirty cents in pennies. Don't tackle Mr. Grimes on the line gale if you still wish to retain the belief of your ancestors on this point.

Inquirer and Mirror,
October 14, 1905.

Wreck of Lightship 58 in 1905

Lightship 58 on Nantucket South Shoals wrecked — shore near Great Point littered with wreckage. Worst ever seen. Occurred on December 10, 1905.

Inquirer and Mirror,
December 31, 1980.

Relief Lightship 58 was on temporary duty on South Shoals when a severe storm hit on December 10, 1905. The weather bureau on Nantucket recorded a maximum wind speed of 50 miles per hour from the north at 10:06 a.m. on the 10th, and the wind averaged 32.5 miles per hour for the twenty-four hours. Rain fell through the day and changed to snow in the evening. Total precipitation was 0.80 inch.

A Dense Fog of 76 Hours' Duration, November 1908

November 8 — Heavy fog from 10:00 p.m.
November 9 — Heavy fog all day.
November 10 — Fog so dense on Sound steamer did not make return trip.
November 11 — Heavy fog all day.
November 12 — Fog lifted at 2:00 a.m.

U.S. Weather Bureau records.

The First S.O.S. Message, November 1909

On January 23, 1909, in dense fog 26 miles southwest of Nantucket Island, the Italian liner *Florida* sliced into the side of the British steamer *Republic* ripping open the hull to the cold Atlantic. Six lives were lost but, more important, it was the first use of the new radio wireless to call for help. The collision bulkhead on the *Florida* held up but she lost thirty feet of her bow. The *Republic* was a doomed ship and the radio operator Jack Binns became famous as he stood by his radio key tapping out the S.O.S. messages to bring aid to the sinking ship. The steamer *Baltic* arrived on the scene and rescued 1,650 passengers from the two vessels — a vast undertaking using small boats at sea. The *Republic* was sinking and the Revenue cutter *Gresham* took her in tow for shoal water but she sank before they could save her. All hands except the six killed in the initial collision were saved. Jack Binns had transmitted more than 200 messages during the ordeal. He was lauded around the world. Unique was the magic of the new radio and its ability to save lives at sea in a disaster. Binns' messages brought nearby ships to the scene of the accident quickly.

William P. Quinn,
Shipwrecks Around New England, 1979.

December Storm at the Haulover, 1909

On the 26th of December 1909, the writer visited the Haulover Beach to investigate the changes there. There had been a gale from the east which started about 8 o'clock in the evening of the 25th and lasted until the next morning. This was accompanied by the highest tide ever witnessed by any of the natives then living. The wind continued very fresh during the day and at about four o'clock on the 26th it shifted into the northeast. For the next twelve hours the wind blew at an average rate of 50 miles per hour and the tide remained very high. It was at the beginning of this second gale that the writer was at the Haulover. The flood tide was running along the ocean shore nearly opposite to the large storm waves which were rolling in from the northeast slightly oblique to the shore. The waves were very high, rugged and irregular, but, on account of the tide, the water did not run up the beach as waves usually do when they strike the shore but seemed to tumble to pieces and splash around. The shore just east and south of Wauwinet was entirely destitute

Hot Boston, Cool Nantucket, July 1911

Boston's greatest July heat wave occurred in the early part of 1911 when nine days soared to readings of 90°F or more from the 1st to 12th. On four days the mercury hit 100° or more, with an all-time Boston maximum record of 104°F on the Fourth of July. The nine very hot days, July 2–6 and 9–12 averaged a maximum of 98.4°F at Boston. The same days at Nantucket averaged a maximum of only 80°F, a difference of 18.4 degrees.

A Good Summer, 1913

The summer of 1913 produced some of the best weather that Nantucket has ever experienced in that season. In the three months of June, July, and August, there were only nine cloudy days, 35 rated partly cloudy, and 48 were clear.

The temperature departure from normal was −0.6 degree in June, + 2.3 degrees in July, and −0.2 degree in August. The maximum temperature for the entire summer attained only 87°F.

Precipitation proved deficient. The measurement for the three months totaled only 5.43 inches. June received 54 percent, July 21 percent, and August 100 percent of normal. Six days had measurable rain in June, four in July, and eight in August, or 18 during the season, compared with a normal of 27 days.

From U.S. Weather Bureau records.

"Crossing Nantucket Sound in a Blizzard,"1914

It was a nasty day with large snowflakes falling steadily and the people of Nantucket did not expect the *Sankaty* to make the run from New Bedford. It was a foregone conclusion that she would remain on the other side. Even at Woods Hole, the people

of sand so that only the hard, dark glacial deposits were left for a beach. The cliffs along this part of the shore had been attacked and great quantities of the material washed away. Sand was being blown from the north like snow and the few houses that stand near the shore were buried to the windows. The narrow beach north of the hamlet had been swept by the waves during the previous storm but as it was low tide at this time, the waves did not reach the crest of the beach.

The writer visited the Haulover again a week later to make more observations and measurements. The cliffs abreast of Wauwinet had been cut back about thirty-five feet, but the adjacent shore had by this time recovered with sand. The narrow grassless strip of beach had widened about one hundred feet on the harbor side. All this added sand was brought from the cliffs and beach to the south by the flood tide and was washed over into the harbor by the storm waves. Across the beach were numerous gullies which were cut out by the water flowing across it. If the water had been confined into one narrow portion of the beach instead of being spread over a quarter of a mile, there would have been, very likely, another opening formed. At another point north of this open beach the waves had washed over the beach into the harbor. The path of the water was very crooked so that it had little chance to scour a channel. All along the harbor shore there were numerous apron beaches of considerable size which were not there before the storms. These also showed that quantities of sand must have washed over the beach during these storms.

Harold Sharp,
"A discussion of the changes in the Haulover Beach at Nantucket,"
unpublished essay on microfilm,
Nantucket Atheneum.

The Haulover path, first cut by fishermen sometime in the early nineteenth century, was transformed into a shallow channel by the winter storm of December 16–17, 1896. A November 1908 storm permanently closed up the channel.

did not expect her, for the weather was boisterous and the air was filled with heavy snow. Conditions were not right for following the crooked course into Woods Hole.

At New Bedford, the crew of the *Sankaty* had been busy for four hours loading freight and at 11:00 o'clock, they got underway. The dim outlines of the shore on either side of the harbor could be made out, but that was about all. To a novice, a snow storm on the water is rather eerie and everything looks spooky and somewhat "out of this world." . . .

The tide tended to carry the steamer to the westward as she churned her way along her regular course to Woods Hole. Just how far off to the west she would be was uncertain. Suddenly the hump of Naushon Island appeared and a little over an hour's run brought the *Sankaty* through the dogleg into Great Harbor.

The wharf was completely dead with not a soul in sight. The *Sankaty* tooted for assistance in handling her docking lines and shortly thereafter agent Veedler appeared and puffed his way through the snow. He seemed to be the only person alive in Woods Hole.

After she was secure, the crew loaded some Chestnut posts and other miscellaneous freight and in fifteen minutes time got underway again. Captain John Merriman took a look out over the bow; the snow was blinding. Off in the distance came the dismal sound of the steam whistle on West Chop at the Vineyard. Soon Vineyard Haven Harbor was made out. A few large barges at anchor could be seen, but not one single vessel underway. Off to the east came the dulcet tones of the Hedge Fence Lightship.

The high bank of the Vineyard became visible through the swirl and finally the faint outline of Oak Bluffs wharf. This was enough to enable pilot James O. Sandsbury to set his course for Cross Rip and the *Sankaty* headed off in an easterly direction. The pilot house windows were plastered with slush as mate Craig, clad in oilskins, took a position, along with the lookout, on the bow . . . .

The *Sankaty* continued to call for the lightship hidden somewhere ahead and finally a faint reply was heard in the distance. It was not clear enough yet to determine its location . . . .

Soon the lightship appeared.

The pilot looked over and asked, "Better to leeward of her, Sir?"

"Yes, might just as well let them know we are around," said the Captain. "Looks like they are all asleep . . . . didn't expect callers in a storm like this. Guess we'll wake 'em up."

The *Sankaty* gave a long blast with her whistle. The covering of snow made the tiny lightship look even smaller. A man emerged from below on the stationary vessel and shuffled his way along the deck to the bow where he rang the bell in an answering salute . . . .

From the lightship, a course was set for the buoy off Tuckernuck Shoal, located several miles to the southeast. Off to the west, a sloop was seen tossing about.

"That's the *Reliance*," said Captain Merriman, "can tell by her cut." He continued, "Those fellows are takin' an awful chance. It's bad enough us bein' out here . . . . . there's the buoy. Tryin' to split it in two, ain't we?"

Then came a call from the deckhand on watch. "There it is, off there," pointing his hand.

"Yes, we see it. You've got a good eye, Joe. See the Jetty yet?"

A moment later, "Bell buoy on the weather bow, Sir!"

"All right, we see 'ah," replied Merriman, as he gave the signal to the engine room to slow down. "There ought to be a whistle on the end of one of these Jetties. It's a wonder the government hasn't done it long ago . . . the bar is a bad, narrow place . . . lots a 'times the bell buoy is not ringin', in fog especially, and a whistle would be a great help in makin' port."

"There's a quahogger dead ahead!" called the bow watch.

"I see him runnin' in. Guess I'd better let him know we are behind 'em," said Merriman. "Yes, it's Jim the Frenchman. He's a lucky fellow . . . always comes in with all he can carry."

The *Sankaty's* whistle brought an immediate swerve to port from the odd looking digger and the steamer rapidly pulled up on her. Two men could be seen on board, one at the wheel, the other huddled in the lee of the pilot house. Through the snow, big black heaps showed up on the little boat's deck. These were quahogs that could not be stowed below. From the *Sankaty's* decks the quahogger looked as though her deck was awash. In spite of the storm, Jim was returning with a big haul.

Brant Point appeared and the outline of the familiar town was seen; quiet and peaceful and buried in snow. There was little sign of life apparent on the wharf. A few fishermen were heading up barrels of quahogs some distance up the wharf. Three men made up the "crowd" that was usually on hand to greet the steamer. It was for good reason . . . no one knew that the *Sankaty* was coming. Her lines were secured and the plank put out. Only two passengers trudged off onto the snow-covered dock.

P.C. Morris and Joseph Morin,
The Island Steamers, 1977.

"A Peculiar Sky," The Yellow Day, July 1916

Sunday was a peculiar day. The sky was heavily overcast and everything had a decidedly yellowish hue, with almost a supernatural effect, while the wind blew freshly from the westward. Vegetation and foliage took on a strange color, the grass and trees seemingly being much greener than usual, while everybody seemed to have a feeling akin to depression if not to awe. It was an unusual condition which nobody seemed able to explain locally, but it seems this section of the country was all under the same spell and the city papers alluded to Sunday as a "yellow day," the condition being due presumably to the heavy forest fires which have been sweeping the Canadian border for some time.

Inquirer and Mirror,
August 5, 1916.

Cloudy July, 1916

There was an unusual amount of cloudy weather. The average amount of sunshine received was one of the lowest of record, particularly in the southern states where the deficiency varied from 20 to 30 percent below normal. The total average rainfall for the section for the months of May, June, and July of the present year has been 14.00 inches, which has been exceeded but twice since the beginning of the record in 1888. This was in 1889, when the average for these months was 14.88 inches, and in 1897, when it was 15.39 inches.

New England climatologist.

July data on Nantucket:
  Humidity at 8:00 a.m. and 8 p.m. averaged 93 percent.
  Sky condition: 4 clear, 10 partly cloudy, and 17 cloudy days.
  Temperature averaged 65.4°, or −2.1 degrees below normal.
  Total precipitation, or 188 percent of normal.
  Measurable rain fell on 16 days plus 3 traces.
  Rain for 8 consecutive days from 20th to 27th.

Weather bureau records.

Weather Sayings

The varieties of weather known to Nantucketers often surprise the inland visitor, who recognizes only two kinds, good and bad. We have fair, good, fine, foul, dirty, nasty, bad, thick, rough, heavy and several other sorts, including "owlish" and "mirogenous." Wind conditions are described as dead calm, stark calm, calm, light, puffy, squally, heavy, single-reef, two- , three- and close-reef breezes, half-a-gale, gale, hurricane, etc.; or a wind may be described as a six-or-eight-knot-breeze, and so on. Among those to the [sic] manner born, a "tempest" means a thunder-storm.

Boxing the Compass

We have our own names for the points of the compass. Many writers persist in making the sailor man say "nor'east" and "sou'east." None such ever used the words. He does say "nor'west" and "sou'west," but north is "no'the," with a long "o" and a soft "th." Northeast is "no'theast," pronounced the same way (the "no'the" like the verb "loathe.") South is pronounced with the same soft "th" (like "mouth" when used as a verb).

When either north or south is used as an adjective before the noun, however, each takes its ordinary dictionary pronunciation, as a "north wind," or the "south shore." It is only when used without the noun that the long "o" sound in "no'the" and the soft "th" in both words are heard. Thus we say the wind is "out southe," or "about no'the"— never a "no'the wind" or the "southe shore." It is a curious distinction, for which there seems to be no reason except custom itself. Then we have "no-no'theast," and "sou'southeast," but always "nor'nor'west" and "sou'sou'west." Writers who wish to apply the local color correctly are urged to study these forms carefully, and not slip up, as most of them do, on such simple matters. "Southe" is sometimes used as a verb, when speaking of the moon, as "when the moon southes"; and the word "easting" is sometimes heard.

Underground Moon

And we must not let another lunar phase pass unheeded, as a part of the island's weather curriculum — the "underground moon." Here we have a strictly local phase of the orb of night. When the moon makes a change between the hours of 12 and 1 o'clock, she is classed as an "underground moon," and the claim is made that foul weather is sure to accompany. Careful notes indicate that such conditions do result, but that the rule is not infallible. The *real* "underground" moon is when that heavenly body makes its change between the time of setting and rising, and between the hours of 12 and 1 o'clock, being at the time below the horizon — or underground. The real weatherwise Nantucketer holds quite tenaciously to the theory.

William F. Macy and Roland B. Hussey,
The Nantucket Scrap Basket, 1916.

Devastating Snowstorm, April 1917

Sleighing on the 10th of April! History does not record such an event ever before on Nantucket — at least not within the memory of the present generation.

Inquirer and Mirror,
April 14, 1917.

Nantucket's Coldest Day, 1918

February 5 — Worst cold wave in history of local weather bureau. Temperature of 6.2 below zero recorded — lowest of record. Wind attained 46 miles an hour during night. Boat at dock.

U.S. Weather Bureau record.

The maximum temperature on the 5th attained only 4°, giving a daily mean temperature of −1°F. At 6:00 a.m. the thermometer read −6° with the wind gusting to 43 miles per hour, the combination making the windchill factor the equivalent of −63°F.

The temperature remained below zero from 1:00 to 11:00 a.m., and from 9:00 to 11:00 p.m. The wind from west or northwest averaged 28 miles per hour for the 24 hours, hitting an extreme speed of 56 miles at 2:27

a.m. With a decrease in the force of the wind before midnight, the temperature rose to 2°F. This was the bitterest day and night experienced thus far in the twentieth century by Nantucket residents.

Disappearance of the Cross Rip Lightship, 1918

February 1, 1918, the Cross Rip lightship was torn from her moorings in Nantucket sound by the heavy ice-fields and was carried helpless out to sea when the field started moving eastward. Was last seen from Great Point lighthouse on the morning of the 5th [the coldest morning in modern Nantucket records]. Lightship was without power or sail and helpless, beyond the reach of tugs or cutters. Disappeared with her crew of eight men.

Gardner,
Wrecks Around Nantucket, 1915.

The Driest Month, October 1924

The marked feature of the month was the small amount of precipitation, the average of the New England section, 0.44 inch, being the smallest of record for October, and with the exception of an average of 0.21 inch in March 1915, the least for any month in the section record, beginning in 1888.

New England climatologist.

Nantucket received only 0.10 inch during October 1924, the least for any month to date. The only rain period extended from the 7th to 10th with a trace, 0.07 inch, .01 inch, .02 inch, and a trace on those days, for a total of 0.10 inch.

September ran below normal also with 2.89 inches, but mostly coming prior to the 19th. A fall of 0.50 inch was measured on the 23d and 0.17 inch on the 30th.

November continued dry until the 22d. Only 0.31 inch falling between the 1st and the

The Cross Rip Lightship, *stationed near the center of Nantucket Sound, tore loose from its mooring during a storm on February 1, 1918. The ship drifted in heavy icefields and was last seen from Great Point on the 5th. The ship and crew of eight disappeared without a trace.*
Photograph by Harry B. Turner.

21st. Then 2.40 inches broke the drought on the 22d and 23d.

The average rainfall of the previous driest months was: 0.14 inch in June 1912, 0.25 inch in March 1915, and 0.27 inch in August 1902.

The driest in recent years has been 0.07 inch in August 1974, when .04 inch fell on the 7th and .03 inch on the 10th.

Snow Plowing, 1928 Style

A heavy snowstorm hit the island on March 9 and 10 [1928], the heaviest March snowfall, 9.1 inches, since 1916. Superintendent of Streets Tice had the snow plough pulled out and attached to one of Henry Chase's motor trucks. It was operated constantly during the storm, keeping the streets open and the road to 'Sconset clear, in case of fire. The need for a motor-driven snow plough was proven.

Merle Orleans,
"Looking Backward,"
Inquirer and Mirror, n.d.

The Coldest Day in Modern Records, December 29, 1933

The temperature fell from 19°F just after midnight on December 29, 1933, to an even zero at 7:00 a.m. It continued its descent to a minimum of –3°F between 8:00 and 9:00 a.m. With the wind blowing at 25 miles per hour, this was equivalent to a windchill temperature of –49°F.

The thermometer stood at –2° at noon, rose to zero at 4:00 p.m. and to 1°F at 9:00 p.m. It had remained at zero or below for 13 consecutive hours, mainly during daylight. By midnight the mercury climbed to 2°F.

This was the coldest daylight period on Nantucket since February 8, 1861, when the thermometer ranged during the day from –6.5° to 3.0°F. The mean for December 29, 1933, however, was not the lowest mean temperature for a day according to the method employed by the weather bureau. Actually, the maximum on the 29th was 19° just after midnight and the minimum was –3° about 8:30 a.m. This gave a mean of 8°, or half the sum of the maximum and minimum.

From U.S. Weather Bureau records.

Frozen Beach, December 1933

The beach was frozen over so hard Saturday and Sunday [Dec. 30–31] that cars were driven over it all the way to Eel Point.

Inquirer and Mirror,
January 6, 1934.

The S.S. *Olympic* Sinks the Nantucket Lightship, 1934

The Nantucket lightship is moored at one of the most isolated and exposed stations in the world. On May 15, 1934, the White Star liner *Olympic* was proceeding in dense fog toward New York City and following the lightship's radio beacon, a combination radio-compass signal, used by ships with radio direction finders to proceed on their course in limited visibility. The instrument aboard the liner was extremely accurate that morning when about eleven a.m. the *Olympic* loomed out of the fog and cut the lightship in half. The crewmen aboard the lightship had only a 30-second warning of the disaster and hardly had time to don life jackets. Seven men died, and the lightship sank in less then a minute at her station 43 miles southeast of Nantucket Island. The *Olympic* stopped and picked up four survivors and three bodies. The bodies of the other four men went down with the ship and were not recovered. Survivor Captain George Braithwaite of the lightship told of the crew having been up all night, as there were two close calls with other steamers on the previous evening. Normally, ships using the RDF would pass no closer than a quarter of a mile away from the lightship. It was ironic that the radio beacons and direction finders that were designed to save lives would be the major cause of the disaster.

Quinn,
Shipwrecks Around New England, 1979.

Towhill Spent Night Alone in Ice-Fields, 1934

Jeremiah Towhill, one of four men isolated on Muskeget island, tried to reach Nantucket when there appeared to be open water.

He was caught in the ice about five hundred feet from Eel Point when darkness fell and iced him in. Coast Guard could not reach him until morning when they brought him safely to land. The night was calm without wind or snow, and he withstood the low temperature without serious injury [night of Feb. 9].

Inquirer and Mirror,
February 17, 1934.

Absolute Calm, February 1936

The anemometer cups atop the weather bureau building hardly turned for over 24 hours on February 20 and 21, 1936. From 1:49 p.m. to 2:02 p.m. on the 20th, no wind movement was registered. The average for the entire 24 hours was only 3.6 miles per hour, and the maximum only 12 miles per hour.

U.S. Weather Bureau records.

Highest Minimum Temperature for an Entire Winter, 1937 and 1949

In the winter of 1936–37, the thermometer sank only to 16°F during the three months. January was the second warmest first month with an average of 40°F. The entire winter averaged 38.5°F, or 5.9 degrees above the town normal.

In the winter of 1948–49, the same high minimum of 16° was reached. The winter averaged 36.6°F or 3.7 degrees above the airport normal.

The Long Thunderstorm, September 15, 1938

A thunderstorm of moderate energy came from the west (Madaket Coast Guard heard first thunder at 2:00 p.m.) at 3:35 p.m. [at Nantucket Town]. Storm moved up very slowly and hung over the station from 5:00 p.m. to 11:00 p.m., then it moved very slowly forward to SE. Lightning was excessive, also precipitation, and the last thunder was heard at 1:00 a.m. [on 16th].

U.S. Weather Bureau record.

Excessive rain fell as follows: 4:00–5:00 p.m., 0.87 inch; 6:00–7:00 p.m., 1.08 inches; and 9:00–10:00 p.m., 0.86 inch. The total fall from 3:48 p.m. to 11:45 p.m. was a large 4.04

inches, one of Nantucket's greatest one-day amounts. The highest wind was only 21 miles per hour from the south.

Dunham Had a Terrible Accident: The Hurricane of 1938

From the account given by Mr. Marcus Dunham upon his return to Nantucket he had the most thrilling experience of any islander, during the gale. Muskeget suffered the most damage of any place on or around the island.

Mr. Dunham reported that the wind assumed gale proportions around 3:00 o'clock Wednesday afternoon. He had seen to it that his boats were taken care of and then had retired to his house, little realizing what was in store. When the gale increased the seas began to pound up the beach.

"I watched it rise," said Mr. Dunham, "and I never saw it rise so fast. The first thing I knew it was all about the house. Then I decided to get out.

"By this time the wind was wicked. It blew Jim Dennis' shanty away as if it were paper. Then Ed Rose's place went. While I watched I felt my own place moving, and before I could get up the seas had washed it out and the wind blew it back into a bog in the middle of the island. I got out of a window and made for the ridge to the west'ard. It was then the only place out of water.

"Muskeget was clean under water — with the sea breaking everywhere. I went through water up to my neck in the hollows of the dunes and finally reached the ridge. I had to lay down in a hole there to keep from blowing away.

"When the wind dropped, late at night, the water went down. I spent the night walking the beach. It was pitch dark, and I was wet and tired. I tell you the sight of the island at daybreak was almost unbelievable. The shanties were gone. My house and Robbie's had been blown back on their beam ends, way up in the sand-dunes. But it was the

Beachgoers at Siasconset ca. 1900.
Nantucket Historical Association
Collection.

September: 8 clear days, 10 partly cloudy, 12 cloudy; southwest wind; sunshine 68% of possible.

Rainfall: 2.14 inches fell from June 27 to September 11, 77 days; June 24–26, 1.37 inches; July, 1.04 inches; August, 0.57 inch; and September 1–7, 0.53 inch.

U.S. Weather Bureau records.

Hot Boston, Cool Nantucket in August 1944

Boston's greatest August heat wave occurred during the middle of August 1944 when the thermometer averaged a maximum of 97.4°F over an eight-day period. A maximum of 101°F occurred on the 12th. Meantime, Nantucket's maximums on these days averaged 80.1°F, or 17.3 degrees lower than Boston's. The highest on the island was only 82°F.

From U.S. Weather Bureau records.

The Wettest Month, August 1946

The rainfall during August 1946 totaled 12.92 inches, which exceeded the former record month of August 1889 with 11.05 inches. Only two other months have reported more than 10.00 inches: October 1894, 10.05 inches, and May 1967, 10.38 inches.

Rain fell on Nantucket on 18 days in August 1946. Measurable amounts came on 14 days and the remaining four were only traces. Two major storms occurred: 3.67 inches on the 6–7th and 3.69 inches on the 26–27th. These were general storms over southeastern New England and considerable damage was reported on the mainland. No tropical storms came north during the month;

clubhouse that was the worst sight. The building — which is quite heavily-built, you know — was a wreck; the windows all smashed in; the doors out; the furniture and bedding all washed around inside; some of it out-of-doors. The big phonograph and radio was up in the sand-dunes, a long distance away.

"A plane circled around and I waved to it. I was getting my littlenecks into the dory, getting ready to go over to Madaket, when the coast guards came. No, sir — I never want to go through that experience again."

Inquirer and Mirror,
September 22, 1938.

Sunny Summer, 1944

June: 8 clear days, 5 partly cloudy, 17 cloudy; sunshine 62% of possible.

July: 16 clear days, 5 partly cloudy, 10 cloudy; southwest wind; sunshine 79% of possible.

August: 16 clear days, 8 partly cloudy, 7 cloudy; southwest wind; sunshine 74% of possible.

the heavy rainfall resulted from cyclonic storms and thunderstorms. Rainfall was also heavy on the Vineyard and Cape Cod: Sandwich 17.85 inches, Fall River 16.10 inches, Hyannis 14.16 inches, and Edgartown 13.84 inches. Nantucket's greatest amount in 24 hours was 3.67 inches on the 6–7th.

The island had 6 clear days in August, 8 partly cloudy days, and 17 cloudy days. Percentage of possible sunshine was only 45 percent.

The mean temperature was 64.9°F, or a −2.9 degrees departure from normal. The maximum of 78°F reached on the 11th and 21st was the lowest August maximum of record. The minimum of 50°F occurred on the 31st.

From U.S. Weather Bureau records.

The Driest Month, June 1949

The only measurable rain to fall during the month of June 1949 was a minuscule 0.01 inch on the 5th. Traces, or too little to measure, fell on the 21st and 28th. Some stations in southeastern New England had no measureable falls. These included East Wareham, Edgartown, and Hyannis.

May had run close to normal in rainfall with the latest fall coming on the 27–28th with 0.66 inch. July continued the drought of June with only 0.87 inch all month. Light amounts fell on the 2d, 5–7th, 13th, 17th, 22d, and 25th; the heaviest was only 0.34 inch on the 17th. The July temperature at Nantucket ran 3.3 degrees above normal.

Other dry months: August 1971, .07 inch; July 1974, .07 inch; August 1980, .33 inch.

From U.S. Weather Bureau records.

Waterspout off South Beach, September 1949

A "small" waterspout was sighted by several persons off the south shore of Nantucket Friday afternoon (Sept. 9), the first to be seen from the island for several years . . . several miles offshore east of Hummock Pond . . . spout was extremely tall—at least 2500 feet, and rather thin . . . located 3 or 4 miles from Nantucket . . . the spout grew larger and blacker . . . the spout was of short duration and did not last more than 5 minutes. . . .

Inquirer and Mirror,
September 10, 1949.

The Tragic Sinking of the *Constance*, September 1949

One of the worst disasters in the maritime history of these waters took place late in the afternoon of Friday, September 9, in the shoals of Nantucket Sound. Coming out of the heavy thunder-clouds which then completely masked the sky, a series of squalls swept the 38-foot cabin cruiser *Constance*, of Falmouth, into the dreaded reaches of Tuckernuck shoals, and the pleasure craft became the focal point in a grim drama of agonizing death as she was gradually foundered and swamped in the welter of waves in this graveyard of the sea. . . .

The skipper of the *Constance*, 26-year old Russell Palmer, related the weather conditions during the last minutes of his boat:

"The weather got squally and the seas rough and around 5 minutes to 5 the spray began coming over us. . . .

"The wind had risen and it was blowing from 25 to 30 miles an hour. The sea was coming in about 3 points off our starboard and I had to head into it. . . .

"The sea was coming in 6-foot swells, with foaming tops, and hitting the bow of the cruiser pretty hard. . . .

"The sea was pretty rough now, and the waves pounding over us. We took water in our front cock-pit and the bow began dragging under. I ordered everyone aft, but the bow kept sinking. The seas began coming aboard and we drifted broadside to. One sea took the cabin windows right out. . . .

"We began to veer crazily. The boat made two complete circles. She was practically awash at this time. . . .

"The boat went down stern first—although she didn't sink completely. . . .

"I grabbed part of the top of the cabin and drifted all night." (he came ashore at Dionis).

Inquirer and Mirror,
September 17, 1949.

Nine of the 11 aboard perished. They were forced into the raging water with life belts, but after struggling with wind and wave for hours they succumbed, "a saga of human courage with a harrowing finale when rescue was so near at hand," in the words of the New England climatologist.

Hurricane Salt Spray, September 1950

Between four and five o'clock the visibility grew steadily worse as the storm drew closer. As the velocity of the wind increased, the fog was supplemented with flying salt spray, making the atmosphere nearly white.

The morning after the storm the owners of white-painted houses hardly recognized their homes. The heavy salt spray, combined with flying sand and leaves, had created a yellow and green effect, which was not pleasing to the eye. Evidently the salt caused a chemical reaction of some kind, for the white paint had turned yellow only where it was exposed to the full force of the storm. Some houses had a one-sided look, with half of the front yellow, and the other half white. One house on upper Main Street was divided in this manner, the white and yellow being separated neatly by the front door and upstairs window.

Inquirer and Mirror,
September 16, 1950.

Blue Sun, September 1950

Nantucket received its share of the smoke, or "smog," from the Canadian forest fires this week, the sun barely shining through thick haze."

Inquirer and Mirror,
September 30, 1950.

During the last days of September, 1950, a smoke pall spread over portions of Canada, the eastern United States, and western Europe. Although there have been many large smoke palls observed in the past, this one was unusual in the following respects: the large area affected; the high concentration of smoke which so obscured the sun that it was visible to the naked eye without discomfort; the violet or lavender color of the sun, and to a lesser extent, of the moon; and the persistence of the smoke in the Middle Atlantic states for nearly a week.

The smoke originated in northwestern Alberta and northeastern British Columbia where, accompanying unseasonably warm weather and three weeks of drought, over 100 forest fires were burning during the week of September 17, reaching their peak from the 22d to the 24th; after the 27th rain and snow extinguished most of them.

Harry Wexler,
Weatherwise, December 1950.

The Great Easterly Gale of November 1950

The new wind-speed and direction indicator, installed at the CAA station at Nantucket Airport only a week or so ago, fell prey to the gale-force winds which the island experienced on Saturday week [Nov. 25]. . . .

The speed indicator had been registering around 65 m.p.h. mark when a vibrating noise was heard Saturday night and upon investigation it was found that one of the four-inch cups on the anemometer installation had

Twelve hours after a collision with the Swedish ship Stockholm, *the Italian luxury liner* Andrea Doria *neared her end about 45 miles south of Nantucket on July 25, 1956. Thick fog and faulty use of radar caused the accident.* Photograph courtesy of the U. S. Coast Guard.

been torn right off. It was found the next day, far out in the center of the field.

Inquirer and Mirror,
December 2, 1950.

The *Andrea Doria* Disaster, July 1956

The Italian luxury liner *Andrea Doria* (29,000 tons) was rammed by the Swedish liner *Stockholm* (12,644 tons) near Nantucket lightship on July 25, 1956. The *Inquirer,* report described extremely calm seas and warm weather, and a night that "was mild with thick fog" around the island waters. The *Stockholm* was proceeding at normal speed of 18 knots in "clear moonlight with stars visible" eastward from New York, while the *Andrea Doria* was approaching the American coast from Europe. Both ships made confused avoidance maneuvers when the *Andrea Doria* emerged from the fog bank across the bow of the *Stockholm.* A deep vertical gash was cut in the former; she lost stability, and slowly sank, making the final plunge twelve hours after the crash. The human toll was fifty-two,

either killed by the impact or drowned before or during the rescue operations.

Inquirer and Mirror,
July 28, 1956.

UFOs sighted, September 1957

UFOs (unidentified flying objects) were being seen by numerous persons on the island, all of them being persons who did not believe in the UFOs, including one or two of the FAA personnel and some airline pilots.

Merle Orleans, "Looking Backward,"
Inquirer and Mirror,
September 15, 1977.

Tragedy at the Airport, 1958

On August 15, 1958, a Northeast Convair 240, bound from New York to Nantucket, crashed at Nantucket Airport. As the aircraft approached at low altitude, a heavy fog bank was encountered. A special observation was transmitted to the plane, reported below minimum ceiling and visibility on the field. The aircraft struck at a point 1450 feet short of the runway and about 600 feet to the left of its extended center line. A ball of fire was observed from a waiting aircraft at 11:38 p.m., the probable time of the crash. Twenty-five of the 34 aboard were killed.

The National Transportation Safety Board in its investigation stated: "The probable cause of this accident was partial obscuration, one-eighth mile visibility, and fog."

Weather Bureau observations at the time of the crash:

10:58 p.m. Scattered clouds at 500 feet, ceiling 12,000 feet, visibility 4 miles, fog.

11:12 p.m. Special report: sky partially obscured, visibility ½ mile, fog.

11:27 p.m. Special observation: sky partially obscured, visibility ½ mile, fog. (This observation transmitted to pilot and acknowledged).

11:31 p.m. Special observation: sky partially obscured, visibility 1/8 miles, fog (This observation transmitted but not acknowledged).

11:36 p.m. Sky partially obscured, visibility 3/16 mile, fog.

11:40 p.m. Weather Bureau notified of crash. Observation: sky partially obscured, visibility 3/16 mile, fog.

Inquirer and Mirror,
August 22, 1958.

Cessna Crash, June 28, 1961

On Friday, June 28, 1961, at, 6:42 p.m. four people were killed instantly in the crash of a single-engine Cessna. Wisps of fog had been visible on the field. The plane made a sharp climb and veered left into a fog bank. Weather Bureau records showed the ceiling was above limits at time of take-off. "Apparently, the plane [was] caught in a quick rolling fog that swept in seconds after the plane was airborne."

Inquirer and Mirror,
August 4, 1961.

Winter Wonderland, 1961

On Sunday the weather was beautiful and the bright sun turned the island into a veritable winter wonderland. The east side of practically every house and building was coated with snow and the icy covering it received from the rain and sleet of the storm made everything sparkle like a forest of diamonds. This created a rush of camera lovers all about the town anxious to record the many beautiful scenes on film before the warm sun melted the snow and ice cover from the buildings, the tall, stately trees lining the streets and the smaller trees and bushes in front of the homes and estates on the island.

Inquirer and Mirror,
February 10, 1961

Nantucket's Worst Windchill, December 1962

How would you like to have been abroad at Nantucket on December 30, 1962, with the temperature at –3°F and the wind blowing at 47 miles per hour? This is a windchill equivalent of a reading of –30°F.

At 1:00 a.m. on December 30, the thermometer read 44°F, but a windshift from south to northwest took place about 2:00 a.m. and the mercury began to plummet. By 5:00 a.m. it was down to 32°F, and continued the descent all day despite a strong sun. The reading was 16° at noon and 8°F at 6:00 p.m. The mercury reached 0° at 11:00 p.m. and sank to a low of –3°F before 6:00 a.m. on the 31st.

The wind averaged 33.8 miles per hour on the 30th with a peak gust to 47 miles per hour; and on the 31st the average was 33.2 miles per hour with a peak gust at 43 miles per hour.

Never had such wind blown across the island under such frigid circumstances!

From National Weather Service records and U.S. Weather Bureau records.

Four Waterspouts, September 1963

Aircraft out of Otis Air Force Base on Cape Cod reported the presence of at least four waterspouts in Nantucket Sound between 11:00 a.m. and 1:00 p.m. on September 23, 1963. The most prominent formed about 12 miles southeast of the Air Force Base off Succonesset Point and moved southward out of Muskeget Channel before a no'therly breeze.

Inquirer and Mirror,
September 26, 1963.

The Northeaster of May 24–26, 1967, Nantucket's Heaviest Rainstorm

A storm center formed in the Gulf of Mexico on May 21 and moved slowly eastward to off the northeast coast of Florida. Instead of continuing an east-northeast direction, the cyclonic system felt the influence of a strong ridge of high pressure in the mid-Atlantic Ocean and turned north-northeast.

Rain began to fall on Nantucket soon after 6:00 p.m. on the 24th, became moderate on the morning of the 25th as the storm center approached from the south, and increased to excessive on the afternoon of the 25th when the center stalled about 100 miles to the south of the island. Lowest pressure was estimated at 29.30 inches.

In all, 7.08 inches of rain fell — 6.53 inches came in a 24-hour period. Other nearby stations also received heavy amounts: Falmouth 5.19, Sandwich 5.99, Edgartown 4.41, and Provincetown 5.23 inches.

National Weather Service records.

Foggy July, 1967

July was very humid, with this feature perhaps being the key to the extreme cloudiness of the month and frequent rains. It was especially the key, combined with resultant unusual cloudiness, to the lack of usual July temperature ranges, both depressing daytime highs and preventing the usual amount of cooling at night. The most obvious result of the extreme humidity was fog. New fog records were set not only in coastal areas, but inland areas were plagued most every night. While the fog usually disappeared inland by mid-morning, it left a haze with poor visibility for July frequently throughout the day . . . .At Nantucket, fog is expected on only 14 days in July. This July it persisted 27 days, a record number.

New England climatologist.

July 1967 was the worst month ever on Nantucket as far as vacation weather goes. Twenty-seven of the 31 days reported heavy fog at some time of the day. This compared with a normal of thirteen. Skies were cloudy during the daytime 85 percent of the time. The percentage of possible sunshine was 42, or 18 less than normal. The month's rainfall amounted to 6.58 inches, or 243 percent of the normal. Measurable rain fell on sixteen days, and on five others a trace was reported. From the 12th to 20th it rained every day. Only once did the temperature exceed 80°, with 82°. The minimum of 51°F came on the 7th. The July average was 1.8 degrees below normal.

To the beach anyone?

"Hot Saturday," Nantucket's Only Century Reading, August 2, 1975

A stagnant high pressure area hovered over the Northeast during the first days of August 1975 with a center over the central Appalachians. Temperatures rose to 100° and more on Hot Saturday, August 2, and set all-time maximum records in Massachusetts and Rhode Island and closely approached record readings in New Hampshire and Maine.

On Nantucket, the previous high reading at the Airport had been 95° on August 28, 1948, during a three-day heat wave with the mercury above 90° each day. But the heat burst on August 2, 1975, saw the only century-degree reading in the history of weather recording on the island.

Nantucket endured a six-day heat wave from July 29 to August 3 with daily maximums of : 85°, 85°, 83°, 88°, 100°, and 97°F. On the century-degree day, the island thermometer dropped to an early morning low of 77°, but rose rapidly to 92° by 9:00 a.m. and to 99° by 12:00 noon. The maximum of 100° was registered at 2:00 p.m. At that observation, the dew point stood at 69°F and the barometer at 29.90 inches. The wind, as it had for several hours previously, came out of the north at 13 miles per hour. The sky was obscured by clouds until after the maximum reading at 2:00 p.m.

Next day the mercury climbed from an overnight low of 71° to 97° by 10:00 a.m., and it looked as though Nantucket was in for another record-breaker day, but the wind backed from north to west and brought cooler air, conditioned over the ocean. The mercury dropped to 87°F within an hour and by 3:00 p.m. was down to 80° with the wind now coming out of the southeast.

"The Mud Bowl," October 1982

October 9 — Nantucket had a rainy day. From about 11 o'clock on until mid or late afternoon over two inches of rain fell. The Nantucket Whalers and the Blue Hill team played in the "mud bowl," the Whalers winning 6-0.

Inquirer and Mirror,
January 27, 1983.

Brilliant Sunsets, December 1982

Without doubt the most beautiful and spectacular sunset for this year was that last evening. The sky went from a lovely shade of blue to a light violet, to a light pink to an orangish-red and finally to a deep purplish red which extended across the western sky for nearly 180 degrees. The beauty lasted for nearly an hour. Our lovely sunsets are partially due to the effects of Mt. St. Helens in the state of Washington; of El Chicon, in Mexico; or the most recent one [Mauna Loa] occurring in Hawaii.

Merle Orleans, "Here and There,"
Inquirer and Mirror,
December 9, 1982.

Arctic Sea Smoke, 1983

Yesterday morning Nantucketers woke up to see a cloud of sea smoke arising from the harbor. This morning we all opened our eyes to the sight of the lovely white fluffy snowflakes slowly covering the ground — snowflakes occurring only over the Cape and Islands while the rest of the area north of the Canal was being treated to blue sky and bright sunshine. We are being assured that these are flurries only, but—where have we heard that tale before!

Inquirer and Mirror,
January 20, 1983.

Quahog Day, February 2, 1983

While the rest of the nation waited for the word on winter from Punxatawney Phil the groundhog, Nantucketers waited for the word on the island winter from Quentin the Quahog.

Wednesday morning, in front of a small gathering down at Steamboat Wharf, Shellfish

Warden Allen Holdgate pried open a quahog to find out the real word on the remainder of the Nantucket winter.

Unlike last year when the mollusk squirted its announcement from its left side, the 1983 quahog dribbled its contents "straight down."

"It's gonna be an open winter," Holdgate announced. "We may see a couple more bad storms, but the remainder of the winter will be mild."

Nancy Burns,
Inquirer and Mirror,
February 3, 1983.

Great Point Light Succumbs to the Sea, March 29, 1984

That storm last Thursday, which has been called "the worst of the century," brought us a total of 2.60 inches of precipitation, with our barometer dropping to a low of 28.80 about mid-afternoon. The highest wind we recorded was 63 m.p.h. from the north-northeast, but we know that some anemometers in other parts of the island showed higher winds.

That storm last Thursday surprised islanders in more ways than one. There was one bright spot on the scene. In the worst storm in years and years the Nantucket Electric Company came through with flying colors. For only one brief moment did the power go off. We were fortunate that we received rain and not the heavy wet snow that hit our mainland neighbors—some places near Boston had no power, and consequently no lights, no heat, for several days . . . .

And Nantucket? Nantucket had its own disaster, winds from 60 to 70 m.p.h., extreme high tides, the creeks turned into a lake at high tide, Easy Street covered with vicious waves breaking over the bulkhead, parts of Steamboat Wharf under water, Washington Street Extension area flooded to include the cellars and first floors (in some instances), trees blown over etc.—and then came the disaster! Great Point Lighthouse was gone, undermined by fierce waves and left mainly in one huge pile of rubble washed by the ocean.

There are literally millions of people—natives and visitors, year-round and summer residents—who have been coming to Nantucket by sea or air. There has been scarcely anyone who has not watched anxiously for that first glimpse of our beloved island—Great Point standing firmly against the blue sky and the ocean by day, its light blinking regularly at night, welcoming travelers home to Nantucket. How many of us can remember almost fighting with our best friends for a place in the bow of the steamer in order to be the first to cry out: "I see it! There she is! There's the light—I saw it first!"

Inquirer and Mirror,
April 15, 1984.

Christmas 1985

Nantucket almost had a white Christmas as recently as 1985. Over five inches of snow fell on Friday, December 21, but above-freezing temperatures and light rain melted away the white blanket on Sunday and Monday, so Christmas Eve came in foggy with bare ground and temperatures in the 40s.

ASTRONOMIA MISCELLANEA
Auroras, Comets, Eclipses, and Meteors

Nineteenth Century

"Darkness at Noon," The Great Eclipse of June 1806

Simple and well known though the fact may be, according to the explanations of astronomical science, that a solar eclipse is caused by the intervention of the moon between the sun and the earth during the daytime, and that the effect of such interposition is to obstruct the sun's rays—the light being turned into darkness while the phenomenon lasts—a *total* eclipse is, without doubt, the most sublime and awe-inspiring spectacle upon which the eye of man is permitted to gaze. By far the most remarkable exhibition of this kind was that which occurred June 16, 1806, when the sun in the northern states was totally eclipsed nearly five minutes, about a half hour before noon, the width of the moon's shadow being about one hundred and fifty miles, or about seventy-five [miles] on each side of the central line. Since 1806 [to 1876], only one total eclipse of the sun occurred in the Atlantic States, namely in South Carolina and Georgia, November 30, 1834; but the eclipse of June 16, 1806, is regarded by astronomers as the most memorable ever known in the United States,—that of August 7, 1869, being the next in grandeur and interest.

Devens,
Our First Century, 1880.

A total eclipse of the sun occurs when the moon passes between the earth and the sun, and is close enough to the earth so that its umbra, or shadow cone, reaches the earth's surface. As the disc of the moon centers over the sun in its journey it appears to cover the entire orb of the sun. The duration of the

The total eclipse of the sun over Nantucket as photographed at the Maria Mitchell Observatory on January 24, 1925.
Photograph courtesy of the Maria Mitchell Observatory.

eclipse and the size of the eclipsed area depend on the season of the year, the distance of the moon from the earth, and the geographic position of the observer on earth. The maximum duration in the latitude of Nantucket is about five minutes, and the greatest possible diameter of the moon's shadow on earth is about 163 miles. The maximum duration possible anywhere on earth is 7 minutes and 31 seconds.

The geographical and astronomical details of the eclipse of June 16, 1806, were outlined in a popular pamphlet, *Darkness at Noon*, which went through several editions prior to the day of the eclipse. The event was of special note because the path crossed the entire

country from Mexican California to the shores of New England. It also occurred near the summer solstice when the moon was at one of its closest approaches to the Earth, giving both a maximum duration and a large width of totality. Both Boston and Salem lay almost on the line of centrality where the duration of the eclipse was about four minutes and fifty seconds, roughly, double the usual time for that latitude.

The Great American eclipse began in the ocean well off Lower California. The line of centrality crossed southern California, then tracked northeast over Colorado, Kansas, northern Illinois, Lake Erie, central New York State, and northern Massachusetts, entering the Atlantic Ocean near Cape Ann.

The zone of totality, about 163 miles wide, included most of central and northern Connecticut and almost all of Rhode Island. All of Cape Cod fell within the zone, as confirmed by reports from Woods Hole and Naushon, the largest of the Elizabeth Islands. A questionable report of totality came from West Chop, the northwest extremity of Martha's Vineyard. The southern edge of totality crossed Nantucket Sound on an east-northeast trending line and included Monomoy Point, but not Great Point. This placed Nantucket Town about 20 miles outside the zone of totality.

Nathaniel Bowditch, the Salem astronomer and author of the *New American Practical Navigator* (1802), gathered all available observations and published the results in the *Memoirs of the American Academy of Arts and Sciences* (Boston, 1809). He stated, "The eclipse was not total at Nantucket in the latitude 41° 15′ 32″ N and in longitude of 4h 40′ 0″ W of Greenwich, as was observed by Mr. Walter Folger, jun."

Bowditch commented on the weather conditions at Salem: "On the day of the eclipse the weather was remarkably fine, scarcely a cloud being visible in any part of the heavens." All other reports from the Northeast spoke of fine viewing conditions. In view of Folger's report, we can assume that they were equally good on Nantucket.

Great Comet of 1807

A comet is an astronomical body composed of a nucleus of condensed material and gases surrounded by a nebulous, hazy light called the coma. It has been likened to a dirty snowball of the sky. When a comet approaches or leaves the sun, a distinctive tail often forms, usually pointing directly away from the sun. These celestial bodies are members of the solar system and have highly elliptical orbits. Some return to earth periodically, such as Halley's comet which appears every 76 years, but others vanish into space. Comets may be seen on Nantucket, but often their orbits take them into the Southern Hemisphere and below the horizon.

Comets are generally described in terms of magnitude, which refers to the relative brightness of a celestial body. The lower the numerical value of the magnitude of a body the brighter it is relative to others. The brightest stars are determined to be magnitude 1. A body of magnitude 1 is 2.512 times brighter than a body of magnitude 2, which in turn is 2.512 times brighter than a body of magnitude 3.

The magnitudes of celestial bodies vary greatly. Naked-eye stars are classed from magnitude 1 to 6. With the best telescopes we can see stars of the 20th magnitude, and photograph those of the 23d. Planets may have minus magnitudes, i.e., Venus at its brightest is -4.4. The sun is of visual magnitude -26.72, and the full moon -12.

The Great Comet of 1807 was discovered in Sicily on September 9, 1807, with a magnitude of 1, or that of a bright star. It passed perihelion [closest to the sun] on September 19. In October, the tail split into a long straight tail and a short curved one. The long tail reached a maximum length of 10 degrees on October 22. [A comet tail that reached halfway from horizon to zenith would be described as 45 degrees long.] At that time the magnitude was judged to be 2. European astronomers followed the comet by telescope until March 27, 1808.

William Mitchell of Nantucket mentioned viewing the Great Comet of 1807 with the naked eye in an article published in the *American Journal of Science* (1840). The "Observations of Walter Folger, jun., on Nantucket" were employed by Nathaniel Bowditch in composing a table of the comet's orbit, which appeared in the *Memoirs of the American Academy of Arts and Sciences* (1809). In Massachusetts the first sighting of the comet was reported at Salem on September 25 and it was last detected on January 30, 1808. Presumably a telescope was used to observe it on these dates.

"Great Bright Comet" of 1811

The Comet of 1811 was discovered in France on March 25, but was not seen in New England until September 6 when about to pass perihelion on the 12th. It then brightened considerably to magnitude 0, or equal to the brightest stars, on October 20. Two tails soon developed, one growing to a length of 70 degrees in December. In January, its brilliance dropped below naked-eye visibility. It was last seen in New England on January 16, 1812, and viewed with a telescope from earth for the last time on August 17. It had been seen from the earth for a total of 512 days.

William Mitchell of Nantucket listed this comet as one he had seen in his youth. Nathaniel Bowditch of Salem, Massachusetts, included "Observations made by Walter Folger, jun., on Nantucket" in a summary article in the *Memoirs of the American Academy of Arts and Sciences* (1815).

Annular Eclipse of September 17, 1811

An annular eclipse occurs when the moon is so far from the earth that its disc does not appear to cover the entire orb of the sun. This permits a thin ring of sunlight to be visible surrounding the perimeter of the moon as it centers over the disc of the sun.

The morning of Sept. 17 was clear, with a small air from the SE: In the afternoon it shifted WSW, and blew fresher.

Walter Folger, jun.
"Observations of the Solar Eclipse of September 11, 1811, made at Nantucket," *Memoirs of the American Academy of Arts and Sciences* (1815).

The annular (ring) eclipse traveled southeast from the southern Alaskan coast over the Dakotas to the Virginia coast.

Sunspots, 1816

Some spots are at present visible on the sun's disc. One of them is of considerable magnitude, and resembles a cluster of islands situated very near to each other. Its breadth is at least equal to the diameter of the earth. Another of them is very dark, and surrounded by an umbra or fainter shade.

Nantucket Mirror
June 24, 1816.

Great Comet of 1819

The observations of Hon. Walter Folger, then Congressman from Massachusetts, were hindered during the month of July by adverse weather conditions. Nevertheless, he sent his results to Nathaniel Bowditch who published them in the *Salem Gazette* on September 28, 1819, and then later in the *Memoirs of the American Academy of Arts and Sciences* (1821). William Mitchell included this in his list of naked-eye comets visible on Nantucket. Comet 1819 II was discovered at Berlin on July 1. Its nuclear magnitude was estimated at nearly 1 and the tail about 8 degrees long. It was a naked-eye object through July. In early August its brightness began to fade. It was last observed on October 25. The comet seems to have crossed the face of the sun on June 26, and at that time, the earth may have been involved in its tail.

Comets of 1825

Comet 1825 IV was seen at Portsmouth, New Hampshire, on September 18, and at Boston the next night.

It also was seen from this place at half past [undecipherable] the same morning [Sept. 19] near the Pleiades.

Nantucket Inquirer,
September 26, 1825.

There are now two visible—one bearing southerly at about 10 p.m. and the other appears in the zenith at the same hour. The latter is scarcely distinguishable by the naked eye—and from its situation the train tail cannot be easily discerned.

Nantucket Inquirer,
October 10, 1825.

William Mitchell included Comet 1825 IV among those he had viewed in his younger days with the naked eye.

Comet 1825 IV was discovered by Jean Louis Pons at Marseilles, France, on July 15. By October the magnitude increased to 2 and the tail was estimated at 12 degrees in length. In November the tail split into five branches. It was lost in the sun's glare after December, but reappeared in April 1826. The last observation came on July 8. The second comet mentioned in the *Inquirer* has not been identified.

Luminous Arch, August 28, 1827

Substance of a Dissertation concerning the celestial phenomenon of August 28, 1827—delivered before the Nantucket Philosophical Institute, Oct. 11, 1827—By William Mitchell, Vice President.

I allude to the luminous arch which encompassed the hemisphere on the 28th of the 8th month last.

It was a well defined, radiant belt extending itself from the east to the west point of the horizon, and passing the zenith from north to south with the most brilliant magnificence; affording to the superstitious, the idlest fancies, and to philosophy, the noblest range of powers.

On this and several preceding evenings, there had been for this latitude, an unusual display of the Aurora Borealis, and although the zone of light was undoubtedly an affect or a modification of that phenomenon, yet there seemed, at this time, to be no connection between them, for during the appearance of the zone, the Aurora Borealis had subsided into an appearance of twilight, and the intervening region of the heavens appeared unusually dark.

I first noticed this extraordinary appearance at ten o'clock. At that time it was completely formed; but individuals who saw it at an earlier period, testify, that it was formed by the union of columns of luminous matter rising simultaneously from opposite points of the horizon, and meeting nearly on the meridian. At ten, the summit, or apex of the arch, had attained an altitude of about 84 degrees from the north point of the horizon. Its width on the meridian was about 9 degrees, but its cusps or extremities appeared to be much more contracted, subtending an angle of two degrees only, probably the effect of distance. Its centre passed the bright star Deneb in the constellation of the Swan, at 15 minutes past ten; at 25 minutes past ten, the western extremity passed the bright star Arcturus in the constellation Bootes. While it moved with a slow and majestic motion toward the south, there was a quick undulating motion of its component parts from east to west comparable to the rippling of the surface of the sea in a steady wind. Neither its width nor its progressive motion was strictly uniform. At one time it is contracted, that its width did not exceed the apparent diameter of the moon, nor was it at this period, scarcely less brilliant than that luminary.

Nantucket Inquirer,
October 20, 1827.

Annular Eclipse, February 12, 1831

The day was cloudless and everything seemed to conspire to render the scene delightfully interesting.

The degree of darkness was far less than had been anticipated by many. The small portion of the sun's disk which was visible during the greatest obscuration kept the day light, and served to relieve the anxiety of the superstitious who had supposed not only, that the darkness would be such as anciently overshadowed Egypt, but also that it would be the awful presage of the dissolution of all things.

The nearest approach of the southern limb was estimated at 15 sec., that of the northern 30 sec. The center of the eclipse must therefore have passed about 16 or 17 miles south of this town, and about 10 miles south of the southeast extremity of our island.

William Mitchell,
Nantucket Inquirer
February 19, 1831.

The air was clear, but about the middle and end of the eclipse there was a tremendous motion of the limbs of the sun.

During the greatest obscuration, the planet Venus was visible about +3 degrees east of the Sun.

Walter Folger.

At Siasconset the eclipse began at 11:50:4, local mean time, was central at 1:27:20.6, and ended at 2:53:4.7. The duration of the ring phase was 2 minutes and 1.7 seconds when the sun was 97.8 percent obscured, leaving a ring of light equal to 2.2 percent around the solar disc.

The annular (ring) eclipse swept across southern United States from the Gulf of California to Texas on an easterly track, then headed east-northeast over the Southeastern states to the coast of Virginia, and finally northeast over the ocean, passing over Nantucket and part of Cape Cod. The eclipse was central over Catawba, North Carolina; Petersburg, Virginia; near Siasconset; and Halifax, Nova Scotia.

Great Meteor Shower, November 12–13, 1833

Extensive and magnificent showers of shooting stars have been known to occur at various places in modern times; but the most universal and wonderful which has ever been recorded is that of the thirteenth of November, 1833, the whole firmament, over all the United States, being then, for hours, in fiery commotion! No celestial phenomenon has ever occurred in this country, since its first settlement, which was viewed with such intense admiration by one class in the community, or with so much dread and alarm by another. It was the all-engrossing theme of conversation and of scientific disquisition, for weeks and months. Indeed, it could not be otherwise, than that such a rare phenomenon, — next in grandeur and sublimity to that of a total solar eclipse, or a great comet stretched athwart the starry heavens, in full view of a wonder-struck universe — should awaken the deepest interest among all beholding it.

Devens,
Our First Century, 1880.

An old woodcut of the Great Meteor Shower in the early morning hours of November 13, 1833. The display was visible from about 60°W in the Atlantic Ocean to about 100°W in the Great Plains, and from the Great Lakes to the southern shore of Jamaica in the Caribbean Sea. Reproduced from The Romance of Astronomy, *by Florence A. Grondal.*

The most famous meteor shower to occur in nineteenth-century America reached its peak during the early morning hours of November 13, 1833, until sunrise brought an end to the spectacular display. No descriptive account of the event by a Nantucket witness has been located, though the *Inquirer*, in carrying an item on the phenomenon from the Boston *Evening Transcript*, stated that "the wonderful aerial spectacle was observed from this place at the same time." The paper later published an explanatory account by Professor Denison Olmstead of Yale College. In referring to his Nantucket correspondent on astronomical matters, he stated that Walter Folger was "not present in town." The Folger meteorological record, presumably with an associate or family member filling in as observer, indicated "fair" weather at 10:00 p.m. on the 12th and at 7:00 a.m. on the 13th. Since the barometer was rising and the wind blowing from the west, high pressure conditions with clear skies and cool temperatures in the 40s prevailed overnight.

A meteor is a small particle of matter, thought to be the debris of a disintegrated comet that follows the orbit of that body and intercepts the path of the earth periodically. Of varying sizes, they are invisible until striking our upper atmosphere where friction with air molecules causes them to glow and assume the effect of a shooting star. Large meteors that make spectacular streaks across the sky are called fireballs and bolides. A meteorite is the rare meteor which is not completely consumed by heat in the atmosphere and falls to earth as a solid body, varying in size from a small stone to many tons. A few meteors may be seen on any clear night on Nantucket, but are most frequent in the annual Perseid shower about August 12 and the Leonid shower about November 17.

Partial Eclipse, November 30, 1834

A partial eclipse of the sun occurs when the disc of the moon is not centered on the sun and obscures only part of the solar surface. The effect on earth resembles one of the various phases of the moon during a month, from a thin crescent to an almost full sphere. A partial eclipse is visible as far as 2200 miles on each side of the path of centrality of a total eclipse.

The day nearly cloudless as were the great eclipses of 1806, 1811, and 1831. The weather was unusually mild for the season.

Began at 1h 29m 13s
Ended at 4h 00m 43s
Duration 2h 31m 30s
Temperature dropped 19°

Nantucket Inquirer
December 3, 1834.

The eclipse began in the Yukon Territory and followed a parabolic course to the southeast to Kansas and then east to the Carolinas where it was total. Nantucket witnessed a coverage of 11 digits, or 92 percent.

Return of Halley's Comet, 1835–36

During the month of August 1835, William Mitchell swept the skies nightly from his observatory atop the Pacific National Bank building, when weather permitted, in an attempt to be the first to capture the return of Halley's Comet in its swing through our inner planetary system once every 76 years. He commented later in a lecture on comets which was published in the *Inquirer*.

The whole month passed and the comet did not come. On the fourth of the succeeding month Sept. the air was uncommonly good, and as I pointed the telescope to the little spot in which I knew it must appear, I was greeted by the stranger, and I shall never forget the sensation which I felt. No man in the world to my knowledge had seen it. Seventy-six years had rolled away since it darted in from immeasurable distance and glanced off again into the infinite depth of space.

Mitchell noted further details of the early sighting in his notebook:

Halley's comet was first discovered in this country by Professors Olmstead & Loomis of Yale College on the morning of the 31st of 8th month (August 31) 1835 & by myself on the 4th of the 9th month (September 4) of the same year, again on the 18th being hindered by the light of the moon it was telescopic till the 26th when to the naked eye it appeared like a star of the fifth magnitude. This morning 10 mon 3 (October 3) it was sufficiently distinct or rather apparent to admit my taking angles with the Sextant & at 4h 41 minutes AM (October 4 at 12:41 a.m.) the angle between the Comet and Capella was 19:56.50" — 40 ...

The comet is now clearly visible, near the most northerly part of its course, in the constellation of the Great Bear. It was on Saturday evening [10th] near the star a, known as one of the Pointers, nearest to the Pole Star. Its motion is in a southeasterly direction.

Nantucket Inquirer,
October 14, 1835.

Other items followed in the *Inquirer*, most likely supplied by Mitchell:

December 30, 1835. It is found that Halley's orbit is quite defective and the perihelion was by no means fixed at the later part of October. [The influence of the newly discovered planet Uranus caused the early calculations to be defective].

January 20, 1836. The comet is again visible, but cannot be seen — i.e. with the naked eye.

Comet 1835 III (Halley) was first sighted in Rome on August 6, 1835, by Father M. Dumouchel. During October it passed within 37 million miles of the earth. Perihelion came on November 16. It reached a maximum magnitude of 1, the tail extended 30 degrees. Halley was last viewed on May 16, 1836.

"Radiated Light in November 1835"

Phenomenon. There was last evening at 11 o'clock, a most astonishing display of radiated light in the heavens — of all hues between white and scarlet. The point from which the rays proceeded was exactly in the zenith, and they stretched North and East, enveloping nearly one half the celestial hemisphere. Astronomers will doubtless notice and explain this exhibition more particularly.

The brilliant bow of 1827 was an image of superlative beauty, but the late phenomenon exceeded it by far, in point of awful grandeur.

Nantucket Inquirer,
November 21, 1835.

Three days later the *Inquirer* gave a more detailed description and expressed the opinion that the light was a reflection from high clouds of an aurora seen through the clouds from 9:00 to 11:00 p.m.

Annular Eclipse, May 15, 1836

The solar eclipse of the 15th inst. was observed in this place under very favorable circumstances, the day being cloudless and the air clear.

William Mitchell
Nantucket Inquirer,
May 18, 1836.

The line of centrality of this annular (ring) eclipse crossed Yucatan and Cuba and continued into the Atlantic Ocean on an easterly track. At Boston, it was judged that 8 and 7/60th digits, or 67 percent, of the sun's disc was eclipsed. The duration on Nantucket was 2h 36m 17.9s. Two sunspots were seen; one was eclipsed for about 17 minutes.

"Sublime and Gorgeous Spectacles," Aurora, July 1, 1837

The Heavens, on Saturday night last [July 1], presented one of those sublime and gorgeous spectacles which in this latter days have not been uncommon. The entire firmament was more or less illuminated for about two hours preceding midnight, by a preternatural brightness — now streaming upward from the Northern and Western horizon, in continuous rays, displaying transiently some of the hues of the rainbow; and sweeping irregularly across the East and West, in white transparent coruscations, suddenly flaring and flickering in all directions, and changing position and shape at every instant. At one period, when these mysterious phenomena seemed congregated for the grandest exhibition, there appeared directly in the zenith, a magnificent scroll of golden-tinted vapor, far more brilliant than the surrounding emissions of light, better defined in form, and more stationary. This occupied some 15 or 20 degrees of arch, from East to West and perhaps one third of that space between North and South; and resembled in its contour, the outstretched wings of an immense Eagle, traced upon the spangled azure, as it were with a pencil of living flame. The night was one of the lovliest of the season — no envious cloud of earth obscured the assembled stars, which clearly sparkled beyond the interlucent flashes. Hundreds of admiring mortals were in the streets, and on house tops, marveling at this stupendous illustration of the ancient minstrel's theme — "The Heavens declare the Glory of God."

Nantucket Inquirer,
July 5, 1837

The aurora is a diffused glow in the upper atmosphere consisting of bright patches, streamers, bands, arches, or "merry dancer" patterns, sometimes white and sometimes in red, green, yellow, or blue colors. They are most frequently seen at high geographic latitudes near the parallels of the magnetic poles. The aurora's electrical source results from the solar wind, racing outward, whose gaseous particles push around the earth's magnetic field forming a cone and creating an electric voltage. The gases in our upper atmosphere are ionized and illuminated at elevations above 70 miles, creating the dazzling display of the aurora borealis (north) or aurora australis (south). The aurora is seen infrequently in the latitude of Nantucket; moonlight, cloudiness, and nighttime fog often obscure those that do occur.

"Eclipsed by Fog and Vapors," September 18, 1838

But the morning would have amounted to naught; for the phenomenon itself was eclipsed by the dense fog and vapors congregated within the nether atmosphere.

Nantucket Inquirer,
September 18, 1838.

The annular (ring) eclipse originated near the North Pole. In a curving track, it moved west of Hudson Bay, then to the south, across the Great Lakes, over Washington, D.C., and into the Atlantic Ocean on a southeast track. At Boston, the coverage was 10 52/60th digits, or 91 percent.

Great March Comet of 1843, "A Most Magnificent Visitor"

Sudden Appearance of a Great and Fiery Comet in the Skies at Noonday, 1843

The comet of 1843 is regarded, perhaps, the most marvelous of the present age, having been observed in the day-time even before it was visible at night, — passing very near the sun, — exhibiting an enormous length of tail,

A representation of the Great March Comet of 1843, which was visible in the Nantucket sky on several occasions that month with the unaided eye.

— and arousing an interest in the public mind as universal and deep as it was unprecedented. It startled the world by its sudden apparition in the spring, in the western heavens, like a streak of aurora, streaming from the region of the sun, below the constellation of Orion. It was at first mistaken, by multitudes, for the zodiacal light; but its aspects and movements soon proved it to be a comet of the very largest class. There were, too, some persons who, without regarding it, like many of the then numerous sect called Millerites, (a sect of Second Adventists, founded by William Miller, that believed the second coming of Christ was to occur in 1843), as foretokening the speedy destruction of the world, still could not gaze at it untroubled by a certain nameless feeling of doubt and fear.

Devens,
Our First Century, 1880.

On the evening of the 5th last, an appearance was visible near the South Western horizon, resembling an immense cometary train, but the intervention of clouds which it somewhat resembled and the illusions so common in such cases directed my attention from the phenomenon. The clear evening of the 7th inst., however, gave an earnest of the presence of a most magnificent visitor. The change of its position from the 5th, was favorable and a stream of well defined white light rising obliquely from a point of the heavens near *Aries,* stretched off to the south, and terminated near the star *Rho* in the constellation of the *River,* subtending in its prolongation, an angle of nearly 40 degrees, what portion of the train was below the horizon in connection with the nucleus, or hidden by the vapours of the earth can only be conjectured. With or without the invisible portion, its aspect was probably more imposing than any recorded comet since that of 1744 or perhaps the great comet of 1680 observed by Newton of which it is a striking likeness . . .

Since writing the above, Capt. Luce of the sloop Portugal, has informed me, that on the 28th ult., at 2 P.M. he saw the nucleus and train of the Comet, a "handspike's length" (four degrees probably) at the left and below the sun.

William Mitchell,
Nantucket Inquirer,
March 11, 1843.

The nucleus of the great comet was seen by our learned correspondent William Mitchell Esq. on the 10th inst. and its Right Ascension and Declination were obtained. It was again visible on the evening of the 12th, but too frequently obscured by the passage of clouds to admit of taking accurate observations. Its apparent motion is very rapid in a south-easterly direction. It is receding from the sun, and while its distance from the earth is probably increasing, the change in its apparent position will afford us a delightful view of it in the absence of the moon.

Nantucket Inquirer,
March 15, 1843.

Additional observations of the comet were made by Nantucketers on March 11, 17, 18, 20, and 21. On March 22, the *Inquirer* commented: "Brilliance diminishing."

Comet 1843 I was discovered on February 5, but no good measurements were obtained until perihelion on February 27. It was of the family of sungrazers, passing within 558,000 miles of that body. It was visible in broad daylight when only one degree from the sun's limb, with a probable magnitude of –7. Estimates of the tail length varied from 69 to 90 degrees, the latter the distance from the horizon to the zenith. The whole comet and tail were visible in the Northern Hemisphere on March 16. In late March the tail decreased to 38 degrees, and by the end of the month the nucleus had dropped below naked-eye visibility. The comet was last seen on April 19.

Meteor Shower, 1844

Aug. 9–10, 1844. William Mitchell on evening of August 9 — about 80 [per hour]

— point of radiation head of Aquarius toward the horizon.

Clipping in Mitchell Mss.
probably published in *Nantucket Inquirer,* August 12, 1844.

Transit of Mercury, May 8, 1845

William Mitchell observed a transit of the planet Mercury across the face of the Sun on May 8, 1845, at 19 hours and 36 minutes, Ephemeris Time. The next transit would occur on November 9, 1848, but would be in a poor position.

Clipping in Mitchell Mss. from *Inquirer.*

A transit is the passage of a small body across the face of a larger one. Mercury and Venus, being inferior planets, transit the face of the Sun, but the exterior planets do not.

Partial Eclipse, April 25, 1846

A partial eclipse was observed "under very favorable conditions." The sun was eclipsed for 6 and 43/60th digits, or 56 percent of its surface, at Boston. The path of totality crossed the Yucatan peninsula, western Cuba, the Florida Straits, and the central Bahamas. The duration of the eclipse was 2 hours 42 minutes.

Clipping in Mitchell Mss., probably from *Inquirer.*

Mitchell's Comet, 1847

Comet 1847 VI was discovered by Maria Mitchell of Nantucket on the evening of October 2. Three other searchers in other countries independently found it within the next ten days. On the 7th, an observer described the new comet as resembling "a hazy star of the 5th magnitude" to the naked eye. The comet passed perigee (the point nearest the earth) on October 12 and was given a magnitude of 3.5. A tail seemed non-existent at this time. It was lost in the twilight on November 14 and passed perihelion that day. Observations resumed on December 10 and continued until January 4, as a telescopic object.

Partial Solar Eclipse, July 28, 1851

[July 29, 1851].

At the beginning, the sky was perfectly clear, but the wind high; and the best instruments used in the open air, was much affected by it. At the end, the wind had fallen, and though threatened by passing clouds, the observation was all that could be desired.

William Mitchell,
Nantucket Inquirer,
August 1, 1851.

Maria Mitchell sighting the heavens for new comets, 1851. Collection of Virginia Barney.

The morning was without a cloud, but the wind was so high at the beginning of the eclipse that I have less confidence in the observation, though even this result may be considered fair.

At the end the wind had fallen, and at the moment of the event the telescope was without tremor.
Beginning 7h, 55m, 34.6s
End 9h, 33m, 47.1s
Duration 1h, 38m, 12.5s

Professor W. Mitchell to Lieutenant C.H. Davis in *The Astronomical Journal,* II, 7 (October 1851), Cambridge, Mass.

The path of totality led from the coast of British Columbia across the Northwest Territories, north of Hudson Bay, and over central Greenland. At Boston, the eclipse was judged to be 3 and 42/60th digits, equal to 31 percent totality.

"Northern Lights," February 19, 1852

The attention of our citizens was arrested on the evening of the 19th inst., by one of the most magnificent displays of the Auroral phenomena that have occurred in the present age. It commenced, or, at least, was manifest a few minutes after sunset and continued until rendered invisible by the returning light of the succeeding day. The previous day had been overcast, but at sundown the clouds brushed away leaving a sky of great serenity. The barometer rose from 30.50 to 30.65, and the thermometer fell during the night from 20 to 15.

In the course of this great exhibition, every modification of the Aurora was displayed from the soft and radiant twilight bordering the smoky bank in the north, to the fanciful and amusing vagaries of the *streamers* and *merry dancers.* It encompassed the entire hemisphere, and the *merry dancers* (as the northern sailors call them) were as plentiful in the south as in the north. At a quarter past seven, a segment of an ellipse was formed in the southwest, whose major axis lay parallel with the horizon at an altitude not more than ten or twelve degrees, and having the planet Venus so nearly in its northern foci that one could scarcely persuade himself that it was merely an apparent and accidental position. Later in the evening a beautiful corona was formed about 10 degrees south of the zenith displaying a symmetry of form and a most delightful variety of colors. Having its apex in the head of Leo, it radiated to every point of the horizon, meeting in this course the upshooting streamers, from which it seemed to drive fresh accumulations of light.

Nothing more prominently marked this beautiful display than the *flashings,* a modification much less common than the *streamers* or the *twilight* form. They resemble flame skipping from point to point of some combustible *matter.* Sometimes indeed, though rarely, the whole exhibition consists of *these* and the twilight modification; such was the first Aurora in the present century; viz. in November 1814.

Nantucket Inquirer,
February 23, 1852.

Father and daughter, William and Maria Mitchell, Nantucket astronomers and weather observers from 1830 to 1861.
Photograph courtesy of the Maria Mitchell Observatory.

Nantucket's Only "Clouded-Out" Major Eclipse, May 26, 1854

The storm of rain on Friday afternoon [May 26] rendered the great eclipse invisible here, except to close observers, for a few seconds after the commencement. As it was pretty well understood that the eclipse would certainly come off, "rain or shine," and not, like most exhibitions, be "postponed on account of the weather," a great deal of regret was expressed during the day by those who had made great dependence upon scrutinizing closely the rare phenomenon. We feel very

sorry for them but as we learn this is the only eclipse which has been hidden by clouds at this place for the last seventy years, we do not feel like making much complaint. We fear that many others in New England may have shared the disappointment expressed by our friends.

Nantucket Inquirer,
May 29, 1854

This annular (ring) eclipse crossed northern United States from the state of Washington to southern Maine. At Boston, it was estimated at 11 and 20/60th digits, or 93 percent of totality.

Comet Discovery, September 1854

A faint telescopic comet was discovered by Miss Mitchell near the head of Ursa Major at 20 minutes past 8 on the evening of the 18th inst. A circular received by her last evening

announced its discovery by Mr. Robert Van Arsdale of Newark, N.J., on the 13th.

Nantucket Inquirer,
September 29, 1854.

Comet 1854 IV was first seen by Klinkerfues at Gottingen on September 11, by Bruhns at Berlin on the 12th, by Van Arsdale at Newark on the 13th, and by Mitchell at Nantucket on the 18th. The comet was generally described as faint, diffuse, and large. The comet remained at magnitude 7.5 up to perihelion. Thereafter, the comet rapidly faded and was last seen on December 3.

Maria Mitchell's Observations on Algol, 1856

Maria Mitchell made observations on the variable star Algol from 1853 to 1856. Her letter on the subject, dated Nantucket, November 3, 1856, was published in *The Astronomical Journal,* 5–1 (November 1856).

Donati's Comet, 1858

Telescopic Comet. A faint telescopic comet was discovered by Miss Mitchell of this town, on the evening of the 5th inst., in the constellation of Leo. It was also seen on the 4th, 5th, and 6th. Its position is so low that she is unable to obtain such measurements as will prove it to be a new one, or show that it is one hitherto seen.

Nantucket Inquirer,
July 9, 1858

The comet shone with unusual brilliancy on Saturday night [Oct. 2], the atmosphere being remarkably clear, until a cloud intervened to prevent a full view of the interesting stranger.

Nantucket Inquirer,
October 5, 1858.

Three of these mysterious night visitors now appear in the heavens, two of which are very feeble, and not discoverable with the naked eye. One is exceedingly brilliant, and has been viewed with enthusiasm by countless thousands during a few weeks past.
Enke's comet is barely visible, and Tuttle's can be seen with a telescope.

Nantucket Inquirer,
October 12, 1858.

William Mitchell's meteorological note books record his observations of the comet on October 9, 10, 11, 14, and 15, 1858. Using a sextant, he measured the angles between the comet and Vega, Arcturus, and Antares.
Comet 1858 VI, known as Donati's Comet, was discovered on June 2. This was confirmed in the United States between June 28 and July 1 by several astronomers, one being Maria Mitchell. The comet developed into one of the most impressive comets of the century, during September, beginning with the appearance of a distinctive curved tail on the 6th. Perihelion came on September 30, and afterwards the comet became even more spectacular as it headed for perigee near October 9. The comet was described as being most spectacular on October 10, when nearest the Earth. The tail stretched 60 degrees across the sky in a "magnificent scimitar-like curve," and the nucleus was described as being as prominent as a 1st magnitude star. It was still visible with the naked eye on November 10 and with a telescope until March 4, 1859.

The Great Aurora, August 28, 1859

The Aurora Borealis. — The beautiful appearance of the heavens on Sunday [28th] night is a subject of general remark, and from all points our exchanges represent the phenomenon as being nearly the same. There was a brilliant light in the East, which illuminated the sky with splendor of a full moon, then flickering lights from all parts of the horizon, which gradually rose higher and higher until they reunited near the zenith, and formed a crown. The whole firmament was stained with rapidly varying hues.

Nantucket Inquirer,
September 2, 1859.

Comet of 1860, "A Conspicuous Object"

The comet is very plainly visible to the naked eye about nine o'clock. It is in fact quite a conspicuous object in the heavens. Not only the nucleus, but also a considerable portion of the tail may be seen. It is in the northwest, and a few degrees above the horizon.

Nantucket Inquirer,
July 3, 1860.

Comet 1860 III passed perihelion on June 16 and was "discovered" in different parts of the world during the next three days. On June 28 the estimated magnitude attained 1.5 and the tail reached 15° long. After July 6 the magnitude declined rapidly as it moved into the Southern Hemisphere. It was listed as a "Great Comet" of the nineteenth century.

Partial Eclipse, July 18, 1860

The eclipse of the Sun, which according to the predictions of the Astronomers was to come off on the 18th, occurred with usual promptness, although few to whom the circumstance was known would have perceived that one-half of the Sun's disk was "shorn of its beam." The day was beautiful and afforded a fine opportunity to those who wished to make scientific observations.

Nantucket Inquirer,
July 20, 1860.

The path of totality led from the state of Washington northeast across southern Hudson Bay and northern Labrador. It was estimated at 6 and 12/60th digits, or 52 percent at Boston. This was the third return of the Great Eclipse of 1806.

Great Comet of 1861

July 2 — The great comet, now visible in the north . . . The nucleus is brighter and its apparent magnitude is greater than that of any comet in this remarkable cometary age, affording at this hour as much light as the moon at octant [a phase halfway between new moon and either first or last quarter]. Its principal train is 75 deg. in length, slightly bending to the right. Other trains consisting of pencils of light, rise from the nucleus on the left, about one third of the primary train, with a more decided course to the left. The sudden appearance of this comet, and its extreme brightness, indicate a rapid apparent motion and close proximity to the Sun, and not a very distant neighbor to the Sun.

Clipping from *Nantucket Mirror* in Mitchell Mss.

Mitchell added in a note that the comet appeared suddenly in the sky on July 2 and was equal to a 1st or 2d magnitude star. "It is a beautiful object. The gibbous form of the nucleus is easily detected," he wrote.

The Great Comet of 1861

Comet — A large, brilliant comet was seen in the heavens last evening, apparently directly over our office. We hope it was a precursor of good luck to some of the types over whose heads it so brightly shone. Who can tell?

Nantucket Inquirer,
July 3, 1861.

No more mention of comet during July; some August issues are missing from the Atheneum file.

Comet 1861 II was discovered with the naked eye in New South Wales, Australia, on May 13. Perihelion followed on June 12. On the last day of June, the comet was described as being as bright as Saturn, or 1st magnitude, and having a tail 100° long. During that day the Earth apparently passed through the tail without any noticeable effects. The tail length and brightness decreased rapidly during July, and naked-eye visibility ended in mid-August, though the comet continued to be observed telescopically through the end of the year. It was also classified as a "Great Comet" of the century.

Annular Eclipse, October 19, 1865

The eclipse of the sun, on Thursday forenoon [Oct. 19], came off according to the prediction of the almanac makers. The sun was obscured by clouds at the beginning of the eclipse, but before its greatest obscuration, the clouds passed away and gave all an opportunity to bring their smoked glasses into requisition, which were pretty generally improved. There will be no other eclipse of the sun of any magnitude until 1869.

Inquirer and Mirror,
October 21, 1865.

The path of the annular eclipse originated in Oregon and swept southeast to northern Florida and into the Atlantic Ocean on a curving easterly track. The solar disc coverage at Boston was 69 percent.

Meteor Shower, November 1866

We were delighted witnesses of ten or more very lustrous meteors on the morning of Tuesday last [Nov. 13]. Their course, mainly, was from east to west, and there were two which deserve more than mere mention. Swift as lightning, these glittering orbs sailed athwart the heavens, and their phosphorescent track was intensely luminous. They were like silver arrows, their heads dipped in liquid fire, their long trails like shafts, many so many spires of light shot from the arrow of Aurora, breaking and falling among the cloud mountains. One exploded over our heads, bright and sizzling as the fiery mane of Pegasus.

It is said by the wise ones that such phenomena as meteoric showers cannot be predicted with the certainty which precedes an eclipse or the advent of a comet. No one has any correct knowledge of the "meteoric ring," or any definite idea of the disposition of the meteors. So we shall have to be in the dark, until we see the light of them.

Inquirer and Mirror,
November 17, 1866.

This was a display of the Leonid meteors emanating from the constellation Leo, which in mid-November rises about 1:00 a.m. Their period is about 33 years, so a greater than normal display was anticipated in 1866. Professor H. A. Newton of Yale College at New Haven, Connecticut, described the event:

... They came upon us in crowds. Over 1000 were counted in an hour. By nine o'clock the display was over ... We saw only the last drops of a heavy shower. Before the Sun had set with us (in USA) the shooting stars were seen throughout all Europe, coming too fast to be counted. At least 50,000, perhaps 100,000 could have been seen there by a single party of observers.

Meteor Seen from Siasconset, June 1, 1868

A meteor was observed at Siasconset on Monday forenoon [June 1], moving from north to south. It "apparently fell into water at a distance as was estimated of a mile and a half."

Inquirer and Mirror,
June 6, 1868.

Great Solar Eclipse, August 7, 1869

The Great Solar Eclipse came off on Saturday afternoon [Aug. 7], and although at the beginning the face of the sun was somewhat obscured by clouds, they soon passed away, and at the time of the greatest obscuration a magnificent view of the eclipse by every person who could procure a piece of smoked glass for the occasion. About four-fifths of the sun's disc was obscured.

Inquirer and Mirror,
August 14, 1869

The path of totality led from southern Alaska southeast over northeast Montana and central Illinois, and to the Atlantic coast near Cape Lookout, North Carolina. Maria Mitchell viewed the eclipse at Burlington, Iowa. The estimated phase at Boston was 10 and 14/60th digits, or 85 percent.

Annular Eclipse, September 29, 1875

The solar eclipse Wednesday morning [Sept. 29] came off according to prediction, but owing to the heavy clouds which obscured the sun, was not very satisfactorily observed.

Inquirer and Mirror,
October 2, 1875.

The annular (ring) eclipse on September 29, 1875, originated over New York State and passed into the Atlantic Ocean south of Nantucket. The estimated maximum phase at Boston was 11 digits and 25/60th, or 92 percent.

Great Comet of 1881

Comet-gazers have had a rare treat the past week, watching the celestial visitor, which first appeared here on the night of the 24th ult. Whether it is a young comet or an old one, and how long it will continue to shine are questions which are agitating the astronomical world.

Inquirer and Mirror,
July 30, 1881.

Comet 1881 III was discovered in New South Wales, Australia, on May 22. Perihelion came on June 16, and the comet appeared in northern skies on June 22, possessing a total magnitude of 1 and a noticeable tail which grew to 20 degrees by the 25th. The total and nuclear magnitudes were estimated consistently at 1. Three jet-like plumes were detected at the end of the month. During July the magnitude faded from 2 to 5, but it was an easy object to find only 8 degrees from the celestial pole. It was last seen telescopically on February 15, 1882.

Great Comet of September 1882

The comet, which for several mornings past has furnished a brilliant spectacle in the eastern sky just previous to sunrise, has been the means of drawing many confirmed sleepers from their beds at an early hour; but they have been fully repaid for their trouble in the delightful view obtained of the long-tailed stranger. The entire sky has presented a picture of remarkable beauty, previous to sunrise, during the week.

Inquirer and Mirror,
October 7, 1882

"The Great September Comet" of 1882 was first discovered on September 1 by a group of Italian sailors in the Southern Hemisphere. By September 10, when the magnitude had grown to −2, numerous astronomers began to study the comet. By the 14th while approaching the sun, it could be seen in broad daylight with a magnitude near −4. Perihelion came on the 14th. By the 17th astronomers' estimates of the magnitude ranged from −15 to −20. Many observers watched the comet as it passed right into the boiling limb of the sun. By October the nucleus was split into four or five parts. The tail remained longer than 20 degrees throughout October, but by the end of the month the comet had diminished to magnitude 3. Naked-eye visibility ended in mid-February, and was observed by telescope on June 1, 1883.

The Comet — Our Skeezix is full of comet, and has risen at four o'clock every morning for a week in order to see the wonderful spectre of the skies, now traversing the southeastern heavens at the rate of 600 miles per second . . .
Early morning comet gazers have been foiled by rising clouds nearly every morning this week.

Inquirer and Mirror,
October 14, 1882.

Darkness in Forenoon: Eclipse of July 29, 1897

But the darkness of last Thursday forenoon July 29th, occasioned by the moon's disk passing across the sun, was intensified by an electrical storm accompanied by rain. It was an annular [ring] eclipse.

Inquirer and Mirror,
July 31, 1897

The annular eclipse path crossed Yucatan peninusla, the south coast of Cuba, and on an east-southeast track into the tropical North Atlantic Ocean. The estimated phase at Boston was 4 digits and 26/60th, or 33 percent.

Eclipse, May 28, 1900

Next Monday look out for the eclipse of the sun. Have smoked glass prepared. There was a total [annular] eclipse visible on Feb. 12, 1831, which will be remembered by many of our older citizens.

Inquirer and Mirror,
May 26, 1900.

No mention of viewing the eclipse appeared in the next issue of the paper. The weather bureau records indicated that a northeaster prevailed on May 28 with misting in the morning and cloudy conditions in the evening. The character of the day was listed as cloudy.
The path of centrality crossed northern Mexico, coastal Texas, the Southeastern states from Louisiana to Virginia, and left the continent in the vicinity of Norfolk, Virginia. The estimated phase at Boston was 11 digits and 1/60th, or 92 percent.

Twentieth Century

Comet of 1901

The new comet has three tails and is the most brilliant of any seen for nineteen years. To observe it one must be awake about 4 o'clock in the morning.

Inquirer and Mirror,
May 4, 1901.

Comet 1901 I was discovered on April 12 in Uruguay. At perihelion on April 24, the nucleus was at magnitude 0 and had a tail 10 degrees long. The comet seemed yellow in appearance and remained visible for some time after sunrise. After the 24th, the comet moved into the evening sky and apparently remained lost in the sun's glare until May 2, when it was described as rivaling Sirius in brightness (–1.5). As the comet moved rapidly away from both the sun and earth, it faded rapidly, down to magnitude 1.0 on May 5, and to 6 by the 24th. The tail reached a maximum length of 10 degrees on May 6. The comet was followed with telescopes until June 14.

Great January Comet, 1910

The comet discovered in South America last week was seen here first on Sunday evening [Jan. 23], and was a brilliant object in the western sky just before sunset. It is said to be the brightest comet since 1882, and is called Innes comet. Keeper Remsen of Sankaty light [house] who is an ardent student of astronomy and alert for all sorts of phenomena was the first person on Nantucket to catch a glimpse of the comet, and telephoned word to town about 5:30 Sunday evening that its brilliancy could be seen in the western sky. The phenomenon was viewed by hundreds that evening and was a most interesting sight.

Inquirer and Mirror,
January 29, 1910.

Comet 1910 was first seen on the early morning of January 13 by a group of mine workers in South Africa. It approached the sun and reached perihelion on the 17th, at magnitude –4. As January neared its end, the comet moved into the evening sky and became a brilliant object visible in the Northern Hemisphere. Its tail reached 30 degrees, with some estimates as long as 50 degrees. After the 27th, a rapid fading took place; it was last seen with a telescope on July 15.

Return of Halley's Comet, 1910

April 30. The Maria Mitchell Observatory will be open Monday evening, May 2d, from 8 to 9 o'clock. On the 2nd, Halley's Comet may be seen about 4:00 a.m. near Venus, the bright star in the southeast.

May 14. Much interest is aroused all over the world in the appearance of Halley's Comet, which is visible to the naked eye in the early morning hours.

May 21. The comet will be at its brightest this evening, but the full brilliancy of the phenomenon will not be apparent, owing to moonlight nights . . . .

What a relief. The comet has passed us safely by. Now we can all breathe easy again.

May 28. The comet has shown its face once or twice this week, and might behave real well if the clouds and mist would keep away.

Inquirer and Mirror,
1910.

Comet 1910 (Halley) was first located photographically at Heidelberg, Germany, on September 11, 1909. It remained a faint, diffuse object through its passage behind the sun in February 1910. Halley reappeared in April and rapidly approached the earth, increasing in brightness. The tail began to grow and reached 55 degrees by May 14, 107 degrees by May 17, and 120 degrees by May 20. As the comet whipped in front of the sun, the tail passed over the earth on May 18. The extent of the tail remained about 50 degrees throughout the remainder of May, then began to decrease in June. The maximum magnitude was 0.

"A Magnificent Display," March 1920

Not a display of automobiles, nor millinery, nor feathery aigrettes for my lady's hair, but a grand display of "Northern Lights" marched and beckoned and flashed celestial signals, from eight to ten o'clock on Monday evening last. I wonder how many of us were "stepping heavenward" — or rather looking heavenward on that crisp starlight evening of March 22d!

The grandest of these pictures moved across the northern sky about 8:30 o'clock, when the streamers rose as if coming out of the very house tops below, and the waving plumes of light seemed like weird geysers from haunted regions of glory. So near to the approaching sacred Sunday these signals flashed to my vision they seemed to me almost a "motion picture" of the hallowed Palms of Jerusalem.

Ann Starbuck Jones,
Inquirer and Mirror,
March 27, 1920.

Total Solar Eclipse, January 24, 1925

The weather man certainly did his very best, even if the temperature was rather low for Nantucket. A clear air and a cloudless sky were what everyone had been praying for, and the conditions could not have been improved upon, with the possible exception of the chilly morning. That was one time when everything worked together, something that does not always happen for "world's series," football games, community festivals, etc. This time it was a nation-wide "show" that could not have been improved upon . . . .

The coldest place on earth just then — in the minds of the five persons there last Saturday morning — was the loft in the south tower. Temperature 5 above zero; wind blowing fresh from the northwest, everything open below, above and around, cold feet, cold hands, cold noses.

Inquirer and Mirror,
January 31, 1925.

The path of totality originated in northern Minnesota and swept southeast over lakes Michigan, Huron, Ontario, and through New York State and Connecticut. Montauk Point at the eastern extremity of Long Island was exactly on the central line of totality.

The northern edge of totality ran from Marion on the mainland across Buzzards Bay and the southwest tip of Cape Cod, on a line from Otis Air Force Base to Cotuit and east-southeast across Nantucket Sound. The line just missed Monomoy Point by about a mile, but encompassed Great Point and all of Nantucket. The Town lay about 16 miles within the zone of totality, which included all the Elizabeth Islands, Martha's Vineyard, Woods Hole, and the Falmouths. The zone of totality covered a strip about 120 miles wide; its southern edge crossed uptown New York City at the Hudson River and 96th Street. At Nantucket totality occurred at 9:15 a.m. and lasted for 89 seconds.

The partial eclipse of the sun on August 31, 1932, as seen from Nantucket. Much of Cape Cod lay within the zone of full totality where it was witnessed at Provincetown by members of the staff of the Maria Mitchell Observatory.
Photograph courtesy of the Maria Mitchell Observatory.

Almost Total Eclipse, August 31, 1932

The weather was made to order for observing the phenomenon. Before the maximum phase was reached, however, one of the white clouds present in the sky all day drifted across the sun's portion of the sky, so that a curious rainbow effect resulted. The little wedge of the sun which was left in sight at the "99 percent totality" gave much more light than expected. Another strange effect was provided by two seagulls, who flew slowly over the town into the northwest, apparently bewildered by the sudden darkening of the sun.

At one of the beaches, a small flock of sandpipers made their way along the water's edge without their usual weak piping cries. The seagulls, too, were strangely silent, a good many being perched on the jetties and remaining there during the dark phase.
Inquirer and Mirror,
September 3, 1932

George C. Grimes at the weather bureau agreed that conditions were close to perfect: "The weather was ideal for the eclipse. The predominating clouds, 3 to 4 tenths of cirrus-stratus, kept well to the eastward and only one little patch passed across the sun's portion of the sky which gave a rainbow effect." The temperature stood at 80° at the start of the eclipse with a light wind blowing at 8 miles per hour from the west.

The path of totality originated in the Arctic Ocean near Siberia, crossed the Arctic Archipelago of Canada, northern Hudson Bay, and central Quebec. It entered the United States over the Northeast Kingdom of Vermont, crossed north-central New Hampshire, and southern Maine.

The southern edge of totality cut from Salem across Massachusetts Bay and Cape Cod Bay to Brewster, then made a short land traverse to South Chatham on Nantucket Sound. Northern Monomoy Island lay within the darkened zone, but south of Inward Point, Monomoy Island across from Great Point lay outside totality. Nantucket Town lay about 16 miles outside of the southern edge of the zone of total eclipse. Across Nantucket Sound on Cape Cod, totality lasted 32 seconds at Chatham and 52 seconds at Provincetown. The maximum coverage of the sun's disc at the Nantucket Observatory was 99 percent at 4:35 p.m.

Giacobini Meteor Shower, October 9–10, 1933

On the evening of October 10 three girls from the High School and the writer witnessed a short shower of at least ten meteors a minute for about five minutes. Word had not yet reached us of the fine and unexpected display of meteors from Giacobini's comet which were seen in all parts of Europe on the evening of October 9. The meteors we observed seem to have been the rear guard of that shower, which, with the possible exception of a few meteors seen in New York and Iowa on the night of the ninth, was seen nowhere else in the western hemisphere. It was cloudy in Nantucket on October 9. This experience again impresses that because of its eastern outpost position Nantucket is an important place for the observation of meteors. This Observatory stands ready to receive all data concerning meteors seen at Nantucket.

The Nantucket Maria Mitchell Association, *Thirty-second Annual Report (1934)*.

Great Aurora, September 18, 1941

One of the most brilliant aurora displays of the present century occurred on a pleasantly crisp evening in September 1941. "It was one of the most glorious ever witnessed and was quite general everywhere in this section," declared the *Inquirer and Mirror* on September 20.

Partial Eclipse, July 9, 1945

Conditions were clear Monday morning [July 9], but comparatively few of our residents took the trouble to hunt up a smoked glass and look at the partial eclipse of the sun. Those who did take a glimpse, however, found there were no clouds to obstruct the view.

Inquirer and Mirror, July 14, 1945.

The path of the eclipse lead from Nevada northeast over central Hudson Bay, and central Greenland.

"Eclipse Eclipsed," June 30, 1954

Eclipse Eclipsed. Like a good part of the people who wanted to watch the partial

Comet Arend-Roland as photographed telescopically by Margaret Harwood at the Maria Mitchell Observatory on April 30, 1957. The comet was photographed on four occasions. Photograph courtesy of the Maria Mitchell Observatory.

eclipse of the sun Wednesday morning [June 30], we here on Nantucket had to be satisfied with an occasional glimpse of the phenomenon when the sun peered through the clouds.

Inquirer and Mirror, July 3, 1954.

The path of the total eclipse began in Nebraska and traveled northeast, passing near Duluth, Minnesota, southern James Bay, and southern Greenland.

Arend-Roland Comet, 1957

The Arend-Roland Comet was seen on Wednesday evening to the northwest, west and south of Cassiopeia. It could be seen by eight o'clock in Nantucket. It has a sharp, bright head and a fuzzy tail at least 10 degrees long, slanting upwards. A thin beam of light streams in the opposite direction to the head. Since the comet is moving away from the sun, it goes "tail first," getting gradually fainter. This is the brightest comet since Halley's left us in 1910.

Inquirer and Mirror,
April 27, 1957.

We saw the Arend-Roland comet again very briefly and faintly Tuesday evening [April 30], the first night the skies had been clear enough since last Wednesday [April 24].

Inquirer and Mirror,
May 4, 1957.

Comet 1957 III (Arend-Roland) was found on astrograph plates taken on November 8, 1956. By late December, the comet increased to magnitude 9 and developed a short tail. The comet brightened gradually as it approached the earth. Perihelion was reached on April 8 and perigee on April 12. The comet then had a magnitude between 1 and 2 and was easily observed in the Northern Hemisphere. The comet developed an unusual feature: an additional sunward tail (15 degrees long) that was as bright as the main tail (30 degrees). Thereafter, the comet faded to 7.8 magnitude on June 3.

Sunrise Eclipse, October 1, 1959

Nantucketers, who rose earlier than usual on Friday morning (October 10) to witness the total eclipse of the sun, saw no more of the spectacle than did anyone else in the New England area. A linesquall passing through eastern New England provided heavy clouds, drizzle, and strong northerly winds, thereby eclipsing the eclipse.

"Here and There,"
Inquirer and Mirror,
October 2, 1959.

The total eclipse of the sun over Nantucket as photographed at the Maria Mitchell Observatory on March 7, 1970.
Photograph courtesy of the Maria Mitchell Observatory.

Total Solar Eclipse, March 7, 1970

A day which will go down in Island history as the most unusual in recent times — Saturday, March 7 — provided an estimated 5,000 visitors an opportunity to witness one of nature's rarest spectacles, a total solar eclipse. Favored with ideal weather conditions, a clear blue sky and a northerly breeze to keep the atmosphere sharp, Nantucket gave both islanders and visitors a close to perfect period for the viewing.

The temperature fell at least 10 degrees at the moment of totality (1:45 + 2 min. 6 sec.).

Timing of eclipse:

start partial phase	12 h	21 m	19 s
start totality	1	45	33
end totality	1	47	50
end partial phase	2	58	05

Inquirer and Mirror,
March 12, 1970.

A *New York Times* reporter composed a dispatch with some local color:

Nantucket, Mass., March 7
A chilling northeast breeze swept over the bayberry-covered dunes of this picturesque island today, but it might have been a balmy Fourth of July holiday to judge from the throngs in the narrow cobbled streets. For Nantucket was the only spot in the Northeastern United States that lay in the narrow path of total solar eclipse. And here a rare winter day was provided for eclipse watchers. Nearly cloudless skies let the sun shine brightly all day except for the two minutes and six seconds when the moon blocked its direct light before the path of darkness left the United States and headed to Nova Scotia.

At 1:30 p.m. as the sunlight thinned and all activity stopped, sea gulls perched on the tops of the dockside buildings sensed that all was not normal. They began to screech and flutter aimlessly in the air.

Nearby, a group of Columbia University students wrapped in blankets gathered around telescopes for the dramatic moment of totality — 1:46 p.m. As darkness grew and the corona burst into view they began to squeal with excitement.

The eclipse originated in the mid-Pacific Ocean near 15°N, crossed southern Mexico and the Yucatan peninsula, the Gulf of Mexico, and came ashore near St. Marks, Florida. The path then led northeast just inland from the coast to the center of totality across Nantucket at 1:46 p.m.

Comet Kohoutek of 1973-74

The comet "Kohoutek" is now visible in the early evening sky just after sunset, below the planet Venus and just above the spot where the sun went down . . . Its faint tail trailing up and to the left, away from the sun. It has been termed a fizzle — only visible with binoculars or telescope.

Inquirer and Mirror,
January 3, 1974.

Comet 1973 XII (Kohoutek) was discovered at the Hamburg Observatory by the Czechoslovakian astronomer Kohoutek from photographic plates taken on March 7 and 9, and was later identified from plates taken on January 28 and 29, 1973. Kohoutek was the last to photograph the comet before it entered the sun's glare. It was recovered in the morning sky at magnitude near 10.5 on September 23. During November the comet brightened to 5.5 on the 30th and revealed a tail about four degrees long. December was the month of its perihelion passage; the comet brightened to 4th magnitude and the tail lengthened to 18 degrees by the 18th. It was rated 3d magnitude in South Africa on the 22d. Perihelion was reached on December 28. The much heralded "Christmas Comet" turned out to be barely visible and was a great disappointment to the public. Kohoutek faded more during January to magnitude 7 by the 30th. A photograph was obtained on April 26 at Kitt Peak Observatory, Arizona, which gave the nuclear magnitude at 18.

Halley's Comet, as photographed at the Maria Mitchell Observatory on January 12, 1986.
Photograph courtesy of the Maria Mitchell Observatory.

Comet West, March 1976

Nantucketers have had a good opportunity to view West's Comet, which has been clearly visible about 30 degrees above the horizon early in the morning (about 5 a.m.!) in the eastern sky. The comet is presently going away from us and, when we once more have a clear early morning sky, it will be visible only with binoculars. It had a brilliant tail and was much more satisfactory than was the much-touted Kohoutek two years ago.

Merle Orleans, "Here and There,"
Inquirer and Mirror,
March 11, 1976.

Comet 1976 VI was discovered by Richard M. West at Geneva, Switzerland, on November 5, 1975. Perihelion came on February 25, 1976. It was visible with the unaided eye through March. The magnitude estimates were 4.7 on March 31 and the tail extended 30 degrees on March 8. The comet continued to be photographed until September 25.

Bright Aurora, April 20, 1985

Bright aurora, including a streak 2–3° wide across the whole sky (auroral arch?). Light low in Northwest, Cassiopeia to Perseus. Sky very bright in Orion-Gemini.

Note of Dr. Emilia Belserene, director of the Maria Mitchell Observatory.

Tattered hurricane-warning flags, red with square black centers, are raised at Brant Point Coast Guard station. Photograph courtesy of Bill Haddon.

Part Two:
Historic Storms of Nantucket

HURRICANES
AND TROPICAL STORMS

Hurricanes and their Pacific cousins have been rightly called "the greatest storms on earth." Not only do they possess massive physical structures and cover enormous geographic areas, but they can also cause natural disasters that take huge tolls in human lives and property.

The word hurricane is derived from the Spanish *huracan*, a term thought to have originated from similar words employed by the Caribbean Indian tribes for storm god, evil spirit, and devil.

A hurricane represents the full development of a tropical disturbance when its rotating wind system attains speeds of 74 miles per hour or more. If the winds register from 39 to 73 miles per hour, it is designated a tropical storm, and, if the winds are below 38 miles an hour, a tropical depression.

The hurricane is essentially a "heat engine," possessing a central core warmer than the surrounding atmosphere. It derives its vast energies from the condensation of water vapor into water droplets visible as cloud and rainfall. The attendant release of latent heat in this process provides the fuel to drive the storm system and create its enormous wind force.

Tropical storms require the proper combination of warmth, moisture, and instability of the atmosphere to generate. The exact process has been under extensive study in recent years but is not yet fully understood. Most storms are born in an easterly wave situation when a low-pressure trough in the upper atmosphere travels westward from Africa across the central Atlantic Ocean to the vicinity of the West Indies. This disturbs the normal homogeneous tropical air mass, causing convection and cloud formation. The rotation of the earth provides a deflecting force to the wind flow aloft, convection increases, precipitation takes place, winds accelerate in a circular pattern, a central eye forms at the surface, and a tropical storm is born.

There is a definite hurricane season. June storms are usually small and of minor intensity. The Gulf of Mexico and the Caribbean Sea spawn many of the early-season storms. Activity increases slightly in July and storms grow in size, but major hurricanes are infrequent. A marked increase takes place in August in both frequency and intensity, and the scene of the major activity shifts eastward.

The height of the hurricane season is reached in early September when the broad Atlantic Ocean is the principal breeding place. A third of all Atlantic tropical storms occur in this month, and some giant ones may cross all the way from West Africa to North America. There is a slight decrease in the second half of September, then a decided increase in the first two weeks of October. At this time the Caribbean Sea becomes an active source region again. The season goes into a steady decline in the second half of October and few November storms are charted.

Viewed from Nantucket, a tropical storm or hurricane is a living entity with a definite life cycle consisting of several stages: birth, growth, maturity, decline, and old age. In meteorological terms the stages up through maturity are: easterly wave, cyclogenesis, disturbance, tropical depression, tropical storm, and full hurricane. Eventually, when the storm system is deprived of its energy source over warm waters, the winds lessen, the barometric depth begins to increase, and the central eye dissipates. It transforms into the extratropical stage and becomes an ordinary cyclonic storm traveling the North Atlantic Ocean toward northern Europe.

Full hurricanes have been known to have lives of a few hours to many days, occasionally extending as long as a month. Tropical storm Ginger in 1971 wandered over the west-central North Atlantic, the Bermuda Triangle, and the coasts of North Carolina and Virginia for a full 31 days from September 5 to October 5. On 20 of these days it was classified as a hurricane, on the remainder as a tropical storm. Many hurricanes begin to decline in strength as they move northward along the Atlantic seaboard and encounter the colder waters south of Long Island. A full hurricane with a tropical structure is a rarity as far north as the latitude of Nantucket.

When the first bulletin of a new tropical storm in the low latitude of the North Atlantic is issued by the National Hurricane Center at Miami, Florida, residents of Nantucket take notice. Then they follow the periodic updates of the advisories carrying information as to the course, strength, and expected developments. The critical time comes when the storm center arrives in the vicinity of the West Indies. Here it will either continue on a westerly course and pass into the Caribbean Sea or Gulf of Mexico, perhaps with a passage over the Florida peninsula, or it will recurve to the northwest and north. A few storms originate in the Caribbean Sea and Gulf of Mexico and come directly northward.

If the westerly steering current is strong and a trough of low pressure extends southward from Canada to the tropics, the hurricane may find a congenial path along the Atlantic seaboard and accelerate its northward movement while curving gradually more toward the northeast. Then all residents of the New England seaboard must take heed and prepare for the possibility of a blow varying in intensity from an ordinary gale to a full hurricane blast.

Despite its exposed position as an island outpost of the New England landmass, Nantucket has been spared the ravages that have attended New England's most destructive hurricane visitations. In both the Great September Gale of 1815 and the New England Hurricane of 1938, the island lay too far to the west of the landfall of these two monsters to suffer hurricane-force winds. The Great Atlantic Hurricane in 1944 came nearer when it cut across Rhode Island to near Boston Harbor and caused some minor punishment on the island. Even Hurricane Edna in 1954 passing directly over the Vineyard and the nearby Sound did little structural damage; most of the losses were confined to the erosion of beaches and bluffs. No doubt, the most destructive hurricane in Nantucket history was the October Gale of

1841 whose center must have passed only a few miles to the eastward and whose winds, estimated in the hurricane category, swept the island for many hours.

The physical structure of the island tends to limit hurricane damage. Nantucket harbor, the only worthwhile commercial opening to the sea, has a northwesterly exposure. Thus an approaching hurricane, with winds usually from the northeast through southeast, operates over a body of water which is protected from a storm surge from the open sea. It is true that the ponds along the south shore and at the western end may be broken into by the sea during a storm surge, but they are sparsely populated, unlike the southward-opening estuaries on the mainland in Rhode Island and Connecticut where there is an immense potential for death and destruction. The buildings of Nantucket and Siasconset have withstood many hurricane blasts with little structural damage. The main effect of storm winds on the island has been the erosion of beaches and bluffs, and the shifting of sand along the shore between Great Point and Smiths Point. The topography of the island is gradually being transformed and the sea level is rising each year. It will eventually disappear with all its real estate, but the arrival of that time, fortunately, is measured in geological epochs, not by centuries.

The *United States Coast Pilot*, published by the National Ocean Survey, has summarized the action of a hurricane upon landfall:

The high winds of a hurricane inflict widespread damage when such a storm leaves the ocean and crosses land. Aids to navigation may be blown out of position or destroyed. Crafts in harbor, unless they are properly secured, drag anchor or are blown against obstructions. Ashore, trees are blown over, houses are damaged, power lines are blown down, etc. The greatest damage usually occurs in the dangerous semicircle a short distance from the center, where the strongest winds occur. As the storm continues on across land, its fury subsides faster than it would if it had remained over water.

Along the coast, particularly, greater damage may be inflicted by water than by wind. There are at least four sources of water damage. First, the unusually high seas generated by the storm winds pound against shore installations and craft in their way. Second, the continued blowing of the wind toward land causes the water level to increase perhaps three to ten feet above its normal level. This *storm tide*, which may begin when the storm center is 500 miles or even farther from the shore, gradually increases until the storm passes. The highest storm tides are caused by a slow-moving hurricane of larger diameter, because both of these effects result in greater duration of wind in the same direction. The effect is greatest in a partly enclosed body of water, such as the Gulf of Mexico, where the concave coastline does not readily permit the escape of water. It is least on small islands, which present little obstruction to the flow of water.

Third, the furious winds which blow around the wall of the eye often create a ridge of water called a *storm surge*, which strikes the coast and often inflicts heavy damage. The effect is similar to that of a *Tsunami* (*seismic sea wave*) caused by an earthquake in ocean floor. Both of these waves are popularly called *tidal waves*. Storm surges of 20 feet or more have occurred. About three or four feet of this is due to the decrease of atmospheric pressure, and the rest to winds. Like the damage caused by wind, that due to high seas, the storm tide, and the storm surge is greatest in the dangerous semicircle, near the center (to the east, in the case of Nantucket).

The fourth source of water damage is the heavy rain that accompanies a tropical cyclone. This causes floods that add to the damage caused in other ways.

Is Nantucket hurricane-proof? This question naturally arises in view of the relatively little serious damage the island has experienced. Only two hurricanes in the nineteenth century, in October 1841 and 1878, have inflicted substantial losses to the island's buildings and shipping. In the present century, the worst experiences were in the Atlantic Hurricane in September 1944, Carol in August 1954, and Edna in September 1954.

A satellite view of Nantucket gives the impression that the glacial forces that shaped the present structure of the island did so with the hurricane threat in mind, contoured to repel an offensive from the open Atlantic Ocean. First, there are the shoals off the southern shore which cause waves to break at a distance of several miles. These shallows effectively reduce the power of the storm surge and lower the size of waves that can be generated by hurricane-force winds.

Second, Sankaty Head and Tom Nevers Head stand as bastions, high on bluffs of 30 to 50 feet above the ordinary surf, and they are flanked by lesser banks and high sand dunes to the east and west. Though they give a little ground each year, they seem capable of holding their main defensive positions for many decades and even centuries.

The ocean does occasionally break into the ponds on either side of this "nose-guard" position: Sesachacha, Miacomet, Hummock, and Long ponds, and though the ocean water floods their shores, it is contained in their basins and little permanent damage is done.

The flanks of this defensive perimeter at Great Point to the northeast and at Smiths Point to the southwest have received heavy blows from the sea that have changed their size and shape. Varying ocean and tides are constantly changing the contours of these sandspits, even without the presence of severe storms. Great Point occasionally becomes an island when the sea breaks across the Galls, and Esther Island at Smiths Point is an example of the transformations wrought by wind and tide. No doubt these flanks of the island's defenses will continue to change their landform from storm to storm and from year to year.

The geographical orientation of Nantucket

harbor, which opens to the north-northwest through two jetties, lessens the hurricane threat there. The approach of a hurricane toward Nantucket usually causes gales from the northeast to arise if the center is to pass to the east of the island, and from the southeast if passing to the west. To the northeast of the harbor lies Cape Cod, a barrier which greatly shortens the wind fetch and reduces the size of wave buildup borne by northeast gales. Sizable waves can be produced in the short run from the Head of the Harbor southwest into the wharf area of the town, but these are relatively small in comparison to those that arise on the open sea during hurricanes. The wharves may be inundated and the nearby streets flooded, but there is no damaging surge of the sea. No estuaries exist on Nantucket similar to Narragansett Bay and Buzzards Bay, where the constantly narrowing breadth of the water surface inland causes higher and higher storm surges to mount and inundate inhabited areas along the shores.

The eastward location of Nantucket in regard to the paths of large hurricanes during this century has allowed the island to escape the damages that have been experienced to the westward in Rhode Island, Connecticut, and Long Island. The Great Long Island-New England Hurricane in September 1938 struck with a central track about 150 miles to the west, Carol in 1954 about 110 miles, Donna in 1944 about 100 miles, and the Atlantic Hurricane in 1944 about 65 miles. The only direct hits in the Martha's Vineyard and Nantucket area came with Edna's passage overhead in September 1954 and Esther's menacing meanders in September 1961. The latter had lost much of its energy prior to landfall.

The radius of hurricane-force winds of 74 miles an hour or more around the center is usually about 75 miles in a powerful storm. A storm center that placed Nantucket on the very fringe of destructive winds would pass very close to Block Island. In this century, only hurricanes Edna in 1954 and Esther in 1961 have approached Nantucket directly from the open ocean to the south.

It is apparent from the meteorological data and from contemporary reports of damage that both the October Gale of 1841 and the Storm of October 1878 moved very close, but to the east of Nantucket, and were very destructive, especially to shipping. No similar storms have been experienced this century.

The worst scenario for Nantucket would have a large hurricane packing great energy move directly from the south or west-southwest into the Bight of Rhode Island between Block Island and Martha's Vineyard. This would place the island in the dangerous eastern semicircle of the storm where the forward momentum of the mass of whirling wind and water moving at 40 to 50 miles per hour is added to the existing wind speed. If the center of the hurricane arrived at the time of astronomical high tide accompanied by a strong storm surge, the inundation of the ponds might be extremely high and the damage to the island's flanks might be extensive and permanent.

Perhaps our recorded hurricane history is too short to make any reliable statement about possible hurricane tracks in regard to Nantucket. We should have 500 years of good records instead of the 150 years that we now possess. Certainly, it is meteorologically possible for a monster hurricane, such as those in 1815 and 1938, to make a direct or close hit on Nantucket from the sea. None have done so in our recorded history, and thence comes the prevailing idea that Nantucket may be hurricane-proof. But remember, "It can happen here!"

Legendary Hurricanes of Early New England

Tropical storms of varying intensity have swept along the Atlantic coastal plain and over the continental shelf offshore for countless ages, many passing over or near Nantucket once this sandy landform emerged from the sea. In later years the native population, no doubt, suffered severely from these visitations, but they had no means of recording for posterity the destruction wrought and the personal discomforts endured.

The European settlers of New England had hardly established their communities along the coast before a full-fledged West Indian hurricane struck the scattered settlements and caused extensive forest and structural damage in 1635. Nantucket, first occupied by white settlers in 1659, must have suffered the battering of tropical storms through many generations; but, like their native predecessors, they left no written record of their trials. No details of storm effects on the island are available for the historian until well into the nineteenth century. The earlier hurricanes during the seventeenth and eighteenth centuries, therefore, must be considered legendary storms as far as their effect on Nantucket. Mention will be made of several of the major ones that passed over the area, and our imagination may describe their probable impact from Great Point to Smith's Point in this undocumented period of Nantucket history.

Seventeenth Century

Two extreme hurricanes occurred during the first century of European settlements in New England. Reverend Increase Mather recalled in his tract "Remarkable Providences" that he had heard of "no storm more dismal than the great hurricane which was in August [1635]." This constituted the most celebrated meteorological event of the entire colonial period, and fascinating and informative accounts have been preserved in the writings of Governor William Bradford of Plymouth Plantation and Governor John Winthrop of Massachusetts Bay Colony. Judging from their testimony of wind shifts at their localities, the center of the vigorous storm passed on a northeast course from the Narragansett Bay region of Rhode Island to the South Shore area of Boston Harbor. This placed Nantucket in the eastern sector of the storm where the island would be exposed to southeast gales. Eight Indians were drowned in Rhode Island, "flying from their wigwams," according to Governor John Winthrop's journal, as the storm surge raised tides to mighty heights. Near Plymouth the hurricane blasts "blew down many hundreds of trees, near the towns, overthrew some houses, and drove ships from their anchors."

A hurricane of almost equal intensity struck forty years later on September 7, 1675 (new style). At Stonington, Connecticut, ships were wrecked and there was "much loss of hay and corn. Multitudes of trees were blown down," according to the diary of Thomas Minor. On Rhode Island in Narragansett Bay Peter Easton noted in his diary that "a windmill was blown down," and compared the storm with that of 1635. Nantucket must have been within the perimeter of at least gale-force winds on this occasion.

Eighteenth Century

Major hurricanes affected southeastern New England in 1716, 1727, 1743, 1761, 1769, and 1778, and also in 1806 early in the next century.

The 1727 hurricane lived long in the memories of residents of coastal New England. It was described by the Reverend Samuel Phillips of Boston: "Then the Lord sent a great rain and horrible wind; hereby much hurt was done, both on the water and on the land." At Swansea near Fall River, "It blew up trees by the roots in abundance; blew down several chimneys, and blew off the roof of a house, and blew sundry vessels on shore," according to the diary of John Comer.

Ben Franklin's Hurricane in 1743 must be mentioned because of his mother's onetime residence on Nantucket and because of its importance to the history of meteorology. Franklin planned to observe an eclipse of the moon at Philadelphia on the evening of November 2, 1743 (new style), but was prevented from viewing the spectacle by the onset of a northeast storm with wind, clouds, and rain. Since the wind was blowing from the northeast, he assumed his brother in Boston would also be unable to witness the lunar event. Some days later he received a letter from his brother saying that he had enjoyed a perfect view of the eclipse, but that several hours later a northeast storm arrived. Franklin correctly surmised that the storm was moving along the coast from southwest to northeast despite the seemingly contrary winds blowing from the northeast. This was the first morsel of intelligence elucidated in American scientific annals about the puzzling problem of storm movement.

The hurricane on October 23–24, 1761, struck a severe blow at the Rhode Island coastline where it was judged the worst in thirty years. The gales blew down the steeple of Trinity Church at Newport, wrecked the bridge across the river at Providence, and did sundry damage: "On both roads east and west, so far as we have heard, the roofs of houses, tops of barns, and fences have been blown down, and it is said thousands of trees have been torn up by the roots by the violence of the storm," according to S. G. Arnold, an early historian of the colony and state. Such a mighty storm must have been of wide expanse and included Nantucket in its windy clutches.

The entire coastline from North Carolina to Maine suffered in the hard blow on September 8, 1769. Winds held to northeast throughout the storm at Boston, indicating that the center passed to the east a short distance offshore, probably very near Nantucket and Cape Cod.

The hurricane on October 20, 1770, raised the highest tide known since the Great Tide of February 1723 at Boston and again knocked the spire from its position atop Trinity Church at Newport, Rhode Island.

Another hurricane of historical significance swept up the coast on August 11–12, 1778, and caught the French and British fleets off the Rhode Island coast, both maneuvering to engage in what might have been a most decisive encounter. As the French with the wind-gauge in their favor were overhauling their withdrawing adversary, the blasts of an approaching hurricane began to whip the waters into huge waves and soon it was each ship for herself to stay afloat. During the gathering dusk the fleets separated. Many lost their sails and masts. Next morning the ships were widely separated, and all chance of a battle and a decision lost.

A report from Martha's Vineyard told of extensive damage to the corn crop at this critical time of the Revolution when food was short on the Vineyard and Nantucket. The northeast gales were noticed by weather observers at Boston, Salem, and Dover in New Hampshire, so the hurricane center remained at sea during its northward passage.

After battering the Atlantic seaboard from Charleston, South Carolina, northward, the August hurricane of 1806 gave Cape Cod and the Islands a blow on the 23d and 24th. The marine reporter for the *Boston Gazette* noticed a hard rain and wind in the harbor, but mentioned that the gale raged much higher out on Massachusetts Bay. From Barnstable on Cape Cod and Edgartown on Martha's Vineyard, much closer to the track of the storm, the reports spoke of a tremendous deluge of rain and of winds severe enough to cause structural damage.

At Edgartown an observer related that the wind went into the east, then veered to northeast early in the night and "increased to one of the severest gales I have ever experienced." His rainfall report would seem incredible; he noticed a barrel filled to a depth of 30 inches. From this and the sheet of water standing on the ground, he estimated that 36 inches fell during the storm. There was great crop destruction on Martha's Vineyard and five coasters were driven ashore there.

These reports received confirmation from Barnstable on Cape Cod across Nantucket Sound. From Brewster came accounts of great destruction to crops and to the valuable salt works. The observer wrote: "It is supposed there is 18 inches of water on a level."

Nineteenth Century

The September Gale of 1815

Lord! how the ponds and rivers boiled,
  And how the shingles rattled!
And oaks were scattered on the ground
  As if the Titans battled;
And all above was in a howl,
  And all below a clatter,
The earth was like a frying-pan,
  Or some such hissing matter.

Oliver Wendell Holmes,
The September Gale.

Judging from all the information, historical and traditional, relating to the great American gales during the last hundred years [1776–1876], it would appear that the one which occurred in New England, on the 23d of September, 1815, was and still is without a parallel, in the extraordinary characteristics of violence and destructiveness. In the history of the country, dating back to its earliest annals, there is no account of any gale or hurricane equaling this, in its various phenomena of suddenness, severity and power. As distinguishing it, therefore, above all others of its class, this has ever been called *the Great September Gale.*

Devens,
Our First Century, 1880.

Of all the storms in New England's history, the Great September Gale of 1815 was long accorded first place by nineteenth-century writers. It won a permanent shrine in the region's folklore through the descriptive poetry of Oliver Wendell Holmes, who witnessed the storm at the age of six, and its authenticity was vouched for by none other than Noah Webster, whose diary shows he was a watcher of the weather as well as of words: "The storm was a proper hurricane."

The path of the center of this unexpected visitor from the tropical seas cut southern New England into two almost equal segments as it roared northward over hill and dale on the morning of September 23, 1815. It arrived at community after community without warning and took an unprecedented toll of buildings, trees, and crops. Few local historians in the nineteenth century failed to mention some incident or tale connected with the most destructive atmospheric disturbance to visit the region since the Great Colonial Hurricane in August 1635. Another century and a quarter would pass before a great storm of equal dimensions and intensity would spread havoc over the countryside: The New England Hurricane in September 1938.

Of definite tropical origin, this mightiest storm of a very active hurricane season probably developed over the eastern Atlantic Ocean near the coast of West Africa when an easterly wave moved outward from the hot sands of the Sahara Desert. In a journey of perhaps a week across the broad stretches of the central Atlantic, the developing whirl of winds acquired the vast quantities of warmth and moisture from the ocean surface needed to supply the energy to sustain its momentum. It travelled westward to the West Indies, then northwest to the offshore waters of the continent, and finally northward from the tropical seas to the normally temperate waters of the Atlantic shelf south of Long Island.

The first reported landfall came in the West Indies at little St. Barthelemy, an *entrepot* of trade lying in the northeast quarter of the exposed Leeward Islands group, where great destruction to shipping and shore installations was reported on September 18. Spinning and curving to the northwest now, the whirling winds then lashed at Turks Island in the extreme southeast of the Bahama Islands two days later. Its forward movement at this time was relatively slow as is characteristic of large developing hurricanes in these latitudes. But once a steering current aloft appears and a congenial trough of low pressure lies to the north, the way is open for a greatly accelerated dash to higher latitudes.

The next coastal crossing came some 1300 miles northward on the south shore of the east-central part of Long Island, very close to Moriches Inlet in the Great South Bay. The whole eastern tip of Long Island lay exposed to the dangerous eastern semicircle, where the forward speed of the storm system is added to the regular wind force of the great atmospheric whirl. Speeds approaching 100 miles per hour wrought great destruction on land and tides of six feet and more surged into bays and harbors.

After a quick churn across the waters of Long Island Sound, the center or eye of the hurricane burst ashore again very close to Saybrook at the mouth of the Connecticut River between New Haven and New London. Its path then advanced inexorably northward, passing over the plateau of eastern Connecticut near Storrs and Willimantic, then through central Massachusetts west of Worcester, and finally into New Hampshire close to Jaffrey and Hillsboro. All of the Cape Cod and Islands area lay in the eastern semicircle of the hurricane and far enough east of the central storm track to escape the effects of extreme winds and dangerously high tides.

Sidney Perley has described some of the storm effects in the area:

Some slight damage was done at Falmouth, but in Vineyard sound the water was not so much affected by the wind as in Buzzard's bay. At Hyannis, a brig was driven upon the shore by the wind. At Sandwich, a vessel bound for Newport was dashed furiously against a wharf while the captain was endeavoring to enter the harbor of New Bedford, and a young lady passenger, Miss Temperance Perry, was drowned in spite of strenuous efforts that were made to save her. Farther out on Cape Cod the wind blew much more moderately, and at Provincetown nothing suffered from it.

A paucity of on-the-spot information exists about the storm effects on Nantucket. The harbor lay about 125 miles west of the path of the hurricane center and well outside the circle of hurricane-force winds. William Mitchell, then a young man of thirty years, later wrote to his friend, William Redfield, the pioneer investigator of hurricanes, that "the gale was not severe" on Nantucket. A press dispatch in the *New Bedford Mercury* on September 29, 1815, declared: "At Nantucket, we are informed, very little damage was sustained; the tide being down, did no injury to the wharves—One barn was blown down and some other buildings a little shattered."

The schooner *America* came ashore somewhere on the island, according to Arthur H. Gardner in *Wrecks Around Nantucket*, but details are lacking. Not so to the westward. At Martha's Vineyard the salt works suffered extensive damage and from 12 to 15 schooners and sloops were driven ashore.

The September Gale of 1821

Six years after the Great September Gale, another major hurricane of somewhat less intensity crossed western New England on September 3, 1821. After passing very close to Norfolk, Virginia, where extensive damage to harbor installations and other buildings occurred, the center of the hurricane moved along the immediate coastline in a north-northeast direction. The calm passage of the storm's eye was reported at Cape Henlopen, Delaware, and Cape May, New Jersey, at the entrance to Delaware Bay. The center then came ashore on the western end of Long Island very close to the present location of Kennedy Airport on Jamaica Bay, about 60 miles west of the landfall of the 1815 gale. After whirling across western Long Island Sound, it passed through Fairfield County, Connecticut, and caused extensive damage in the Greenwich-Stamford-Bridgeport area. The path was very close to that followed by Hurricane Gloria on September 27, 1985.

Again Nantucket lay well east of the area of high winds and destruction. The *Nantucket Inquirer* had been in existence for only three months, and began to furnish information about the local impact of storms. Three days after the blow, the issue of September 6 carried only one item concerning the storm:

The schooner *William*, Capt. Harris, 31 days from Jamaica for Halifax went ashore at Tookoonook (north part of this island) in the gale Monday night [Sept. 3]. —We learn he had no cargo on board. The Capt., passengers and crew are now ashore on the Island, and the wreck is advertised to be sold tommorow.

The issue a week later informed: "A sloop and a schooner arrived on Monday [Sept. 10]. No [storm] damage to eastward."

End-of-August Hurricane of 1839

A major hurricane moved north along the Atlantic seaboard in the last week of August 1839. It was reported at Charleston, South Carolina, on the 28th, at Wilmington and Cape Hatteras on the 29th, and at Norfolk late on the 29th and 30th. Apparently, it curved northeast from the latter location and brushed the southern shores of Long Island and the eastern exposures of Nantucket and Cape Cod, passing close enough to cause some damage.

At Nantucket, the wind came out of the northeast all day on the 30th with heavy rain falling and the temperature hanging in the cool 50s. Honorable William Mitchell, one-time Congressman, astronomer, and meteorologist, observed: "We have not had so severe a gale for many years." At his 7:00 a.m. observation on the 31st Mitchell's barometer was down to 29.48 inches, the thermometer stood at 54°F, and the wind had backed from northeast to north-northwest, indicating the passage of the storm center northward of the latitude of Nantucket.

"On land, the trees, shrubbery, corn, and other vegetables suffered greatly," reported the *Inquirer*. In a follow-up account in mid-October, the editor declared: "The severe storm of the 30th and 31st August seemed to operate on most of the plants in our vicinity, withering and killing the foliage which generally soon dropped off, leaving the limbs and trunks in a great measure denuded. [They were] succeeded by new dress."

The *Inquirer* listed a long account of shipping disasters along the coast. Those on the island were noticed by Gardner in his listing of wrecks:

August 30th, brig "Nelson," of Eastport, with a cargo of coal, struck on Great Point Rip during a severe N.E. gale. The captain, with his wife and crew, landed on Great Point, and the vessel broke up immediately.

August 30th, whaling schooner "Amazon," Pinkham, of this port, which had left here for a cruise, was driven from her moorings at the Cape and went ashore high and dry at the Cliff, but was subsequently gotten off.

August 30th, schooner "Penobscot," Thompson, of and for this port, from Bangor, with a load of lumber, in coming in over the Bar, struck heavily, sprang a leak and partly sank after reaching the dock, but was subsequently raised and repaired.

August 30th, schooner "Lion," from Portland to this port, with a cargo of lumber, bricks and hay, drove from her anchorage back of the Bar, and bilged. The crew were taken off in a whale boat and the vessel finally stranded near Brant Point. The cargo was mostly saved, but the vessel went to pieces.

The Memorable October Gale of 1841

One of the most intense hurricanes of the century came out of the tropics and raced northward through the shipping lanes off the Middle Atlantic seaboard on the morning of October 3, 1841. The dangerous whirl of wind and wave arrived almost unheralded soon after noon on that fateful Sunday and caught a large portion of the Cape Cod fishing fleet on their favorite grounds, the Georges Bank, southeast of Nantucket.

Still known as the "October Gale," the storm's terrible reputation has lived long in the memory of those who go "down to sea" in ships from Cape Cod and the Islands, since so many seafaring youths of the small ports along Cape Cod Bay and Nantucket Sound went to watery graves on that wild night on Georges Bank. The easterly gales, quickly rising to full hurricane strength, prevented the small vessels from either rounding the Cape or entering the Sound. They were either overwhelmed by the huge waves at sea or dashed to pieces in the cruel breakers along the beaches.

The center of the hurricane remained offshore during its entire advance along the Atlantic seaboard. It passed close enough to the Outer Banks of North Carolina to drive several ships ashore on the 2d and to cause similar beachings at Cape Henry in Virginia as the western semicircle of the rotating winds raked the coastal shipping lanes with destructive gales. The east-northeast winds backing to northeast and to north indicated that the center passed to the east of Nantucket, but we have no means of knowing how far. A scientific surmise might place it 25 to 50 miles distant.

Cape Cod and the Islands bore the full brunt of the hurricane force winds on the afternoon and evening of the 3d and the early morning of the 4th. Fortunately, William Mitchell's excellent observations gave a full account of the impact of the storm on Nantucket. Mitchell wrote to his frequent meteorological correspondent, William C. Redfield, on the day following the event:

Our island having been visited with far the most disastrous storm known in its whole history, I send herewith, before learning anything from the continent, my meteorological observations during the whole period. It commenced at 8 A.M. of the 3d, and its termination may be stated at 8 P.M. of the fourth. The height of the wind, the duration of its violence, & its disastrous effects are without parallel in this region. Sixteen wrecks have already been described from the observatories, though the weather is still very thick . . . .

The editor of the *Inquirer* also took notice of the effect of the storm on the island and islanders:

The Line Gale, this year, though some ten days in arrear of the almanac, made up for its tardiness by its violence. It commenced on early Sunday morning last [Oct. 3], and continued to increase in severity for some hours, until it had grown into a tremendous hurricane, which lasted until yesterday [Oct. 5] without essential abatement. The wind came directly from that storehouse of storms as of sunshine, the East; and was accompanied almost unintermittently by driving and drenching squalls of rain. Immense damage has been occasioned to the shipping in port, to the wharves, to property lying thereon and near them, to buildings in various parts of the town and vicinity—the details of which would occupy columns of our paper . . . .
During the night of Sunday, especially, when every building trembled under the pressure of the furious elements, there were but few families free from alarm and consternation. On that night, literally, not many slept without rocking . . . .
A great number of chimneys, some of them from buildings nearly new, were thrown down by force of the wind. The walks upon the roofs of some thirty dwelling houses in various quarters of the town were blown off.—Trees of large dimensions, flag-staffs, fences, and other exposed objects, were prostrated. The tide rose to a height almost unprecedented—reaching from two to three feet above the surface of the wharves, and extending into most of the lower streets, strewing in various directions quantities of lumber, cord wood, and other buoyant objects. [The moon had been full on September 30 at 11:19 a.m.]

Mitchell also transmitted his complete meteorological log to Redfield. It showed the storm at its height from soon after midnight until about sunrise (the town clock stopped at 1:29 a.m. on the 4th), as the wind slowly backed and the barometer reached its lowest point.

Writing in 1924 in his classic *The History of Nantucket,* Alexander Starbuck stated that "on October 3, 1841 occurred what was doubtless the severest gale recorded in the history of the island." This judgment has been well documented by Arthur H. Gardner in *Wrecks Around Nantucket*: "On the morning after the gale, nineteen vessels lay stranded on or near the island, and within sight of shore, the masts of two others protruded from the water—such a sight was never witnessed before or since upon the island."

Severe Gale, August 2, 1867

Nantucket—The gale on the 2d instant was very severe at Nantucket. The *Inquirer and Mirror* [Aug. 10] says: "The corn and other vegetables were prostrated, large trees torn up by the roots, chimneys and fences blown down, and much other damage was done." The sea at the south side of the island broke over the banks, raising Hummock Pond to such a height that it cut a channel through the beach 100 yards wide. Parties at Squanimus fared hard, but, though numbers were out in boats, not an accident occurred.

New Bedford Mercury,
August 12, 1867.

For information on the early August hurricane we must depend on the *New Bedford Mercury* since the issue of the *Inquirer and Mirror* following the storm is missing from the files in the Atheneum. The *Mercury* also went on to report that the gale made "great havoc" at Provincetown among the shipping and that many trees were broken down. In the vicinity of New Bedford the high winds lasted only about two hours. All this pointed to a small hurricane of considerable intensity passing just a short distance off the coast.

No local meteorological report was available since William Mitchell had accompanied his daughter, Maria, first to Lynn, Massachusetts, to be near relatives, and then to the newly-founded Vassar College at Poughkeepsie, New York.

September Gale of 1869

On the late afternoon of September 8, 1869, a hurricane of unique size and structure raised full hurricane blasts over parts of southern New England for a brief time. It marked the first time since September 1815 that inland locations had experienced the full fury of a tropical visitor.

The central path of the northward-rushing storm cut across the extreme eastern tip of Long Island before striking the mainland close to the Connecticut-Rhode Island border near Stonington and Watch Hill. Continuing north-northeast, the path traversed the length of western Rhode Island, passing to the west of both Newport and Providence, then moved through Massachusetts between Worcester and Boston, and finally over southeast New Hampshire into Maine.

Though Cape Cod and the Islands lay at least 70 miles west of the path of the central eye of the storm, the Buzzards Bay area, which separates Cape Cod from the mainland, experienced a storm tide of almost unprecedented height and suffered severe damage to shore installations, as did the south shores.

Cape Cod's *Yarmouth Register* described the storm as "of great severity, rivaling in violence and destructiveness, the great gale of September 1815. It commenced to blow in this vicinity about 2 o'clock from the S.S.E. and by 4 o'clock the wind had increased to a furious gale, which continued two or three hours." The *Barnstable Patriot* thought "the

Hurricane Carol at Brant Point, August 1954.
Photograph courtesy of
H. Flint Ranney.

storm will long be remembered as the *great gale,* and the injury it has caused will not speedily be repaired."

The *Inquirer and Mirror* compared the effect of the gale on Nantucket to the fate of the mainland:

"September Gale"—A severe gale was experienced here on Wednesday last [Sept. 8], more violent than any other since the gale of 1867, which brought in the sea on our South Shore, swept corn fields and did other damage. The wind which blew from the Southeast increased from the morning until about 3 p.m.; from which time it may be said to have commenced in earnest. It continued from the Southeast until about 7 p.m. when the wind veered to the Southwest, from which quarter it continued to blow during the night with great though diminishing force. We have not heard of any wrecks, or of any damage being done in this vicinity, where the gale was

nothing in comparison to what it must have been on the main land.

Saxby's Gale, October 1869

In December of 1868, Lieutenant S. M. Saxby of the Royal Navy forwarded a letter to the London press predicting that the earth would be visited by a storm of unusual violence, attended by an extraordinary rise of tide at 7:00 a.m. on the morning of October 5, 1869, or some eleven months hence. He based his prophecy on a lunar coincidence which would place the moon directly over the earth's equator at the very time that the satellite's orbit would be at its closest approach. Since the sun and moon would be exerting their maximum forces in unison and to an almost unprecedented degree, Saxby reasoned that a tide of record proportions should be expected; and if a storm occurred at the same time, the tide would be much augmented. This dire prediction caused considerable comment and excitement in both scientific and popular circles since the naval officer had a previous success with this sort of prediction.

The communication of Lieutenant Saxby to the *London Standard* of December 21, 1868, read:

At 7 a.m. (GMT) on the ensuing 5th of October the moon will be at the part of her orbit which is nearest the earth; her attraction, therefore, will be at its maximum force. At noon the moon will be on the earth's equator—a circumstance which never occurs without marked atmospheric disturbance. At 2 p.m. of the same day, lines drawn from the earth's center will cut the sun and moon in the same arc of right ascension (syzygy). The moon's attraction and the sun's will, therefore, be acting in the same direction. In other words, the new moon will be on the earth's equator when in perigee, and nothing more threatening of high tides and destructive storms can occur.

The place of origin and the track northward of the early October hurricane is lost in historical silence. This was just a year before the founding of the Signal Service Storm Warning system, so we have no series of coordinated reports along the Atlantic seaboard to trace the storm's movement. It was not reported at any land station until reaching the Cape Cod and Islands area. Its arrival in these waters was obscured by the presence of a deep trough of low pressure over the Northeast which produced an amazing quantity of precipitation on the morning of the 4th: more than six inches in all the New England states except Rhode Island.

This same trough of low pressure, moving eastward over the mainland, broke up the usual wind formations in the western sector of the hurricane circulation so that no high wind speeds were recorded.

Our best evidence of the hurricane's movement appears in Nantucket's *Inquirer and Mirror* which, in the absence of a regular meteorological observer, supplied some local details:

The Latest Gale—The gale of Monday last was much more violent here than that of Sept. 8th, but did no material damage. The occurrence of the gale within a day of the time predicted by Capt. Crocker of Sandwich must have been quite gratifying to that gentleman, and its violence at this place, at least, identifies it with the veritable one intended by the prophet. The mercury of the barometer fell to a very low degree, 28.7, and about 3 o'clock, when the wind changed from S.E. to S.W. it rose rapidly. The rain fell fast as well as furiously for a couple of hours, and was grateful to the thirsty land, which has been watered but sparingly since July. Our farmers have been obliged to feed their cows with roots and stalks, pasturage being very scanty . . . .

The occurrence of two such storms as those of September 8th and October 4th, so near each other is very remarkable; and that the last should have been predicted, is also striking. Was it guess work or had Capt. Crocker some meteorological science not in the books?

Inquirer and Mirror,
October 9, 1869.

It is not known whether Captain Crocker arrived at his forecast independently or applied Lt. Saxby's data to the local Cape Cod scene.

The Great Hurricane of October 1878

Since the October gale of 1841, all of our aged inhabitants admit that no storm has prevailed here of equal severity with that of Saturday last [Oct. 12], while many who have made note of such events, declare that never in the memory of the oldest inhabitant, has any wind storm prevailed at Nantucket for so long a period of time and with such disastrous results to private property. Commencing early on Saturday morning, the wind increased gradually during the day, a large amount of rain descending, until about 7 o'clock in the evening when the gale was terrific. Trees were uprooted and branches shivered from their trunks, chimneys were hurled from buildings and trees were demolished, and roofs rolled up in chaotic confusion, appalling to contemplate. An unrestrained fury possessed the atmosphere and destruction seemed to be the order of its coming. Devastation has followed storms in Nantucket before, and while our wharves swarmed with the messengers of commerce, it was possible for greater damage to property afloat to ensue. We had little of value at tidewater, compared to that we had during the gale of 1841, and in many subsequent years, yet the late gale was far more universal in its ranges, sparing neither section of the town and having no regard for the condition of its victims. Scarcely a house but has suffered some damage and the aggregate of such damages cannot be safely estimated at present.

Nantucket Journal,
October 17, 1878.

Arthur Gardner, the editor of the *Nantucket Journal* and an authority on storm damage around the island, rated the Hurricane of 1878 at the top of Nantucket's hurricane experiences. He also listed the damages street by street, among the wharves, and along the shore.

The *Inquirer and Mirror* agreed as to the storm's historic status:

The storm which visited our island Saturday [Oct. 12] was one that will long be remembered both from the serious consequences which followed in its wake, and for its extreme severity. Not since the October gale of 1841 has anything occurred here to equal it, the gale of a year ago being but a gentle zephyr compared to it.

The active tropical storm season of 1878 witnessed ten full hurricanes develop. The sixth of these was first charted in the central Gulf of Mexico on October 9. This area has been the birthplace of many mighty October storms that have passed over parts of the Southeastern states and then gone on to wrack the Atlantic coast shipping lanes from Florida to Newfoundland. On October 10, the hurricane center crossed from near Apalachicola, Florida, to Brunswick, Georgia, passed about 75 miles east of Cape Hatteras late on the 11th and headed straight northeast at a fast clip. On the night of the 12–13th, the central eye passed about 150 miles southeast of Nantucket, moving through the Atlantic shipping lanes toward Newfoundland.

Saturday morning of the 12th dawned on Nantucket with cloudy skies and a light rain. The wind, coming out of the east, began to increase in force around noon. Two hours later as the main force of the hurricane arrived, "fierce blasts drove the rain in blinding sheets." The fury of the storm reached a peak about 11:00 p.m. with winds of hurricane force out of the northeast. By 4:00 a.m. the gale was reported to have been well spent, though rain continued to 7:00 a.m. During the height of the storm, the tide rose until it covered Steamboat Wharf to a depth of one foot. The *Island Home* lost a portion of her hurricane deck and awning stanchions, and the *River Queen* had her flagstaff carried away. Damage on the island was estimated by the *Inquirer and Mirror* at $50,000, a substantial sum for those times.

Rainfall in the area proved very heavy: Newport reported 3.11 inches on the 12th and 3.31 inches on the 13th. Individual day totals were: Woods Hole 2.56 inches on the 12th and Fall River 3.30 inches on the 13th. Captain Charles Coleman, the keeper of the Nantucket rain gauge at this time, recorded a total of 3.28 inches.

Late-Season Hurricane, November 1888

Not for years has the Storm King paid his respects to this remote little island with such intense fury as he dealt during Sunday, Monday and Tuesday last [Nov. 25–27], and the changes wrought along the beaches by the raging elements is simply wonderful. Many people are also sufferers by the effect upon their property, though in no individual case will the losses be great. The Nantucket Railroad Company will be the heaviest loser, its tracks having been annihilated in long sections by the raging water.

The storm broke upon us Saturday evening with a little snow, followed by rain. Sunday morning [Nov. 25] dawned with a howling northeaster and torrents of rain. All day long the howling blasts swept over sea and land, and the sheets of water poured down. The waters rose in the bay and harbor, and the dull roar on the beaches told that something terrific was raging there. It was a day that few cared to venture forth: but those who did seek the shores of the harbor witnessed a rare picture of wild tumult. It was not until the gale had somewhat abated the following day that any idea of what mischief Nature's pranks had caused could be gathered.

Inquirer and Mirror,
December 1, 1888.

November 28th, schooner "David Faust," for Boston, with a cargo of cement, struck on Great Point Rip during the night. The following day she was boarded by a crew in the underwriters' boat, who contracted to float her for $300 and she was gotten off after throwing overboard 150 barrels of her cargo.

Gardner,
Wrecks Around Nantucket, 1915.

This ninth and last hurricane of the 1888 season proved outstanding in a number of ways. It formed at the very late date of November 17 and in an unusual area for the birth of a tropical storm. In addition, its track paralleled the offshore shipping lanes of North America and then those of the broad North Atlantic to Europe. The storm was first charted in the central North Atlantic about 700 miles southeast of Bermuda and the same distance northeast of Puerto Rico, near 56.5°W and 24.5°N. For five days the developing circulation moved slowly west-northwest to about 75°W where it made an unusual move; an abrupt right-angle turn to the north on the 22d. After two days at a slow pace along the prime meridian of Eastern Standard Time, the whole system accelerated on the 25th, curved to the north-northeast, and took a bead on the Cape Cod and Islands area. According to the historical hurricane charts prepared by George Cry and his associates, the center passed approximately 30 to 50 miles southeast of Nantucket, which placed the island within the dangerous wind zone.

Some meteorological details were supplied by the weather bureau:

	8:00 a.m.	8:00 p.m.	
Nov. 25	42°	46°	
	NE 21	NE 21	maximum 22 mi/h
	.09″	1.27″	tot. precipitation 1.36″
Nov. 26	52°	53°	
	E 11	E 21	maximum 40 mi/h
	.82″	.20″	tot. precipitation 1.02″

The great surf attending the storm on the south shore was vividly described by the editor of the *Inquirer and Mirror:*

Those who witnessed the great waves off Surfside during the 29th day of August, 1883, well remember their grand and formidable appearance as they swept onward to the beach, which suffered seriously from the inroads of the raging waters; but that grand spectacle and attendant damage were fairly eclipsed last Sunday; at least, those who saw both so state and there is every reason to think that the statement is correct. During the storm of 1883 huge masses of the bluff were washed away along the shore of Surfside and to the eastward, and the great billows dashed against the bluff, sending their clouds of spray high in the air over the bank; but on Sunday the billows went even farther breaking on top of the bluff, and in one or two instances sending the water to the gates of Surfside Hotel.

There were certain remarkable features attendant upon that great disturbance of the elements that were apparent in the storm on Sunday, viz; that the wind was blowing a gale from the northeast, and the waves all came from the southeast, which has always been explained by the direst result of the tidal waves in the Straits of Sunda which occurred but a short time previous to it. With Sunday's storm, as stated, these same peculiarities were noticed, and the fishermen also remarked a few days prior to it, while launching their dories, the sea being quiet on the beach, that an occasional wall of water would come tumbling in and go rolling way up the back and quiet would immediately follow.

Five-Day Blow of October 1896

High winds occurred generally on the 11th, 12th, and 13th [October] during the prevalence of a tropical storm. This storm, which was of great severity, first came under notice off the southern coast of Florida on the 9th. It moved slowly up the coast, its center being off Cape Hatteras for two days, 11th and 12th. At this stage the gales and general effects of the storm on shore were at their most ominous point. In New England, Sunday, the 12th, was noted as a day practically without precipitation, but with destructive easterly gales, high tides, and an unusually heavy surf on the coast.

On the 13th, the storm center lay about 200 miles southeast of Cape Cod, slowly diminishing in force. It passed onward to the Gulf of St. Lawrence by the 14th.

New England climatologist.

On Nantucket, the *Inquirer and Mirror* declared: Wind was on a rampage on Sunday, Monday, and Tuesday [Oct. 11–13] last . . . It developed a wind velocity at times unequalled in the history of the weather station . . . on Monday the average velocity was 38 miles per hour with a maximum gust to 59 miles per hour . . . At flood tide waves were breaking savagely against wharves. Brant Point was flooded . . . rainfall .02 inch on 11th, .04 inch on the 12th, .08 inch on 13th—total 0.14 inch.

From a high barometer reading of 30.54 inches on Saturday morning, October 10, the pressure fell during the day and the wind came out of the northeast at moderate speeds. The sky was clear. On Sunday morning the barometer fell 0.18 inch and the wind mounted to 26 miles per hour. The day was cloudy but rainless.

On Monday morning, the 12th, the wind increased to 38 miles per hour and to 47 miles in the evening, still steady from the northeast. Skies were cloudy all day, and a very light rain of 0.02 inch fell.

On Tuesday morning, the 13th, the barometer dropped further to 29.73 inches and the winds continued from the northeast at slightly lower speeds, measuring 35 miles per hour at the evening observation. Only 0.04 inch more rain fell.

On the morning of the 14th, the barometer slipped another 0.05 inch and the wind continued to diminish, still out of the northeast. The lowest reading, 29.50 inches, occurred at 7:00 a.m. on the 15th. The wind remained in the northeast, but 0.58 inch of rain fell, the largest daily amount during the five-day windstorm.

Twentieth Century

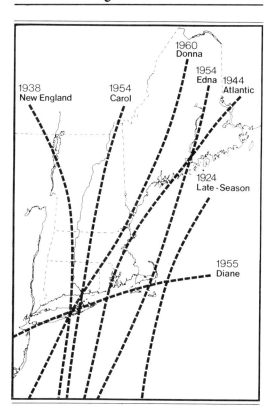

Tracks of damaging twentieth-century hurricanes that have struck New England. No major hurricanes have visited since 1960.

Ex-hurricane, September 1904

The conspicuous features of the September weather were the severe and general storm of the 14–15th, and the heavy frosts and freezing weather in many sections on the 22d and 23d. During the storm heavy rains fell in about all, except some of the southeastern sections, the fall at many stations being more than half the total amount of the month, and high northeast winds and gales occurred along the coast, reaching hurricane force on the southern portion.

New England climatologist

The hurricane came from the mid-Atlantic northeast of the Leeward Islands on September 8. Recurvature took place over the Carolinas, then the storm lost its tropical form and tracked across central Chesapeake Bay, lower Delaware Bay, the eastern tip of Long Island, and across southeastern Massachusetts on roughly a Fall River-Plymouth line.

The barometer at Nantucket dropped to 29.44 inches, and the wind mounted to 46 miles per hour from the south. Winds throughout were from the southeast or south, until the shift to northwest after 8:00 a.m. Rainfall amounted to only 0.01 inch, but only 85 miles to the northwest at Norfolk near Foxboro the catch was 5.08 inches. Boston reported 3.47 inches and Provincetown 0.32 inches. Winds mounted to 65 miles per hour at Block Island.

The *Inquirer and Mirror* described the storm's passage over Nantucket:

A fierce wind storm; appeared to be a veritable tornado, breaking forth from the S.E. and sweeping around the compass to N.W. before it had spent its force.

Storm warnings had been issued, but damage wrought was almost as great as that of the memorable storm of November 1898.

It was not accompanied by rain, but was one of the worst wind storms on record at the local weather bureau [since 1886], with an extreme of 56 miles per hour.

The Quidnet Inn was moved bodily about 6 inches from its foundation. Large trees, barns, roofs off all over the Island . . . The seas made terrible inroads into the beach, the topography of which was more or less changed as a result of the tempest.

The Blow in 1917: "The Worst September Storm of Record"

The first thirty years of U.S. Weather Bureau observations on Nantucket, 1886–1916, coincided with a period of lessened tropical storm activity in the North Atlantic that marked the last decade of the nineteenth century and the first years of the twentieth century. Consequently, few storms of tropical origin are recorded in the early annals of Nantucket's weather bureau history. The first big weather event of this nature to affect Nantucket in the twentieth century, labeled the "worst September storm of record," by observer George E. Grimes of the weather bureau, occurred in 1917.

"It is three years since Nantucket has experienced a 'heavy blow' in the month of September of sufficient intensity as to prevent the operation of the steamboat schedule," declared the *Inquirer and Mirror*. But on the 17th and practically all of the 18th of September the sailing schedule of the steamer was interrupted by winds of a severe tropical disturbance.

The storm pursued a steady course almost due north from eastern Cuba where it was first tracked on the morning of September 13. After brushing past Cape Hatteras on the morning of the 16th, it reached a position near Nantucket lightship on the evening of the 17th. Peak winds on the island occurred about midnight, gusting to 62 miles per hour and sustaining 52 miles per hour for up to five minutes. Winds came from the northeast, but backed to north as the center drew abreast. Fortunately, the tide was low at the time of highest winds.

The *Inquirer and Mirror* commented on the local impact of the storm:

Along south beach, there was quite an assortment of small boats cast ashore, but no serious damage resulted . . . About town the trees suffered severely, and the streets were littered with broken twigs and branches, many of which showed the work of the 'borer' on the elm trees . . . But other than these slight disasters (small boats) the water front emerged from the storm much better than is usual in disturbances with such high wind.

August Storm, 1924

The most severe storm [in August] was the tropical disturbance which moved up the Atlantic Coast on the 25th and 26th and developed great intensity on the southeast New England coast with exceptionally heavy rainfall and gales of 47 to 62 miles per hour. The gale blew down hundreds of trees in eastern Massachusetts and Rhode Island, causing temporary damage to wire systems, much minor damage to houses, and wrecked many small pleasure boats. Much damage also occurred to corn and fruit; the rainfall was more than six inches at some stations.

New England climatologist.

The tropical storm of August 1924 came from very low latitudes, first being charted on August 16 at 11°N and 55°W, or about 350 miles southeast of Barbados. It moved northwest at a normal pace for six days until reaching 75°W in the latitude of Cape Canaveral, Florida on the night of the 21st–22d. Here a hesitation took place until late on the 24th when a steering current in the upper atmosphere carried the disturbance rapidly north-northeast. On the morning of the 26th, the center was off the Virginia Capes and heading for the tip of southeast New England at a 50-mile-per-hour clip.

George E. Grimes, described the storm's impact:

The storm was of great intensity doing extensive damage to the water front. The surf was terrific on the Ocean side of the Island breaking over the beach into the ponds and washing away bridges and small buildings.

The small boats in the harbor were driven ashore and one large steam yacht was dragged on the rocks. Big trees were uprooted and the telephone system prostrated.

Through the courtesy of the U.S. Compass Station the cipher reports from this station were sent out on time.

Fishing sloops *Five Brothers* and *Thelma Snow* (of this port) were wrecked off Eaton Neck, Long Island, but suffered no loss of life; all the small fishing crafts were more or less damaged.

Vegetable gardens and trees were blasted by the wind and rain, the foliage blackened as if visited by a killing frost. The corn crop was badly damaged and the second crop of alfalfa was absolutely ruined.

The highest winds gusted to 47 miles per hour, and the barometer sank to a low of 28.70 inches at 2:00 p.m. on the 26th. Rainfall amounted to 2.95 inches with the bulk, 2.08 inches, falling between midnight and 12:30 p.m. on the 26th.

The *Inquirer and Mirror* described the storm with the headline:

Greatest Summer Storm in the History of the Weather Bureau

The heavy-easterly storm which swept this section of the coast Tuesday [Aug. 26, 1924] did not miss Nantucket, and it brought a disturbance which was most unusual for the month of August. The heavy foliage on the trees, weighted down by the rain, was responsible for much of the damage wrought about town. Although the wind velocity was not great, compared to what Nantucket has experienced in winter storms, the conditions were such that the beautiful shade trees in the center of town suffered severely . . . .

The water front received the full brunt of the storm, especially during the morning and early afternoon, while the wind was in the eastward, and it was lively around the docks for several hours. The fleet of small boats moored inside of Brant Point rode heavily at

their anchors and many parted from their moorings.

Fortunately the storm was not at its height at high water, else the wharves would have been washed but as it was the boats at the docks chafed badly and everyone was kept busy to prevent injury.

The fleet of summer boats at anchor in the harbor received a terrible raking, many of them breaking from their moorings and sweeping ashore, some landing on the harbor beach, others against the Yacht Club bulkhead, and others on other parts of the water front.

Unquestionably the worst part of the storm was felt at Great Neck on the west end of the Island near the Maddaquet Coast Guard station where the stretch of beach below the bluff is much narrower than at Surfside. This section has been eating away steadily for the last twenty years, each successive storm making great inroads into the bluff. Twice the government has found it necessary to move the station and now another move will be necessary.

Between 1:00 and 2:00 o'clock Tuesday afternoon the surf was at its worst at Madaket, breaking upon the beach continuously, the heavy seas surging the around the station building and across the roadway several hundred feet. Captain Norcross and his men at one time thought they would have to abandon the station, as the surf was pounding its way through the bluff and the surging water sweeping under and around the building.

A tremendous surf was heaving on the south shore of the island and hundreds of persons braved the elements and went out to see the unusual sight. The direction of the wind was such, however, that at Surfside it had the tendency to sweep the top off the waves before they broke, which prevented the heavy rollers that sometimes accompany a storm like this. The surf was very pretty, however, and the breakers showing up far offshore and the seas surging up into the bank, cutting it away considerably in several sections.

The September Storm, 1933

The storm of the 16–17th [September] was exceedingly severe, with attending damage both at sea and on land. Excessive rain, high storm tides, and gales, caused notable destruction on the Massachusetts coast. 9.92 inches of rain fell at Provincetown in 24 consecutive hours, and there were many occurrences of 4 to over 6 inches in that period in eastern Massachusetts and Rhode Island.

New England climatologist

The 1933 tropical storm season ranked among the busiest of record with 21 individual disturbances charted. Storm number 13 was the only one to affect Nantucket. First observed on September 8 east of the Windward Islands near latitude 10°N, it followed a sinuous track to the north, much like a slalom course, then northwest for nine days before making a landfall on the Outer Banks of North Carolina on the 16th. After a momentary hesitation while recurving, the storm system turned northeast, accelerated, and passed about 75 miles southeast of Nantucket in the early afternoon of September 17.

Gale-force winds lashed the island for 17 hours beginning at 3:30 a.m. on the 17th. The greatest wind strength was exhibited about 11:00 a.m. when a sustained five-minute speed of 46 miles per hour and a peak gust of 54 miles were clocked.

Wind direction was east until 9:00 a.m. when it shifted to northeast; then it went into the north for two hours for two observations at 3:00 and 4:00 p.m.; and finally backed to the northwest at 8:00 p.m. For the 24 hours of the 17th, it averaged 31.9 miles per hour. The lowest barometer reading of 29.16 inches was reached about 2:00 p.m. when the storm center was at its closest approach.

Rain began to fall at 12:45 a.m. and continued to 8:45 p.m. A moderately heavy amount fell between 7:00 and 8:00 a.m. From

9:00 a.m. until noon hourly amounts were : 0.26, 0.57, and 0.27 inch. The storm total was 1.65 inches.

Since a trough of low pressure hovered over New England at that time, rain fell for four days at most stations, adding to the very heavy amounts contributed by the tropical storm passage. Daily amounts measured on Nantucket from the 14th to 17th were: 1.26, 1.16, 0.66, and 2.29 inches, for a storm total of 5.37 inches. Provincetown reported 12.32 inches on the 16th and 17th. The Block Island catch was 6.46 inches and East Wareham totaled 9.04 inches — all very heavy amounts for a hurricane.

The *Inquirer and Mirror* reported little damage from "the northeast storm" on September 17:

Four days of an easterly storm, with heavy rain, high wind, and a rugged sea put a damper on the last weekend and upset the steamboat schedule and about everything and everybody else. It was a severe storm all along the coast, but was well heralded by the Weather Bureau, even though it did come from out to sea and apparently resulted from a tropical disturbance of great intensity.

Nantucket got its full share of the fury of the elements, but comparatively little damage resulted, except to the eastern shore-line of the island, into which the big seas ate their way for hours. The direction of the wind was such that the harbor front was protected more than in the storm of July 4th, and about all the damage to shipping was the sinking of a number of small pleasure boats, which filled with water and sank at their moorings.

New England Hurricane Of 1938

The Great Hurricane of September 1938 stands as the most memorable meteorological event of the present century for almost all of New England. Within a few hours on the late afternoon and evening of September 21, a mass of whirling wind, surging sea, and flooding rain, all unheralded to those who became its victims, swept in from the Atlantic Ocean and caused unprecedented damage from Long Island Sound and Block Island Sound northward to the Canadian border. Over six hundred people who were alive and going about their daily tasks at 3:00 p.m. that day failed to survive until sunset that evening, having succumbed in various ways to the thrusts of wind, wave, and water. Damage to man's structures and nature's forests was estimated at $306 million dollars. These figures of death and destruction combined to produce the greatest natural catastrophe in New England's history.

The center of the tropical intruder came ashore near Patchogue in central Long Island and, after churning across Long Island Sound, it struck land near Milford a short distance west of New Haven, Connecticut. Only the eastern fringe of New England escaped major losses, the lucky list included Nantucket, outer Cape Cod, and most of Maine. Though Cape Cod and the Islands lay within the sweep of gale-force winds, they were beyond the close circle of hurricane-force blasts of 74 or more miles per hour which extended about 50 or 60 miles east of the central eye of the hurricane vortex. Nantucket lay some 150 miles east of the center and clocked sustained winds of 52 miles per hour, compared to Block Island's 82 miles and Providence's 87 miles. Furthermore, the area lay in the dry eastern semicircle of the storm system. Nantucket received only 0.04 inch of rain, Hyannis 0.25 inch, and Provincetown 0.35 inch, while some areas of western New England were deluged with over 10 inches.

The wind came out of the southeast all morning of the 21st, blowing from 20 to 29 miles per hour. It increased to gale force at 11:49 a.m. and continued above 31 miles for 14 hours. The peak one-minute sustained speed of 57 miles per hour was recorded at 3:54 p.m. from the southeast as the hurricane center raced north from New Haven to Hartford, Connecticut. This occurred just before the wind shifted to south where it settled for three hours, before veering to southwest about 9:00 p.m. Speeds gradually decreased until dropping below gale force at 3:00 a.m. on the 22d.

Very light rain fell intermittently from 1:32 to 4:00 p.m. with a storm total of only 0.04 inch measured. A brief shower without a measurable amount occurred at 7:00 p.m., and this was all the precipitation deposited by the tropical intruder.

The temperature amounted to 75°F at 11:00 a.m. in the tropical air flowing north from the Gulf Stream area of the Atlantic Ocean. During the afternoon and evening the thermometer gradually fell, reaching 61° by midnight as a cool airstream from the continent circled south of the hurricane center, then moving northward from Vermont into Canada.

The barometer began to drop at 9:00 p.m. on the 20th, falling very slowly until 10:00 a.m. on the 21st when the influence of the approaching hurricane was first felt. A steep decline began in the late morning and reached a low point of 29.38 inches at 3:15 p.m. This contrasted greatly with the lowest reported in the eye of the storm on Long Island: 27.97 inches at the Bellport Coast Guard Station near Patchogue, New York.

The *Inquirer and Mirror* assessed the storm experience:

While islanders sat in their comfortable homes, listening to the wind whistling out-of-doors, and well aware that the strong southerly was of more than ordinary intensity, it was not until they tuned in their radios and heard the reports of the devastation throughout New England that they realized the full extent of the storm.

The coast-line of the island had suffered, it is true, but the damage here could not be compared to anything on either the Vineyard or Cape or the mainland. It became a contrast instead.

Surrounded by shoals, which acted as natural bulwarks to the sweep of the waves,

Surf breaks over the Nantucket Yacht Club bulkhead during the Great Storm of March 1984. Photograph courtesy of H. Flint Ranney.

the island's east and north shores are more protected, perhaps, than the south and west ends, which bore the brunt of the seas. But in the town, aside from a few branches ripped off trees, the tops of several chimneys shorn of a few bricks, and a few fences toppling, the storm did little damage. The telephone, electric power, and lighting service was not interrupted; and the old houses merely took the blow as just another storm.

When the cable connections with the mainland went "by the board," fears for the island's safety were expressed with a number of news broadcasters announcing that "there was no news from Nantucket." Through the medium of the U.S. Compass Station at Surfside the government coast guard headquarters were notified that "Nantucket was all right."

The gigantic seas broke into the ponds. Long Pond received the greatest amount of water, submerging both bridges and

undermining their approaches. Along Hummock Pond the former property of the Humane Society, which had been remodeled into a home, was demolished. Houses on Cisco were surrounded by water and residents evacuated in time. The bars at the heads of ponds disappeared and became part of the Atlantic. Several families were marooned on the other side of Broad Creek when the roadway was washed out. Electric power on Nantucket was not interrupted anywhere on the island by the storm and it was possible to telephone to Falmouth during the height of the storm.

The passage of the New England Hurricane about 150 miles west of Nantucket Town on September 21, 1938, is demonstrated by the weather elements as recorded by the weather bureau:

Time	Wind		Cloud cover	Precip	Temp
	Steady	Gusts			
	(mi/h)		(tenths)	(inches)	°F
7:00am	SE 21		5		70
10:00	SE 26		10		74
12:00n	SE 29	32	10		74
1:00pm	SE 32	38	10		73
2:00	E 35	38	10	T	73
3:00	SE 41	47	10	T	71
4:00	SE 43	52	10	.04	72
5:00	SE 42	47	10		71
6:00	S 38	43	10		69
9:00	SW 37	44	10		65
12:00am	SW 33	38	0		61

Lowest barometer: 29.38 inches at 3:15 p.m. Wind: highest sustained for 5 minutes at 52 mi/h at 3:54 p.m.; highest sustained for 1 minute at 57 mi/h.
Total precipitation: 0.04 inch.

Great Atlantic Hurricane of September 14–15, 1944

One of the great hurricanes of the modern era, with respect to size and physical force, was first detected in the tropics on 8 September 1944 northeast of the Windward Islands close to 55°W, or about the longitude of east-central Newfoundland. During the next seven days the system of whirling winds and condensing moisture performed a vast parabolic journey that would take its destructive central core along the Outer Banks of North Carolina, over the eastern end of Long Island, into Rhode Island and Massachusetts, across the Gulf of Maine and the Bay of Fundy, through the Atlantic Provinces of Canada, and finally back to the longitude of its starting place, but some 1700 miles to the northward.

The storm track cut across extreme eastern Long Island close to Montauk Point about 9:00 p.m. on September 14. The center then churned across Long Island Sound, passing between Fishers Island and Block Island to make a New England landfall about 10:00 p.m. on the Rhode Island shore between Charlestown and Point Judith, 75 miles west of Nantucket harbor.

The hurricane center continued almost directly northeast, passing between Providence and Fall River, across what is now Route 195 near Swansea, and then through southeast Massachusetts over a Taunton-Brockton-South Weymouth line. The 67-mile land traverse took one hour and 50 minutes, at a forward speed of about 36 miles per hour. The eye of the storm, with its lull in winds and starlit sky, was experienced over Providence at 11:20 p.m. and at South Weymouth, just south of Boston, about 12:15 a.m. The Naval Air Station at the latter witnessed an interesting wind shift about 12:05 a.m. from the southeast to west with the wind diminishing to 4 miles per hour for three minutes and blowing at less than 10 miles for 25 minutes. The calm eye of the hurricane was about 15 miles in diameter.

Nantucket's lowest barometer reading of 29.04 inches occurred at 11:28 p.m. on the 14th, about the time that Providence, Rhode Island, in the eye of the storm, hit a low of 28.56 inches. The lowest barometer reported in New England, 28.31 inches, came at Point Judith, Rhode Island at the entrance to Narragansett Bay.

The first wind of gale force hit Nantucket at 7:45 p.m. from the southeast and gradually increased to a peak of 55 miles per hour at 12:13 a.m. on the 15th. The highest blow came from the southwest after the barometer commenced to rise; an extreme gust of 79 miles per hour was registered at 12:46 a.m. The force gradually diminished to a steady 30 miles per hour by 3:00 a.m. Block Island, Rhode Island had an extreme wind of 88 miles per hour from the southeast, and Chatham, Massachusetts reported 85 miles per hour with an extreme gust estimated at 100 miles per hour. The passage of the Great Atlantic Hurricane about 65 miles northwest of Nantucket Town is demonstrated by the weather elements as recorded by the weather bureau on September 14 and 15, 1944:

| Time | Wind Steady | Gusts | Cloud cover | Precip. | Temp. |
	(mi/h)		(tenths)	(inches)	°F
Sept. 14					
6:00 pm	SE 20		10		70
7:00	SE 25		10		71
8:00	SE 28	31	10	.01	71
9:00	SE 35	42	10	.08	70
10:00	SE 37	42	10	.02	73
11:00	SE 44	49	10		68
12:00	SE 57	57	10		67
Sept. 15					
1:00 am	SW 49	55	10		68
2:00	SW 46	49	10		68
3:00	SW 41	44	8		68
4:00	SW 30	34	4		68
5:00	SW 26	30	3		68
6:00	SW 26		1		68
7:00	SW 20		0		71

Lowest barometer: 29.04 inches at 11:28 p.m., Sept. 14.
Wind: highest sustained for 5 minutes at 57 mi/h at 11:47 p.m., Sept. 14; highest gust at 79 mi/h at 12:45 a.m. on Sept. 15.
Total precipitation: 0.11 inch.

The *Inquirer and Mirror* described the local scene:

The disturbance increased as the evening advanced and the wind reached high velocity and the local Weather Bureau recorded gusts as high as 65 miles. The greatest damage was done to trees and as a result the streets were littered with leaves and broken branches, several of the large shade trees being uprooted. The time for high water was around 10:45 o'clock, but the water did not rise much above normal and did not reach the level of the wharves or cover the roadway on Beach or Washington streets, as sometimes occurs on an extreme high tide.

The heavy foliage on the trees this year was the reason for so much damage about the central streets, and the extreme heavy gusts was probably what brought such serious injury to roofs and small buildings. . . .

Compared to other storms experienced on Nantucket, this one broke no records. . . .

'Sconset had its share of damage. The fence and trees around the Casino property were shattered; the roof of the 'Sconset Golf Club building was damaged; Dorothy Webster's garage was lifted from its moorings and landed on the MacArthur property. The shingles were torn from the roof of the Hilts house, and there was quite a lot of damage to small buildings all over the village. Christy Psaradelis had his garage demolished, but his house was uninjured and cars undamaged. . . .

At Madaket, only a few of the craft moored in the creek or hauled up were damaged. A number of chimneys were blown away, and roofs were damaged all along the way. The shore line was badly battered, as usual, and denizens of Smith's Point would have been marooned had they not come over the bridge before midnight.

The paper a week later supplied more information and comments:

Nantucket was fortunate, indeed, and, as in the hurricane of September 21, 1938, the full force of the disturbance was not felt here....

Hummock Pond was opened to the sea, the surf pounding its way through the beach and letting the pond run out to a low level. Other ponds were invaded by the sea along the south shore and in places the water came up through the low places a quarter of a mile or more.

Hurricane Carol, August 31, 1954

Hurricane Carol was a killer second only to the Great New England Hurricane of September 1938. Sixty persons lost their lives on that tragic last day of August 1954, and more than one thousand received serious injuries. Property and crop losses totaled an estimated $460 million, well in excess of any other hurricane disaster in the United States up to that time.

Carol formed in an easterly wave over the Atlantic Ocean east of the northern Bahamas on August 25–26. Its movement was sluggish for the next three days, as its size and intensity expanded greatly. Late on the 30th, the center passed a few miles east of Cape Hatteras where winds mounted to 78 miles an hour in gusts and the lowest pressure reached 29.52 inches. Since the storm's path lay some 75 to 100 miles offshore, the most destructive winds remained at sea and their full force was not realized by weather forecasters.

The impact of the great mass of whirling winds and condensing moisture on eastern Long Island and New England proved catastrophic. The center struck the south shore of eastern Long Island about 8:30 a.m. on the morning of the 31st; the landfall was east of Westhampton in the Shinnecock Bay area about 130 miles west-southwest of Nantucket harbor.

After traversing Great Peconic Bay, Carol lashed across Long Island Sound and arrived on the Connecticut shore close to the mouth of the Connecticut River at Saybrook about 10:30 a.m. This was similar to the path followed by the Great September Gale of 1815.

Curving slightly to the north, the center passed about 5 to 10 miles west of Worcester in central Massachusetts about noon and then raced into south-central New Hampshire in early afternoon, roughly the schedule of the September 1815 storm.

When most New England residents went to bed on the night of the 30th, there had been no hurricane warnings broadcast. Not until the weather bureau's 6:00 a.m. advisory was it suggested that the storm path might cross Long Island and burst into New England. Then gale rather than hurricane warnings were issued. It was apparent that no one knew what lurked in the dangerous eastern semicircle of Carol. By the time warnings were received, powerlines were down and hurricane blasts were wreaking havoc with buildings, foliage, and forests, and smashing small boats. As in September 1938, storm tides surged up the southern estuaries of eastern Connecticut and Rhode Island, wrecking shore installations and invading resort homes.

The editor of the *Inquirer & Mirror* described the hurricane's impact on Nantucket Island:

Carol ... caught New England by surprise at the last moment as the storm suddenly changed direction and struck the area with winds far exceeding gale force Tuesday morning [Aug. 31].

Hurricanes for the past 10 years have passed Nantucket some distance out in the Atlantic, but Hurricane Carol, in passing to the west, presented the quarter with the highest winds to the island. Although missing Nantucket by a good many miles, the hurricane caused a SE wind which occurred Tuesday morning and reached a high of 77 miles per hour in gusts, accompanied by a heavy rain for a short while.

Fortunately, the tides were not high when Nantucket underwent the highest winds. Harbor damage was at a minimum for such a strong blow, but the western end of the Island suffered considerable erosion. Smith Point was cut off from the rest of the island by a deep channel while the Point, itself, was cut in two parts by a shallower passage. "A good blow from any standpoint," concluded the newspaper editor.

Carol's passage about 115 miles to the west of Nantucket is demonstrated by the weather elements as recorded by the weather bureau on August 31, 1954:

Time	Wind Steady	Gusts	Bar.	Cloud cover	Precip.	Temp.
	(mi/h)		(inches)	(tenths)	(inches)	°F
5:25am	ENE 24	31	29.81	10		64
6:25	ENE 25	30	.74	10		67
7:25	ESE 38	42	.63	10	.12	69
8:25	ESE 50	69	.45	10	.37	69
9:25	SE 48	60	.38	10	.03	69
10:25	SSE 49	60	.33	10	T	71
11:25	S 55	73	.35	10	T	70
12:25pm	SSW 50	60	.43	9		68
1:25	SSW 45	50	.51	9		70
2:25	SW 38	49	.59	8		69
3:25	SSW 29	35	.64	0		69
4:25	SW 28	42	.68	0		69

Lowest barometer: 29.33 inches at 10:25 a.m. Highest wind: SE 54 mi/h at 8:35 a.m.; gust at 72 mi/h at 9:00 a.m.

Hurricane Edna, September 11, 1954

Hurricane Edna took its place among the memorable hurricane visitations in Nantucket's history when its center came nearer to passing directly over the island than that of any other storm of the present century, and the barometer dropped to the lowest point ever reported by a local instrument. The slightly lower barometer readings at Edgartown and Hyannis and the attendant wind behavior at the Nantucket Airport indicated that the island remained in the eastern sector of the storm system throughout. The center or eye of the hurricane passed over

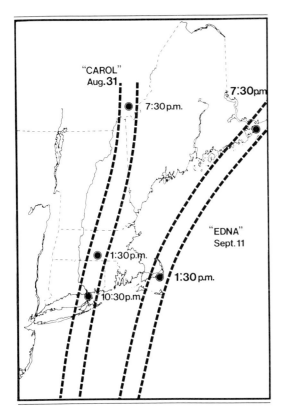

the waters separating Martha's Vineyard and Nantucket, then across Nantucket Sound, and along the hook of Cape Cod. Though other tropical storms and winter northeasters have done greater damage, the unique meteorological aspects of Edna deserve close scrutiny.

The first indication of a fifth tropical storm circulation of the 1954 season appeared between Puerto Rico and the southeastern Bahama Islands on the night of September 5. Spawned by an easterly wave in the upper atmosphere, Edna moved slowly northwest, then north until the 10th. There its forward progress suddenly accelerated. By 10:00 p.m., the center stood about 60 miles east of Cape Hatteras, now moving north-northeast. The central pressure dropped toward 28.00 inches and the winds were spinning around the center at 125 miles per hour. By 6:00 a.m. on the morning of the 11th, Edna reached a

position about 135 miles southeast of Atlantic City and directly south of the southern tip of Long Island, with a bead drawn on Nantucket and Cape Cod to the northeast.

During the morning hours Edna moved over the continental shelf waters at 40 miles per hour, still somewhat slower than Carol's fast pace two weeks before. The position of the center can be judged by the times of lowest pressures during the early afternoon: Block Island, 12:25 p.m., Edgartown 1:30 p.m., Nantucket 1:45 p.m., Hyannis 2:14 p.m., and Chatham 2:20 p.m.

Edna's tight-knit, circular vortex possessed a very low barometric depth. Lowest pressures on Martha's Vineyard were reported close to 28.00 inches: 28.02 inches on a tested instrument, while some private observers, as usual, proudly pointed to lower readings, slightly below 28.00 inches. Chatham at the southwest tip of Cape Cod registered 28.05 inches. Nantucket recorded 28.17 inches, the lowest by 0.15 inch in the island's history.

Winds over the area were well above the hurricane criterion of 73 miles per hour. Peak gusts hit 88 miles per hour on Nantucket, 110 miles on Block Island, 100 miles at Hyannis, and 120 miles on Martha's Vineyard. After the center passed, Boston received its highest blast at 87 miles from the northwest. Most stations on the mainland clocked their highest winds during the backlash of the storm after it had progressed northward and winds had shifted into the west and northwest.

The *Inquirer and Mirror* described the near passage of the hurricane center:

The fact that the "eye" passed close to the island was evident by the fact that for an hour Saturday afternoon the sun shone, and blue sky could be seen. At the same time the winds shifted but did not give Nantucket the period of calm which generally shows that the center of a hurricane is at hand. The winds definitely decreased at this time, and when the "eye" had passed, turned to the northwest and blew with sustained velocities of 50 to 60 miles per hour. . . .

The highest tides did not compare with those experienced during hurricane Carol, as wharf top levels were barely reached. The higher winds did drive the water further inland in several areas and bulkheads along the waterfront were particularly damaged by the action of the waves. . . .

Along the ocean shores of Nantucket much heavier damage was experienced as the surf literally "walked into the bank." Some forty to fifty feet of the bluffs disappeared during the storm at various places. . . .

Smith's Point was further washed away but its shape was not changed greatly from that shown in the photograph published in our last week's issue. The channels were deepened and remaining sand dunes were flattened out.

Edna's approach to and passage over the Islands and Cape Cod is demonstrated by the hourly report of the weather elements on Nantucket as recorded by the weather bureau on September 11, 1954:

Time	Wind				Cloud		
	Steady	Gusts	Bar.	cover	Precip.	Temp.
	(mi/h)		(inches)	(tenths)	(inches)	°F
12:28am	SE	13		29.89	10		68
1:25	SE	15		.84	10	67	
2:25	SE	15		.81	10	.07	67
3:25	ESE	17	22	.76	10	T	67
4:25	ESE	19	24	.70	10		67
5:25	ESE	23	30	.67	10		67
6:26	SE	24	36	.61	10		68
7:26	SE	31	42	.52	10	.01	68
8:28	ESE	33	46	.40	10	.03	69
9:26	E	45	68	.25	10	.21	69
10:28	E	45	72	.06	10	.64	69
11:27	ESE	50	71	28.83	10	.48	69
12:25pm	SSE	52	72	.53	10	.18	69
1:26	SSE	60	88	.17	10	.02	68
2:29	W	40	60	.35	9	T	70
3:26	WNW	40	65	.61	10		67
4:26	WNW	40	60	.97	10		69
5:29	W	45	50	29.23	7		68
6:28	W	30	38	.33	7	T	70
7:28	W	28	36	.46	4		67
8:28	W	22	28	.57	2		67
9:25	WNW	25	36	.64	1		67
10:25	WNW	25	33	.69	0		66

T = trace, or less than a measurable amount.
Lowest barometer: 28.17 inches at 1:45 p.m.
Highest wind: SE at 64 mi/h at 12:50 p.m.; gust at 73 mi/h at 1:04 p.m.

Hurricane Donna, September 12, 1960

Hurricane Donna proved a vigorous and long-lived lady, though a bit disorganized in the appearance and arrangement of her meteorological dress. Nothing approaching her size and energy has been seen by current residents of the New England coast since the visitation of this tropical intruder on September 12, 1960. Several threats have appeared on the weather maps, but no combination of wind and wave force comparable with the great series of hurricane appearances from 1924 to 1960 has ventured so far north in the past 25 years.

First detected off the coast of West Africa on August 30, 1960, Donna crossed the broad North Atlantic Ocean, passed just north of the Greater Antilles on a west-northwest track, and made a landfall on the Florida Keys early on September 10. A recurve to the north carried the center of the storm over south and central Florida where major damage resulted to crops and buildings. Trending to the north-northeast, Donna made an overwater passage from northeast Florida to the Outer Banks of North Carolina, brushing the Cape Hatteras area about midnight of the 11th. The central core of the hurricane, after lashing the entire Middle Atlantic seaboard, arrived on the Long Island shore early in the afternoon of the 12th.

A well-defined, circular eye was not in evidence at this northerly latitude, rather a wide oblong of practically equal low pressure stretched from New York City on the west to the Brookhaven area in the east-central part of Long Island. Lulls in wind force were experienced between 1:00 and 3:00 p.m. at various places, earlier to the west and later to the east. Having lost her forward momentum, Donna was adjusting to the new meteorological environment prevailing over the cool waters surrounding Long Island. Brookhaven in the east-central part of Long Island registered a low pressure of 28.375 inches at 2:50 p.m. and a highest gust of 90

miles per hour about 1:30 p.m.

The Weather Bureau charted the path of lowest pressure crossing from Orient Point on eastern Long Island to the beaches of Saybrook and New London, and then across eastern Connecticut, over the northwest tip of Rhode Island, and then through Massachusetts on a Milford-Framingham-Lowell line. The oblong of lowest pressure had narrowed somewhat in its movement over land. The nearest approach of the path to Nantucket harbor was about 115 miles to the northwest.

Block Island, lying about 75 miles west of Nantucket, received the brunt of the wind and waves in the dangerous eastern sector of the storm. Sustained speeds of 95 miles per hour were measured at 4:15 p.m., along with a gust of 135 miles per hour. Point Judith on the Rhode Island mainland clocked gusts up to 100 miles per hour. The minimum pressure recorded at Block Island was 28.58 inches, or almost half an inch lower than Nantucket's barometric nadir.

"Donna Washes Out Madaket Road," was the headline in the *Inquirer and Mirror*:

Hurricane Donna gave Nantucket a terrific wind lashing, but spared the island the severe damage it caused sections of Rhode Island and southeastern Massachusetts. . . .

At Madaket, huge waves . . . cut a path across a dirt road leading to Broad Creek crossing. The road washout was about 4 ft. deep and 30 ft. wide.

The fact that the wind was from the SE and then shifted to the W kept the harbor area from suffering damage from an excessive high tide and, with the exception of the Brant Point area, along Easton St. and at Madaket there was no flooding reported.

Damage on the island was confined to boats breaking loose from moorings, tree limbs broken, and television antennas downed. Negligible waterfront losses were reported.

The Weather Bureau had warned that Nantucket would get the worst of the approaching hurricane, but the editor thought the winds of 45 to 65 miles per hour were no

worse than experienced in winter northeasters. In the morning winds blew from the east-southeast, but did not reach speeds of 40 miles per hour until near 1:00 p.m. The highest wind speed, 65 miles per hour, was recorded at 4:30 p.m. just before the wind shifted to the south. High gusts continued through the evening, with a peak of 73 miles per hour coming out of the southwest at 7:05 p.m. Over the 24-hour period the wind averaged 27.4 miles per hour.

Though there were intermittent showers from 12:20 to 4:21 p.m., the only measurable amount, 0.14 inch, fell between 2:00 and 3:00 p.m.

Donna's passage about 100 miles west of Nantucket is demonstrated by the weather elements as recorded by the weather bureau on September 12, 1960:

Time	Wind Steady Gusts		Bar.	Cloud cover	Precip	Temp
	(mi/h)		(inches)	(tenths)	(inches)	°F
12:55am	SSE	6	29.88	10		68
3:58	SSE	12	.83	10		68
6:58	SE	18	.78	10		69
8:57	ESE 16	23	.69	10		69
10:58	ESE	33	.55	10		70
12:56pm	ESE 33	46	.34	10	T	67
1:55	ESE 44	63	.18	10	.01	71
2:55	SSE 41	56	.14	10	.13	70
3:59	S 46	59	.09	10	T	73
4:58	S 48	73	.06	8	T	66
5:53	SSW 44	69	.15	10	T	69
6:58	SSW 44	70	.22	8		67
7:59	SW 43	67	.30	2		67
9:58	WSW 35	55	.44	0		66

T = trace, or less than a measurable amount.
Lowest barometer: 29.04 inches at 4:47 p.m.
Highest wind: S 56 mi/h at 4:34 p.m.; gust at 73 mi/h at 7:05 and 7:07 p.m.
Total precipitation: 0.14 inch.

Ex-Hurricane Esther's Loop, September 1961

As Hurricane Esther approached the southern New England mainland during the early morning of the 21st, winds increased to near or slightly above hurricane force in gusts along the coast and over some of the offshore islands. Block Island, Rhode Island, experienced peak speed of 83 miles per hour, while a few coastal areas reported gusts over 70 miles per hour. Farther north over southeastern New England peak gusts ranged from 40 to 65 miles per hour.

When the storm center reached a point about 50 miles south-southeast of Block Island, it suddenly stalled and weakened, after which it made a slow turn to the east. This action of the storm was unique in the history of New England hurricanes. As a result this area was spared much of the impact that had been anticipated. Another saving feature was that the time of heaviest surf occurrence did not coincide with that of the regular high tide.

Esther's path after leaving the waters south of Block Island took it south of Nantucket. While describing a slow clockwise loop [it] crossed the original track a short distance southeast of Nantucket on the 25th. Packing heavy rain but no damaging winds, the storm moved north and northeastward passing east of Cape Cod and crossing Maine from near Brunswick to eastern Aroostock County.

New England climatologist.

Hurricane Esther was the fourth of six hurricanes that formed in September 1961. It came from the eastern North Atlantic Ocean, first charted at 32°W and 12°N on the 12th. Esther followed a west-northwest and northwest track until north of Hispaniola and east of southern Florida on the 17th when it recurved to the north. Off Cape Hatteras on the 20th, it turned north-northeast toward southeastern New England.

Esther approached to within 100 miles of Nantucket on the 21st before degenerating into a tropical storm. Little damage resulted to the island except by erosion from high seas. About 1.5 miles of the western tip of the island was cut off by a channel of approximately one-quarter mile width, turning Smith's Point into Esther Island.

The *Inquirer and Mirror*'s reporter witnessed the scene:

Hurricane Esther hit Nantucket Wednes-day night [Sept. 20] and all day yesterday and although it had been labeled "large and dangerous" by the Miami Weather Bureau, it caused little damage except to Madaket shoreline and at Broad Creek crossing.

Huge 20-foot waves rolled in one on top of the other, battered the sand dunes at the crossing and by late Wednesday had flattened the area, washing out the road and knocking down the utility poles carrying the telephone lines. Where the road left the Madaket side there is now a 10 to 15-foot drop which extends about a quarter of a mile across to the Smith's Point side. The Smith's Point area is virtually an island today.

The first sign of the hurricane getting nearer to the island came Tuesday night [Sept. 19] when high breakers came rolling in on the beaches along the South Shore, especially at Surfside, Cisco, Siasconset, and Madaket. The roar of the breakers crashing on the beaches could be heard very clearly in town all through the night.

The surf at the South Shore broke through Nobadeer Valley on Thursday [Sept. 21], and the water headed for the pine grove. Who knows, if the South Shore continues to be eaten away by successive storms, we may someday have a passage from the harbor to Surfside! Sounds bizarre, but stranger things have happened.

The presence of Hurricane Esther in the vicinity of Nantucket from September 20 to 26, 1961, is demonstrated by the records of the weather bureau:

Date	Average	Wind (mi/h)	1=minute	Precip (inches)
20	NE	18.3	34	.04
21	E	29.5	40	1.21
22	N	22.6	29	.01
23	N	19.5	26	T
24	NE	19.0	20	T
25	E	20.5	27	1.58
26	W	16.6	20	.02

T trace, or less than a measurable amount. Lowest barometer: 29.33 inches on 21st. Highest wind: sustained 1 = minute 40 mi/h; unofficial reports from South Shore at 70 mi/h
Total precipitation: 2.89 inches.

Tropical Storm Carrie on Labor Day Weekend: September 2–3, 1972

Tropical storm Carrie achieved notoriety because it chose to arrive on the New England shore in the middle of the Labor Day weekend. Travel plans for many had to be altered on land, sea, and air. Those planning to spend the holiday on the islands were especially inconvenienced since boat schedules were completely disrupted by cancelled trips when the demand was greatest.

Carrie, spawned in a tropical wave east of central Florida on August 29, pursued a sinuous course at a slow pace northward while remaining well offshore. On September 2 and 3, the center tracked along 71°W meridian reaching 40°N latitude where it turned northeast. Early on the 3d, the size expanded and the barometric depth deepened when the disturbance was about 100 miles south of Nantucket. At this point, the estimated lowest pressure was 29.30 inches, not unusual for a well-developed northeast storm at this time of the year. What gave Carrie its wind punch was a blocking high pressure area hovering south of Newfoundland with a barometer reading of 30.27 inches. Neither the high nor the low was extreme for the season, but the proximity of the two over the offshore waters created a strong wind circulation, the fringe of which lashed coastal New England all weekend.

High winds and wind-generated seas, along with heavy rains and flooding, did most of the damage. A gust of 84 miles per hour was reported at Point Judith, Rhode Island, one of 69 miles per hour on Cape Cod.

The New England climatologist summarized Carrie's impact on the region during the Labor Day weekend:

Storm Carrie brought sustained winds of 40 to 50 m.p.h. to many coastal sections and islands, with gusts of 60 to 80 m.p.h. Great loss to boats and damage to coastal installations occurred. Many buildings damaged by wind or falling trees or limbs. Many walls and buildings under construction collapsed, including a large structure in Boston, a shopping mall at Taunton, a garage in New Bedford, and walls in Hyannis. Homes were undermined on Plum Island and 15 people were evacuated. Many autos damaged by falling trees and limbs along and near the coast. Many utility outages also. Roads blocked by fallen trees in some communities.

Record-breaking rains in many coastal and island communities, with a storm total of 12.50 inches at Tashmoo on Martha's Vineyard in 16 hours. Totals of 4 to 9 inches at most coastal sections but amounts fell off rapidly inland to mostly 1 to 2 inches in eastern Worcester County and to a trace or none in extreme northwestern Worcester County. Heavy flood and erosion damage in the heavy rain area. Plymouth was declared a local disaster area with many homes damaged or undermined. Thousands of cellars flooded. Two deaths and one injury from boats swamped by wind. One injured by a falling tree and one by flying debris.

Rains were confined to a strip within 70 miles of the coast and ranged from 2.0 to 10.0 inches. Some heavy amounts recorded were: Nantucket 5.02, Edgartown 7.06, Hyannis 5.02, Chatham 6.12, and East Wareham 8.89. An unconfirmed report from Tashmoo on Martha's Vineyard claimed 12.50 inches fell in about 16 hours.

Hurricane Gloria 1985

When Hurricane Gloria passed over Cape Hatteras soon after midnight on September 27, its central barometric pressure read 27.82 inches and winds in its eastern sector gusted to 120 miles per hour. A major hurricane, Gloria posed a threat to the entire North Atlantic seaboard. Full hurricane warnings were issued north to Portsmouth, New Hampshire. During the next 12 hours Gloria accelerated on a north-northeast path, but in passing over the cool Atlantic waters off the Middle Atlantic states its energy decreased and its winds lessened somewhat. Hurricane Belle in August 1976 had undergone the same decrease in force in the same area.

About noontime on the 27th, Gloria made a landfall on Long Island over Jones Inlet and then pursued a path northward across the island very close to the boundary of Nassau and Suffolk counties. The landfall was only about 12 miles east of the International Arrivals Building at Kennedy International Airport and about 175 miles west of Nantucket Harbor. The barometric pressure read 28.28 inches and winds gusted to 90 miles per hour. The major hurricanes of the twentieth century in 1938, 1944, 1954, and 1960 had made their entries into Long Island well to the east of Gloria and closer to Nantucket.

The threat of Gloria and its impact were described by the three regular columnists of the *Inquirer and Mirror* on October 3. Merle T. Orleans presented the general situation:

Hurricane "Gloria" gave Nantucket only a passing glance, winds not really reaching hurricane force and only 0.10 inch of rain. That was the amount of rain received also on the Cape and in Providence. . . . Nantucket fared well, but the entire community was ready to cope with most any emergency. . . . Everyone on Nantucket should be proud of the way the people pulled together—Police, Fire Department, Hospital, School Officials, and the Center for the Elderly, and the Churches—and planned what to do if it struck us.

Charles F. Sayle, "Waterfront News" covered the marine aspects:

It [Gloria] was delayed a day or so finally arriving at noon Friday and following pretty close on the track of the 1938 breeze. The wind got up to 50 to 55 m.p.h. by noon, just as the tide began to fall, so we had a pretty much normal high water as the breeze went across Long Island and up inside us, we had a south-east wind, hauling to south around mid afternoon, and by 5 p.m. the wind hauled west and blew 60 to 70 m.p.h. for a while as the center passed by way to the west, and headed up through New Hampshire and Canada. As expected four or five boats moored off Brant Point, on a lee shore, landed on the beach and a 25' to 30' power cruiser was reported ashore up on Coatue between 3rd and 4th points. By low water around 6:30 p.m. the whole thing was past us.

Tom Giffin in "Flight Deck" provided the aviation perspective:

The wind stayed southeast through the morning, rising as a low cloud layer broke up and was replaced by a hazy obscuration. When the tower closed at 11:30 a.m. the wind was still southeast, now 30 gusting to 45, pressure falling rapidly, but no long after that the pressure began to bottom out, levelling off at our place at 29.54. That's about the time Gloria was passing abeam, and a long way off as hurricanes go—170 statute miles. That's why the pressure stayed so high. Peak winds here didn't get above the 80s as far as I have heard, or about 70 knots. . . . If the hurricane had gone up over New London, as looked likely for a while, we would have seen some damage here. We were lucky. . . .

We weren't quite close enough to the center to get more than one brief shower, but that little was welcome as it laid the worst of the dust. Late that afternoon, about 4:15, I noticed the first momentary lull in the wind, and by 4:45 the slow abatement seemed to be established. The sun came out an hour before sunset and we had a clear, moonlit night with diminishing winds. So much for Gloria on Nantucket. The most spectacular aspect of it had been the fact that before noon the island shut up shop and went home, everyone but the safety services. We've never done that before.

Hurricane flags fly over Brant Point to warn of the possible approach of Hurricane Gloria on September 27, 1985. Photograph courtesy of H. Flint Ranney.

Lesser Hurricanes And Tropical Storms, 1951–1985

All data and references are to Nantucket unless otherwise stated. An ex-hurricane is one whose winds in northerly latitudes have diminished below the hurricane criterion of 74 miles per hour. All quotations are from the *Inquirer and Mirror*. An asterisk (*) indicates a full discussion is included in previous section.

1951   No tropical storms approached Nantucket.

1952   September 4. Ex-hurricane Able moved over Pennsylvania and central New England while rapidly losing energy; wind 30 mi/h south; barometer 29.74 inches; only 0.02 inch rain on 3d.

1953   August 15. Hurricane Barbara lost its tropical structure when about 100 miles southeast of Nantucket; barometer 29.33 inches; wind 47 mi/h northwest; 2.54 inches rain on 15th, 2.54 inches total 14th-16th; "no serious damage occurred."

1953   September 7. Hurricane Carol passed about 50 miles east; barometer 29.33 inches; wind 54 mi/h north; 1.77 inches rain.

1954   August 31. Hurricane Carol*

1954   September 11. Hurricane Edna*

1955   August 18-19. Ex-hurricane Diane moved along south shore of Long Island and over Nantucket on an east-northeast track; barometer 29.54 inches; wind 38 mi/h northwest; 2.50 inches rain, but 12.51 inches at Boston and 19.45 inches at Westfield, Massachusetts

1955   September 20. Ex-hurricane Ione; passed 175 miles southeast; barometer 29.58

inches; wind 31 mi/h northwest; 0.39 inch; "a brief but heavy squall passed quickly over."

1956   No tropical storms approached.

1957   No tropical storms approached.

1958   August 29. Hurricane Daisy passed about 65 miles southeast; barometer 29.56 inches; wind 42 mi/h north-northeast, gusts to 55 mi/h; 3.26 inches rain; "nothing more than a weak northeaster as far as Nantucket was concerned."

1959   July 11. Ex-hurricane Cindy moved over Nantucket about 7 a.m.; barometer 29.56 inches; wind 34 mi/h south; 1.54 inches rain; no mention in press.

1960   September 12. Hurricane Donna*

1961   September 21-25. Ex-hurricane Esther*

1962   August 29. Hurricane Alma became a tropical storm about 60 miles to the southeast; barometer 29.36 inches; wind 37 mi/h northwest; 2.74 inches rain on 29th, 0.36 inch on 30th; "damage on island was very light."

1963   October 29. Hurricane Ginny passed about 160 miles southeast; barometer 29.12 inches; 65 mi/h north, gust to 76 mi/h, average 32.6 mi/h; 2.55 inches rain on 29th, total 3.82 inches 28-30th; waves pounded Madaket, cutting 25 feet from sand bar and widening Broad Creek; "high winds and heavy rain inflicted little damage."

1964   September 23-24. Hurricane Gladys passed about 150 miles southeast; barometer 29.29 inches; little wind and no rain; considerable beach erosion from heavy surf.

1965   No tropical storms approached Nantucket.

1966   June 14. Tropical storm Alma dissipated over Rhode Island; its remnants drifted over Islands and Cape Cod; only 0.24 inch rain; "degenerated into a diffuse low pressure area."

1967   No tropical storms approached Nantucket.

1968   October 20. Hurricane Gladys passed about 250 miles southeast; wind 32 mi/h northwest; 1.59 inches rain.

1969   September 9. Hurricane Gerda passed about 60 miles southeast; barometer 29.94 inches; wind 40 mi/h north; Nantucket Shoals Lightship, 40 miles to southeast, reported wind gusts to 98 mi/h; an excessive rainfall of 5.06 inches in 24 hours was the heaviest from a hurricane this century; "Once again Nantucket was fortunate in escaping the brunt of a hurricane."

1970   No tropical storms approached Nantucket.

1971   September 14. Tropical storm Heidi, in a weakened condition, passed about 60 miles east; barometer 29.51 inches; wind 22 mi/h southeast; only 0.04 inch rain.

1972   September 2-3. Tropical storm Carrie*

1973   No tropical storms approached Nantucket.

1974   September 4. Tropical storm Dolly passed about 150 miles east; barometer 29.86 inches; wind gusts to 27 mi/h

1975   July 27-28. Hurricane Blanche passed about 150 miles east; barometer 29.83 inches; wind 24 mi/h west-southwest; no rain.

1976   August 9-10. Ex-hurricane Belle crossed Long Island near Jones Beach early on 10th; barometer 29.90 inches; wind 25 mi/h south-southwest, gust to 45 mi/h; no rain; "heavy swells sent massive 15-foot breakers on Nobadeer Beach ... surf changed the character of the beach, grading it smoothly from bank to surf"; called the "visitor who never arrived."

1977   No tropical storms approached Nantucket.

1978   No tropical storms approached Nantucket.

1979   September 6. Ex-hurricane David moved from central Pennsylvania to northern New England; barometer 29.48 inches; wind gusts to 40 mi/h south and southwest; 0.39 inch rain; all boat trips cancelled; "Nantucket came out pretty lucky again."

1979   September 14. Ex-hurricane Frederic, after smashing Mobile, Alabama, came north over Pennsylvania and Vermont a short distance west of David's track; barometer 29.69 inches; wind gust to 35 mi/h southwest; "All Nantucket got ... was about 0.25 inch of rainfall."

1980   No tropical storms approached Nantucket.

1981   No tropical storms approached Nantucket.

1982   No tropical storms approached Nantucket.

Hurricanes continue to reshape Nantucket's western end. Esther Island in left foreground was severed from the mainland during Hurricane Esther in September 1961; Smith's Point was severed from Nantucket as an aftermath of Hurricane Gloria in late September 1985. Photograph courtesy of Thomas Giffin.

1983   No tropical storms approached Nantucket.

1984   October 13-14. Hurricane Josephine moved north over the ocean to a position directly south of Nantucket at 71.5°W and 36.8°N, or about 270 miles from the island by noon October 14. Highest winds near the storm center were 85 mi/h. A continuation of this path would have brought the center of Josephine across the southeastern New England coast. However, after a short pause, the center moved southeast and then east-northeast away from the mainland. Winds on Nantucket increased on the 14th from about 35 mi/h to about 45 mi/h in the late afternoon when the barometer reached its lowest reading of 29.76 inches. Winds continued through the night at speeds from 30 to 40 mi/h and gradually backed to the north as Josephine passed well to the east.

SNOWSTORMS

A snowfall consists of myriads of minute ice crystals whose birthplace lies in the subfreezing strata of the middle and upper atmosphere when there is an adequate supply of moisture present. At the core of every ice crystal is a minuscule nucleus, a solid particle of matter of varying composition, around which moisture condenses and freezes. Liquid water droplets floating in the supercooled atmosphere and free ice crystals cannot coexist within the same cloud since the vapor pressure of molecules of ice is less than that of water molecules. This enables the ice crystal to rob the liquid droplets of their moisture and to grow continuously and rapidly by accretion, quickly creating larger ice crystals. Some of these larger crystals adhere to each other to create an aggregate of ice crystals or a snowflake. Simple flakes possess a variety of beautiful forms, usually hexagonal, though the symmetrical shapes reproduced in most photomicrographs are not found in actual snowfalls. Most snowflakes in a typical snowstorm consist of broken fragments and clusters of ice crystals.

For a snowfall to continue once it starts, there must be a constant inflow of moisture to feed the hungry condensation nuclei. This occurs when an airstream passes over a water surface and subsequently raises moisture to an upper level of the atmosphere. For Nantucket, the Atlantic Ocean is the chief source of water vapor for storms moving from the south, while the Gulf of Mexico serves as a secondary source for storms moving from the west.

The thermodynamics and hygrodynamics of large cyclonic storm systems govern snowmaking through the successive processes of warming, convection, cooling, condensation, and precipitation. In additon to general snowstorms, the lee shores of large bodies of water can initiate snowfalls when cool airstreams flow over warmer bodies of water. These produce the lake-effect snows that make the Great Lakes a famous snow belt, and the same process can produce a sea-effect snowfall along the lee shores of the Atlantic

Mitchell's Book Corner on Main Street after a heavy snowstorm. Photograph courtesy of H. Flint Ranney.

Ocean and its appendages such as Nantucket Sound and Cape Cod Bay. These falls may amount to only a few flakes, or a flurry, but on occasion they may amount to several inches, much to the consternation of forecasters and weather followers.

Many elements in the atmosphere must be brought together in the right proportion at the right time for a snowstorm to occur. The main ingredients are moisture and cold. There is an inflow of a moist airstream which must continue over a period of time with below-freezing conditions prevailing aloft. The airstream lifts the moist air so that precipitation can be initiated under freezing conditions.

A general snowstorm is an exceptional happenstance for Nantucket, due to its location and watery surroundings. Cold air must be borne to the scene from central or northern New England or from the cool waters off the Atlantic Provinces of Canada, and moisture must be borne to the scene on an easterly or northeasterly wind flow.

A genuine snowstorm with a continued fall of dry snowflakes is a rarity for the island. Most often the snow-lover is disappointed when a classic snowstorm turns either to wet snow or to rain, spoiling the winter scene and creating a sloppy mess of slush and slop. The reason for this is that warmer air is being advected to the area, either on the surface or in the upper air, and the process of producing dry snowflakes has become disordered. Nantucket's deepest snowfall in a single storm of 31.3 inches was of the dry-to-wet type, and after continual surface melting only 19.0 inches remained on the ground at the end of the storm. Nantucket's greatest snowstorm without melting took place in January 1905 when 21.5 inches fell under dry blizzard conditions of high winds and low temperatures and that amount remained on the ground at the end of the snowfall.

More so than a snowstorm, winter's worst menace to islanders is a freezing rain that coats all outside objects with an icy sheath known to meteorologists as glaze. With the island's almost complete dependence on electric power for heating, cooking, communications, and even entertainment, the disruption attending an ice storm can cause widespread discomfort and malaise. One may escape the effects of a big snowstorm by seeking shelter, but the chill and discomfort of an ice storm can make themselves felt indoors as well as outdoors.

Freezing rain occurs when water droplets fall from an above-freezing layer of air aloft through a shallow layer of below-freezing air at the surface of the earth. Upon impact or shortly thereafter the droplets freeze on all exposed objects, coating them with varying thicknesses of glaze ice. If the layer of cold air at the surface is deep, the rain droplets will freeze in their descent and form small ice pellets, known as sleet. Sometimes both sleet and freezing rain will occur at different times during one storm, congealing into an icy mass that covers the ground and all exposed objects. Despite the damage and inconvenience caused by an ice storm, it presents a most spectacular scene as the rays of the rising sun reveal thousands of beautiful spangles glinting on ice-coated trees and shrubs.

Though I would like to be the historian of every snowflake which has fallen on Nantucket during the past centuries, limitations imposed by editors and publishers will confine our study of snowstorms to the major ones of which we have record. During the present century Nantucket's snowstorms have occurred primarily in two clusters: from 1903 to 1916 and from 1950 to 1970, with a major storm in 1940. When the 1950s and 1960s came along, the island's snow-lovers were more than satisfied, particularly in the winter of 1960–61 when no less than three ranking snowstorms took place within a seven-week period.

Eighteenth Century

Great Storm and Tide of December 1786

The first snowstorm in Nantucket to be authentically recorded was the first of a series of three which fell within a week in early December 1786. Two major storms occurred on the 4th and 5th and on the 8th and 9th, with a minor fall on the 7th and 8th. The editor of the Boston *Independent Chronicle* wrote at the conclusion of these pre-winter snowstorms: "The quantity of snow is supposed to be greater, now, than has been seen in this country at any time since that which fell about 70 years ago, commonly termed the *great snow.*" The Great Snow of 1717 was reported to have left three feet at Boston and four to five feet to the north. No report of its depth on the Islands has been uncovered.

Reports from all over eastern New England during early December 1786 told of roads blocked with huge snowdrifts. A Boston paper estimated the depth as "nearly four feet deep upon a level." A diary keeper at Kingston on Plymouth Bay gave the same figure for snow at the end of the seven days of snowfalls.

By good chance, we have a reference to the snowstorm and its impact on Nantucket written by the hand of an islander. Kezia Coffin Fanning began a diary upon her marriage in 1776 and jotted down almost daily references to local happenings until 1820. Unfortunately only extracts made sometime in the 1870s survive, the original manuscript having been lost. But among these are several pertaining to the weather and historic storms. She wrote:

Dec. 5 — Wind extreme   Tide as high as ever known   Snowed very fast all day.

Dec. 6 — very pleasant overhead   a vast deal of snow has fallen   'tis said it has been a harder storm than has been known for a number of years   Vast deal of shipwreck among the vessels at the wharfs   the wharfs swept of everything   'tis said 150 cords of wood carried off the wharfs & it will take 2 Brazel Voyages to make up the loss the Island has sustained in stock and shipping.

Long Storm of November 1798

The long and severe winter of 1798–99 began on the morning of Saturday, the seventeenth of November, 1798, with one of the severest snow storms that has ever been known in New England.

On Sunday it became quite moderate, and for a time appeared to be clearing off, but when night came on the snow began to fall fast again, and the wind blew from the northeast with the force of a gale. The storm continued all day Monday and Tuesday and until the night of Wednesday [the 21st], when the weather cleared, the wind ceased to blow and the snow to fall.

The great quantity of snow that fell was unprecedented so early in the winter, and in but few instances had the settlers experienced such a snow storm during any part of the year. The mail carriers, or postboys, as they were called, were obliged to ride through fields for miles at a time, the roads being impassable in all parts of the country. The snow was so deep that in some places where highways had been shovelled out the banks of snow on both sides of the road were so high that men on horseback could not look over them. Many houses were so deeply buried in the snow that the families which lived in them found it very difficult to make an egress without tunnelling through the drifts.

Sidney Perley,
Historic Storms of New England, 1891.

The November 1798 storm also struck hard at sea, taking a human toll that would not be equaled until the Portland Storm of November 1898. Many vessels were wrecked on the shores of Cape Cod, as cemetery tombstones will testify. At least seven vessels went to pieces on that sandy promontory with the loss of all aboard, and the bodies of 25 sailors later were taken from bilged ships and buried ashore.

A Nantucket reference is found in Arthur Gardner's *Wrecks Around Nantucket:*

The winter of 1798–99 set in cold and blustering early, accompanied by a number of storms, in which many have suffered shipwreck, and two strangers were cast ashore at the back of Great Point.

Nineteenth Century

Great Snowstorm, February 1802

The winter of 1801–02 was very mild, the month of January being so warm that on the twenty-fourth, the ice on the Merrimack river began to move down the stream, and on the twenty-eighth at Salem, Mass., the thermometer indicated sixty degrees above zero. It was the warmest January that people remembered. There had been but little snow, and they congratulated themselves upon the pleasant winter and the prospect of an early spring.

On Sunday, the twenty-first of February, the aspect of the weather wholly changed. The first part of the day was remarkably pleasant, but the wind soon changed to the northeast, and a fierce snow storm came on. The storm continued for nearly a week, covering the earth with snow and sleet to the depth of several feet. Intense cold prevailed, which produced much suffering among all classes, and caused the sleet to freeze upon the snow, forming a crust so hard and thick that the people, not distinguishing the location of the roads, drove in their sleighs across lots over fences and walls.

Thus did Sidney Perley in *Historic Storms of New England* describe the series of northeasters which dropped a snow blanket of three feet and more in the hill country of central and eastern New England and spread havoc and destruction along the coastline.

The weather situation on the morning of February 21 was what is known as a "weather breeder" in Yankee dialect. At that very time a coastal storm was gathering energy as it swept northeast along the Carolina and Virginia coasts. Its progress was very swift. Dawn of the 22d found all southern and eastern New England locked in a furious northeast snowstorm. Without the benefit of modern weather forecasting and radio communication, three full-rigged Indiamen had sailed from Salem harbor under the sunny skies and fair weather on the 21st. The next day the rising storm caught the *Ulysses, Brutus,* and *Volusia* off Cape Cod where they were wrecked on the Truro shoals. The hulks were carried over the bar and onto the beach and the crews were able to scramble ashore, but found themselves on a snow-covered beach in near-zero temperature. During the following night the famished and frozen men wandered over the sand hills between Truro and Provincetown seeking shelter from the cruel elements. Of the fourteen-member crew of the *Brutus* only five survived that night.

A brief mention of this storm on Nantucket was made by the pen of an anonymous diarist which appeared in several New England newspapers several years later:

Jan. 30. More like spring than winter.
Feb. 22. A great snow storm with the heaviest

gale of wind known for many years.
Feb. 24. Weather very cold; harbor frozen up; stormy, cold weather ends the month.
Mar. 15. Cold snow storm all day; it is supposed 3,000 sheep have died during the late storms.

Big Storm, March 1806

The March storm in 1806 acquired a lasting reputation. In 1829 after a particularly heavy northeast snowstorm, the editor of the *Inquirer* thought it "to have been more violent than any other that has occurred since 1806."

Kezia Fanning took notice of this storm in her diary:

Monday. Mar. 24. Extreme winds at N.E. Storms abated toward eve. very racking works among the shipping at the wharf 'tis said such a storm has not been known for more than 20 years [1786?].

Arthur Gardner in *Wrecks Around Nantucket* wrote of a "heavy gale accompanied by snow." He listed the sloop *Julian* cast ashore on Great Point; a brig from Virginia anchored seven miles northeast of the Point with masts cut off, but never seen again; considerable damage in port; several vessels sunk, many otherwise injured; and the ship *Fame* just arrived from a Cape Horn voyage driven ashore southward of Great Point.

Three Snowstorms in the Severe Winter of 1829

Snow began in the afternoon of January 2, 1829, became heavy about 8:00 p.m., and continued all night. The barometer dropped to 29.54 inches by 10:00 p.m. on the morning of the 3d, Walter Folger's thermometer read 2°F at sunrise and climbed only to 9°F by noontime. The snowfall was the greatest for several years, according to the *Inquirer;* the 1820s were a notoriously snowless period in

southern New England. Sleighing took place on the island, "a rare occurrence on Nantucket," according to the editor.

A severe coastal storm struck on the afternoon of Friday, February 20, and continued to Saturday noon. It was said "to have been more violent than any other that has occurred since 1806," according to the *Inquirer.* Walter Folger's barometer dropped to 28.54 inches, a very low reading, and it may have been lower during the night than this 7:00 a.m. reading on the 21st. Rain was falling at 9:00 p.m. on the 21st with a southeast wind, but the next morning snow had taken over, and the wind was out of the northwest.

The *Inquirer* added to its article the opinion: "We believe no winter for the last twenty years has been so severe at Nantucket, as the present." Walter Folger's temperature records indicated that average temperatures in January 1829 were lower than normal by 0.7 degree and February by 4.1 degrees.

Walter Folger's meteorological log:

		7:00 a.m.	12:00	9:00 p.m.
Feb. 20	bar.	29.73″	29.65″	28.78″
	temp.	16°	24°	35°
	wind	NNW	SE	SE
	sky	cloudy	snow	rain
Feb. 21	bar.	28.64″	28.92″	29.37″
	temp.	24°	24°	24°
	wind	NW	WNW	WNW
	sky	snow	fair	fair

The month of March seldom leaves Nantucket without a return to winter, and so it was in 1829, as the *Inquirer* reported:

Storm & Shipwreck — On Sunday last [Mar. 22], a snow storm commenced about sunrise, and soon became very furious, and continued with unabated severity through the day and following evening. The quantity of snow had it fallen even, would probably have been more than a foot in depth; but owing to the violence of the wind, it was heaped up in prodigious drifts in many places, while others were swept clean and not a flake suffered to remain.

"The Great Snowstorm of January 1831"

This was "The Great Snowstorm" according to Samuel Hazard of Philadelphia, who published in his *Register of Pennsylvania* a collection of press notices for readers "some twenty or thirty years hence, when the next great storm occurs, to inform them when the like had happened." It rated as the greatest snowstorm of the nineteenth century along the entire Atlantic seaboard. Other great storms such as those of March 23, 1806, December 23–24, 1811, January 18–19, 1857, March 12–13, 1888, and February 11–14, 1899, may have been superior in limited areas with regard to sustained gales and excessive snowfalls, but none matched the January 1831 event in the grandeur of its physical structure or in the magnitude of energy as expended along the entire Atlantic coastal plain from the Gulf of Mexico to the Gulf of Maine. It produced the heaviest snowfall over the largest area of any storm during the century.

The impact of the great storm on southeast Massachusetts was well described by the *New Bedford Mercury:*

The storm of Saturday and Sunday last is without a parallel in the memory of the present generation; to find an equal, some of our sexagenarians carry us back to the winter of 1779–80 to what is called in this part of the country the Magee Storm . . . The oldest citizens of the town do not recollect any of so long continuance, or when such a quantity has fallen. Its duration was for thirty-six hours, from Saturday morning 15th till Sunday evening 16th. It is supposed the snow fell four feet deep on a level. During the first twelve or fifteen hours the wind was very high, and occasioned an uncommon high tide.

Samuel Rodman of New Bedford, who with his son carried on local weather observations for over ninety years, was on hand to record some of the meteorological details of the historic storm:

The quantity of snow noted on the 15th and 16th is not derived from actual measurement. The snow began about one half past 7 a.m. of the 15th and continued without cessation till toward the end of the 16th. The roads were blocked up for many days and drifts 10 or 12 feet high formed in some places — from the best information which I could obtain as to the depth on the average I judge that it was about three feet deep in the woods and applying the rule which my observations have heretofore suggested of taking the corresponding quantity of water as one tenth of that of snow I get the quantity noted in the column of rainfall (3.60 inches).

The storm raged on Nantucket for more than forty hours according to the weather log of Walter Folger, from before 7:00 a.m. on the 15th to after 9:00 p.m. on the 16th. Unfortunately, no actual measurement was recorded. The *Inquirer* merely stated a week later that "the snow has been and is still very deep here, with fine sleighing, and weather so cold that the harbor is closed beyond Brant Point." At 7:00 a.m. Folger's barometer read 29.06 inches, and may have been lower in the early hours of the 16th. The wind blew from the east-northeast all day on the 15th, and from the northeast all day on the 16th. The temperature hovered very close to 32 °F, a degree or two below on the 15th and a degree or two above on the 16th, so the snow pack must have been wet and heavy with some settling perhaps during the snowfall.

The *Inquirer* described the storm:

The weather — The advices which we have received from the continent, inform us of very heavy falls of snow, and of severe weather. — the Mails have been delayed several days in consequence of this, so that by the Hyannis Packet on Wednesday last [19th] we only received Saturday's mail. The snow has been and is still very deep here, with fine sleighing, and weather so cold that the harbor is closed beyond Brant Point.

Walter Folger, Jr., kept track of the meteorological details on Nantucket:

		7:00 a.m.	12:00	9:00 p.m.
Jan. 14	Temp.	17°	26°	25°
	Bar.	30.13″	30.09″	29.98″
	Wind	NNW	NE	ENE
	Sky	Fair	Fair	Cloudy
Jan. 15		30°	32°	32°
		29.57″	29.36″	29.12″
		ENE	ENE	ENE
		Snow	Snow	Snow
Jan. 16		33°	34°	32°
		29.06″	29.12″	29.35″
		NE	NE	NE
		Snow	Snow	Snow
Jan. 17		27°	28°	22°
		29.49″	29.45″	29.48″
		NNE	N	NNW
		Cloudy	Cloudy	Fair

Snow very deep — fine sleighing — harbor closed beyond Brant Point.

"The Most Violent Snowstorm . . . For more than 25 Years," 1846

On Sunday last [Feb. 15] we in Nantucket were visited by the most violent snowstorm which has been experienced here for more than 25 years. It commenced snowing about daybreak, and continued without intermission throughout the whole day and evening. Nearly all church-going was intercepted, and none but the most zealous and hardy were induced to leave their comfortable firesides to breast the tempest. The snow is so badly drifted, however, as to prevent the gay ones from enjoying it by way of sleighriding. We are indebted to our Friend Hon. Wm. Mitchell, for the following barometrical account of the day:

2d mo. 14 at 11 p.m.
Barometer 29.90; calm
2d mo. 15,

7:30 a.m.	Bar. 29.33″ High wind at East
12:00 noon	29.12″ E. by N.
1:00 p.m.	29.03″ E.N.E.
2:30 p.m.	29.03″ N.E.
3:30 p.m.	29.04″ N.E.

Quoted from the *Nantucket Inquirer* in the *New York Herald,* February 23, 1846. The files of the *Inquirer* for 1846 are missing from the Atheneum.

"Furious Snowstorm, February 1855

A memorable cold snap descended on New England from February 5 to 7, 1855, and departed as a severe snowstorm engulfed the region. In Vermont, thermometers dropped to the lowest point in 45 years with readings below –40 °F, and in southern New England February 6 was one of the bitterest days of record with the mercury remaining below zero all day. The readings on Samuel Rodman's thermometer at New Bedford indicate the severity of the day along coastal Massachusetts: 7:00 a.m., –3.5 °F; 2:00 p.m, –6 °F; and 9:00 p.m., –14 °F.

Out at Nantucket the severe airmass made itself felt with more modified readings as the result of the passage of the frigid airstream over open water. The Smithsonian instrument of Hon. William Mitchell was down to 4 °F at 9:00 p.m. on the 6th, but the absolute minimum was not in his records. The *Inquirer's* reading ran lower, down to a minimum of –2 °F at an unspecified time, probably on the 7th.

A major snowstorm followed on the heels of the cold wave, apparently spawned along the southern edge of the cold air mass. Over southern New England depths were quite uniform. Both Providence and Boston reported 14 inches. Out on the Islands and the Cape the storm raged more furiously. Both the *Vineyard Gazette* and the *Inquirer* declared the storm the worst in thirty years, though they were probably referring to the Great Snowstorm of January 1831, with a journalist's often lack of historic and arithmetic accuracy.

Snow began to fall on Nantucket about 6:00 p.m. on the 7th and continued until 5:00 p.m on the 9th. A depth of 18 inches fell and the melted precipitation amounted to the equivalent of 1.50 inches. The *Inquirer* estimated the depth at two feet on the level, "more than has fallen before at one time for 30 years, it is said." So furious was the storm that the Atheneum did not open, though Maria Mitchell, the librarian, did make her usual weather observation: barometer 29.50 inches, thermometer about 29°F, wind east-northeast, and "snow great."

William Mitchell's thermometer at home indicated readings close to freezing during all but the latter stages of the storm when they commenced to drop into the middle 20s.

Just a month later another major snowstorm hit. The *Inquirer* gave an adequate description. It started as rain about midnight on Friday, March 9, and soon turned to snow:

. . . it was very damp, and of course much of it melted as fast as it fell. — The previous rain which had made the streets very wet also aided very much in dispersing the snow, so that the whole amount must otherwise have been considerably greater, probably not much less than three and a half feet. Taken as a whole, it may safely be regarded as an "old fashioned snow storm."

William Mitchell's rain gauge caught 1.62 inches on the 8th and 2.22 inches on the 9th for a total of 3.84 inches, a very large amount for a winter storm, though about equal to that on March 3–5, 1960. His notes contained the following: "Horrid storm throughout last night and through the day," and "dreadful, snowing, raging storm . . . 2 feet deep."

At the conclusion of the storm, Maria Mitchell painted a scene of Nantucket's snow-clogged streets. When entered later in the year in a contest for local paintings at Nantucket's first county fair, it won first prize.

Great "Cold Storm," January 1857

"The fury of this storm has been unequalled for many years. Never since the establishment of railroads has there been such an interruption of travel or hindrance to the mails." This was the judgment of Lieutenant Matthew Fontaine Maury, U.S.N., the pioneer hydrographer of the United States. He had set for himself the task of compiling an on-the-spot account of the "Great Storm of 1857," as it was called in Virginia. In New Jersey it was named the "Cold Storm" from the combined heavy snowfall, zero temperatures, and whole gale winds. The term "blizzard" had not yet been applied to a meteorological phenomenon. In New England the storm was long remembered for the complete paralysis of transportation on land, shipwrecks at sea, and structural damage caused by what one editor described as a "winter hurricane." This was the great storm of the mid-century: a worthy companion to the earlier Great Snowstorm of 1831 and the later February Blizzard of 1899.

As the storm system drove rapidly northeast from its birthplace in the Gulf of Mexico, the precipitation changed to snow in the Carolinas. Snowflakes began to fall about daybreak of January 18 in the Chesapeake Bay area, at "breakfast" in Washington, D.C., at noon in Delaware and southern New Jersey, at 1:00 p.m. in the Philadelphia area, at 2:00 p.m in New York City, at 7:00 p.m. in Boston, and at 10:00 p.m. in Portland Maine.

The impact of the storm along the coast of southern New England was carefully noted by veteran weather observers in Providence and New Bedford. Professor Alexis Caswell of Brown University witnessed "a storm of extreme severity" from late afternoon on the 18th until almost noon on the 19th. He thought about 18 inches fell, but drifting prevented an accurate measurement. At New Bedford, Samuel Rodman described "the most severe gale & snow storm for many years."

His thermometer rose from a low of –9°F at sunrise on the 18th to a noon reading of –3°. Snow began to fall at 5:00 p.m., and by 9:00 p.m. a northeast gale was raging and the temperature had risen rapidly to 11.5° as the wind shifted seaward.

On Cape Cod, the tower of a new Catholic church at Sandwich was blown over. Drifts on the tracks of the Cape Cod Railroad were said to have been 18 feet deep and some of them 100 feet in length. All communication with Boston by rail was severed for ten days. "Old people assert that such a succession of severe snowstorms have been unprecedented for the past forty years," declared the *Yarmouth Register*. So furiously did the gale turn the windmill on the Cape Cod property of Stephen Smith that the moving parts caught fire and the entire structure was consumed by flames at the height of the storm. At Provincetown it was the greatest wind storm in many years, probably since the October Gale of 1841, with all but three of a fleet of 20 ships driven high on the beaches.

The *Inquirer* carried a notice of the storm:

A severe gale from the NE accompanied with snow, commenced here on Sunday afternoon [18th] and continued throughout the night and exceeded in violence any storm experienced here for several years . . . Our streets on Monday morning were impassable . . . The ice in the Sound being very hard was not much affected by the storm.

A study of William Mitchell's weather log supplies a key to some of the peculiarities of the storm and definitely establishes the fact that the barometric center moved close, but slightly to the southeast, of the island. Mitchell reported that the wind was at its greatest strength at about 3:30 a.m. on the 19th. At 8:30 a.m., there was calm in town accompanied by considerable fogginess, though the roar of wind and wave on the south shore of the island could be distinctly heard.

Similar lulls during the storm were reported at Sag Harbor near the tip of Long Island about 120 miles to the west where the sun broke through for an hour and a half, and later at Boston, 80 miles to the north, where the snow stopped and the sky became partly clear in the early afternoon. These lulls, quite unusual in a winter storm, point to a vast expansion of the central core. This caused an "eye" condition to develop and permitted the sun to break through as the slow-moving center drifted over southeast New England. The relatively warm temperature of 38.5 °F at Nantucket at 2:00 p.m. and the very light winds indicated the near proximity of the calm center of the disturbance.

Mitchell's thrice daily observations on these days:

		7:00 a.m.	2:00 p.m.	9:00 p.m.
Jan. 18	Temp.	8°	16°	20°
	Bar.	30.33"	30.18"	29.97"
	Wind	NNE 6	NE 7	NE 8
	Sky	Snow	Snow	Snow
Jan. 19		33°	38.5°	26°
		29.01"	29.14"	29.16"
		NE 5	NW 1	NNW 7
		Cloudy	Snow	Snow

Hardest wind at 3:30 a.m. At 8:30 a.m., calm and fog, though roaring at the south [beach]. Observatory much damage.

The numbers following the notations of wind direction are derived from Beaufort Scale, with 0 equal to calm, and 10 to hurricane, and 12 to severe hurricane.

The Snowless Period: 1858 to 1898

For nearly forty years, from 1857 to 1898, Nantucket winters were noteworthy for the lack of very deep snowstorms. There were severe northeasters with very high winds, but they seem to have been accompanied mostly by rain and not snow. Though we have no authentic records until the establishment of the Weather Bureau on the island in 1886, the newspapers of the day carry no accounts of storms such as those of the mid-1850s. This snowless period of the late nineteenth century was matched by a similar lack of snow during the early twentieth century, from 1911 to 1951.

Non-Blizzard of '88

The Blizzard of '88 stands unique in the storm annals of the northeast corner of the United States. No other atmospheric disturbance has brought together in such extreme degree the combination of deep snowfall, gale-force winds, and bitter cold, the three ingredients of an eastern blizzard. The late-winter storm, coming only ten days before the spring equinox, claimed over 400 victims on land and sea as it raged east of the Appalachian Mountains from North Carolina to the Atlantic Provinces of Canada and out over the ocean for hundreds of miles.

Yet on Nantucket and over extreme southeast Massachusetts, it was a non-blizzard: temperatures remained above freezing during the heavy precipitation, so rain fell instead of snow; and the wind, though of gale force at times, came from a southerly quarter and not the direction from which Old Boreas usually rages. Nantucket received only two inches of snow, and that only as an aftermath once the battling elements had settled down and ceased their turmoil. Little damage resulted on the island beyond what usually occurs during a moderately hard blow.

The meteorological events of March 1888 presented a classic example of Nantucket Island's unique position in the atmospheric geography of North America. The convulsion of the elements over the Northeast at that time was caused by atmospheric forces lying many hundreds of miles distant from the scene where the final action took place.

A cold air mass resided over the Great Lakes which fed the necessary frigidity into the developing storm system along the Atlantic Coast. Contrasting airstreams over the Southeast developed the cyclonic circulation that gave birth to the storm system. A great reservoir of warm, moist air over the sub-tropical Atlantic Ocean supplied the moisture required for heavy precipitation. A vast anticyclone to the northeast over the Atlantic Provinces of Canada slowed the northward progress of the developing storm center along the Carolina coast and caused the normal north-south axis of a low pressure system to swing into a west-east axis, an orientation that resulted in greatly increased precipitation over New England and New York than normally occurs with a coastal storm.

On Nantucket the barometer fell steadily all day on Sunday, March 11, from the relatively high reading of 30.38 inches, to 29.70 inches at 8:00 a.m. on the 12th. The wind blew out of the southeast at 25 miles per hour. The thermometer stood five degrees above freezing at 37 °F. At this hour the New York temperature read 22 °F with a very dry snow being blown by gales in blizzard fashion, and at Boston the reading was 35 °F with rain about to change to a wet snow.

Heavy rain began to fall at Nantucket at 7:05 a.m. on the 12th. A high southeast wind raged all day, peaking at 43 miles per hour. The temperature rose to 43 °F in the afternoon. The gale out of the southeast diminished by 6:00 a.m. on the 13th, about the time the barometer reached its lowest reading of 28.93 inches on the island. The wind soon shifted to the south bringing with it the cold airstream that had left the continent on the Middle Atlantic coast. By circling south of the storm center over Rhode Island Sound it reached Nantucket. The wind dropped to only 11 miles per hour at 9:00 p.m. and a heavy fog settled over the harbor.

During the night of the 12–13th, the temperature fell to 19 °F, under the continued advection of cold air arriving on the wings of a south wind blowing at 23 miles per hour. At New York City the temperature was much colder at 6 °F and at Boston, warmer at 24 °F. The barometer recovered by 7:00 a.m. to 29.07 inches, and continued to rise all day. The wind remained in the south and the temperature stayed in the 20s, rising as high as 28 °F by evening. A light snow continued all day, but with an accumulation of only 1.3

inches. The wind dropped below storm force at 1:30 p.m., and the three-day blow was over.

The *Inquirer and Mirror* devoted a good deal of space to the details of the storm on the island:

The Weather— If ever the weather was fickle, it was early the present week, when it assumed a variety of aspects. Sunday, for the greater part of the day, heavy clouds betokened an approaching storm which developed into a rain storm and howling southeast gale the following day. The wind at 4 p.m. attained the greatest velocity reached since the establishment of the signal station — 80 [62 corrected] miles per hour, and strong trees bent and large buildings trembled before the violence of the whispering blasts. The scene about the harbor and along the south shore of the island was one of grandeur, the huge billows at the latter point dashing heavily at the base of the bluffs with terrible roar, breaking away the heavy fill on the railroad track at Nobadeer, and tumbling the rails inshore, while at Madequecham the water found its way well up into the valley. The harbor scene was one of great tumult on a smaller scale. The weak parts of the several piers were sadly wrecked, and the railroad bulkhead across the head of the steamboat dock also suffered from the inroads of the seas, being at times submerged. This furious state of the weather lasted but a brief time, however; but it caused in that period some slight damage about town, blowing the walks from the roofs of the houses of Thomas B. Field, Esq., and Mr. Henry H. Crocker, demolishing them sadly. A chimney on the Town Hall was blown over, necessitating dismissing the school held in the building until damages could be repaired. The car houses of the Nantucket Railroad company were flooded during the high tide, necessitating running the rolling stock out to prevent damage thereto. A portion of the roof of the barn at the farm of Charles G.S. Austin was blown off and numerous chimneys on buildings about town were more or less demoralized, while weak fences were

prostrated and stout ones strained by the fitful blasts.

Tuesday morning developed a change, the mercury having dropped to 24°, with a slight snow falling. The wind still blew from the southeast, and the day was cold and cheerless, with frequent flights of snow and a strong breeze. Again on Wednesday a clouded sky, with light snow, was the morning greeting, but warmer weather followed, carrying away the little snow remaining on the ground.

Great Eastern Blizzard of February 1899

The Great Arctic Outbreak just prior to midmonth of February 1899 stands preeminent in the history of American weather events for its energy, degree of severity, and extent of influence. Propelled by a massive anticylone of a record magnitude of 31.42 inches over the Prairie Provinces of Canada, the most frigid airstream ever to descend into the latitudes of the United States in recorded meteorological history carried below-zero temperatures to every state east of the Rocky Mountains. Even Florida was affected; the all-time low reading for the Sunshine State was recorded at Tallahassee: −2°F.

Upon reaching the warm waters of the Gulf of Mexico, the cold air flow lost its momentum and the advancing front slowed its forward progress and eventually stalled over the Gulf. Along this stationary front, stretching from the lower Texas coast northeast and east to south-central Florida, two waves developed along the front and gradually organized into cyclonic circulations. They set into motion deep southerly currents of warm, humid, tropical airmasses from the southern Gulf of Mexico and the Caribbean Sea south of Cuba. These glided up over the very cold air hugging the surface of the northern Gulf waters and the adjacent coastal plain. All of the South, with the exception of extreme south Florida, was treated to a rare snowstorm. Snow fell in an arc that reached

from southeast Texas to Florida. As much as 3.0 inches whitened the coastline of Florida's panhandle near Pensacola.

By the morning of the 11th, the first disturbance advanced northeast to a position off the coast of Georgia, while the second was crossing the central part of the Gulf of Mexico. The cyclonic action of the dual centers now drew on Atlantic Ocean moisture rapidly causing precipitation northward along the Atlantic coastal plain. The snowfall reached southern New Jersey at 7:45 p.m. on the 11th and Boston at 8:45 a.m. on the 12th. On that morning the first storm center had moved to the latitude of Norfolk, Virginia, while the second was still developing in the Gulf of Mexico south of Pensacola. During this day, a Sunday, very heavy snowfall at the rate of an inch an hour developed over the Middle Atlantic region and spread into southern New England as the first storm center stalled for a few hours south of Long Island, in an ideal position to supply Atlantic Ocean moisture for snowmaking all over the Northeast.

The northern center increased its barometric depth while maintaining a trough of low pressure to the south through which the second center advanced northeast. By the morning of the 14th, the system had consolidated somewhat with the main center, at about 28.90 inches, a short distance east of Boston and the second center near Cape Hatteras.

Earlier, the arctic airstreams from the northwest had arrived in southern New England late on the 8th, following the northeast passage of a coastal disturbance which had dropped 7.8 inches of snow on Nantucket. This fell on top of the 8.5 inches remaining from two lesser storms in the month. Temperatures tumbled to readings of 6°, 4°, and 2°F on the mornings of the 9th, 10th, and 11th. The 10th was one of the bitterest days in Nantucket's history with the thermometer climbing from a morning low of 4° to a high of only 8° in the afternoon. This was the frigid situation on the island as the storm threat from the south approached.

The *Inquirer and Mirror* reported on the ice

conditions that resulted from the cold wave on February 9th to 11th, and then described the snowstorm of the next two days:

Sunday [the 12th] followed with a heavy snow storm with the temperature ranging about 24°. There was but little wind until late in the evening, when it breezed from the northeast and a smothering snow storm raged during the night, continuing with increasing fury all day Monday, with blinding clouds of snow and hail, which drifted in huge piles, rendering locomotion anything but pleasant. There was no let-up in the fierceness of the storm, which in intensity and duration, exceeded anything we can recall. The mercury held at a point between 20° and 26° most of the day, but by 5:30 p.m. had risen to 29°. Suddenly at about that hour the wind ceased and but little snow fell. The barometer, which had registered 29 most of the day, commenced to rise, and rapidly ran up one-tenth and there halted. It then dropped back rapidly to 28.85, and after playing about that point for a few moments, continued to drop until it touched the lowest point we have ever seen it record — 28.56. To the weather sharp this was ominous of a westerly gale with cold, and he was not to be disappointed. At 9 p.m. it was almost calm, and the mercury registered at the freezing point, rising slowly until 11 o'clock, when the record was 34°, and the wind had swung into the southwest. At 11:30 the wind swung into the northwest with a roar, and blew fitfully, attaining a velocity of 45 miles, with an extreme of 50 miles. The mercury dropped quickly, and at 3:00 a.m. recorded 14° where it remained until 8:00 a.m. Tuesday, when it rose gradually.

The wind continued to blow freshly from the northwest, but the clouds had dispersed and the sun shone on a scene of grandeur. Bell-ringer Hall, from the tower lookout, descried seven unfortunate vessels in the ice off Tuckernuck and Muskeget, one, a small craft, being reported from the Great Neck Station as being off Eel Point, while a large three-masted schooner evidently stranded on Swile island shoal, displayed distress signals.

It was impossible for the life savers to reach the poor fellows.

Lowest barometer: 28.90 inches on evening of 13th.
Highest wind: 41 miles per hour on 13th.

Snow fell from 2:30 a.m. on the 12th to 9:30 a.m. on the 13th; then sleet (ice pellets) from 9:30 a.m. to 9:10 p.m. on the 13th. The snow depth on the 11th measured 8.3 inches. On the 12th, 6.6 inches of new snow fell, and on the 13th, 7.0 inches — a storm total of 13.6 inches. The maximum depth on the ground was measured on the evening of the 13th at 21.9 inches. At least an inch remained on the ground until February 22.

Twentieth Century

Big Ten Snowstorms of the Twentieth Century
(measured in inches of snowfall)

1. 1905	January 25–26	21.4
2. 1952	February 27–28	20.1
3. 1964	January 13–14	19.2
4. 1960	March 3–5	19.0
5. 1910	January 14–15	16.4
6. 1961	January 19–20	16.0
7. 1951	February 3–4	15.9
8. 1960	December 11–12	15.7
9. 1963	December 18–19	15.1
10. 1904	January 2–3	14.6

Greatest in 24 hours:
 20.1, February 27–28, 1952
Greatest single month:
 40.2, March 1960
Greatest single season:
 82.0, 1903–04
Greatest depth on ground:
 23.0, February 28, 1952

During the snowfall of March 3–5, 1960, much melting and settling occurred, the depth never amounting to more than 19.0 inches; but the weather bureau observers judged that 31.3 inches had fallen by adding together all of the six-hour measurements. The storm on January 25–26, 1905, consisted of dry snowflakes with no melting taking place, while that on February 27–28, 1952, was a wet snow with some settling of the snow pack. Therefore, the 1905 storm should be considered Nantucket's greatest snowstorm of the twentieth century.

Blizzard of Early January 1904

"It is a long time since Nantucket has been visited by a blizzard of the magnitude of that of Sunday [Jan.3], when the wind howled, hurling the snow in smothering clouds and making outdoor life unbearable," declared the editor of the *Inquirer and Mirror*. "Between 8:15 and 9:15 a.m. the wind blew continuously at the rate of 47 miles per hour, and gave Mr. Grimes' anemometer a continuous whirl. The amount of snow on the ground at 8 p.m Sunday the weather bureau office records as 16 inches."

The snowstorm on January 2–3, 1904, dropped 14.6 inches of snow. This was the highlight of a wintry fortnight on the island with an introductory snowfall of 6.4 inches on December 26–27 and cold wave preview which dropped the mercury to 8°F at the tail end of the storm.

The big storm at the opening of January was first charted in the Oklahoma area on New Year's morning. Taking a more northerly route than other such storms, it headed east-northeast on a Fort Smith, Arkansas, Lexingtion, Kentucky, Cape May, New Jersey track. Pressure at the latter station where the storm center met ocean influences measured 29.54 inches. Since no blocking high pressure stood to the north or northeast, the storm center turned northeast and deepened gradually as it continued at a fast pace. When passing Nantucket at dawn on January 3, the barometer on the island dropped to 29.31 inches.

The island was still covered with about one inch of snow from the post-Christmas storm as the new snow arrived. This time Nantucket was in the heavy snow zone which usually lies about 125 to 150 miles to the northwest of the storm center's path.

When melted for measurement the precipitation amounted to 0.65 inch on Saturday and 1.08 inches on Sunday, for a storm total of 1.73 inches. The 14.6 inches of snow measured during the storm raised the depth on the ground to 16.0 inches, then a record for weather bureau figures on the island since 1886–87. Blizzard conditions prevailed during the latter stages of the storm.

The temperature followed the pattern of a week before by dropping sharply during the concluding phases of the snowfall. It fell to 7°F by 3:00 p.m. on Sunday afternoon, and then reached a low of 2° at 11:00 p.m. on Monday morning when the core of the cold wave was over the island. These low temperatures froze the harbor and caused an "Ice Embargo," preventing the steamer from leaving for the mainland until a week later on Monday, the 11th.

The 16.0 inches of snow on the ground was augmented by a fall of 8.2 inches on the 9th, raising the cover to 17.2 inches, a new record. Another 2.2 inches fell on the 20th and 21st, but by then warm weather had already reduced the depth to 3.2 inches. After a week of bare ground it snowed again from February 1 to 6 and 11 to 21, yielding a record 46 days of snow cover for the 1903–04 season. The January snowfall total of 32.4 inches established an all-time record for any month and the 82.0 inches total for the 1903–04 season still stands as the seasonal record for Nantucket.

Nantucket's Worst Blizzard, January 1905

"The most severe storms of the month were those of the 3d–4th, 6–7th, and 24–25th. The last-named one was the worst for several years on account of the very low temperature and the winds of hurricane force that attended it. Several persons are known to have perished from the cold, at least fifteen vessels were driven ashore by the violent winds, and the damage to property along the beach from the wind and high water amounted to thousands of dollars. The heavy snow drifts caused by the storm were from three to eight feet deep in some places, while in others there was bare ground," summarized the New England climatologist about one of the greatest snowstorms ever experienced by Cape Cod and the Islands.

The storm center took an unusual course in reaching the New England offshore waters. It first appeared as a weak low pressure area over Lake Superior on the evening of January 23. Though no blocking anticyclone was present to the east or northeast, the storm center headed southeast and arrived on the morning of January 25 in the vicinity of Atlantic City, New Jersey, where the pressure dropped to 29.34 inches. There it joined with a developing coastal low and turned to the northeast. By evening the center lay off Cape Cod, as indicated by the Nantucket barometer reading of 29.23 inches.

Nantucket and the Cape shared the brunt of the savage storm. On the island light snow falling with a southeast wind gave way soon before midnight to "a howling gale and blinding snow" from the northeast. The snowfall on the 25th amounted to a record 24-hour fall of 17.8 inches, to which was added another 3.6 inches next morning, for a storm total of 21.4 inches. The temperature during the snowfall period remained close to 26°F, but toward the conclusion on the morning of the 26th dropped to a low of 11.7°F.

With moderate snow falling during the morning of the 25th, the wind averaged 43 miles per hour and sustained peak speeds above 45 miles each hour during the 24 hours. A maximum of 54 miles was clocked at 11:10 a.m.

For three hours after noontime the snow fell heavily at a rate of 2 inches per hour, and then dropped to a more moderate rate of 1 inch per hour. The snow tapered off soon after midnight and ceased by 2:00 a.m. of the 26th.

Since the moon had been full on January 21, the tides were already running high without a storm and its northeast gales. "Have seen nobody who recalls a time when the tide reached such a height," declared the editor of the *Inquirer and Mirror*. The normal tide augmented by the storm tide rose to 7.4 feet above low water and inundated every wharf around the harbor. On the oceanfront of the island, "the topography was considerably changed" at Wauwinet where some cottages were carried 200 yards from their foundations.

The steamer *Nantucket* did not leave her berth on the 25th, and the steamer *Georgetown* went ashore on the south side of Great Point. The telegraph line carrying weather messages became grounded.

George E. Grimes of the United States Weather Bureau declared that the "storm was the most severe in the history of the station, although no serious damage was reported, and no marine disasters, except to local shipping."

Wind, Snow, and Tide on January 24–25, 1908

The "worst storm" in Weather Bureau records occurred on January 24–25, 1908, surpassing that of 1905, in the opinion of observer George E. Grimes when writing in 1938. It was a northeaster of the severest type with the wind averaging 41 miles per hour for the 24 hours of the 24th. A peak wind sustained for five minutes averaged 50 miles and a one-minute sustained speed of 73 miles occurred at 7:31 a.m. on the 24th at the height of the blow. Gale-force winds began at 6:15 p.m on Thursday, the 24th, and continued for over 21 hours until 3:41 p.m. on the following afternoon.

The snowfall began at 12:20 a.m. on the 24th and ended at 4:45 a.m. on the 25th. Eight inches fell on the 24th and another 2.9 inches on the 25th, for a storm total of 10.9 inches. Temperatures remained just low enough to keep the precipitation all snow, ranging from 34° to 27°F on the 24th, and from 31° to 22°F on the 25th. On the next day the thermometer soared to 42°F and melted much of the snow.

The barometer fell to a low of 29.11 inches when the storm center offshore was at its greatest development in the latitude of Nantucket.

The most damaging aspect of the storm was the extremely high tide, even though the moon was six days past full. Observer Grimes described the scene:

During the great storm of 1908, an unprecedented sea was raised in the harbor, which is open to a northeaster. A tide some seven feet above the normal swept the wharves, inundating the wharf streets for some distance. The small craft tied up between Old South and Commercial wharves suffered great damage.

The editor of the *Inquirer and Mirror* supplied additional details of the effects of the raging ocean:

The heavy storm of last week made great inroads in the south shore of the island between Surfside life saving station and Nobadeer, and the configuration of the shore line for several miles has been greatly changed. For 20 hours surf heavier than at any time in last 25 years. Bank eaten away 25 feet in some places. Surfside life savers said only once before sometime in the 1880s did they experience such a storm.

Big Snowstorm of January 1910

The forty-hour snow and wind storm on January 14–15, 1910, made a distinct impression on the islanders. "One of the worst snow storms in memory of the present

Snow piles along the sidewalks of Lower Main Street looking toward the Pacific National Bank, 1912. Collection of the Nantucket Historical Association.

generation," declared the *Inquirer and Mirror,* and then continued, "A blizzard which was undoubtedly the worst Nantucket has experienced for many years. In fact, it is said it closely resembled the blizzard of 1898 — the year the steamer *Portland* was lost — but some folks claim the storm hereabouts was even worse than on that memorable date."

Despite the contemporary opinion, the January Snowstorm of 1910 bore no resemblance to the Great Storm of November 1898. The genesis of the 1910 storm lay in the Texas panhandle area. Instead of taking the usual loop southeast into the Gulf of Mexico, the storm system sped east-northeast on a Kansas City, Missouri, Columbus, Ohio, Cape May, New Jersey path. With pressure on the New Jersey coast down to 30.02 inches on the evening of the 14th, the storm did not

appear very dangerous, but a great development took place overnight. Next morning the center was located about 75 miles southeast of Nantucket where the barometer reached a minimum of 29.24 inches.

The heaviest precipitation fell on the 14th when 1.07 inches of melted snow were measured, and another 0.50 inch was added on the 15th. Total snowfall amounted to 16.4 inches, and at the end of the storm the total on the ground had increased to 17.3 inches.

Temperatures remained in the maximum snowmaking range, from 33° to 29°F, throughout the snowfall. On the 16th, the thermometer soared to 45°, as it often does when south or southwest onshore winds prevail, and much of the snow melted.

Christmas Eve Snowstorm, 1912

Nantucket's whitest Christmas came as the aftermath of a heavy snowstorm on December 24, 1912. Flakes began to fall at 4:15 a.m. and kept up until 8:20 p.m. when 8.7 inches covered the ground.

"The storm was severe, the moist snow clung to the wires and poles which were snapped like pipe stems. All wires down by 8:00 p.m.," declared the weather bureau observer.

Northeast winds picked up gradually during the morning, reaching gale force at about 11:00 a.m. The peak speed of 38 miles per hour was reached at 2:45 p.m. The average for the day came to 28.6 miles.

The barometer dropped to 29.59 inches at 4:00 p.m. and the wind soon shifted from northeast to north. The temperature had been up to 34°F at 11:00 a.m., making the snow very moist, but dropped to 28°F by 9:00 p.m.

Christmas Day was clear and sunny with the temperature running up to 34°F. Many sleighs appeared on Main Street, but such sport was short-lived as the snow melted rapidly the next day and was gone by the 27th.

Wet, Clinging Snow,
March 26–27, 1933

It was the worst storm of this character that Nantucket has experienced since the heavy snowfall of April 9,1917, which was recorded as the worst wet-snow storm since the Weather Bureau station was established in 1886. There have been many storms with greater wind velocity and with heavier snowfall during the last 45 years, but the storm on Sunday [March 26] did more actual damage to telephone and electric light lines than any storm heretofore.

George E. Grimes of the Weather Bureau, in a summary of severe winter storms on the island presented the details:

Northeast storm began at 12:33 p.m. on the 26th and ended at 4:36 a.m. on the 27th. Storm was accompanied by heavy, moist snow and during late evening it began to cling to the wires and by 8:00 p.m. all wires to mainland were down. The snow was unusually moist with large flakes which froze and accumulated. On the morning of the 27th some wires were 1½ inches in diameter and several thousand dollars damage was done. The piazza roof [of the weather station] over the upper piazza crashed when a large bunch of snow slid from the main roof. When the roof left the house, a piece of timber smashed through the storm window.

The 5.6 inches of snow that remained at the end of the storm would have amounted to 13.1 inches if not for the concluding rain which melted down most of it.

The wind mounted to 45 miles per hour on the 26th and blew down all the wires leading to the cable connecting the island with the mainland. The total damage was estimated at $20–25,000 by the *Inquirer and Mirror*.

Coastal Storm,
January 23, 1935

A moderate snow storm on the 13–14th was followed by further snows, so that the ground remained covered during the remainder of the month. A coastal storm on the 23d was attended by deep snow over nearly all portions of the Section except Vermont and northern New Hampshire. This storm caused considerable interruption to traffic, principally on account of the rapid rate of fall, which exceeded, in most instances, snow removal equipment capacity. The accumulated snow depths varied from some 10 to 14 inches in about ten hours, and these amounts were not record-breaking. The demands of motorized traffic, however, for cleared roads and streets, resulted in the storm being the cause of great expense for snow-removal.

New England climatologist.

Snow and sleet began to fall on Nantucket at 6:10 a.m. on January 23 and continued at a light intensity all morning. After noon the snow fell at a rate of an inch an hour, for about nine hours. By 7:45 p.m., ten inches lay on the ground and this increased during the late evening to 13.6 inches. The temperature varied during the storm from 30°F to 32°F. Wind came out of the northeast at an average hourly rate of 29.8 miles. An extreme speed of 56 miles occurred at 10:23 p.m. Gale-force winds continued on the 24th until 7:19 a.m. when a shift from north to northwest took place.

Under the heading, "Severe 'Sleet Storm' Sweeps Across Nantucket," the *Inquirer and Mirror* described local conditions:

The severe storm which visited New England on Wednesday this week [Jan. 23] had its effect on Nantucket. Whereas the mainland got more snow, the storm as experienced on this island was recorded by the Weather Bureau as a 'sleet storm' — that is, it was for the greater part frozen rain [ice

pellets]. As a result the accumulation on the ground was not as great as though it had been all snow. The amount of recorded precipitation was 1.12 inches, according to the government record.

Sleet has a much larger water content than snow, and as the storm was mostly sleet on Nantucket, it probably did not accumulate to much more than 6 inches on a level, although recording a total of 11.2 inches.

The wind was from the northeast and was at its worst about 10:30 Wednesday evening, when a velocity of 55 miles an hour was recorded, with an extreme of 61 miles. All day the temperature had ranged from 30 to 32 degrees and the conditions were decidedly uncomfortable, with the sleet driving and cutting fiercely for hours.

Owing to the fact that it was sleet and not frozen snow, there was comparatively little damage done to telephone and electric wires, although Wednesday evening the current was cut off for a moment or two several times. Had the storm brought wet snow to freeze with the lowering temperature, there would have unquestionably been a large amount of wire damage all over the island.

Valentine's Day Storm, 1940

In the memory of many old time residents of eastern Massachusetts, the storm on St. Valentine's Day in 1940 earned a reputation for viciousness unequalled by any other of their generation. Often it is recalled in conversation and in the press in comparison with contemporary severe storms. Its meteorological data and newspaper coverage certainly confirm that the combination of heavy, dense flakes and gale-force winds produced a driving snowstorm of the severest kind. Nineteenth-century editors on Nantucket would have called it a "smotherer." The almost complete paralysis of all forms of transportation in southeast Massachusetts was its distinguishing feature. It lacked only near-zero temperatures to qualify as a classic example of a New England blizzard.

The storm's impact across the region was described by the New England climatologist:

The weather in New England in February 1940, was notable for the severe northeast snow-storm of the 14th and 15th. The disturbance, which originated in New Mexico on the evening of the 11th, moved slowly eastward across the western Gulf States, picking up a great amount of moisture; its path of movement during the 13th was slightly north of east with increasing intensity and velocity; on the night of the 14th its center was just off the southern Massachusetts coast with the barometer reading below 975 millibars [28.79 inches]: the storm passed out to sea during the morning of the 15th, and snow ended in New England generally before noon of that day. The influence of the storm was experienced for the most part over southern and central portions of the Section, with snow depths ranging from 10 to 18 inches. It was most severe along the central and southern New England coasts where winds of gale and whole-gale force drifted the snow to extraordinary depths. All types of transportation were either seriously hampered or were unable to operate for several days following the storm, and a number of lives were lost.

"Undoubtedly the worst winter storms, in point of damage since the January sleet storm of 1935, occurred on Wednesday and Thursday [February 14–15] of this week, when a fierce sleet and snow storm swept the island," was the assessment of the *Inquirer and Mirror.* It was described locally as a "howling northeaster of 50 miles per hour velocity, driving rain, hail, sleet and snow before it."

The northeast gales caused high water in the harbor. The waves smashed at Straight Wharf, breaking many piles and doing considerable damage to the structures along the south side. The report in the *Inquirer and Mirror* continued:

The wharves took on a wild appearance as the tide rose, the spray being driven many

yards through the air. Workmen at Island Service wharf had a busy time of it shifting the *Isco*'s berth across the slip near the gasoline shed. Three small boats in the basin between South and Straight wharfs were sunk during the night; a power dory belonging to Robert Blair, a scallop boat belonging to George Garnett and Harold Mills.

News came that the heavy seas, beating the easterly shoreline of the island, had cut through Great Point at the Gauls, isolating the keepers at Great Point station. Keeper E.V. Haskins and Assistant Keeper Gerald Lowther stated, via the telephone, that a channel 100 feet wide and 4 feet deep was cut across the Gauls. At 5:30 Thursday [Feb. 15] afternoon, Keeper Haskins reported the sea washing all around the light and buildings, flooding the basin in which the tower and structures are located.

Before the afternoon had waned, the wind had mounted to gale force. Rain and hail hit against windows like bird-shot, and the sound of the water rushing up through the streets of the town, off the open harbor, was the best indication of the power of the storm.

At dusk, the sleet was mixed with snow and the trees and wires became weighted down with the frozen stuff. The electric power lines were interrupted intermittently all through the evening, but there was no period longer that 15 minutes with town circuits completely out-of-order until later in the night.

Tuesday, February 13, 1940, was a "weather breeder" day on Nantucket. The sunshine recorder logged 9.4 hours of direct solar rays or 89 percent of the possible. The wind averaged 11.1 miles per hour and in the evening dropped as low as 7 miles. During the day it shifted gradually from north to northeast and finally settled in the east: an ominous sign.

Through most of the day the temperature hovered above freezing, but in mid-evening dipped down into the upper twenties, another condition to be considered. Finally, in late evening the barometer reversed a rising trend and began to fall gradually, a third warning

to the forecasters. These indications during the evening wer the harbingers of a distant disturbance located at that time some 800 miles away in northeastern Tennessee.

On the morning of February 14, the wind remained in the east but gradually increased in speed, reaching gale force at 7:55 a.m. Winds blew at 32 or more miles per hour for the next 31 hours until 2:03 p.m. on the 15th. Maximum sustained force on the 14th was 51 miles with an extreme gust of 57 miles. The wind averaged 30.6 miles for the 24 hours of the 14th.

Precipitation began at 10:40 a.m. and fell variously as a mixture of rain and snow, rain and sleet, rain only, and sleet only, until 9:13 p.m., when it changed to snow only and continued all night until 10:50 a.m. the next morning. Very large amounts fell from 1:00 to 9:00 p.m., mainly as a sleety mixture. Had so much of it not fallen in partly frozen form, the rate of precipitation would have produced a total of 14 inches of snow. But by 7:30 p.m., only 1.3 inches of mixed sleet and snow lay on the ground. The snowfall early on the 15th brought the storm total to 4.4 inches and the depth on the ground to 4.1 inches. The total precipitation — snow, sleet, and rain — amounted to 1.74 inches when melted, a sizable figure for a winter storm.

The most remarkable phenomenon of the storm was exhibited by the barometer which dropped more than an inch in the 12 hours ending at 7:30 p.m., from 29.68 to 28.67 inches. The absolute minimum reading was 28.66 inches, among the ten lowest barometric readings ever observed on Nantucket.

The wind shifted to north at 1:00 a.m. on the 15th and continued in that direction until mid-afternoon when it backed farther into northwest. A maximum sustained speed of 49 miles per hour was registered at 2:35 a.m. The average hourly speed was just below that of the day before, at 28.9 miles.

During the early part of the storm on the 14th, temperatures hovered very close to freezing, either a degree above or below. On Thursday morning, the 15th, the thermometer gradually slipped down to a low of 28°F, the minimum during the storm period.

Light snow fell all morning until 10:50 a.m. in the amount of 0.20 inch. The barometer recovered during the day from 29.17 inches to 29.75 inches at 7:30 p.m. By this time the storm center had moved to near Nova Scotia.

Big Coastal Snowstorm, February 1951

Peculiarly, the conspicuous snowstorm of the winter was on February 3–4th in the extreme southeast corner of the section, when Nantucket was burdened with 15.9 inches, Greenville, R.I., 15.3 inches, and Hyannis 12 inches. Other parts of the section were little affected. On rare occasions, as in this instance, coast-skirting storms pass at just the right distance off-shore, with temperature at the critical point, to place southeastern Massachusetts in the sector of maximum snowfall. Conversely, some of the heaviest snowstorms of the interior, commonly those with low pressure centers passing to the north, give rain only or a wet mixture on the southeast coast.

New England climatologist.

The early February storm of 1951 had an unusual place of origin. Instead of the Gulf of Mexico or the Carolina coast it was first charted well off the coast of northern Florida at 75°W and 29°N, or 350 miles east of Daytona Beach. It moved very rapidly north-northeast and by 7:00 a.m. the next morning it had reached the latitude of Nantucket, about 150 miles to the east. It continued this rapid pace to the northeast on the 4th and 5th and was southeast of Newfoundland at 7:00 a.m. on the 5th. The central barometric pressure when nearest Nantucket was about 29.50 inches.

"When the storm started to break Tuesday evening with the wind breezing from the eastward, the weatherwise predicted a (round-turn,) as the Nantucketers call a

sudden change in the weather. Rain first then snow all night and all day on the 4th," reported the *Inquirer and Mirror.*

Snow described as "very fine" began about 4:47 p.m. on February 3, 1951. The temperature stood at 31°F and the wind was blowing from the east-northeast at 15 miles per hour. The snowfall became moderate at 7:20 p.m and began to accumulate. By midnight, 8.0 inches covered the ground. The wind backed into the northeast and increased to a steady 30 miles. The temperature remained at 31°F. Blowing snow was recorded after 9:00 p.m. and drifts on the 4th were reported to have reached two to three feet.

During the early morning hours of the 4th, moderate and sometimes heavy snow fell with occasional periods of sleet mixed in. At 1:00 a.m. the depth on the ground reached 10 inches and at 7:15 a.m. the maximum of 15 inches was measured. The total snowfall was 15.9 inches, and the melted water equivalent of the snow amounted to 1.62 inches.

The barometer reached its lowest point of 29.84 inches at 5:27 a.m. on thc 4th when the wind was roaring out of the northeast at a 41 mile per hour clip, with gusts to 47 miles. Soon after this, the wind backed to north and diminished gradually to 20 miles by 9:30 a.m.

Temperature remained in the proper range for heavy snow production, with a maximum of 32°F and a minimum of 24°F.

Since the Town of Nantucket had available only four snowplows, tractors were used to help clear the roads. June Bartlett, with his horses and sidewalk plows, spent long hours clearing the sidewalks of heavy snow. On Wednesday, February 6, heavy rains came, washing away all the snow.

"The Great Storm of '52"

One of the memorable weather events of the region, the "Great Storm of '52" was described by the New England climatologist:

Again on the 27th, a coastal storm developed great energy off Nantucket. The

average snow measurement on the Island was 23 inches [actually 20], but the gales piled up such drifts there as on Martha's Vineyard and Cape Cod that communication and travel were completely disrupted.... Martha's Vineyard records show no such snowstorm in the past 30 or more years. There was considerable damage to utilities and many narrow escapes from disaster. In this Great Storm of '52, the brunt of the heavy snow was borne by Nantucket. The 120-ft. Loran tower near Sankaty Head toppled as the wind attained an 80 m.p.h. rate in gusts. Abnormal high tides damaged several buildings near Brant Point. At Martha's Vineyard and the mainland from Cape Cod to Plymouth, there was a 15- to 20-inch cover. The estimates of damage range from a quarter- to a half-million dollars, mostly as cost of repairs and clearing roads.

Plowing equipment was brought from the Berkshires, to aid over-taxed local machinery. Some 3,000 autoists were stranded on the lower Cape; most communities were without power and lights, communications, or transportation.

The local impact of the great blizzard was related in the columns of the *Inquirer and Mirror:*

The Island of Nantucket was almost completely paralyzed by one of the worst storms in its history, this week, when a roaring blizzard blanketed the island with 20 inches of snow. 'Sconset, Madaket, Wauwinet, Surfside ... all were cut off by drifts as high as 12 to 14 feet across roads, and snapped telephone poles and broken power lines cut off electricity and communications.

The storm started as a gentle snowfall, Wednesday morning [Feb. 27], and within a very few hours had turned into a storm almost unbelievable in its fury. The winds rose to an average of 45 miles per hour, with gusts estimated at over 80 miles per hour, which drove the wet snow with tremendous force, breaking power lines and plunging the town into darkness.

p.m. on the 27th until 5:30 a.m. on the 28th, a remarkably long period for sustained gales. Only two observations during that period of 14 hours and a half dropped below the 40-mile clip.

The crisis of the storm came soon after midnight when the barometer reached its lowest point and the wind shifted. From blowing steadily for hours at north-northeast, it changed to west-northwest at 1:30 a.m. on the 28th. At that time sustained winds reached 61 miles per hour, with gusts to 72 miles. Heavy snow fell, the visibility lowered to only 1/8 mile, and blowing and drifting snow prevailed. The barometer dipped to 29.09 inches and then began to rise. A ship close to the center of the storm reported a very low reading of 28.02 inches, which would place the center a good distance offshore.

The heavy snowfall continued through the 28th and into the next morning until 2:30 a.m. It decreased to a moderate fall at 3:00 a.m. and finally ceased completely at 4:42 a.m. on the 29th, after almost 44 hours of continuous snowfall. The wind was now roaring out of the west-northwest at 40 miles per hour with gusts to 52 miles.

Nantucket had received 14.9 inches on the 27th, 5.2 inches on the 28th, and 1.3 inches on the 29th, for a total of 21.4 inches, earning this storm an equal rank with the big storm of February 1905 as Nantucket's deepest snowstorm of record. On the 28th the depth on the ground measured 23 inches, an all-time record for Nantucket. Despite the additional 1.4 inches on the 29th, the actual depth diminished to 17 inches as the result of the settling of the wet snow pack. The temperture rose to 38°F on the 29th.

The total snowfall for the period February 18 to March 1 was 42.6 inches, according to Don K. Halligan of the weather bureau. The snow cover of 23 inches in late February reduced to only a trace by March 6 since the thermometer mounted into the high 30s each day and rapid melting ensued.

After forming in the Gulf of Mexico, the disturbance cut across Florida and Georgia to the Atlantic coast, apparently headed well out to sea. Forecasters along the Middle Atlantic seaboard were in a quandary, confronted with the problem as to how far inland the canopy of snow would reach. As the center sped northeast over the offshore waters, the edge of the snowfall just missed Washington, D.C., gave Atlantic City a dusting, New York City only a trace. Bridgehampton, near the eastern tip of Long Island, received 3.0 inches before the increasing heavy snow zone cut across extreme southeastern New England. Hyannis reported 20.0 inches, Edgartown 14.0 inches, New Bedford 11.0 inches, Plymouth 10 inches, Boston 5.2 inches, and Providence 4.9 inches.

Light snow began to fall on Nantucket at 9:08 a.m. on February 27 with the temperature at 35°F. The wind came out of the east-northeast at 25 miles per hour with gusts to 29 miles. The snowfall alternated between light and moderate until 11:05 a.m. when it became heavy and continued so. The temperature soon dropped to an even 32°F and remained at that figure throughout the duration of the storm. Three inches had been on the ground at the outset of this snowfall. The depth increased to 5.0 inches by 1:30 p.m., to 13 inches by 7:30 p.m., and to 18 inches by midnight when 14.9 inches of new snow had been added to the ground cover.

The barometer fell rapidly all afternoon and evening of the 27th. The wind increased at a steady rate to 50 miles per hour at 9:42 p.m. with gusts to 67 miles per hour. Blowing snow became one of the chief ingredients of the storm after 3:00 p.m. The wind remained at a steady rate of 40 miles per hour from 3:00

Snowy Mid-March of 1956

"Snow, snow, and more snow, topped by terrific snowstorms of the 16–17th and 19th, coupled with unusual cold, made this month's weather distinctly unpleasant except for winter enthusiasts," declared the New England climatologist.

Cyclonic activity was marked on the weather maps following the middle of March. Storms developed very quickly and moved very rapidly. Late on the 15th a large area of precipitation spread over the Gulf States with a low centered in Mississippi at 1:30 a.m. on the 16th. Twenty-four hours later the center had made an amazing dash to the northeast and was off the Nova Scotia coast, having moved offshore in southern Maryland and skirted Cape Cod. It dumped 10.1 inches of wet stuff on Nantucket between noon of the 16th and 6:00 a.m. of the 17th. Its water equivalent was 1.68 inches, but the depth on the ground amounted to only 2.0 inches at the conclusion of the fall. Temperature rose to 37°F and 36°F on both days. The Nantucket barometer sank to 28.80 inches at 12:57 a.m on the 17th.

A second major storm followed closely on the heels of that of the 16–17th. This center, however, originated in the Northwest, and, as an innocent looking depression, moved at a normal pace southeast during the 17th and 18th to a position in southern Virginia. Here it began to pick up moisture from the Atlantic Ocean and a remarkable regeneration took place. Snow broke out in West Virginia and southern Pennsylvania and extended to the coast. Making the usual turn to the north, the center commenced to deepen rapidly, but did not move off with the accustomed speed of a coastal low. Indeed, it appeared to become almost stationary when just south of Nantucket, permitting a whirl of moist northeast winds to pour over the land. A heavy snow belt developed from northern New Jersey to the Massachusetts coast with snowfall measurements in many places just under 20.0 inches.

Traces of snow were recorded on Nantucket each hour from 10:00 p.m. to 1:00 a.m. on the 19th, then increased to a light snowfall. The density of the flakes became heavy at 9:00 a.m. and within an hour turned very heavy and continued to 1:00 p.m. Shortly thereafter, the intensity lightened and the snowfall continued until 5:00 p.m when it was estimated that 11.2 inches of wet snow had accumulated. By 7:00 p.m. the evening observation noted only 5.0 inches remaining on the ground. Some insignificant amounts continued to fall at intervals through the 25th.

Temperatures on the 19th varied from 29°F to 35°F. Wind blew at an average of 25 miles per hour on the 19th and hit a peak of 47 miles per hour. The barometer dropped to the low reading of 28.81 inches.

The conditions attending the storm were summarized by the *Inquirer and Mirror:*

Heavy snow, winds 80 miles per hour. Began Friday afternoon, 16th, and continued until early Saturday afternoon. Extreme high tide at 1:00 a.m. Saturday morning flooded Brant Point and Washington street areas — almost unprecedented evacuation of families. Two feet deep in places on Washington street. Another heavy snowfall on Sunday night and Monday 18–19th. Gully 20–30 feet wide and 3–5 feet deep on east side of Children's beach. Second storm on Sunday and Monday, not as severe as on mainland and no high tide. Water on 17th rose higher than it had for 25 years — even compares with 1915 according to old timers. Tide rose quickly.

Damage to homes equaling or surpassing that done by the heaviest of the much-publicized hurricanes occurred Friday night and Saturday morning [March 16 and 17] when a heavy snowstorm accompanied by winds clocked at better than 80 miles per hour struck the island almost without warning. Beginning as a light snow Friday afternoon, the storm grew to blizzard proportions by nightfall, continuing to early afternoon on Saturday.

Great Snowstorm of February 1958

Once in a lifetime a great snowstorm will occur and thereafter supplies an unlimited source of reminiscences and material for ever-growing tall tales. Writing in 1831 about a great storm, Ebenezer Niles, the Baltimore editor of the leading news weekly of the country, declared it "a genuine old-fashioned snowstorm" and "worthy of the best days of our fathers."

The storm which swept the entire length of the Atlantic seaboard and the eastern slopes of the Appalachians on February 14 to 16, 1958, was of major stature. It spread a blanket of snow 12 inches or more deep in a broad band from northern Alabama to the Canadian border and beyond. Some states and areas have had heavier falls of snow within memory, but no storm of the present century combined the magnitude of areal extent and the intensity of the falling frozen precipitation as did the Great Snowstorm of Mid-Februray 1958.

The genesis of the storm lay in a low pressure impulse which moved across the western intermountain region and Rocky Mountain states on February 13, 1958. It joined the semi-permanent front along the eastern slopes of the Rockies which during most of January and February forms the boundary between mild Pacific and cold polar air from Canada. The center slid rapidly south on the 14th to the Texas panhandle under the influence of a strong southerly jetstream, then rushed southeast to the Gulf of Mexico where it emerged around noon of the 14th as a low center of 29.77 inches on the barometer. Twenty-four hours later it was on the South Carolina coast at 29.42 inches, and another 24 hours carried it to a position off Nantucket where its central pressure had deepened greatly to 28.68 inches.

The storm assumed blizzard proportions in many areas of the Middle Atlantic states and western New England on February 17th, toward the end of the storm. Gale-force winds from the northeast increased in speed as they backed to the north and northwest. The dry snow, which fell mostly with temperatures in the low 20s and upper teens, was blown into mountainous drifts, and for 48 hours or more defied the efforts of snow fighters to keep the main arteries open. Many country roads in New England remained closed for 5 to 7 days after the storm with great economic loss to rural communities.

Snowfall was heavy across eastern Massachusetts. Boston's 19.4 inches established a new mark for a single snowstorm in a record dating back to 1871, and Blue Hill Observatory's 22.2 inches broke the record dating back to 1885.

The *Inquirer and Mirror* described the storm's effect on Nantucket with the headline: "Weekend Storm Brings Snow, Low Temperature:"

Early Sunday morning, at 12:20 a.m., snow started to fall and whipped by easterly winds blowing between 65–67 miles in gusts, the storm approached blizzard proportions. By 9:00 a.m. there was six inches of snow recorded but the high winds blew most of it off the highways. Just before 11:00 a.m. the wind let up and the snow stopped. The temperature rose to around the 40 degree mark and there was light intermittent rain that melted the snow down to about one inch on the level.

About 6:00 p.m the temperature dropped again and it started to snow. As the storm passed over the island in the early evening the wind swept in from the northwest and blew in gusts up to 60 miles an hour accompanied by snow squalls.

With conditions on the mainland even worse than on Nantucket all plane service to the island was disrupted by the storm as well as forcing the cancellation of the boat trip for the day.

The strong gale winds blew down the power lines to Siasconset and Madaket and in town areas early Sunday morning. Some power failures were caused by short circuits in transformers. The Nantucket Gas and Electric Company called emergency crews from their homes around 3:00 a.m. to repair the damage and by late afternoon normal electric service was restored everywhere. Street lights were not completely restored until Wednesday.

Siasconset was hardest hit by falling wires and was without power for about 8 hours while Madaket residents lost their electricity for 4 hours.

Highway Department employees were called out by Superintendent of Streets Matthew Jaeckle at 5:00 a.m. to see that the main highways were kept open and to plow the in-town streets.

An unusual feature of the storm was that at the Nantucket Memorial Airport, where there are 8000 feet of runways, the maintenance crew did not have to plow the runways as the gale-force winds blew the snow off as it landed. At the same time, two automobiles in the car parking area outside the administration building were buried in a 12-foot drift.

Under the influence of an anticyclone, the barometer peaked at 30.08 inches on February 15, then began a rapid descent as the rapidly developing cyclonic storm approached. When the center of the "Great Snowstorm of February 1958" passed overhead, at 5:00 p.m. on the 16th, the barometer bottomed at 28.69 inches.

Very light snow began to fall at 12:20 a.m. on the 16th. From 2:55 to 7:35 a.m., it fell at moderate to heavy rates. By 6:45 a.m. 4.0 inches had accumulated on the ground and another 2.0 inches were added during the morning, though melting and settling kept the maximum depth at 4.0 inches. Rain mixed with snow after 8:58 a.m. when the temperature rose to 34°F. All precipitation ceased over the noon hours until 2:50 p.m. when the rain resumed.

The wind remained in the east all morning until noon when a shift to the south-southeast occurred as the storm center approached. The temperature rose to 40°F. When the center of the storm finally passed over Nantucket, at 5:00 p.m., the wind lulled but soon increased to 37 miles per hour with gusts to 56 miles as it shifted gradually to southwest and west-southwest. It finally settled in the west for the evening hours.

Light snow began again at 5:50 p.m. and continued past midnight. The total of the snowfall amounted to 6.4 inches. Next day light snow was in the air most of the time; the fall amounted to 3.5 inches, for a storm total of 9.9 inches.

Record Snowstorm, Early March 1960

The heaviest snowstorm known to a generation of southeastern New England residents staggered the area on March 3–5, 1960, when a coastal northeaster, swirling up from the Cape Hatteras region, hesitated in its poleward dash for a few crucial hours when southeast of Cape Cod. The pause, in this area of convergent ocean currents and atmospheric airstreams, was accompanied by a marked intensification of the whole system. As a result, the precipitation process continued several hours longer than during a normally-paced storm, and record amounts of frozen precipitation descended on Rhode Island, eastern Massachusetts, and the offshore waters during these hours.

The fame of the Early March Storm of 1960 was earned by the excessive snowfall it deposited over southeastern New England, to which the 30 inches of new snow at Blue Hill and the rainfall catch of 3.60 inches at Medway testified. No previous storm during the twentieth century had produced so much snow over this region. It was a worthy rival of the Great Snowstorm of January 1831, which held the record for the nineteenth century. But this was just the start of a series of record-breaking snowstorms. Those in 1969 and 1978 again set all-time records.

A low-pressure center moved from the western Gulf of Mexico to central Kentucky by 1:30 a.m. on March 3 when a secondary low formed over southern Georgia. The latter progressed rapidly northeast in 24 hours to a position about 100 miles south of Nantucket, where the pressure dropped to 28.70 inches at 1:00 a.m. on the 4th. The intense development, the fast movement northeast, and the amazing deepening indicated an energetic disturbance with vast momentum which would only brush the New England coast and move rapidly on. But during the night of the 3–4th the encircling arms of a strong surface anticyclone to the north began applying a restraining force on the rate of advance of the disturbance. During the succeeding 12 hours, daylight of the 4th, the strong center moved only about 180 miles along its northeast track, at a 15 mi/h rate compared to its previous 30 to 40-mile clip. The central pressure offshore further deepened to an estimated 28.47 inches, an extremely low reading even in this stormy area.

On Nantucket, the temperature at the start of the snowfall at 9:10 a.m. on March 3 stood at 27°F, rising to 32° at 10:00 p.m. that evening, and to 35° at 5:00 a.m. on the 4th. It remained above freezing until noon and thereafter hovered either slightly above or slightly below the freezing mark.

Light winds prevailed from the east-northeast on the morning of the 3d, but picked up considerably in the evening to a maximum of 47 miles per hour at 10:53 p.m. The next morning it backed to north-northeast, indicating the passage of the center seaward, and increased to a peak of 59 miles per hour at 8:23 a.m. Earlier, a gust had hit 64 miles per hour. The wind continued to back and gradually diminish during the afternoon and evening, though a gust as high as 41 miles per hour was registered at 7:00 p.m.

"Storm Damage to Wharves Is Considerable" was the headline of the *Inquirer and Mirror*:

A large part of the macadam surface of Commercial Wharf was broken and strewn about the wharf, and the water undermined the area in many places, creating a large number of holes. A large section of the Hyannis boat landing was broken off by the combined efforts of wind and waves.

Along the front end of the Island Service Co. Wharf the macadam surfacing was undermined and the water cut a gully about four feet wide. This end of the wharf has been blocked off to vehicular traffic. There are other depressions along the surface of the wharf that show there was a lot of undermining all along the wharf. BMl Thomas Snell of the Brant Point Lifeboat Station reported early this week that it was necessary to send the Coast Guard Dukw to Great Point Monday to refuel the light station with diesel oil after it was found that the storm-tossed waves had made a cut across the "Galls" and they were covered with water.

ENl Eves Vincent, who had charge of the Dukw on its trip, reported the cut was open across the narrow strip of sand and was about 100 feet wide. He said that at high tide the water is about six inches deep over the area. Mr. Vincent stated that the Dukw had no trouble crossing the cut and that he planned to make another trip across tomorrow morning.

The Highway Department worked against heavy odds to keep the main roads open despite the wind-blown drifting snow. The workers are to be complimented for their efforts.

Only nuisance damage was caused to telephone and electric power cables, and line crews from both companies worked around the clock keeping them in order. Madaket lost its power Friday night and it was not restored until the next day because of the terrific whipping the power cable was receiving along the way.

The lone casualty was a large black and tan dog that in some unknown manner got into the harbor waters and was found Saturday by John McLaughlin Jr., in the water off Commercial Wharf.

Alfred Geddes, chief of the U.S. Weather Bureau station at the Airport, revealed early this week that their computations of the actual amount of snowfall showed 31.3 inches of snow fell on the island during the three day storm but two or three periods of rain and a rise in temperature cut the accumulation to 19 inches.

If the rain and warm temperatures had not caused such a considerable amount of melting, Nantucket would have certainly been buried in snow.

Triple Snowstorms in Winter 1960–61

Few winters of the past have produced three northeasters of such severity and widespread influence as the months of December 1960, January 1961, and February 1961. Nantucket's total snowfall for 1960–61 was 62.1 inches, the greatest since the big snow winter of 1904–05 when 72.2 inches descended. In fact, the total snowfall of the successive winters of 1959–60 and 1960–61, 121.5 inches, most nearly approached the total of 154.2 inches of the winters of 1903–04 and 1904–05. Residents who thought they were back in the days of the fabled old-fashioned winters were right.

Pre-winter Snowstorm, December 1960

On December 12th a major snowstorm brought paralyzing blizzard conditions to nearly all the area of Connecticut, Rhode Island, Massachusetts, extreme southeastern Vermont, southern New Hampshire, and southern Maine. The cause was a rapidly deepening low pressure center which passed at sea. This low moved from the Virginia Capes to Halifax, Nova Scotia, during the 24 hours of the 12th. It brought snow to southern New England beginning during the evening of the 11th and continuing most of the 12th. Farther north, snow began early on the 12th and continued into the 13th . . . .

Especially remarkable was the storm's ocurrence so early in the season. Such a heavy snowfall so early was unprecedented [in modern records]. Also, at many stations in the belt of heavier snowfall, December maximum 24-hour amount records were broken. Nantucket's new record 24-hour snowfall, 15.5 inches, greatly exceeded the former [Dec.] record of 11.6 inches set in 1904.

New England climatologist.

Many atmospheric elements were in action on December 11, 1960, preparing for one of the greatest pre-solstice snowstorms of record. Early in the day a secondary center formed east of the Appalachian Mountains in west-central North Carolina. As the new storm system moved off to the northeast at a rapid clip, a mantle of snow spread along the coast well in advance. It reached Roanoke about 7:00 a.m., Washington at 9:00 a.m., New York City about 2:00 p.m., and Boston at 10:00 p.m. on December 11.

The storm track passed off the coast southeast of Norfolk late on the 11th and by 7:00 a.m. of the 12th had progressed to a position about 250 miles directly east of Atlantic City and 125 miles south-southeast of Nantucket. By that time the central pressure had deepened very rapidly to an estimated 28.86 inches. Nantucket's lowest dropped to 29.11 inches.

Light snow began to fall on Nantucket at 7:50 p.m. with the temperature at 30°F and the wind out of the east at 11 miles per hour. Only a trace accumulated by midnight. The snowfall became moderate at 12:25 a.m. on the 12th and continued at either a moderate or heavy rate, with only one interval of light snowfall, until 2.55 p.m. The total snowfall in 24 hours was estimated at 15.5 inches from 1.37 inches of melted precipitation. This indicated a light density fall, unusual for Nantucket.

The pressure fell rapidly all morning to a low of 29.11 inches at 12:20 p.m. on the 12th. During the morning the wind shifted from a steady northeast to north at noon, and to north-northwest at 3:30 p.m. Steady speeds

were at 46 miles per hour in the late morning with gusts to 70 miles at 11:20 a.m. Visibility was reported at zero from 10:00 to 12:00 a.m., at the height of the storm.

The temperature read 29°F at the time of the noon windshift, and then dropped off to 23°F at 6:00 p.m. and to 14°F at midnight.

Blowing snow was reported at all observations from 4:30 a.m. to midnight when the wind was blowing a steady 29 miles per hour from the west-northwest.

The headline in the *Inquirer and Mirror* on Dec. 15, 1960, read: "Severe Northeaster Hits Nantucket; Power Lines Down; Homes Heatless:"

A severe northeast blizzard accompanied by frigid temperatures and gale winds up to 70 miles per hour in gusts lashed the island last Sunday night and all day Monday, causing a traffic fatality and creating untold damage to the scallop fleet and electric power lines.

The storm deposited 16 inches of snow in its wake and moved out to sea Tuesday night. The high winds and 15-foot waves swept the 65-foot New Bedford fishing dragger, *Sharon Louise,* high on the North Shore in front of the Clancy property and caused the wrecking of the 36-foot Coast Guard patrol boat from the Brant Point Station.

Steamboat service was disrupted Monday and all airplane service was cancelled during the length of the storm. Highway Department employees and emergency crews worked around the clock under the direction of Superintendent of Streets Matthew L. Jaeckle in an effort to keep the main highways and town roads open. Despite their efforts cars became stalled on many of the out-of-town roads and their owners had to abandon them temporarily. Winds caused drifts ranging from two feet in some areas to 10 feet along open sections of the Siasconset, Madaket, Monomoy, Old South, and Polpis roads.

Scores of rooftop antennas were bent and twisted and some fences were blown down. The Nantucket Gas and Electric Company was hard hit and their crews were working throughout the storm trying to keep the

homes supplied with electric current. They were hampered in their work by falling power lines caused by icy conditions combined with high winds and in some cases caused by falling tree limbs snapping the lines.

Siasconset was without electric power for 16 to 18 hours... part of Madaket lost service for several hours...a total of 180 telephones were put out of commission... a tree fell on Centre Street taking down power lines... Fire Department had three calls for oil stove fires... Mrs. T. Handy, 65, was killed when her car had a head-on collision on the State Highway... lifeboat after taking on crew of dragger *Sharon Louise* overturned, but all struggled ashore to safety...two planes at the Airport broke their tiedowns and were carried a distance by the wind before being flipped over... boats in Madaket Harbor were sunk..At Broad Creek ten boats were driven ashore, four demolished... seven boats were flooded and sunk between Old South Wharf and Straight Wharf... ambulance taking expectant mother to hospital had to park 100 yards from house on account of snow drifts... *Nobska* made regular run on Tuesday and one runway at airport was opened... by Wednesday everything was back to normal.

"Kennedy Inaugural Snowstorm," 1961

This second big storm of the winter threatened to white out the inauguration ceremonies of the first president from Massachusetts since Calvin Coolidge. Forecasters at the nation's capital early on the morning of January 19 centered their concerns on a small low-pressure area moving eastward across the northern portion of Tennessee. Up to this time the disturbance had produced only a light dusting of snow in the central Ohio Valley. Its future course and behavior, however, were of the greatest importance since the extensive Kennedy inaugural ceremonies, indoors or out, were scheduled to commence at noon the next day.

As the low pressure area moved east close to the Virginia-North Carolina border on the afternoon of the 19th, snowflakes began to fall to the north, about noon at Washington and in midafternoon at New York City. Upon approaching the coast, the low-pressure center developed "explosively." The clash of cold air west of the center and the warm, maritime air to its east supplied the dynamics for a very rapid deepening of the barometric center and an intensification of the entire wind system. The central pressure fell to 29.06 inches off southern Maryland early on the 20th and down to 28.59 inches twelve hours later when east of Nantucket. The figures recorded on the island attest to the storm's intensity at this time: a low pressure of 28.85 inches, average wind speed of 30 miles per hour, and a peak one-minute gust of 48 miles.

The first snowflakes reached Nantucket at 7:20 p.m. on the 19th and the snowfall intensified to a rate of about one inch per hour. The heavy fall continued through the morning of the 20th with no slackening until about 1:00 p.m. when it tapered off to a light fall for the rest of the afternoon, ending about 7:00 p.m. A total of 16.0 inches fell within 24 hours, setting a January intensive snowfall record for the twentieth century. When melted, the 16 inches of snow yielded the equivalent of 1.65 inches of water, just about the normal density for a snowfall at the ratio of 10 inches of snow for 1.00 inch of precipitation.

At the end of the storm the snow lay 16 inches deep on the ground. Flurries on the 26–27th raised this to a maximum of 17 inches; with the cold wave continuing, the cover lost only one inch during the remainder of the month.

Northeast gales created blizzard conditions across the island. With the wind averaging 30.2 miles per hour, the temperature dropped steadily during the day from a midnight high of 32°F to 12°F twenty-four hours later. Windchill was excessive on the 20th with the wind gusting to 48 miles per hour.

"Island Buried in Snow by Northeast Blizzard," read the headline in the *Inquirer & Mirror:*

Another northeast blizzard hit Nantucket last night and by 9:30 this morning had deposited 12 inches of snow. High winds have caused considerable drifting on streets and out-of-town roads. Snowplows were ordered into action about 11 o'clock last night by Superintendent of Streets Matthew L. Jaeckle in an attempt to keep the main road open. Plows were working on the streets in town in the early hours this morning . . . Cars are stuck in all parts of the island despite efforts of the Highway Department crews to keep the roads open. At the airport automobiles can only get as far as Glowacki's Gasoline Station and airport and Federal employees have to walk the remaining distance through huge drifts. Three cars are reported stuck at that location.

Today's trip of the steamer *Nantucket* has been cancelled and this also apples to Northeast Airlines and the Cape and Islands Flight Service.

A total of 44 persons, many of them children, were taken out of the flooded area around Brant Point by the Coast Guard, Fire Department, and the Red Cross Disaster Committee.

Third Northeaster of Season, February 1961

The third northeast snowstorm of the winter swept over Nantucket last Saturday and deposited 14.4 inches of snow on top of the pile of snow already on the ground from previous storms.

The snowfall would have been much heavier but for the rain and sleet that fell intermittently through the day. As the storm swirled into the island area it brought with it winds that averaged about 43 miles per hour and also sent the temperature rising to about

36 degrees. This marked the first time in 16 straight days that the temperature went above the freezing mark. The cold wave preceding the storm set a new all-time record for consecutive days of below freezing temperatures. The previous record of 15 straight days of sub-freezing weather was set in January 1893 . . .

Many places on the mainland recorded winds of 70 miles per hour and higher but the highest recorded at the Weather Bureau at the airport was 56 miles from the east at 10:20 Saturday morning. By 6 p.m. it was blowing a steady 50 miles per hour and the wind seemed stronger on the wharves as it was almost impossible for a person to move against it. On the Cape at the same time gusts of 72 miles an hour were being recorded at Chatham.

The Steamer *Nobska* was held in port by the storm and was not able to make the return trip to the mainland until Monday morning. All plane service was cancelled for the day.

High tides were recorded in other coastal areas but it is believed the frozen condition of the harbor and outside the jetties prevented the tide from rising above normal. There were no reports of flooding at any place on the island. There was very little storm damage reported. Only 20 telephone customers lost their service temporarily and the Nantucket Gas and Electric Company said they had a few lines down but nothing serious . . .

The only serious property damage caused by the storm was the toppling of a 50-foot metal light pole in the car parking area at the First National Store on Sparks Avenue and the blowing away of a light from another metal pole at the same place.

On Sunday the weather was beautiful and the bright sun turned the island into a veritable winter wonderland. The east side of practically every house and building was coated with snow and the icy covering it received from the rain and sleet of the storm made everything sparkle like a forest of diamonds. This created a rush of camera lovers all about the town anxious to record the many beautiful scenes on film before the warm sun melted the snow and ice cover from the buildings, the tall, stately trees lining the streets and the smaller trees and bushes in front of the homes and estates on the island.

One good result of Saturday's storm was that it broke up the ice field that was holding the island in its grip and most of the broken ice floes went out into the sound. Woods Hole and Vineyard Haven reported a large amount of the ice field entered their harbors and caused delays and some cancellations of trips by the *Nantucket* between these two ports.

The Coast Guard reported the ice pack dragged the *Cross Rip Lightship* off its position and the tug *Acushnet* was sent to tow the lightship to Woods Hole where it will remain until the ice has cleared out of the sound. It is also reported that practically all the buoys are out of position at the present time.

Inquirer and Mirror,
February 10, 1951.

The main force behind the early February storm of 1961 was a massive area of high barometer that dominated southeast Canada during the opening days of the month. Drifting leisurely eastward, on the morning of the 3d it stood astride the Ontario-Quebec border with a central pressure at 30.89 inches. At that point the storm showed a tendency to hold its position and retain its strength. The core was made up of very cold air, with –25 °F in central Quebec, and zero readings as far south as New York City and Philadelphia on the morning of the 2d.

The presence of such cold air in a semi-stationary position soon had repercussions to the south where a vigorous secondary center developed in a low pressure trough off the Georgia coast on the night of the 2–3d. By 1:00 p.m on the 3d, with the low pressure center off southeast North Carolina, light snow fell as far north as New Jersey, though it did not accumulate in quantity until late afternoon. The northeast progress of snow shield proved exasperatingly slow to snow watchers, not reaching Providence or Nantucket with significant amounts until 2:00 a.m. and Boston at 4:00 a.m. on the 4th.

The northward progress of the center began to feel the resisting force of the Quebec anticyclone during the night of the 3–4th as it gradually made a turn to the east-northeast, moving almost parallel to the southern New England coast. This trajectory enabled the developing storm to draw aloft vast quantities of Atlantic Ocean moisture which fell to earth in the form of myriads of snowflakes.

Shortly after noon on the 4th, the center lay about 100 miles offshore, with central pressure at 29.41 inches, and gale-force winds sweeping all the northern sector of the storm.

The cold air from Canada penetrated across the Sound to give Nantucket its first zero temperature since 1943 with an even 0 °F reading on the morning of the 2d. The next morning the mercury read 7°. With the approach of the storm circulation from the southwest, the wind shifted into the northeast, and ocean trajectory brought the reading to 32 °F.

Snow began to filter down just before midnight, but did not really get to work until about 3:00 a.m. For eleven hours until 2:00 p.m., it fell at a rate of an inch an hour, then dropped off for two hours before resuming at about half that rate until 11:00 p.m. The total fall was 14.4 inches, from a melted catch of 2.09 inches. Since the temperature ranged up to 36 °F during the day, it was a wet snow.

Winds were high during the storm, but did not reach the blizzard proportions of the first two storms of the season. Wind speed averaged 27.4 miles per hour from the east-northeast; the peak one-minute sustained speed was 56 miles per hour.

Despite the additional 14.4 inches of snowfall, the total amount on the ground was little affected. From an existing cover of 10 inches on the 3d, the total amounted to only 11 inches by the end of the storm, but as a result of the additional wet snow the water equivalent of the now soggy snow pack increased from 1.5 inches to 2.2 inches. Thereafter, the depth reduced at the rate of about one inch a day until the 18th when only a trace remained. Snow had covered the ground for 29 consecutive days from January

20 to February 17.

The New England climatologist summed up the remarkable season:

February marks the close of the "statistical" winter season. Despite the moderation of severe weather that prevailed after the storm of February 4th, the winter of 1960–61 in central and southern New England, with its 3 or 4 major snowstorms and blizzards and its record or near-record period of enduring intense cold, was the most rigorous this area has experienced in more than 40 years.

Record Snowy December, 1963

Probably the best example of a "sneak snowstorm" which buried Nantucket and spared most of the mainland occurred on December 18 and 19 in 1963. A total of 15.1 inches descended on the island within the short time of 12 hours. The first flakes were noticed at 1:00 p.m. on the 18th, but heavy snow did not start until 8:00 p.m.; it continued to fall heavily until 7:00 a.m. on the 19th before ceasing altogether about 9:00 a.m. The 15.1 inches total marked the second deepest December snowstorm, being exceeded only by 15.5 inches that fell in a single storm in December 1960. The snow cover, later augmented by 4.9 inches that fell on the 23–24th, endured to the end of the month when 1.0 inch remained on the ground. This provided the first white Christmas since 1945.

During the big storm of the 18–19th on Nantucket, Boston reported only 1.7 inches and Providence 4.3 inches. Other measurements on or near Cape Cod in inches were: East Wareham 8.0, Fall River 6.2, New Bedford 8.5, and Sandwich 5.0.

Temperatures at Nantucket on the snow days ranged from 32° down to 18°F. The wind averaged 24.7 miles per hour on the 19th, and the peak one-minute sustained speed hit 40 miles from the northwest.

The total snowfall in December added up

to 24.7 inches, exceeding the old record set in December 1904 by 0.6 inch.

Under the head, "14-inch Snow Hits Nantucket," the *Inquirer and Mirror* describes its effect.

There can be no complaint from anyone who wanted snow, for snow is what Nantucket now has in almost record depths for this time of the year.

Fourteen inches fell on the Island from early evening Wednesday, until 7 this morning. The only heavier fall for December was 15½ inches on December 12, 1960.

Uncounted automobiles were stuck for hours in drifts that piled, in some places, to a depth of three to four feet.

Highway Superintendent Matthew Jaeckle called out all of his department's emergency equipment about 2 a.m., and had the main streets well cleared before the wind, sometimes gusting to 50 miles an hour, shifted from the northeast to north-northwest and blew most of the snow back on the roads again.

The heavy fall caused a 45-minute electric power shut off at Polpis. There was also a break in power lines in the Sankaty section of 'Sconset, but emergency crews repaired the damage.

At the height of the storm, waves at Nantucket Lightship were between 15 and 18 feet.

Police Chief Wendell H. Howes put both police cruisers into service, transporting nurses to and from Nantucket Cottage Hospital and Our Island Home.

Airport Manager Thomas F. Gibson had all of his maintenance men and equipment in service throughout the night, fighting drifts.

Big Snowstorm, January 1964

Nantucket was the hardest hit of any community on the eastern seaboard by the two-day blinding northeast blizzard that deposited 19 inches of snow on the Island and sent temperatures below the freezing mark. Transportation was brought to a halt and schools were closed for a day and a half.

The storm was accompanied by gale force winds that averaged 50 miles per hour with gusts to 60 miles per hour and caused heavy snow drifts to form on roads both in an out of town, making driving hazardous.

Boat transportation was cancelled Monday and Tuesday [Jan. 12 and 13], with partial resumption of services Tuesday afternoon.

Northeast Airlines cancelled all their flights both days, while other airlines were grounded all day Monday and resumed flights Tuesday afternoon.

The worst drifts were encountered by ploughing crews at the entrance to the airport, on the Hummock Pond Road, Old South Road, Sparks Avenue, and Cliff Road, according to Mr. Jaeckle, Superintendent of Streets.

Inquirer and Mirror,
January 16, 1964.

A secondary center of a storm over Tennessee formed off the coast of Georgia near Savannah during the early morning hours of January 12. At 7:00 a.m. the central pressure read 29.71 inches. Twelve hours later the center was southeast of Cape Hatteras, and on the morning of the 13th directly east of Atlantic City and south of the eastern tip of Long Island, the central pressure now down to 29.29 inches. Here the direction of movement changed from northeast to east-northeast. At noon the center lay due south of Nantucket at 39.5°N and 70°W, or about 100 miles distant. This put Nantucket in the center of a newly-developed heavy snow zone.

With the temperature at 28°F, light snow began to fall on Nantucket at 2:20 a.m. on January 13, 1964, and continued throughout the day and night until 11:15 a.m. on the 14th, a period of about 33 hours. The total fall was 19.2 inches, the fourth greatest snowstorm in Nantucket's history.

The accumulation was very gradual on the 13th. Only 3.0 inches at 1:00 p.m. and 8.0 inches at 7:00 p.m. This increased to 13 inches at 1:00 a.m. on the 14th and to the maximum of 19 inches at 11:15 a.m. Thereafter, the snow "drifted off the island," according to the weather bureau log, and the depth reduced slightly. The melted precipitation amounted to 1.80 inches.

The barometric low point occurred between midnight and 1:00 a.m. on the 14th when it read 29.21 inches. At that time the wind backed from northeast to north-northeast. Winds had been blowing as high as 45 miles per hour at 9:00 p.m., but slacked off to 23 miles at midnight.

Blowing snow was a feature throughout the storm, generally limiting visibility from one-eighth to one-quarter mile and occasionally to zero. With the shift to north and north-northwest, the wind picked up and blew at a high speed of 49 miles per hour at 5:22 a.m. on the 14th. The thermometer, dropping all morning, read 20°F at the end of the snowfall and eventually sank to 17°F by midnight. In all, a bitter stormy day with a severe windchill.

Recent Snowfalls, 1970–1984

After the big snow season of 1966–67 when 57.6 inches fell, Nantucket entered an almost snowless period with no major snowstorms visiting the island until the winter of 1981–82. Unfortunately, the official record at the Airport ended with the 1972–73 season. Though the daily reports at the FAA tower continue to list snowfall, they appear to be based on the amount of precipitation falling, employing a standard ratio of 1 inch of precipitation equivalent to 10 inches of snow. Many times even this ratio is not listed.

The station at Chatham on Cape Cod maintained a record from 1970 to the present, and this is helpful in approximating snowfall on the island. As Great Point is closest to the Cape, these figures are probably more accurate for that eastern promontory than for the settled part of the island. The Edgartown station covers some of these years, but many critical months are missing from the record.

Under these circumstances, one must rely on the reports published in the *Inquirer and Mirror* by three of its correspondents, Tom Giffin, Charles Sayle, and Merle Orleans. Their measurements or estimates often differ and state that different amounts were reported from different places on the island. So snowfall data during this recent period are more an act of faith, in the view of climatologists, than when the Weather Bureau measurements on Main Street and Orange Street gave more authenticity to the amounts.

No storms during the period from 1968 to 1985 qualified for a Big Ten rating amount Nantucket snowfalls, which requires a depth of at least 15 inches per storm to be considered. In the Chatham record only the following individual months had a total excess of 15 inches: January 1976, 25.5 inches; January 1981, 22.8 inches; January 1982, 15.7 inches; December 1982, 15.0 inches; February 1983, 22.8 inches; and March 1984, 15.0 inches. The lack of months with excessive snowfall until 1981 and then the clustering of such months is quite evident.

An analysis of these big snow months at Chatham with what can be gathered on Nantucket does not indicate any single big storm on the island until 1983. In January 1976, Nantucket reported only 1.8 inches when Chatham had 11.4 inches. In January 1981, 8 inches fell on January 9–10 at both Chatham and Nantucket, and no subsequent storm that year equaled that amount.

On January 13–14, 1982, Chatham measured 9.3 inches of snow. Nantucket reported 2.00 inches of precipitation, of which only 6.0 inches was snowfall [equivalent to 0.60 inch of precipitation], all coming toward the end of the storm on the morning of the 14th.

On December 10, 1982, rain started before midnight, but soon turned to snow and continued all day Sunday [11th] and into early Monday morning [12th]. The heavy snowfall confined itself to the islands; Edgartown reported 15 inches the *Inquirer*

Main Street under a mantle of white, turn of the century. Collection of the Nantucket Historical Association.

and Mirror stated that the storm left "the island under a 16 inch blanket, with drifts of four to six feet reported." Merle Orleans wrote that the "depths varied from 5 to 12 inches." Tom Giffin commented: "Estimates of how much snow fell Sunday vary with the observer, anything from eight to 14 inches, soft and fluffy, but with that wind it drifted badly, and long after the snowfall and tapered off in the afternoon the blowing snow made it hard to tell the difference." Certainly, this was a major storm in Nantucket's history, but its credentials are not quite enough to accord it a Big Ten rating.

The Blizzard of '83 visited Nantucket on February 11–12. The heaviest snows fell in southern New England with a concentration of 20 inches or more in Connecticut and Rhode Island. Chatham also reported a total of 20 inches, with one inch on the 11th and 19 inches on the 12th. Edgartown had 1.30

inches melted precipitation, the equivalent of at least 13 inches of snow since the temperatures were in the low 20s. Measurements on Nantucket varied. Nancy Burns in the *Inquirer and Mirror* wrote: "it was hard to measure the exact amount of the storm's accumulation. The estimates are that we received somewhere between 10 and 14 inches." Charles Sayle in his "Waterfront News" stated: "By daylight the island was quite a sight after fourteen to sixteen inches had fallen."

The only noteworthy snowstorm of the 1983–84 season occurred on March 9–10 when a coastal storm well offshore caught southern New England within its snowfall canopy. The Islands and Cape Cod received the heaviest falls. Chatham reported 13 inches and Edgartown 12.8 inches. Nantucket's snow depth was estimated at 14.0 inches.

Early Season Snowfalls
October 10–11, 1925

The earliest snowfall in the season occurred on October 10 and 11, 1925. A cold front moved through the area during the early morning hours of the 10th, dropping the temperature from a high of 52°F shortly after midnight to 40° by 9:00 a.m. and eventually to a low of 36°F at 3:00 p.m. Winds from the northwest picked up from only 7 miles per hour to 29 miles at noon and to a peak of 47 miles by 7:00 p.m.

The weather bureau daily record read: "Cold blustery day with snow squalls. Lowest temperature so early in the season since station opened. Unusually rough sea, especially on ocean side." Traces of rain and sleet fell at 8:20 a.m., snow and sleet at 11:25 a.m., and snow and sleet at 3:45 p.m. The total amount of snow was listed as 0.2 inch.

Other occasions when snow has fallen in October were: 15th in 1876, 17th in 1929, 21st in 1899, 25th in 1962, 27th in 1859, 27th in 1869, and 28th in 1934. All were traces with no measurable amounts.

November Snows

A November snowstorm is a rarity on Nantucket. In fact, nothing worthy of the name has occurred since 1903 and 1904. During this month the waters surrounding the island are still warmer than the land, causing most precipitation to fall as rain while snow may be descending on the adjacent mainland.

In the 88 years of snowfall records on the island, only two Novembers have measured more than 3.0 inches during the entire month, and only five have totaled more than 2.0 inches. The average snowfall for November is only 0.6 inch. In 18 Novembers no snow has been reported, and in 45 more the amounts were only traces, or too small to be measured.

The greatest November snowstorm

occurred on the 27th in 1904 when 8.1 inches fell from 12:40 p.m. to 7:10 p.m. It came on a wind shifting from northeast to northwest which gusted to 18 miles per hour. The temperature fell during the day from a morning 38° to an evening 24°.

The *Inquirer and Mirror* commented on December 3:

Winter came upon us in full feather Sunday. Threatening skies of the morning gave forth snow by afternoon and the flakes fell copiously and uninterruptedly until early evening, the wind being moderate from the northeast. It then hauled to northwest and breezed, and the temperature fell, Monday morning revealing the mercury at 22 degrees, with a stiff northwester blowing that was a little too strong for the steamboat to buffet, and she remained at her berth.

Oddly enough, the next heaviest November snowstorm had occurred just a year before. It was a three-day storm with snow falling on the 27th, 28th, and 29th in the amounts of 1.2, 1.4, and 4.3 inches. Though a total of 6.9 inches fell, the amount on the ground never exceeded 4.3 inches at an observation time. The flakes on the 27th were described as dry and those on the 29th as moist. During these days temperatures ranged from 35° down to 26°.

The *Inquirer and Mirror* described the storm in the issue of December 5:

A thick snowstorm developed early Friday afternoon of last week [Nov. 28], continuing at intervals throughout the night, and Saturday morning dawned with a thick mantle of snow and a fresh northeast wind. Steamer *Gay Head* delayed her departure until 10:30 o'clock, the storm having abated sufficiently at that hour to allow the boat to make the passage to Woods Hole, and she arrived here on the return about 5:30 o'clock.

Late Season Snowfalls
Great April Snowstorm, 1841

The deepest April snow blanket ever dropped along the Atlantic seaboard descended from spring skies on April 12–13, 1841. From 10 to 12 inches covered Philadelphia. About 18 inches were reported in New York City where the marshall of a parade to honor the late President William Henry Harrison caught pneumonia and died soon after as a result of exposure to the elements. Next day was Election Day and many went to the polls knee-deep in a melting snow.

The April snowstorm developed even greater fury in New England. At Providence, 16 to 18 inches were reported by Professor Alexis Caswell, and the figure at New Bedford was 18 to 20 inches. There, Samuel Rodman added some notes to his record book to confirm that this was one of the truly great late-season storms:

Many cedars and some other trees broken by the weight of the snow on them — some snow flakes flying at intervals, begins to snow in the evening and continued with violent wind through the night and till the afternoon of the 13th. Snow being very compact and somewhat drifted about 16 inches average. Had it been as light as usual in the winter and level, it would have been 2½ to 3 feet deep.

The approaches to Cape Cod also received the full brunt of the storm. Reverend Thomas Robbins at Mattapoisett on Buzzards Bay on the 12th wrote in his diary:"at evening a severe snow storm." And on the 13th he continued: "it snowed hard during the night until noon. There is as much as 18 inches of heavy snow."

Down Cape at Yarmouth on the 13th, a heavy snow and high wind prevailed. "Snow in the woods about 18 inches deep on the average," reported the *Yarmouth Register,* and drifts in the western part of the town [on

Nantucket Sound] were estimated at eight feet high.

The *Inquirer* gave an eloquent description of the scene on Nantucket:

Winter Returned — At this present writing (Tuesday noon) [13th] we are in the midst of one of the most severest and incalculable storms of wind, snow, sleet, and rain, of which the experience of the past six months furnishes any example. The elements are battling with a sort of fierceness and ferocity that would seem to make up in violence what may peradventure be deficient in duration; although the fury of the warfare, which has continued without abatement some eighteen hours, as yet promises no speedy cessation. The streets were never in so bad plight, possibly since their elevation to the dignity of public highways. They are literally buried in porridge — too "thick and slab" to run off — too "soft and gentle", though half leg deep. Our whole town is one vast theater of slush and slop. There is no business — no locomotion. Houses and shops, to all exterior appearance, are as desolate as though the plague had imprisoned their inmates. The gale, from the northeast, rages so vehemently, as to carry away all hope of navigation. Neither steamboat or packet can reach us; and we must go to press in arrears to the amount of three main mails.

Easter Storm, 1854

The Storm—We were visited with one of the heaviest snow storms last Saturday [April 15] we ever saw so late in the season. It commenced at 3 o'clock in the morning, and the snow continued to fall very fast until afternoon.—We should judge that eighteen inches of snow fell on a level. It disappeared fast yesterday but the air was cold, very cold for the season, and there is still a considerable amount of snow on the ground.

Nantucket Inquirer,
April 17, 1854.

Long and Cold Storm—The storm which we spoke of in Monday's paper subsided for a short time on Sunday [16th], only to commence afresh during Sunday night with renewed vigor, and raged during the whole of the day following. Considerable snow fell on Sunday night and Monday morning, but the storm finally degenerated into one of those northeast drizzles which are always so exceedingly disagreeable and the wind blew furiously until Monday night. No vessel left here on Monday, but the weather becoming a little more tolerable, the steamer left on Tuesday morning at 6 o'clock, wind stiff at northeast, and returned in the evening. The weather, however, was still cold and disagreeable, with occasional squalls of rain and snow.

Nantucket Inquirer,
April 19, 1854.

April Fool's Snowstorm, 1887

April 1—Cloudy cool weather, sunrise 5:23 a.m. Heavy snow from early morning until 9 p.m. when it turned to rain accompanied by warmer weather. Average depth of unmelted snow 4.80 inches. High easterly winds. Cautionary received 7:47 a.m. and ordered down at 11:45 a.m. Sunset 6:07 p.m. Obscured. Foul weather sunset.

April 2—Cloudy sunrise 5:22 a.m. High and stationary temperature. Light rain, sleet and snow continued during the day accompanied by unusually severe and high northeast winds. Average depth of unmelted snow 2:00 inches. Maximum velocity of wind 42 miles per hour from N.E.

April 3—Telegraph line to Vineyard prostrated by severe storm yesterday.

Three masted schooner *Mattie W. Atwood* came ashore early a.m. on the north side of the island, vessel was from Boston for Norfolk Va. in ballast. Probably will be saved.
United States Weather Bureau daily weather report.

Devastating Snowstorm, April 1917

Sleighing on the 10th of April! History does not record such an event ever before on Nantucket—at least not within the memory of the present generation.

Inquirer and Mirror,
April 14, 1917.

The storm of April 9, 1917, will go down as the worst snow-storm that has visited Nantucket since October 18th, 1886; prior to that date we have no record. It was a typical coast storm, with its center near Cape Hatteras on April 8th, at ten p.m. and moving rapidly northeast. At 5:00 a.m. on the 9th, Nantucket began to feel the depression, with heavy, moist snow falling; at 7:27 a.m. a thirty-two mile breeze was blowing; at 10:45 a.m., 46 miles northeast was reached with an extreme of 49 miles. Then it began to diminish gradually, but kept up a good gale until 5:41 p.m.

The total snow-fall during the storm was 11.6 inches, some of which melted as it fell (6.6 inches), but leaving 5 inches on the level at 2:25 p.m.

This storm did considerable damage as the temperature was low 33° and the snow was in large flakes and froze solid to all objects. The telegraph and telephone lines were demolished by the weight of this ice, in some places the diameter being two to three inches, especially on the water front.

The storm will be considered as the worst snow-storm, and possibly by some as the highest wind, but the records show that the wind was a gentle zephyr in comparison with other April wind velocities, but during the other northeasters we were always remembered with a little snow.

George C. Grimes, official record of the U.S. Weather Bureau.

The snow began at 1:10 a.m., became heavy

at 5:00 a.m., and continued so until 2:00 p.m., when it tapered off and ceased to fall at 2:25 p.m. The total of 11.6 inches measured 1.16 inches water equivalent.

Winds of storm force prevailed from 7:27 a.m. to 5:41 p.m. The maximum sustained wind of 59 miles per hour began at 10:45 a.m. from the northeast, and the extreme one-minute wind speed of 62 miles per hour occurred at the same time. The average wind speed for the day was 29.8 miles per hour.

The temperature stood at 40°F at the start of the snowfall, but fell to 33°F at 4:00 a.m. and to 30°F at 2:00 p.m.

The wind behavior indicated that the center of low pressure offshore was nearest Nantucket at 12:00 noon when it backed from northeast to north and finally went to northwest at 7:00 p.m.

Tragic April Storm, 1950

April was not free of storm losses, however. On the 7-8th, a secondary or wave disturbance developed and moved north-northwestward off the coast along a low pressure trough, reaching extraordinary intensity in Nantucket waters and bearing lethal consequences to the fishing and dragging vessels operating there.

The scallop sloop *William J. Landry* with a crew of eight men, and the *Four Sisters* with ten men aboard were overwhelmed as the raging seas, built up by long-continued easterly gales, rendered the small vessels helpless, then tore them asunder and swallowed them up in a period of minutes. All eighteen hands were lost. Masters of other vessels which later limped into port described it as the worst April storm in 77 years [since 1873].

The blinding snow contributing to the calamity covered Cape Cod from Chatham to Wellfleet with four to eight inches.

New England climatologist.

The weather bureau reported 4.0 inches

falling between 2:00 and 7:00 a.m., and the press mentioned drifts of 8.0 inches at the Airport. The temperature varied from 37°F to 26°F on the 8th.

April Snowstorm, 1955

On the 3d and 4th a vigorous offshore low pressure center brought one of the worst April storms of record to many parts of southern New England. High winds, in many instances combined with sleet and wet snow, caused heavy damage to power and telegraph lines and disrupted services to thousands of homes. Snowfalls of 10 inches were fairly common in parts of western Massachusetts, southern Vermont, and northwestern Connecticut, and a few falls exceeded 20 inches.

Snow was drifted to even greater depths by the high winds with peak gusts reported above 70 mi/h. Automobile traffic was stalled, stranding many hundreds of motorists in towns and villages and many autos were abandoned on the highways.

Snowfall was much lighter in eastern Massachusetts with a few spotty falls highlighted by the 9.5 inches on Nantucket Island. Damage on Cape Cod, Martha's Vineyard, and Nantucket Island was due primarily to wind knocking out utilities, and in this area alone losses were estimated at $500,000. An estimate of property losses in other areas was not available.

New England climatologist.

The *Inquirer and Mirror* reported the unusual scene:

A 6 inch snowstorm which had effects equalling or surpassing the now famous storm in the winter of 1952, or even Hurricane Carol or Edna.

Light snow started early Sunday evening April 3—around midnight began to come down heavily.

Heavy snow estimated as weighing 12

pounds per foot collected on electric and telephone wires. Wind shifted after 8 a.m., gusts occasionally exceeded 50 miles per hour.

A total of 40 poles broken—some poles not broken but "when one nearby fell, they twisted like corkscrews from the pull of the wires. Temporary service restored but will take Telephone Company a month for complete restoration.

The unusual thing about the damage was that it was done by soft, wet snow rather than sleet, and that by noon on Monday there were few traces left, except where it had drifted.

Rain began on Nantucket at 12:16 p.m., April 3, 1955. The temperature stood at 41°F. The wind was out of the east at 27 miles per hour with gusts to 32 miles. The temperature dropped steadily all afternoon and evening to reach 33°F at 11:30 p.m. The rain changed to sleet (ice pellets) at 9:55 p.m. and to light snow at 10:10 p.m. Snow mixed with sleet fell until 11:50 p.m. Total precipitation amounted to 0.92 inch during the 24 hours of the 3d, and 0.7 inch of snow fell in the last hour before midnight.

Mixed snow and sleet fell during the early morning hours of the 4th until moderate snow took over at 5:20 a.m. and continued until 11:00 a.m. Though a total of 7.3 inches fell, the maximum accumulation on the ground reached only 5.3 inches as a result of melting. The thermometer hovered at 32°F and 33°F during the morning snow. At the very end, the snow turned to rain for an hour after noon with the temperature at 34°F. The total melted precipitation, rain, sleet, and snow, amounted to 1.70 inches.

The maximum wind on the 4th reached 42 miles per hour with a high speed of 47 miles per hour recorded at 12:28 p.m.

The barometric low of 29.48 inches occurred at 5:25 a.m. with the wind at north-northeast; there was no essential change in wind direction until 7:25 p.m. when it backed to north, then to north-northwest at 10:28.

The weather bureau report commented: "At 10:30 a.m. snow was 2 to 4 inches thick on telephone poles and wires."

"Great Blizzard" of April 1982

The month will be remembered in the Northeast for the "Great Blizzard" of the 6th and 7th [April]. The storm which was to become the blizzard made its way across California on the 3d and 4th, redeveloping over the southern Plains. By the 5th it was already dumping unusually heavy snows in the Midwest. As the storm moved toward the New Jersey coast, it began to pull in the record cold Arctic air which was entrenched across the Northwestern States.

By midday on the 6th a major blizzard was underway from northern New Jersey to Maine. The storm slowed down offshore and continued to be fed by the Arctic air to the north and warm, moist air from the Gulf of Mexico.

By the time it was all over, the storm had dumped a fairly general 8 to 18 inches of snow from northern New Jersey to northern New England. It was the snowiest April in most places in the Northeast since 1916, smashing numerous snowfall records from southern New England to the Middle Atlantic states.

The bitterly cold Arctic air poured down across New England in the wake of the storm and many spots were 25 degrees colder than normal the day after the storm . . . The snow was so deep and the cold so extensive that it took a week to moderate the region and melt the snow cover.

David M. Taylor, climatologist, Weather Services International, Inc. Bedford, Massachusetts.

April Fool's Day Storm, 1983

When we cautioned Nantucketers two weeks ago not to be too smug about there being no more snowstorms since spring had arrived, we didn't really expect the first day of April to carry out our warning. We had an honest-to-goodness blizzard, beautiful while

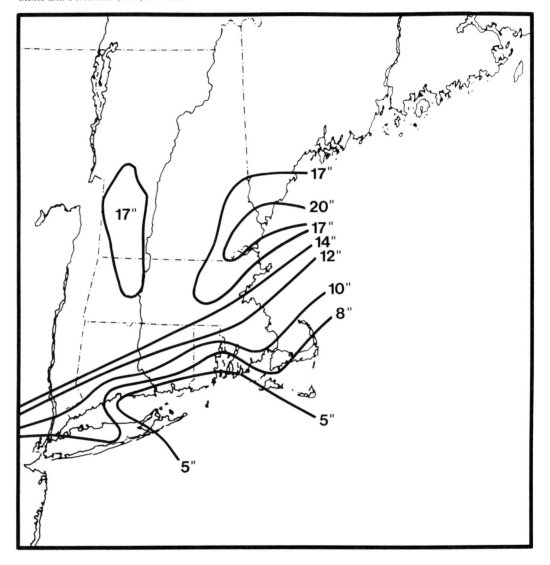

The snowfall distribution over southern New England during the Great April Blizzard of 1982 on the 6th and 7th. Nantucket received only four inches while Boston reported 13.3 inches and Portsmouth, NH, 20 inches.

it lasted. The winds were shifting from northeast to northwest and back until finally settling down to the northwest, with the highest gust we recorded as 56 mph from the northwest. We had about ¾ inch of snow, but again it was hard to measure due to the constant gale of wind whirling it around. The barometer dropped to a low of 29.62 before starting its upward trend early Saturday.
Inquirer and Mirror,
April 7, 1983.

Friday's assault was fairly well forecast, as forecasts go, but the snow lasted longer than we thought it would, which is why plowing wasn't started earlier. The day began with a fresh east-no'theast breeze slightly favoring Runway 15, a mixture of rain and snow falling. Then the wind backed a couple of points to just favoring 33, began to pick up in gusts, and the precip became all snow, great big flakes that stuck only on grass areas at first, but which after a while began to leave a treacherous layer of slush on runways and taxiways. The wind very slowly backed as it strengthened, keeping the crosswind factor nearly constant except for the deepening slush. Weather was at bare [aircraft operational] minimums of 400 [feet ceiling] and 1 [mile visibility], occasionally dipping to 300 [feet] and ¾ [mile], below limits for brief periods.

The wind reached its peak around one o'clock with a logged gust of 52 knots from 0.30, or 60 degrees of right crosswind on 33, and shortly after that the pilots still flying said that was it. (The skipper of the *Nantucket* had reached the same decision at nearly the same time, cancelling the return trip after his noon arrival and laying overnight till Saturday morning.

Tom Giffin,
Inquirer and Mirror,
April 7, 1983.

The storm raged all day on April 6 on Nantucket. When the precipitation began about 8:00 a.m., the wind was southeast blowing a steady 23 miles per hour with gusts to 40. A mixture of rain, freezing rain, and snow fell all day with the temperature rising as high as 41°F. The lowest barometer reading occurred about 6:00 p.m. The rain soon changed to snow and the temperature, with a northwest wind blowing at 40 miles per hour, stood at 28°F. The wind gusted as high as 70 miles per hour. Next morning, the 7th, the thermometer read 20° with the wind gusting to 52 miles per hour.

Snowfall amounts through the region, in inches, were: Hyannis 4.0, Chatham 4.6, Providence 7.6, Plymouth 8.0, New Bedford 9.0, Provincetown 10.0, and Boston 13.3.

White Christmases, 1876-1983

1876. Shortly after noon the sleighs began to increase in number, and Main Street presented an extremely lively appearance. Everything with runners was brought into

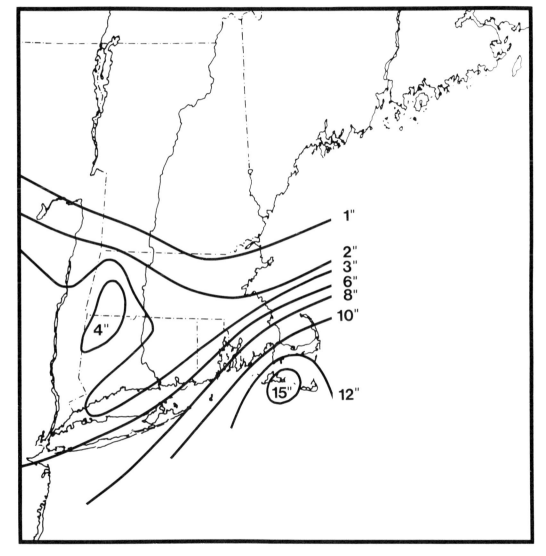

Heavy snowfalls are not limited to Boston and areas to the north as the storm of December 11–12, 1982 illustrates.

active service. Owners of fast teams put in an appearance, and there were some fine sports. These trials of speed drew together a large concourse of spectators who thronged the street on either side, and became more or less demonstrative as the race grew exciting or became devoid of fun.

The cold weather of Sunday [Dec. 24] tended to increase the quality of the sleighing and Monday morning the crisp surface caused a calm smile to o'erspread the countenance of the owners of teams, who (it being Christmas day) could afford to give their time to the sport. The streets were dotted with sleighs, and the merry jingling of the bells added to the general good cheer of Christmas day . . .

We have had the longest period of sleighing known here for many years.

Inquirer and Mirror,
December 30, 1876.

1878. The great festival of the year fell upon a cold, blustering day, and hence there was little to be noticed in the streets. Home gatherings were numerous, and the public services, by the Sunday schools, were among the pleasant features for the children . . .

Sleighing Christmas Day, the first of the season . . .

Inquirer and Mirror,
December 28, 1878.

1892. The Frost King took Nantucket by surprise last week, when he sat severely upon the temperature, forcing the mercury down in the tube to 5° above on Saturday [24th] morning, and creating a gale with his flight feathers that made everybody and everything shiver and shake in his path . . .

Sunday afternoon [25th] afforded a blinding snowstorm, but of short duration [measured 2.5 inches]. A high wind accompanied the snowfall, making locomotion on the streets difficult.

Inquirer and Mirror,
December 31, 1892.

1912. Nantucket's whitest Christmas came as the aftermath of a heavy snowstorm on December 24, 1912. Flakes began to fall at 4:15 a.m. and continued until 8:20 p.m. when 8.7 inches covered the ground. "The storm was severe, the moist snow clung to the wires and poles which were snapped like pipe stems. All wires down by 8:00 p.m.," declared the weather bureau observer.

Northeast winds picked up gradually during the morning, reaching gale force about 11:00 a.m. The peak speed of 38 miles per hour hit at 2:45 p.m. The average for the day was 28.6 miles per hour.

The barometer dropped to 29.59 inches at 4:00 p.m. and soon afterwards the wind shifted from northeast to north. The temperature had been at 34ºF at 11:00 a.m., making the snow very moist, but dropped to 28ºF by 9:00 p.m. and froze the snow clinging to the overhead wires.

Christmas was clear and sunny with the thermometer rising to 34ºF. Many sleighs appeared on Main Street, but the rare sport was short-lived as the snow melted rapidly the next day and was gone by the 27th.

1914. Two inches of snow fell on Christmas eve and morning; the temperature ranged only from 21° to 18°F, remaining below freezing continuously from the 23d through the 26th.

1924. Monday's [22d] snow lasted until Wednesday morning, when it rained steadily and the snow disappeared quickly . . . Shortly after day-break on Thursday [25th] the rain turned to hail and then to snow, and by 8:00 o'clock it was snowing thick and fast again and accumulating rapidly on the ground, bringing the "White Christmas" that everyone enjoys, even those who as a rule do not appreciate snow on the ground at any other time . . . The youngsters had opportunity to enjoy coasting on Christmas day, which is something unusual here on Nantucket Island.

Inquirer and Mirror, December 27, 1924.

The weather bureau reported a fall of 2.8 inches of snow on Christmas day. The temperature ranged from 38° to 21°F.

1925. Nantucket is experiencing another "white Christmas" this year . . . Following on a week of unseasonably warm weather, a change in conditions came Tuesday night and Wednesday [22nd and 23rd] brought a decided drop in temperature with a light snow-fall [1.6 inches] . . . early Thursday [24th] morning snow was falling again [1.8 inches], adding another layer to the whiteness of the snow . . .

The weather this week was not much different than what it was a year ago, although the temperature did not go so low. The cold wave came on almost the corresponding days of the week, however.

Inquirer and Mirror,
December 26, 1925.

Snow began to fall again on Christmas Day but turned to rain (0.22 inch). The temperature ranged from a low of 25° to a high of 38°F. It dropped to 13° on the 26th and 9°F on the 27th.

1935. A White Christmas only Four Times This Century. In the apparent cycle of cold weather which appears to have been launched in 1932, the island has experienced snow storms in December but, somehow, the snow had either come before or after the holiday, so that this year when a quantity fell on the 23d and again on the 26th, the Yuletide season on Nantucket has been given a most appropriate setting.

Inquirer and Mirror,
December 28, 1935.

The temperature on Christmas Day ranged from 30° to 21°F. It remained below freezing continuously from December 22 through 31, then dropping to a low of 10°F on the 29th.

1945. The snowstorm of the 19th–20th this year, however, was the heaviest since 1904—8.8 inches compared to 1904's 11.6 inches on December 12–13th.

Boys threw snowballs on Christmas Eve and "even the police car was stuck in the snow on Christmas day," according to the *Inquirer and Mirror*, December 29, 1945. The temperature on Christmas Day ranged from 42° to 26°F.

1959. "Though the ground was white it was beautiful overhead."

Inquirer and Mirror, January 1, 1960.

A total of 7.8 inches fell on the 22nd, and 4.0 inches remained on the ground at 7:00 a.m. on the 25th. Christmas Day temperatures ranged from 40° to 22°F.

1963. "Nantucket had a white Christmas."
Inquirer and Mirror, January 2, 1964.

A major storm dropped 15.1 inches of snow on December 18–19, and an additional 4.9 inches fell on the 23d and 24th. On the morning of the 24th, 8 inches remained on the ground, but this was reduced to 4 inches on Christmas morning. The temperature on the holiday ranged from 39° to 31°F. A light snow cover of 1 inch remained during Christmas week until New Year's Day.

1967. Though 2.2 inches fell on the 23d, only a trace remained on Christmas morning; that day the temperature ranged from 43° to 17°F.

1969. Of the 1.5 inches that fell on the 24th, only a trace remained on the ground on Christmas morning. The temperature ranged from 35° to 25°F.

1983. While Nantucket did not get the full brunt of the snowy deep freeze over the Christmas weekend, we had more than we needed. Gale force winds and temperatures down to 8° [7° at airport] complicated the clearing of the roads both Christmas Eve and Christmas Day. We had a total of 3½-4 inches of fluffy white snow which caused all sorts of problems, altering the plans of hundreds of Nantucketers either trying to get off the island or to return to spend Christmas here with their families or friends . . .

The snowfall of Christmas, 1983, began about midnight on the 23d, developed into a near blizzard when the northwest winds nearing gale force made plowing almost impossible. The DPW crew were out at 2:00 a.m. Christmas morning, some of them continuing to plow, shovel and sand the roads for 18 hours without a rest. Kids using Christmas sleds? Forget it. The wind was too strong temperature down to 7° and most everyone was content to stay inside. The barometer dropped from 30.79° in the 22nd to 29.40° before starting its upward trend on Christmas Day . . .

Nantucket had 0.81 inches of rain on Thursday, December 22nd, 3.75 inches of snow on the 23d–25th, and 0.35 inch during the rainstorm that ended some time after midnight. As of this morning [Dec. 29] most of the snow has disappeared.

Inquirer and Mirror,
December 29, 1983.

The highest temperature ever registered on Christmas Day was 53°F in 1889 and again in 1979, however, this figure stands as the lowest maximum for any day in the month of December. During Christmas week the temperature has risen as high as 57°F. The lowest Christmas Day reading was 1°F in 1980, and the next lowest was 7° in 1983. During Christmas week of 1933 the mercury dropped to –3°F on the 29th and again to –3°F on the 31st in 1962. The normal range of the thermometer on Christmas Day is a maximum of 40° and a minimum of 27°, for a mean of 33.5°F.

COLD WAVES AND COLD WINTERS

Snow engulfs a whale boat's crew in the wooden relief that hangs outside Nantucket's Whaling Museum.

Photograph courtesy of Cary Hazlegrove.

The first mention of the presence of a thermometer on Nantucket Island came in a 1788 entry in the diary of Kezia Fanning, stating that the cold on February 2, 1788 was several degrees colder than that of the lowest thermometer reading in the Hard Winter of 1780. Unfortunately, she did not state the exact reading of the instrument on either date. No other temperature figures appeared in print until 1806 when in "Notes on Nantucket," the Massachusetts Historical Society published mean monthly thermometer readings from January 1806 to July 1807. The thermometer of the Marine Insurance Office, Nantucket, as observed by Robert Barker, supplied these data. A cold winter in 1806–07 was indicated by the following average temperatures: December 30°F, January 26°F, February 27°F.

Obed Macy mentioned a reading of –11°F in February 1815 and Kezia Fanning told of –12°F and –13°F in the cold February of 1817. These are the only records of actual thermometer readings that have been found prior to 1823, when Walter Folger began his monthly meteorological summaries in the *Inquirer*, which continued until 1843. William Mitchell's observations were made from 1835 to 1861, though until 1847 his records were not of sufficient regularity and frequency to enable monthly means to be calculated.

Following Mitchell's departure for the mainland in 1861 come the "Dark Ages" of Nantucket meteorological history in that no regular series of observations have been found. Not until the founding of the Signal Service weather station in October 1886 do we have a daily run of temperature readings on Nantucket.

Eighteenth Century

The Hard Winter of 1780

During only one winter in recorded American meteorological history have all the salt water harbors of the Atlantic coast northward from the Carolinas frozen over and remained closed to navigation for a period of a month or more. This occurred during what has ever since been called "The Hard Winter of 1780," a crucial year during the War of American Independence when General Washington and his poorly-housed, ill-clad, and under-nourished troops at Morristown in the north Jersey hills were keeping a watchful eye on the British Army much more comfortably quartered in New York some 20 miles distant.

The Hard Winter of 1780 went through three phases: First, Snowbound—there came a series of exceptionally heavy snowstorms in late December and early January which accumulated to depths of two to three feet and more from Pennsylvania and New Jersey northeast over all of New England. Then, Deep Freeze—uninterrupted arctic blasts out of the north and northwest throughout January brought cold wave after cold wave without any sustained intervening thaws; gales drifted the snow into mountainous piles, blocking all communications. Thermometers remained persistently lower for the full month of January than any month since. Finally, Icebound—all navigable waters, both fresh and salt, froze so that the coast of the Northeast became locked inside an icy moat, interrupting the normal communication by boat with the outside world. New York harbor remained closed to navigation for five weeks.

Since Nantucket was joined to the mainland by a bridge of ice during January 1780, little modification of airstreams crossing Nantucket Sound would have occurred. Island temperatures would have ranged, relatively, in the same manner as on the continent.

Accordingly, this critical month during the middle of the War of Independence rates as a prime candidate for the title of Nantucket's "coldest month ever known."

Conditions on Nantucket were recalled by historian Obed Macy, writing fifty-five years later, of events "during the winter of that year, designated the hard winter."

The harbor was closed with ice about the twentieth of the twelfth month, 1779, and continued frozen, without intermission during the winter. The inhabitants soon began to feel the effects of this severity: for the cold increased and the ice was formed on all sides, so that there was no water to be seen from the highest eminences, for the space of several weeks. There was so much ice and snow on the ground and in the swamps as to almost entirely prevent the obtaining of any fuel thence. The shores and creeks were so covered with thick ice, that it was with great difficulty that fish of any kind could be procured.

A sailing ship when about 12 miles south of Block Island in the open Atlantic Ocean encountered "a very large body of ice." A vessel from Europe was turned away from Boston harbor as late as February 14th by an ice blockade. Down East in Maine, the tidal waters of Casco Bay and Penobscot Bay were frozen. "The like was never known by any living," were the words of the eighteenth-century authority on Maine weather, Reverend Thomas Smith.

Nineteenth Century

Cold Friday, 1810

The early morning hours of January 19, 1810, were long remembered in New England for the sudden overnight temperature descent, and the extreme windchill prevailing all day, as the strong northwest gale propelled subzero airstreams across the frigid countryside. For many years thereafter whenever a cold wind whistled outside and the family huddled around the fireplace, the tragic story of the Ellsworth family of Sanborton, New Hampshire, was retold. Their farmhouse was demolished in the early morning and their clothing scattered across the fields by the chilling gale. Three small children were frozen to death when their sleigh upset in the winds and their parents had gone to seek help from a neighbor. Bitter conditions prevailed for the next four days, and then a very mild late winter followed.

No account of the impact of Cold Friday on Nantucket has been found, either in diaries or the mainland press. Such a northwest air flow over New England must have brought zero conditions to the island, an isolated cold period in an otherwise very mild winter.

The Severe Winter of 1815

The winter of 1814–15 struck especially hard at the southern shore of New England and the islands from Long Island to Cape Cod. Frederick Freeman, the able historian of Cape Cod writing in 1860, singled out this season as being very severe. Newspaper editors in the 1850s would hark back to January and February 1815 as a winter comparable with the snows and cold of the mid-fifties.

Temperature records maintained at New Haven and New Bedford indicated greater departures from normal for the months of January and February 1815 than elsewhere in the Northeast. Apparently trough conditions existed not far offshore to maintain a northerly circulation most of the time. New Bedford had lower than normal temperatures for the three winter months: −2.9° in December, −1.8° in January, and −3.7°F in February. The thermometer went below freezing on every night of February, and for three weeks from January 26 to February 16 the maximum reached no higher than 34°. Thus, the heavy snows falling at New Bedford on January 17–18 and 22, and on February 4, 6, and 18 were little diminished by the sun.

The bitter cold wave at the end of January brought surprisingly low readings to southeast New England. The Rodman family at New Bedford, beginning with Samuel Rodman in 1812, kept meteorological records until 1905. During that nearly one century of thermometer readings, none matched those obtained on the below-zero day of January 31, 1815, when the four regular observations read −5°, −2°, −5°, and −9°F.

The *New Bedford Mercury* took notice of the extreme cold in the issue of February 3:

The weather has been unusually inclement for several days past. Yesterday [Tuesday] the mercury in the thermometer was down to 10° deg. below cypher; a degree of cold not experienced here for several years past. The harbour is completely frozen over to Long Island.

With Nantucket Sound and surrounding waters almost solidly congealed, the air flow was little modified when it reached the outer islands. Obed Macy writing of his experiences during the cold of January 31 and February 1 observed: "On the first of the second month, 1815, the weather was remarkably cold. The thermometer was eleven degrees below zero, lower by several degrees than had ever before been known."

Nantucket's Bitterest Daylight: December 16, 1835

The coldest daylight period since thermometers came into use in the northeastern section of the country occurred on December 16, 1835. People had gone to bed the evening before with temperatures at comfortable winter levels, but awoke to find a whole gale out of the northwest raging with the mercury already at zero and dropping rapidly despite the efforts of a sun rising in a clear sky.

Without doubt, this was the most remarkable Arctic blast ever to penetrate the New England countryside. It was similar to the gale of Cold Friday in 1810 though the chill factor was greater than that of its predecessor, and its arrival a week before the winter solstice made it all the more remarkable. All-time records for so early in the season, unequalled to this day, were established across New York State and New England.

The cold airstreams swept southeastward from Canada, where the day was known as "Black Wednesday," unimpeded and unmodified, to engulf the entire region between midnight and dawn. At sunrise on the 16th, Professor Adams at Hanover, NH, arose to find his thermometer at −15° with a gale raging out of the west-northwest.

At Boston similar conditions were unfolding. The *Evening Traveller*'s weatherman, Robert Treat Paine, a noted astronomer and almanac editor, reported a temperature drop of 20 degrees to a sunrise reading of –1.5 °F. It continued to sink, despite a bright sun, to –6° at 2:00 p.m. and finally reached a nadir of –10.8 at 6:00 p.m., a most remarkable early evening reading for The Hub. The core of the frigid air passed eastward at this time, slightly relaxing the grip of the cold wave. Next morning the Boston thermometer had risen to –4 °F.

To reach the island of Nantucket, an airstream at this early date in winter must pass over the open waters of the Sound and thereby undergo modification of its coldness. The intensity of the cold airstream was illustrated by its thermal content upon reaching Nantucket. William Mitchell's thermometer descended to –6° and others were said to have gone to –7 °F.

"There is no such record for the last 30 years which reaches this extent by four or five degrees," declared the *Nantucket Inquirer*. As so often happens when discussing past weather events, the editor was wrong. The mercury had dropped to –11 °F in the great freeze-up of January 1815, according to historian Obed Macy.

The exact data for Nantucket have been preserved in the notebooks of William Mitchell for hourly readings:

Dec. 16	sunrise	5 °F
	9:00 a.m.	3°
	1:00 p.m.	3°
	2:00	2°
	3:00	–2°
	4:00	–5°
	6:00	–6°
	9:00	–6°
	10:00	–5.5°
	11:00	–4°
	12:00 a.m.	–2°
Dec 17	1:00 a.m.	–1°
	3:00	0°
	5:00	1°
	6:00	2°
	10:00	8°
	12:00 noon	10°

At all three of Mitchell's observations on both the 16th and 17th, the wind direction was northwest and the sky condition was fair. His barometer rose steadily at each observation from 29.58 inches at sunrise on December 16 to 30.07 inches at 9:00 p.m. on December 17.

Thomas Burns Marriett in his diary gave some chill facts about the day:

Dec. 16 Fourth day Monthly meeting but so very cold windy and stormy did not go, and Nathan concluded to postpone his going. Thermometer being blown down could not ascertain correctly but about zero when we examined about 7 this morning. Geraniums, some frozen in the Parlour this morning. Gathered snow for washing.

William Mitchell added the sad note that "two women, Priscilla Cartwright & Phebe Coleman, sisters, living together, were found in their chamber frozen to death."

Cold Friday II: January 23, 1857

"The winter of 1856–57 was one of the severest winters ever known in this climate, and is the last very rigorous season that has occurred in New England," wrote Sidney Perley in 1891. "It began much earlier than usual, and continued far into the spring. There were thirty-two snow storms in all, three more than the average number for a score of years, and the snow fell to the depth of six feet two inches, the average depth for twenty years having been but four feet and four inches in eastern Massachusetts."

The first wintry spell of the season arrived in mid-December when the mercury fell below zero on the mainland and to 19 °F on Nantucket. Ice formed in the harbor during the next two weeks, though it did not form a solid sheet and block navigation. Another outbreak of cold weather began on January 4 and kept the thermometer below freezing for nine consecutive days. The floating ice

soon consolidated and on the 5th prevented the *Island Home* from leaving her wharf for the regular run to the mainland. For the next three weeks only four days had temperature readings above freezing in mid-afternoon, and these were in the middle or high thirties.

After a sudden change to above freezing readings on the 21st the authorities decided to try to break a path through the ice and free the *Island Home*, but little did they know that an arctic outbreak was on its way that would sink the thermometer to the lowest readings ever experienced on the island. The cold front arrived soon after noon on the 22d when the thermometer dropped from 24° to 4 °F by 9:00 p.m., and ultimately down to –6.5° in the morning of the 23d on William Mitchell's Smithsonian thermometer. The *Weekly Mirror* called attention to an instrument "with the thermometer at 11° below zero" at 6:30 a.m. and up to zero by noontime. "The coldest ever known," was the opinion of the *Inquirer*, despite the same low reading mentioned in 1815 by Obed Macy and the –12° and –13° temperatures noted in February 1815 by Kezia Fanning. Even so, January 23, 1857, has deservedly been called "Cold Friday II."

Not until the 28th did the mercury rise above freezing, and the last four days of the month were almost continuously above freezing at all observations. Nevertheless, the mean of 23.7° ranked January 1857 as the coldest month during the nineteenth century.

Winter ended after these two cold months. February turned notably mild with a mean of 35.7 °F, or 12 degrees above that of January, and raised the average of the three winter months of 1856–57 to 30.7 °F. In comparison, the average for the previous winter of 1855–56, when all three months were well below normal, was 28.8 °F.

Spectacular Temperature Descent, February 1861

The most precipitous temperature drop of

Stuck in a snowdrift, February 1924.
Collection of the Nantucket
Historical Association.

the century occurred in the otherwise lackluster winter of 1860-61. Residents of northern New England went to bed on the evening of Wednesday, February 6, with the temperature at the freezing point. During the night a cold front from Canada plunged southeastward and carried the mercury steadily downward to –40°F on the morning of the 8th, a Friday—hence Cold Friday III. At Hanover, New Hampshire, the thermometer fell 69 degrees in 18 hours to a low of –32°F.

The Boston area was not spared. The *Traveller*'s thermometer mounted to 46°F at 1:00 p.m. on the 7th. Next morning it had tumbled 60 degrees to a sunrise low of –14°F, the lowest point this thermometer had read since its acquisition in 1824. At Cambridge, the Observatory thermometer reached a nadir of –19°F.

The cold airstreams had swept from the continent to Nantucket, apparently with only minor modification of their chilliness while crossing the unfrozen surface of the Sound. The *Weekly Mirror* described the arrival of the cold airstreams and the occurrence of Arctic sea smoke when the cold air and the warm water interacted:

Great Cold—The first days of the closing week were pleasant and the temperature of the air moderate. But late in the afternoon of Thursday [Feb. 7], winter came back in a snow squall, and the mercury rapidly fell. Early yesterday morning, the mercury stood at ten degrees below zero. The wind blew a gale during the night of Thursday, but abated during yesterday. Ice formed rapidly in the Sound; indeed at ten o'clock yesterday [Feb. 8], no clear water could be seen North of the island. It should be remarked, however, that vision in that direction was very limited, owing to masses of vapor arising from the freezing water. A few days of severe cold weather are desirable for the growth of a crop of ice, which has not yet been secured.

William Mitchell, now in his last year of weather watching on the island, supplied the meteorological details. His thermometer registered a balmy 48°F at 2:00 p.m. on the 7th with a very strong southwest wind blowing. The cold front arrived with a bang about midafternoon. By 9:00 p.m. the thermometer was down to 14°F and dropping very rapidly under the urging of a northwest gale. At force 8 on the Smithsonian scale, the wind speed was that of a "violent gale" or an estimated 75 miles per hour. Imagine the cutting edge of the windchill that greeted Islanders on the morning of the 8th: –6.5° and a nor'wester raging at force 9, a "hurricane." And there was little relief during the day. At 2:00 p.m. the temperature was 1°F, accompanied by "a strong gale." By evening the wind had diminished to less than a gale, force 4 or "strong wind," and the mercury rose to a more comfortable 3°.

As in January 1857, Mitchell's conservative readings were exceeded by other thermometers around the island. The sheltered exposure of his instrument at the Pacific Bank building on Main Street was affected by the warmth of the nearby harbor and by smoke pollution over the town, while others on the outskirts of the town were in more open country and subject to the effect of radiation of heat to outer space which lowered readings by several degrees. The contrast is noticeable today between airport and town temperatures at night.

Twentieth Century

Cold and Snowy Winter, 1903-04

Old-fashioned winter descended on New England in the season of 1903-04 after an absence of some years. The regional climatologist summarized the two opening months of 1904: "January may be safely considered one of the most severe months that has occurred during the last century... The mean temperature for the whole district is the lowest since the New England Climate and

Crop Service was established in 1884." And of the succeeding month, he wrote: "February was a fitting climax to a winter that, so far as mean temperature is concerned, is unprecedented in the records."

Winter settled in on Nantucket at mid-December when the temperature fell from a high of 54°F on the afternoon of the 13th to a midnight low of 30°F and continued down to 22°F next morning. For the next six days the thermometer did not rise above freezing. A respite from the cold followed, with afternoon readings in the 40s and 50s, until Christmas.

Severe arctic conditions descended on the day after Christmas and continued for the next two weeks into the new year. On the heels of a heavy snowstorm on the 26–27th, the thermometer dropped to 8°F on the morning of the 27th and to low figures each night until the end of the month. December averaged 2.4 degrees below the decade's normal.

New Year's Day came in comparatively mild with the thermometer rising to 34°F; then another heavy snowstorm followed by a cold wave brought a return to hard winter. Minimum readings from the 2d through the 6th were: 7°, 2°, 7°, 13°F. Aside from a January thaw from the 20th through 25th when the mercury rose as high as 50°F, the month continued cold and ranked as the third coldest January in the modern record books. January averaged 4.1 degrees below the normal for the decade.

Winter returned again in mid-February to close the harbor for a third time. The 16th proved a bitter day: maximum 8°F and minimum –1°F. The following days of the cold wave had minimums of: 2°, 3°, 20°, 10°, and 12°F. Despite three days with maximums above 40°F, winter paid another visit during the last days of the month to produce a mean of 25.4° that tied 1901 as the coldest February of modern record. February averaged 4.7 degrees below the normal for the decade.

The three months of winter averaged 28.7°F, second only to the 28.3° average of the season of 1892–93. But the total snowfall of 82.0 inches, an all-time record for Nantucket, clinched the title for 1903–04 as the severest winter to date in the records of the weather bureau, which began in the fall of 1886.

Another Severe Winter, Back-to-Back, 1904–05

Though December 1904 at Nantucket averaged 6.4 degrees below normal, there were no severely cold days. The month's minimum reached only 14°F. The post-Christmas days were mild, with the thermometer soaring to 48° and 53°F on the 27th and 28th.

January behaved as a winter month should. The cold averaged 2.0 degrees below normal and snowfall was plentiful. The minimum for the month was only 10°F on the 5th. The winter's main cold spell set in on January 24, with a string of 13 days when the thermometer remained at or below freezing until February 5. During this period of steady cold the maximum reached 29°F and the minimum dropped to 8°F.

February produced 12 more freezing days, but the warmer days were interspersed with the cold ones. The month, as a whole, averaged 6.5 degrees below normal, making it the coldest February to that time. For the entire period of record to the present, February 1905 tied February 1977 for second place, exceeded only by February 1934.

The winter of 1904–05 was the coldest of record to that date with a mean of 27.8°F and placed second to 1917–18 (27°F) in the all-time records.

[Nantucket] The weather was remarkable for its persistent low temperature and high northwesterly winds, which caused the worst ice embargo experienced here since 1857. Ice began forming in the harbor on January 30th, and from February 2d to the 23d, inclusive, navigation was suspended.

George E. Grimes. U.S. Weather Bureau.

Two Colds Days In 1914

A frigid midnight occurred on January 13–14, 1914. A cold wave hit about 10:45 a.m. on the 12th when the thermometer stood at 36°F. The mercury was driven down to 10°F by midnight under the compulsion of winds of 50 miles per hour. Next morning at 8:00 a.m. the reading was 2°F and did not rise above the 5°F registered at 1:00 p.m. The mercury sank gradually to –1°F at 11:00 p.m. where it remained until 1:00 a.m.; then a slow rise began, reaching 3°F at 6:00 a.m. and 19°F at 2:00 p.m. Though the thermometer remained below zero for only two hours, both the 13th and 14th qualified as days having a zero reading in the record books. The mean of 2°F on the 13th comprised one of the coldest days in Nantucket history.

The coldest official temperature since January 1888 hit Nantucket during an arctic outbreak on February 12, 1914, during a month that averaged –5.4 degrees below normal. The cold front arrived late on the 11th and drove the thermometer from a high of 26°F to a midnight low of 4°F. The mercury sank to –4°F by 6:00 a.m. where it remained for two hours. It rose slowly above zero soon after 10:00 a.m. and read 4°F at noontime. The afternoon maximum reached 12°F. A drop-off to 5°F occurred by midnight. The mean for the day was 4°F.

The wind blew at an average of 22 miles per hour all day with an extreme gust of 34 miles per hour. "Owing to the low temperature and strong northwest winds all shipping remained in Harbor," the Weather Bureau reported. "Ice made rapidly all day. At 8:00 p.m. estimated thickness one inch extending from Hussey Shoal to Commercial wharf."

Next day the mercury rose to a maximum of 26°F and to 43°F on the 14th. The cold spell was over and the hard winter ended.

The Severest Winter Of Modern Times: 1917–18

In one season only has the temperature of each winter month averaged below 30°F. This occurred in the single winter of America's participation in World War I when December 1917 averaged 29.4°, January 24.0°, and February 27.7°. The mean for the three months of winter was 27.03°F, the lowest in the Nantucket Weather Bureau records since 1886.

After two days with the thermometer in the 50s, a sharp cold wave introduced true winter conditions to Nantucket on December 10, 1917. The temperature fell below freezing on each night for the remainder of the month except on the 18th and 19th when the minimum reached 34°F. One of the bitterest year-ends in New England weather history arrived on the day after Christmas and brought Nantucket minimums of 8°F on both the 29th and 30th.

The cold spell carried into the New Year until the 6th. Maximums generally remained in the teens and the minimums descended to single figures. The thermal decline reached its nadir on the 2d when a minimum of 5°F was registered.

A relatively mild period prevailed on Nantucket from January 11 to 18. Then hard winter returned for the rest of the month; only one day witnessed the mercury above freezing. No minimums, however, dropped below 12°F. The average minimum for January 1918 of 18.2°F was the lowest in Nantucket records.

Other minimum figures for January in the region were: Provincetown 8°, Block Island 2°, Fall River –3°, Providence –4°, and Plymouth –5°F.

The cold period continued into the first week of February. Though maximums rose above freezing on the 3d and 4th, a cold wave with extremely bitter arctic content arrived late on the 4th, dropping the mercury to 1° by midnight and to –6.2°F by sunrise, the lowest ever registered by the weather bureau on Nantucket. The previous record lows were –3.5° in January 1888 and –4°F in February 1914. Minimum readings in the region on February 5, 1918, were: Block Island and Provincetown –6°, Boston, Fall River, and Plymouth –10°F.

With the island surrounded by ice, no warming maritime winds arrived to bring relief. The temperature dropped to freezing or below on every night of February except two, the 12th and 28th. The February mean of 27.7°F was warmer by 3.2 degrees than the record cold February in 1905.

Christmas Holiday Cold, December 1933

Winter of outstanding severity was the noteworthy characteristic feature of the weather in New England during December 1933. The mean temperature was the third lowest since 1888, when monthly averages for the entire region were first compiled. The two colder occurrences were in 1904 and 1917. The lowest temperature was 50° below zero at Bloomfield, Vermont, which was the lowest ever recorded officially in New England, except upon the summit of Mount Washington.

New England climatologist.

The major cold wave of December reached Nantucket on the 27th when the thermometer fell to 15°F and on the 28th to 14°F. These readings were preliminary to the arrival of a truly arctic airstream which dropped the mercury to –3°F on the 29th, the lowest reading ever recorded in December until that time. Maximums on these days were not exceptionally low as bright sunshine raised the temperature to almost comfortable levels: 31°, 30°, 19°, and 29°F from the 27th through the 30th. On the last day of the year, the thermometer soared to 42°F. The month averaged 2.2 degrees below normal.

Coldest Month Ever: February 1934

"The coldest month ever recorded, since the compilation of regional averages, passed into New England history as the temperatures during February, 1934, are brought into comparison with earlier occurrences," the New England climatologist declared in his monthly survey. "The mean for the region was 11.8° which was 1.4° colder than the previous low-record month of January, 1918 . . . On the 9th, it was below zero throughout the region, and in some of the more distant parts of northern New England it was below freezing every moment of the month."

After a brief respite at the beginning of February, hardcore winter settled down on Nantucket at the start of the second week. On Thursday, the 8th, the thermometer slumped from a reading of 15° at noon to –1°F at midnight. At that hour the wind was blowing at 19 miles per hour from the northwest.

The Nantucket thermometer remained at zero or below for eleven consecutive hours until 10:00 a.m. on the 9th. The minimum of –4°F was noted at both the 7:00 and 8:00 a.m. observations. Despite clear skies all day, the mercury rebounded to only 4°F in the early afternoon. This gave the 9th a daylight mean of exactly zero. It did grow slightly warmer late in the evening, reaching 5°F, and remained there for the rest of the night. At 8:00 a.m. on the 10th the temperature began a rise to a maximum of 22°F at 3:00 p.m. Under the influence of a strong anticyclone, winds were light to moderate from the northwest in the morning and from the west in the afternoon.

The steamer with its few hardy travelers left on time at 6:30 a.m. on the 9th when the thermometer read –4°F. However, ice conditions near the jetties forced it to return, much to the chagrin of the passengers who had foresaken warm beds to brave the arctic cold.

A cold morning at 9:30 on Orange Street. Photograph courtesy of H. Flint Ranney.

February 1934 went into the record books as the coldest month of the century. The average of 22.55° exceeded that of the previous title holder, January 1893 with 23.8°, and February 1905 with 24.5°F. This record cold was not even closely challenged until recently when a 22.60°F mean in January 1981 narrowly missed dethroning King Winter—February 1934.

Cold Surge of February 1943

A spectacular cold wave descended on New England in mid-February 1943 during an otherwise unexciting winter in much the same manner as on Cold Friday in January 1810 and in the Cold Descent of February 1861. In Vermont, the temperature plummeted to –46° and a week later rose to 55°F—a change of 101 degrees! Nantucket experienced the same proportionally, for an island location.

The thermometer stood at 30°F at noon on February 14 and a moderate wind out of the west was blowing across the island. About 5:00 p.m., the wind veered to northwest as a cold front arrived. The wind continued moderate, but the temperature started downward, reaching 11°F by midnight. The descent continued into the early morning hours of the 15th. The mercury reached 0° at 5:00 a.m. on its way to a nadir of –5°F a little before 8:00 a.m. It remained at that low point for more than an hour. This marked the lowest temperature on Nantucket since the all-time low of –6.2°F in February 1918 and still ranks second for low readings in the Weather Bureau records. The wind continued at moderate speeds from the northwest all day. At 6:40 a.m. the wind speed peaked at 30 miles per hour and the thermometer read –4°F, for a windchill factor of –55°.

After eight hours at zero or lower, the thermometer rose by 2 p.m. to an afternoon maximum of 2° before another gradual descent carried the mercury down to –3°F at 7:00 and 8:00 p.m. Fifteen hours of below-zero readings extended from 5:00 p.m. on the 15th to 7:00 a.m. on the 16th—a record string of consecutive below-zero hours for Nantucket. The reading remained fixed at –1°F from 11:00 p.m. to 7:00 a.m.; then a gradual rise to the afternoon's maximum of 13°F took place. Wind movement was low, at an hourly average of 7.7 miles per hour. Some light snow fell intermittently in the morning, total amount being only 0.3 inch.

Despite the cold surge at midmonth, February 1943 averaged 31.2°F, or exactly the normal for the month at that time. Other thermometers in the region registered extreme minimums: –6° at Block Island, –11° at New Bedford and Hyannis, –12° at East Wareham, –14° at Boston, Providence, and Plymouth, –15° at Fall River, and –18°F at Blue Hill Observatory, Milton.

Year-Ending Windchill of 1962

A prime example of what storm activity at considerable distance from Nantucket can do to the local weather occurred on the last two days of December 1962 when the backlash of a very deep cyclonic center over the Gulf of Maine created blizzard conditions over much of New England. Two of Nantucket's bitterest days followed with gale-force winds lashing the island while the thermometer hung close to zero.

The culprit low pressure area had moved off the Carolina coast late on the 29th and took a course to the northeast, passing west of Nantucket shortly after midnight of the 29–30th when the local barometer read 29.73 inches. The storm center deepened rapidly as it sped northeast to a position south of Cape Sable, and well east of the Nova Scotia shoreline by noon of the 30th. Then the center turned north-northwest and performed a counter-clockwise loop over the Bay of Fundy, northeast Maine, and southern Nova Scotia during the night of the 30–31st. Lowest pressure of the deep storm center at a land station, 28.73 inches, was reported at Eastport, Maine. In conjunction with a strong high pressure area extending on a north-south axis from Hudson Bay to the Gulf of Mexico, a very intense circulation whirled around the storm center, bringing a vast flow of cold arctic air into New England with temperatures from about 15°F in Maine to zero on the south coast. Gusts mounted to 95 miles per hour at Block Island and to 75 miles at Point Judith, RI. The highest wind speeds coincided with the minimum temperatures, producing an extremely dangerous windchill comparable to that of 100° to 125°F below zero.

At midnight of the 29–30th, Nantucket basked in a southerly air flow that brought thermometer readings to 44°F. About 2:00 a.m. the wind shifted into the northwest and mounted steadily to gale force. As the wind increased, the temperature fell: to 32° at 5:00

a.m., to 16° by noon, to 8° by 6:00 p.m., and 0°F by 11:00 p.m. of the 30th. The wind mounted to a peak of 47 miles per hour during the day and averaged 33.8 miles per hour for the twenty-four hours.

Early on the morning of the 31st, the mercury sank to a minimum of –3°F and hovered at or below zero until 7:00 a.m. A gradual rise to 8° by noon followed and to 12°F by 3:00 p.m. The wind continued unabated all day from the northwest, averaging only slightly less than the day before, at 33.2 miles per hour. The peak hit 43 miles per hour.

The mark of –3°F equaled the lowest ever registered in December during the modern period on the island and was among the five lowest readings ever made by the Weather Bureau in any month. December averaged 2.1 degrees below normal, and 17 inches of snow fell—a truly wintry month and the start of a severe season.

Temperatures in the region over the night of the 30–31st were rather uniform as the strong advective winds were little modified by the land or sea they passed over: Boston 2°, Edgartown and New Bedford –3°, Block Island –4°, Fall River and Providence –5°, East Wareham –6°, and Hyannis –7°F.

Prolonged Continuous Cold, January 1970

January 1970 on Nantucket proved the coldest month since February 1934 and the coldest January since 1918. In fact, only in 1893 and 1918 had the month of January been colder. The first two weeks were steadily below normal, but no unusually severe days occurred except on the 8th when the thermometer dipped to an even 0°F.

A second cold period, beginning on the 19th and ending on the 25th, brought consecutive minimums of 2°, 2°, –1°, 9°, and 6°F. The reading of –1°F on the 23d marked the coldest registered by an official thermometer on the island since December 1962.

Despite a warm ending of two consecutive days with maximums of 44°, the month averaged 24.8°F, or 8.2 degrees below normal.

"The Memorable Month Of January 1977"

"The 'Memorable Month of January 1977' will take its place among the outstanding winter months in the meteorological annals of North America. Never before has the weather made so many headlines and occupied so much front-page space as during the month under review. This resulted not only from the severity of the weather conditions and their extreme departure from normal, but also from their critical impact on many aspects of the daily health and economic welfare of people in all parts of the country." So read my monthly column in *Weatherwise* magazine.

On Nantucket, January 1977 was a severely cold month, the third coldest in Airport records, January 1970 and 1981 being more severe. The mean of 24.6°F was 7.2 degrees below normal. There were three extremely cold periods; minimums below 10° were registered on the 13th and 14th; 6°, 4°, 8°, and 9° were noted on the 17th to 20th; and 15°, 11°, 9°, and 13°F on the 28th to 31st. The cold continued through the first three days of February. During the month only one day failed to register a freezing temperature at night, and that was the 4th when the minimum reached 33°F. Daytime maximums, however, were above freezing on half the days of the month. January 1977 ranked as the fifth coldest January and the eighth coldest month of any on Nantucket.

Other minimum readings during this cold February of 1979 were: Chatham 1°, Provincetown 1°, Block Island 0°, Martha's Vineyard Airport –1°, Newport –3°, Boston –3°, New Bedford –4°, Hyannis –5°, East Wareham –8°, Taunton –13°, and Plymouth –15°F.

Two-Week Freeze, February 1979

Nantucket's thermometer remained below freezing at all hours during the 14 days from February 5 through 18, the longest such period in this century and exceeded only by 15 days in January 1893.

During this recent cold spell the maximum reading topped at 31° and the minimum sank to an even zero, the coldest reading since –1°F in January 1970. The core of the cold period extended from the 9th to 19th, with daily minimums of: 11°, 5°, 2°, 4°, 7°, 0°, 9°, 12°, 5°, 3°, and 11°—a mean minimum of 6°F.

With a maximum of 41° and a minimum of 34°F, February 21 marked the first day with an overnight thaw since January 30. Subsequently, from the 23d to 27th, the mercury remained continuously above the freezing mark, even at night. Even so, the mean of the month figured 24.5°, for the coldest February since the record of 22.55°F in 1934.

The first 18 days of February 1979 averaged 18°F, while in 1934 the same span of 18 days averaged four degrees higher at 22°F. But the final ten days of these two months brought a very different result. In 1979, they were very warm, averaging 37°, but in 1934 much colder with an average of 24°F. Thus, the month's mean in 1979 of 24.5° ranks second, along with that of February 1905, to February 1934's mean of 22.55°F.

Cold Christmas Day, 1980

Most residents of the northeastern corner of the country were delighted to receive an inch or two of snow on Christmas Eve which provided the proper seasonal setting for the annual holiday. Yet they were not quite prepared for the arctic blasts which greeted them when they arose next morning to see what Santa had brought. The front causing the snowfall on the 24th moved offshore about midnight and introduced one of the coldest advective blasts to descend on New England in many a winter.

The most memorable feature [of the month] was a remarkably large and rapid drop in temperature which hit the northwestern corner [of New England] on the 24th, progressing to the southeast on Christmas Day. This gave northwestern Vermont maximum temperature readings on Christmas of well below zero and minimal mostly 20-to-30° below zero. This was accompanied by very strong wind, which produced dangerous windchill conditions . . . This cold with its bitter windchill, will make Christmas 1980 long remembered in all New England.

New England climatologist.

On the day before Christmas the thermometer on Nantucket ranged from a morning low of 31° to an evening high of 42°F at 8:00 p.m. under the urging of a southwesterly flow. But soon after midnight the leading edge of a sharp cold wave hit the island with winds swinging into the northwest and north-northwest. By 7:00 a.m. the temperature dropped to 14°F and was falling rapidly. At noon it read 4°F, or down 38 degrees from the previous evening. Winds gusted to 40 miles an hour, creating a windchill of about –45°F. The slumping mercury reached a low of 1°F at 8:00 p.m.

The thermometer remained there for several hours until past midnight when a slow rise began. It read 5°F at 6:00 a.m. and continued upward all day to a maximum of 29°F by 11:00 p.m. Winds diminished rapidly during the night and on the 26th were generally 10 miles per hour or lower. The recovery of the mercury was as rapid as had been its drop on the island's bitterest ever Christmas Day.

Other Christmas Day minimums in the region were: Provincetown and Block Island 0°, Edgartown –2°, West Falmouth –3°, New Bedford –5°, East Wareham and Boston –7°, Hyannis –6°, Providence –10°F.

Another Cold January, 1981

Nearly all of New England was extremely cold and extremely dry. Many records were broken or threatened . . .

January in most areas averaged 7° to 9° below normal, setting new record low means at some stations. Over much of the section, this was the coldest January since 1970 or longer.

Extreme lows approached state record minimums in most states, with the –35° at Chester, Massachusetts, on the 12th breaking [the state record] set at Birch Hill Dam on January 18, 1957, with –34°.

New England climatologist.

The temperature on Nantucket dropped below the freezing mark on every night save one during January 1981. The average minimum of 15.7° was almost as low as the 15.4°F registered during the coldest month of February 1934. But the average maximum of 29.5° ran 0.2 degree lower than in 1934. Nevertheless, the mean of January 1981 figured 22.60° as compared with February 1934's 22.55°F. Thus, January 1981 was the second coldest month in the modern records dating from the weather bureau's establishment on the island in October 1886.

The severely cold period in January 1981 extended from the 3d to 14th with the minimum remaining below 20° each night except for 22°F on the 7th. On the 12th the thermometer reached its nadir of 2°F. Since average temperatures in both December and February of that winter ran above normal, January 1981 stood out on the meteorological calendar as an isolated cold period.

Minimum temperatures during the month throughout southeastern New England dropped generally to zero or below: Nantucket 2°, Block Island 1°, Provincetown 0°, Edgartown –2°, Boston and New Bedford –4°, Hyannis –6°, East Wareham –10°, Providence –12°F.

Cold Mid-January Of 1982

January was very cold. It followed the trend of the recent winters with one very cold month in each season. After a rather mild initial week, severe cold reigned almost to the month's end. The cold was accompanied on many days by strong winds, producing a severe windchill.

From January 10 to 22, Nantucket endured a cold period with minimums below 20°F every night except one. The severely cold nights were the 10th, 11th, and 12th with lows of 6°, 6°, and 4°, and the 17th and 18th with 2°F on each night. The month's average of 25.7°F represents a negative departure from normal of 6.1 degrees. This comprised the fourth coldest January in the airport records behind 1970, 1977, and 1981.

Low temperatures around the region in January 1982 were: Nantucket and Block Island 2°, Provincetown 3°, Edgartown and Boston –2°, New Bedford –3°, Hyannis –4°, East Wareham –6°, and Providence –9°F.

Zero and Below on Nantucket

Date	Temp.	Source
1780, Jan.	− 11 °	Macy
1815, Feb. 1	− 11 °	Macy
1826, Jan. 31	0 °	Folger
Feb. 1	− 1 °	Folger
1835, Dec. 16	− 5 °	Mitchell
	− 7 °	*Inquirer*
1846, Feb. 27	0 °	*Inquirer*
	− 1.5°	*Mirror*
1855, Feb. 7	− 2 °	*Inquirer*
1857, Jan. 23	− 6.5°	Mitchell
	− 11.0	*Inquirer*
Jan. 24	0 °	Mitchell
1861, Feb. 8	− 6.5°	Mitchell
	− 10.0°	*Mirror*
1882, Jan. 24	− 6.0°	*Inquirer and Mirror*
1883, Dec. 23	0 °	*Inquirer and Mirror*
1888, Jan. 29	− 3.5°	United States
Feb. 16	− 1 °	Weather Bureau
1895, Feb. 5	− 2 °	*Inquirer*
	+ 0.8°	USWB
1896, Feb. 17	− 1.2°	USWB
1900, Feb. 27	+ 0.5°	USWB
1902, Dec. 9	− 1 °	USWB
1914, Jan. 13	− 1 °	USWB
Jan. 14	− 1 °	USWB
Feb. 12	− 4 °	USWB
1918, Feb. 5	− 6.2°	USWB
1933, Dec. 29	− 3 °	USWB
1934, Feb. 8	− 1 °	USWB
Feb. 9	− 4 °	USWB
1942, Dec. 20	− 3 °	USWB
1943, Feb. 15	− 5 °	USWB
Feb. 16	− 1 °	USWB
1961, Feb. 2	0 °	USWB
1962, Dec. 30	0 °	USWB
Dec. 31	− 3 °	USWB
1970, Jan. 23	− 1 °	USWB
1979, Feb. 14	0 °	USWB
1980, Dec. 25	− 1 °	USWB
	1 °	USWB
1981, Jan. 4	1 °	USWB
1982, Jan. 17	2 °	USWB
Jan. 18	2 °	USWB

HARBOR ICE AND FREEZE-UPS

wished.

The introduction of the airplane greatly reduced the physical effect of a freeze-up. Mail, commodities, and even people could be transported over the ice-solid waterways to the mainland and back. Though the weather might cause a temporary halt in communications, complete "ice-olation" was gone forever.

The history of Nantucket's freeze-ups from 1818 to 1910, as reported in diary and newspaper accounts, has been published by Harry B. Turner in *The Story of the Island Steamers* (1910). The longest tie-up occurred in 1857 when no boats entered or left the harbor from January 5 to February 6, a period of 31 days without direct communications. The second most serious ice blockade occurred in February 1905 when for three weeks, from the 3d to the 23d, no boats could navigate the harbor. Turner could find no account of this period of isolation because the pages of the *Inquirer and Mirror* for this month are missing from the collection in the Atheneum. Fortunately, George E. Grimes of the weather bureau set down a daily account of ice conditions in the harbor so that we can now add this important information to Turner's original work.

The following section describes the more important freeze-ups in Turner's chronicle, and extends the significant accounts from 1910 to the present.

Eighteenth Century

The Hard Winter Of 1780

Ice conditions on Nantucket in 1780 were recalled by historian Obed Macy, writing 55 years later.

The harbor was closed with ice about the twentieth of the twelfth month, 1779, and

Prior to the twentieth century, Nantucketers looked to the surface condition of the harbor waters, whether liquid or solid, for their economic well-being as well as for their feeling of personal security. The parody word, "ice-olation" was created by a newspaper editor to express their situation. The *Inquirer* declared at the end of the January 1857 ice embargo: "At length the joyful hour has come! The period of suspense is ended, and we are no longer Know-Nothing."

The significance of a harbor freeze-up has declined steadily over the years. In the days of sail power, a boat was at the mercy of sheet ice and ice floes since it lacked the power to make headway in any direction. Steam-powered ships often could force their way through thin or rotting ice, and with the increase in motor power around the turn of the century, and the later introduction of diesel fuel and more powerful engines, they could serve as icebreakers to aid less powerful vessels.

Once cable to the mainland was laid in 1886 messages could be sent and received instantly, which greatly reduced the feeling of isolation formerly brought on by a freeze-up. News of events around the world, as well as personal messages could be flashed to and from islanders. Next came the telephone with its instant two-way conversations, and finally the introduction of radio communication in the early part of this century enabled all Nantucketers, whether on ships or ashore, to have immediate contact with whomever they continued frozen, without intermission during the winter. The inhabitants soon began to feel the effects of this severity: for the cold increased and the ice was formed on all sides, so that there was no water to be seen from the highest eminences, for the space of several weeks. There was much snow and ice on the ground.

Kezia Fanning noted in her diary: "Jan. 15   Harbor frozen over. People go to Quaise on the ice. Feb. 6   Juda and Bill came down from Quaise on the ice."

Nineteenth Century

The Winter Of 1814-15

The winter of 1814–15 brought as severe conditions as had prevailed since the Hard Winter. It was especially intense on Cape Cod and the Islands. We have no direct word as to ice conditions on Nantucket except for Obed Macy's statement that the thermometer was down to –11 °F, "lower by several degrees than had ever before been known." The *New Bedford Mercury* reported on February 3 that their harbor was frozen out as far as Long Island. Presumably Nantucket harbor was frozen, too, at this time.

Severe Winter Of 1835-36

A hard winter, Nantucket being surrounded by ice the greater part of the time. On February 6 no water was in sight. Sloop *Barclay* was caught in the ice three miles in back of the bar, and people passed to and fro drawing sleighs, and by this means discharged her cargo.

View of harbor and ice-bound vessels from Clock Tower in the severe winter of 1880–81. Collection of the Nantucket Historical Association.

Harry B. Turner, *The Story of the Island Steamer*, 1910.

In 1835–36 winter temperatures recorded at New Bedford departed from the normal monthly average for the decade by the following amounts: December –5.5°, January +0.6°, February –5.9°, and March –2.4°—a mean departure for the winter of –3.3 degrees Fahrenheit.

Walter Folger's figures for Nantucket largely concurred: December -5.9, January -0.1, February -5.9, and March -4.4—a mean departure of -5.4 degrees Fahrenheit.

Long Freeze-up Of 1836-37

The harbor was frozen over during all the depth of winter. Sloop *Silas Parker* sailed from outside Brant Point on January 2 with twenty passengers, among whom were the town's representatives to the legislature. Schooner *Exact* arrived at Brant Point from Baltimore on January 6, and during the night was carried by the ice into the inner harbor, where she was imprisoned until February 23. Horses and carts were driven over the ice to the schooner and took out the flour and corn, carrying it four miles over the ice to town. There was a shortage of grain and a few provisions that winter.

The mail packet sailed February 8 for the first time in forty days. Steamer *Telegraph* arrived at Nantucket on February 25 for the first time since Christmas.

Turner,
The Story of the Island Steamer,
1910.

The temperature departures from normal at New Bedford for the winter months of 1836-37 were: December -1.5, January -4.3, February -1.6, and March -3.0—a mean departure from normal of -2.9 degrees Fahrenheit for the winter.

Walter Folger's observations on Nantucket were more extreme: December –3.9, January –6.7, February –1.0, and March –2.7—an average departure of –4.8 degrees Fahrenheit.

January
Cold and Ice,
1852

The harbor was closed for five weeks and the winter was very severe. Mails were landed on Great Point on January 25, and two days later the steamer made her way out through the ice to clear water.

Turner,
The Story of the Island Steamers, 1910.

The temperature departures from normal for New Bedford during the winter of 1851–52 were: December –6.1, January –3.2, February +0.3, and March –0.3—a winter departure from normal of –3.1 degrees F.

William Mitchell's observations on Nantucket showed the following departures from normal: December –4.9, January –1.7, February +1.9, and March +0.4—a mean departure of –1.4 degrees.

The First of Three
Cold Winters, 1855

Steamers *Massachusetts* and *Eagle's Wing* were both frozen in the harbor this winter, but were able to resume their trips by the middle of February.

Turner,
The Story of the Island Steamers, 1910.

The temperature departures from normal for the winter months of 1854–55 at New Bedford were: December +2.3, January –7.2, February –6.1, and March –5.8—a winter's mean departure of –5.8 degrees F.

William Mitchell's departures from normal were: December –1.9, January missing, February –3.1, and March –4.3 degrees.

The Long Cold
Winter of 1856

The ice embargo of this year extended over a period from January 4 to February 23. There were several interruptions, when communication was held with the outside world via steamship *Island Home* from Hyannis. The first period was between the 4th and 11th, then from January 25 to February 5, on which latter date eight days' mails and fifteen passengers were landed at Quidnet.

On February 6, twenty-two sleighs were out on the harbor ice at one time. On the 9th, the steamer effected a landing at Great Point. It was snowing at the time, and the townspeople did not know of her coming. The mails and passengers were taken to Polpis in carts by farmers, and then Charles F. Brown rode to Nantucket on horseback and apprised the astonished citizens of what had been doing. On the 12th, the boat reached her pier here; sailing next day, it took her 23 hours to reach Hyannis. She did not return until the 23d, when the harbor was freer of ice than for many weeks.

Turner,
The Story of the Island Steamers, 1910.

The temperature departures from normal at New Bedford were: December +2.3, January –7.8, February –6.1, and March –6.9—a winter's mean departure of –6.2 degrees F.

William Mitchell's figures, though showing a lesser departure, agreed: December +2.2, January –4.4, February –4.2, and March –4.3—a mean departure of –3.8 degrees.

"The Longest Period
of Isolation,"
January 1857

January of 1857 chronicled the longest period of isolation on record, the harbor filling up with ice during the last two weeks of December and finally closing completely on the night of January 5. Steamer *Island Home* was unable to move from her berth the following morning and it was not until Wednesday, the 21st, that any attempt was made to break out the ice. The plan of blowing up the ice was resorted to, but was unsuccessful on account of the extreme thickness, in some places being over ten feet thick. It was then determined to saw a passage through the ice to Brant Point the following day, and a large gang of men were engaged for the work, but a heavy snow storm prevented. The plan was to saw two cuts the width of steamer *Island Home* apart and then blow up the ice between, the expense to be defrayed by voluntary subscription, and but for the severe storm the scheme might have proved effective.

On Tuesday, February 3, the little schooner *Pizarro*, of Hyannis, Capt. Chase, anchored off Quidnet and sent a boat ashore with about thirty passengers and mails, which had been accumulating for twenty-eight days. A thaw set in on the 4th, and aided by a strong southerly wind, steamer *Island Home* forced her way out of the harbor on the afternoon of the 6th, the isolation having lasted just thirty-one days. Steamer *Eagle's Wing* was frozen into Edgartown harbor this winter for nearly six weeks.

Turner,
The Story of the Island Steamers, 1910.

The mean departures from normal at New Bedford were: December –4.3, January –9.6, February +4.4, and March –2.1—a winter's mean departure of –3.7 degrees F.

William Mitchell's figures for Nantucket were: December –4.4, January –8.6, February +3.5, and March –1.4—a mean departure of –3.6 degrees.

Long Freeze-up
Of 1875

January 1875 witnessed the beginning of a long period of isolation for Nantucket that

At the twilight of her career, the Island Home *could still buck ice as she steamed into the harbor during the freeze-up of 1893.* Collection of the Nantucket Historical Association.

nearly equaled the duration of the 1857 freeze-up. The combination of January-February 1875 was the coldest of the century in the New Bedford records and probably was on Nantucket, though we do have not actual figures to substantiate this.

On Saturday, January 16, the steamer *Island Home* forced her way out of the harbor through broken ice and reached the open Sound on the trip to Hyannis, but in attempting to return she did not get close until the following Saturday and was then forced to return to Cape Cod. On the next day the U.S. steamer *Verbena* anchored off Quidnet on the outside on her return passage from South Shoals lightship and landed some passengers.

On Monday, the 25th, *Island Home* succeeded in reaching Brant Point, but not the inner harbor, and landed eight overdue mails. An attempt to blow up the ice in the harbor was made the following day, but the thickness of the ice defeated the project.

On Sunday, the 31st, the steamer made another unsuccessful attempt to enter the harbor, and a large force of men were set to work cutting and sawing the ice with the purpose of clearing a way for the small steamer *River Queen*, which had been lying at her dock all winter. A heavy snowstorm set in, stopping further work in this direction. Two days later *Island Home* went outside and landed seven days of mail at Quidnet, together with a few passengers and a small amount of express. A brief warming trend set in at the beginning of February, and *Island Home* was able to force her way into the harbor and reach her dock on the 3d after a battle of several hours with the ice. She had been absent since January 16.

On her return on the following Saturday, February 6, the steamer grounded on the bar and did not float again until 11:00 p.m. A heavy snowstorm set in that night accompanied by a cold wave that drove the Nantucket thermometer down to –8° on Monday night, the 8th, the coldest temperature since February 1861.

After a lay-up of three weeks, *Island Home*

forced her way around Brant Point on the 26th. A large force of volunteers worked for several days and succeeded in loosening the ice floes on the 24th. But a thick fog settled in the next day, and no attempt was made to gain open water until the 26th, when the steamer experienced but little difficulty in gaining the Sound.

The harbor at Woods Hole had been closed by southerly winds, so it required another battle of several hours to reach her dock. *Island Home* was not able to return to Nantucket until March 6, when eighteen overdue mails were brought, the largest number landed at one time since 1857.

Turner,
The Story of the Island Steamers, 1910.

The New Bedford departures from normal for the winter of 1874–75 were: December –0.7, January –6.6, February –7.0, and March –4.8—a mean departure of –4.8 degrees F. No temperature observations for Nantucket have been located.

Cold February, 1899

The most arctic experience of Nantucketers occurred during the next to last winter of the nineteenth century when near-zero temperatures and four snowstorms recreated scenes from the far North. After a mild month

of January with daily maximums rising as high as 50ºF, cold weather settled over the island on January 27, 1899. Minimums thereafter dropped below freezing for 21 days until February 17th. Readings were not extreme, however, until the greatest arctic outbreak in recorded American meteorological history reached Nantucket on February 8th. Four bitter days followed with daily maximums and minimums from the 9th to 12th ranging from 20º to 6º on the 9th, 8º to 4º on the 10th, 11º to 2º on the 11th, and 24º to 8ºF on the 12th.

Daily minimums continued below freezing through the 17th, while maximums generally reached into the 30s. But then a great reversal in the circulation took place with westerly and southerly airstreams prevailing. The first fourteen days of February averaged very cold at 22.0º, while the last fourteen days had a mean of 34.8º, a difference of 12.8 degrees Fahrenheit.

Temperatures on the mainland went below zero on two or three mornings, the lowest readings being: New Bedford –8°, Providence –2°, and Boston –4°F. Other locations with ocean exposures similar to Nantucket reported: Vineyard Haven 2°, and Block Island 0°F.

The *Inquirer and Mirror* described the wintry scene:

Ice-Bound. We are undergoing one of these ice-found experiences Nantucketers are entirely familiar with, but which the absence of cable communications makes it more difficult to bear. At the hour of going to press on Friday afternoon last week [Feb. 10] steamer *Nantucket* was battling with the ice between the jetty and her berth, reaching the latter about 5 p.m. It was a cold and bitter day, and continued cold during the night, the mercury in some sections touching the zero mark, with a strong westerly wind blowing, and no effort was made to break out on Saturday. Indeed it would have been fruitless, for the channel made in coming in the previous day had been closed up solidly, and the storm-bound sportsmen on Coatue came over to their native shores on ice.

Sunday [Feb. 12] followed with a heavy snowstorm, with the temperature ranging about 24°. There was but little wind until late in the evening when it breezed from the northeast and a smothering snow storm raged during the night, continuing with increasing fury all day Monday, with blinding clouds of snow and hail, which drifted in huge piles, rending locomotion anything but pleasant. There was no let up in the fierceness of the storm, which in intensity and duration, exceeded anything we can recall.

After some trying trips steamer *Nantucket* was frozen in here on February 9. On the 17th, steamer *Monohassett* ran down to the jetty and transferred mails to a dory on the ice. On the 20th, the *Nantucket* started to break her way out, and after nearly five hours' hard service, went clear. On the 23d, the harbor was practically free from ice.

Twentieth Century

Three Periods of Isolation, 1903–04

The winter of 1904, from January 4 to February 26, was notable for the fact that three distinct periods of isolation occurred between those dates, of nine, five, and seventeen days' duration, respectively, the island being without steamboat communication with the continent for 31 days out of 55—an unusual occurrence.

Steamer *Nantucket* left her wharf on Monday, January 4, after a week of frigidity had packed the harbor with ice. After butting the floes for nearly two hours, she gained an exit and made for Woods Hole where she remained for nearly a week. An attempt was made on the 10th to break through the ice at the bar, but with no success. On Wednesday, the 13th the captain succeeded in reaching the wharf and breaking up the ice in the harbor by a few turns. The harbor was kept open until the 19th when a second period of isolation began. *Nantucket* had succeeded in breaking out that day, but was unable to return until Sunday the 24th.

The harbor remained open until February 9th when the third period of isolation began. The temperature fell to 2 °F and no water was in sight from the harbor. Steamer *Nantucket* battled the ice all day and reached a point near the jetties at dusk, but deemed it imprudent to continue and returned to her wharf. The boat remained a prisoner until the 15th, when she was able to break out and reach Woods Hole. Not until the 23d did the *Nantucket* finally make her way through the ice of the Sound to the jetties. She brought one passenger, seventy-eight newspaper sacks, and twenty-three letter pouches, transferring the mails and the provisions over the ice from a point inside the jetties, where she remained about three hours. Seven persons made their way over the mile of ice between the shore and the steamer and thus took passage for the mainland. The following Friday, February 26, the steamer reached her dock at Nantucket, after which date there were no more interruptions in the service on account of ice.

Turner,
The Story of the Island Steamers 1910.

The weather bureau observations for Nantucket gave the following departures from normal: December -1.8, January -4.1, February -3.8, and March -3.5—a winter mean departure of -3.3 degrees Fahrenheit.

Three-Week Freeze-up, 1905

"The weather was remarkable for its persistent low temperature and high northwesterly winds, which caused the worst ice embargo experienced here since 1857. Ice began forming in the harbor on January 30th, and from February 2d to the 23d, inclusive, navigation was suspended," wrote George E. Grimes of the local weather bureau in the February issue of the *Climate and Crop Service for New England*.

On January 30, ice was making in the upper harbor, though the channel remained open. The ice was two inches thick on the first day of February and increased to six inches by the 5th. On the 16th it increased to seven inches and on the 19th to ten inches, the maximum depth. Then the ice began to melt and reduced to 6.7 inches thick by the 25th and to 1.0 inch on March 1.

The temperature during February continued steadily cold with the mercury dropping to 32°F or below on every night of the month. The maximum exceeded freezing on only ten days. The maximum for the month climbed to 40° on the 13th and the minimum dropped to 8°F on the 4th.

The departure from normal for the winter months of 1904–05 on Nantucket were: December –4.5, January –3.2, February –4.7, and March –1.3—a mean departure of –3.4 degrees F for the winter.

Steamers and the Ice, 1917–18

With the temperature down to 8°F, ice began to form in the harbor on December 29, 1917. Next day the harbor closed to sailing vessels, and on the 31st, with the ice five

Passengers of the Sankaty *had to walk over icefields to reach shore during the hard winter of 1917–18, when the temperature dropped to a record low of –6°F in early February.* Collection of Charles F. Sayle.

inches thick, the steamer did not return. On New Year's Day the steamer *Uncatena* forced her way to her dock. On January 4 the steamer *Sankaty* left on schedule, but had to return after encountering ice piled six feet high by the wind near the bar. Harbor ice thickened to ten inches. Southerly winds on the 7th broke up the ice and clear water extended as far as the bar. Four days later, the *Sankaty* ventured out but "walked" all day on the ice and had to be rescued by the *Uncatena*.

On the 12th southerly winds carried ice from the outer harbor into the Sound. A brief thaw on the 15th created air holes in the inner harbor ice and the steamboat channel opened despite eight-inch ice. By the 21st, however, more ice was making in the harbor, though the steamer was able to make her way from Cross Rip to her dock through much slush ice. During the next few days, the *Sankaty* occasionally managed to get out but on the 30th she fought ice all day to no avail.

On February 1st the ice measured ten inches and remained at that thickness for the next twelve days, preventing all steamer trips. Finally, on the 13th the *Sankaty* was able to leave on time and the *Uncatena* arrived with mail and freight. Southwest storms on the 12th and 14th assisted in rotting the ice. The temperature ranged up to 46°F on the 15th, with 34-mile-per-hour winds from the southwest, and most of the ice cleared from the harbor. The embargo was thought to be completely ended. Next day the harbor opened to sailing vessels. On the 25th the weather bureau reported "no snow, no ice."

The temperature departures from normal for the winter months of 1917–18 were: December –6.8, January –7.9, February –2.3 and March –1.4—an average winter departure from normal of –4.6 degrees F.

February Freeze, 1923

Ice began forming on January 30 after three nights of temperatures in the teens. On February 1, thin ice extended to the jetties. Four consecutive days of below-freezing temperatures, from the 4th to 7th, rapidly made ice. On the 5th, the harbor closed to sailing vessels. The ice rotted from the 8th to 12th. Northerly winds on 13th brought ice in from the Sound, but the tide carried it out the next day.

Another series of ice days from the 15th to 21st, accompanied by four nights of temperatures at 10°F or lower, brought on another embargo. The steamer made no attempt to leave from the 20th through 25th. On the 26th the *Sankaty* took an hour and a half to round Great Point, but then found open water and arrived at Woods Hole six hours after departing. Ice in the harbor was eight inches thick. The combination of ice and thick snow forced the *Sankaty* to return to dock on the 28th. On March 1st, after butting a great deal of ice, the *Sankaty* made it to New Bedford, but did not return that day. On the 3d, a southwest wind set all the ice floating and carried out a great deal of harbor ice. The *Sankaty* made a round trip. Next day the inner and outer harbors were clear of ice and the snow was gone, and by the 5th sailing vessels were able to enter and depart.

The monthly temperature departures from the normal for the decade were: December –0.9, January –1.9, February –6.3, and March –4.3—for a winter departure of –3.4 degrees Fahrenheit.

The Coldest Month And Harbor Ice, February 1934

After the temperature plunged from 41° to 1°F on January 29, ice formed all day on the 30th and by the next day extended to the steamboat channel, which remained open. This condition continued for a week until the hard core of the cold wave arrived on the 7th with a drop to 10°F. On that day the steamboats were running but had "some difficulty" with the ice. On the 8th the ice extended to the jetties, and on the 9th the steamboat left her wharf on time at 6:30 a.m. but could not get out of the harbor and returned to home. The temperature dropped to –1°, and to the winter's nadir of –4°F on the 9th. On that day the steamer again could not get out and so returned. "Ice as far as the eye can see. Six to 8 inches thick," was the weather bureau report. The ice embargo remained the same through the 18th. Ice packed up on the bar to a height of 4 to 5 feet.

On the 13th several planes arrived at the Nobadeer landing strip with food and mail. On the 19th, "ice conditions improved" and the steamer came in at 6:00 p.m. On the 20th the boat could not get out, but did succeed on the 21st. The westerly winds brought the ice back into the outer harbor. On the 22d with the ice breaking up, the steamer made her regular trip. The arrival of another cold wave brought temperatures down to 9°F on the 24th and 25th and solidified the ice field. From the 26th of February to March 1, no attempt was made to get out. Finally, on March 2, the steamer left in the morning and the evening boat came in with reports of the ice breaking up outside. Next day the ice would not permit the boat to leave, but on March 4 the ice had cleared from Brant Point outward. The harbor ice was still 4 to 6 inches thick, though softening rapidly. On the 5th, with ice gone from the steamboat wharf and harbor, boats could depart and arrive. The last ice entry in the weather log on March 6: "Ice gone, harbor clear."

Temperature departures from normal for the decade were: December –3.3, January –1.0, February –9.3, and March –2.5—a mean winter departure of –4.0 degrees F. Such steady cold has not occurred since.

The editor of the *Inquirer and Mirror* wrote a nostalgic paragraph for those who found the 1934 freeze-up an "old fashioned winter" and an "enjoyable and exciting" experience:

The trials and tribulations of the old-time freeze-up have passed away, never to return, and the younger generation knows of them only by hearsay. The freeze-up this winter was indeed quite novel and enjoyable. To be sure, the Island has been surrounded by heavy ice fields, the harbor has been sealed up solid, the steamer frozen at her berth, and the customary freeze-up conditions have prevailed, but withal the real thrill of a freeze-up has departed and will never be experienced again.

A February Ice Embargo, 1936

The last eight days of January were ice days with the temperature continuously below freezing. By the 28th six-inch-thick ice had formed, causing difficulty for the steamers. By February 3, all navigation was closed down and mail had to be delivered by plane at the Nobadeer airport.

The *Inquirer and Mirror* described the subsequent ice troubles:

The past week has not been without its troubles for Nantucket, so far as steamboat service was concerned. The steamer *Nantucket* put out on Saturday morning [15th] but was not able to make a return trip to the island until Wednesday [19th].

The boat had little difficulty in breaking out through the ice Saturday, although she had been imprisoned in the harbor since she came in the previous Monday [10th]. A mishap to the *Marthas* [sic] *Vineyard* and a change in weather conditions brought the announcement that no return trip would be attempted until Monday.

Sunday brought thick weather, with neither boat nor plane service either way. A mail plane started from Boston, but ran into heavy fog over Hingham and was forced back. Conditions were unchanged on Monday with dense fog all along the coast, making it impossible for the steamer to venture out, with buoys and aids to navigation either gone or out of position, and ice fields and fog making a combination that made it improvident to even attempt a passage across the sound.

The ice-fields had packed in again on the north side of the island, but were not firm enough to bar the progress of the boat. Leaving New Bedford at 7:00 in the morning, the *Nantucket* proceeded to Woods Hole and was held there 1½ hours loading freight, so that by the time she started across the sound her capacity was packed to the limit.

Tuesday brought more fog and rain, with lowering temperature in the afternoon which brought thick snow squalls. The thermometer commenced to fall steadily and at 8 o'clock Wednesday morning had touched the low point of 7 degrees above zero.

This was the first cargo of freight landed here by steamer since the 10th—a period of nine days—and the supplies were most welcome, as some of the stores were depleted of vegetables and staple goods.

At 2:45 she reached the dock at Nantucket, making steady progress through the ice-field and meeting with no great difficulty until she rounded Brant Point, where Captain Sandsbury butted away for about ten minutes before breaking a passage.

Yesterday [Friday] morning, following a light snowfall the previous evening, the weather conditions were somewhat milder, with almost a touch of spring in the air. Steamer *Martha's Vineyard* put out on time and had not great difficulty in making her way through the ice fields.

Regular steamboat service is now in prospect, unless another cold wave happens along to harden the ice which covers the waters of the sound. The fact that we are entering on the last week in February, however, is almost an assurance that the worst of Nantucket's troubles are over for this winter.

Inquirer and Mirror,
February 22, 1936.

By the 25th the ice was rotting, and open water extended from Brant Point out. On the 26th, water appeared around the wharf, and on the 27th the ice embargo ended after thirty-one days of ice troubles.

The departure from normal winter temperatures for the decade were: December –3.3, January –1.0, February –9.3, and March –2.5—for a winter mean departure of –4.3 degrees Fahrenheit.

Record Cold Spell, January–February 1961

The record cold spell at the end of January and start of February in 1961 caused the first ice problems in the Sound since 1936. For 16 days, from January 19 to February 3, the temperature did not rise above freezing, breaking the fifteen-day record of January 1893. This period also marked the interlude between two major snowstorms of the severe winter of 1960–61. During this time the snow cover on the ground varied from 17 inches to 10 inches, and the temperature reached a minimum of 7°F.

The Sound finally became too ice-clogged to navigate on January 31, and Nantucket had no boat for three days.

Twin Freeze-ups of 1968

January 1968 averaged 4.1 degrees below normal. A severely cold period prevailed from January 8 to 12 with the temperature continuously below 28ºF for the five-day period. The minimums of 3º and 2ºF were registered on the 8th and 9th. In the January 18 issue, the *Inquirer and Mirror* declared the *Nantucket* a good ice-breaker since it had forced its way from the entrance to the jetties to her wharf in a matter of an hour and a half.

February was also a very cold month with temperatures departing from normal an average of –3.9 degrees Fahrenheit. This marked the two coldest consecutive months since January and February 1934. The lowest

reading was 7°F on the 13th, and the longest string of consecutive days with the thermometer continuously below freezing numbered four. Until the 28th, no daily maximum exceeded 40°F.

This winter's second freeze has the scallop fleet tied up again, and over ten days have been lost in this one, also . . .

More of the last 12 days has seen temperatures at 10 to 15 degrees during the nights, getting up around 15 to 20 degrees during the days. Fresh to strong sou'west winds and mild Saturday blew a good part of the ice out of the harbor. Ten degree temperature Saturday night froze most of the harbor over again by daylight.

Inquirer and Mirror,
February 22, 1968

The tanker *F L Hayes* with 10,000 barrels of oil broke through the heavy ice.

The ice field extends clear to the mainland and large masses have been going out by the east end of the island. The Sound is still full although moderating temperatures during the daytime this week have started to soften the ice somewhat.

Charles Sayle, "Waterfront,"
Inquirer and Mirror,
February 29, 1968

March 7. Winter hangs on and it looks as though ice will be in the harbor till the middle of the month . . . This is the 6th week the fleet has been tied up on account of the ice.

March 14. Warm weather and sou'west winds cleared a lot of the ice out but quite a bit was carried back up harbor, where it was jammed across the harbor just above Pocomo.

March 21. The last of the ice has gone . . . ice and cold temperatures have cost the scallopers a good two months fishing out of the five month season.

Inquirer and Mirror.

"Ice-olation," January 1970

With a mean of 24.6°, January 1970 was the coldest first month since January 1918, which averaged 24.0°, while the latter was exceeded only by the 23.8° mean of January 1893. The departure from the contemporary normal in January 1970 amounted to 8.2 degrees F. The minimum of ¹1°F on the 23d was the first below-zero reading since December 1962.

Ice conditions became difficult after midmonth. The *Uncatena* was turned back in its attempt to break out of the harbor on two consecutive days on the 23d and 24th. The ice packed at the jetties and in the harbor measured from six inches to three feet in depth. A Coast Guard tug finally broke through and freed the boat which had been icebound from Tuesday, the 20th, to Sunday, the 25th.

The mainland press, as usual, sensationalized the "ice-olation" and the *Inquirer and Mirror* noted that "Islanders were amused at the suggestion that there was a shortage" of food and fuel.

Two-week Freeze, February 1979

February 1979 was a severely cold month, being 11.1 degrees colder than January 1979. The departure from the contemporary normal was –7.1 degrees. The mercury touched zero on the 14th, the first time since January 1970.

Two Coast Guard cutters were scheduled to attempt a break through to Nantucket today in order to allow the Steamship Authority to complete a passage to the island for the first time since Monday.

The cutters, *Spar* and *Yankton* from Portland, Maine, will try to cut a path through nearly nine miles of ice which is as much as a foot and a half thick in places . . .

The ice is the result of a week long spell of bone chilling weather in which the

The *Uncatena working through the icefields in the Outer Harbor on February 12, 1979. The temperature dropped to 12°F or lower on eleven consecutive days from February 9 to 19, with a minimum of 0°F on the 14th.* Photograph courtesy of H. Flint Ranney.

temperature has seldom climbed into the teens. The Arctic freeze started last Thursday (Feb. 7) following a six inch snowfall and has caused frozen pipes and hazardous driving but no shortage of supplies.

The steamship Authority's problems began Sunday as the freezing temperatures and a northerly wind packed the boat's route with ice . . .

Inquirer and Mirror,
February 15, 1979.

Somewhat regular boat service to the mainland has been resumed by the Steamship Authority following the end of two weeks of frigid Arctic weather.

The *S.S. Naushon* left Woods Hole for Nantucket this morning at 10:30 for what may be the second round trip between the island and the mainland in two days.

Yesterday's round trip was the first one day round trip in nearly ten days. Authority spokesmen say the boatline is planning its trips one day at a time and cannot tell when a schedule of two boat trips a day will begin again.

Sunday, February 11, was the last day of normal boat service before freezing temperatures and northerly winds packed the entrance to Nantucket Harbor with thick ice. The *Uncatena* completed one breakthrough to the island next day but a similar effort on February 13 proved futile and the boat was forced to return to Woods Hole.

Finally last Thursday, the *Uncatena* with truckloads of supplies and about 20 passengers aboard, finished a grueling twelve and a half hour voyage with the assistance of the Coast Guard cutter *Yankton.*

Commanded by Captain Edward "Buddy"

Nemeth, the *Uncatena* had left Woods Hole at 10:30 that morning. By early afternoon the boat had reached the *Yankton* and was visible from Nantucket. But progress had slowed to a crawl and all day long, in bitterly cold temperatures, Nantucketers watched the two vessels inch along. Viewing spots on the cliff and Jetties Beach were crowded with curious islanders, and those who could receive the Authority's radio frequency on their scanners listened to the conversation between Nantucket and the *Uncatena.*

Finally, a few minutes after 11 p.m., the *Uncatena* docked at Steamboat Wharf and unloaded her weary passengers, including a boys' basketball team from the Roberto Clemente School in New Haven, Connecticut. The small crowd waiting at the wharf cheered as the passengers walked onto the dock.

The *Uncatena* left for the mainland the next morning, once again following the 110-foot *Yankton* and the path she cut through the ice.

Inquirer and Mirror,
February 22, 1979.

Cold January, 1981

January 1981 with a mean of 22.6° was the coldest month since February 1934. For the first 15 days, the minimums were extremely low, averaging 10.7°F. The low figure of 1°F was reached on the 4th.

"On Monday [Jan. 12], accompanied by the *Yankton*, the *Uncatena* made it to Nantucket [from Woods Hole] in roughly 15 hours. The Captain was quoted: 'as saying it was the longest trip he had made in his forty years in the business,'" reported the *Inquirer and Mirror.* The final stretch from the Jetties to the wharf took about six hours.

Again the mainland press devoted much attention to the situation, declaring that the island was about to be evacuated.

Fuel ran low, but no cutback was needed since a fuel barge arrived. Air New England cut freight rates by 50 percent during the freeze-up.

The cold continued almost to the end of the month, and there were two substantial snowstorms, one of 8 inches on the 10th, another of 9 inches on the 17–18th.

On January 22, the *Inquirer and Mirror* declared: "The brief moment in the national spotlight brought on by the freeze seems to have ended."

Another Cold January, 1982

January 1982 was another severely cold period with an average departure from normal of –6.1 degrees Fahrenheit. The coldest period extended from the 8th to 22d with an average minimum of 12.9°F. Single-digit minimums were registered on the following dates: 6° on the 10th and 11th, 4° on the 12th, and 2°F on the 17th and 18th.

Though ice formed, it did not impede the steamer. The *Nantucket* was making one round trip each day with "little trouble." The Coast Guard tug *Yankton* remained in the area to assist vessels if needed.

The opening of February 1978 was a stormy period. Boston was buried under 27 inches of snow on the 6–7th and all travel in eastern Massachusetts was banned for a week by the Governor's decree. Nantucket had only about 7 inches.
Photograph courtesy of H. Flint Ranney.

SPRING STORMS

March is frequently a wintry month along the New England coast. Not until the close of the month do the chances of a heavy snowstorm and single-figure temperatures diminish to a low percentage possibility. Yet there can be evidences of spring in the air even before the vernal equinox. Many mighty storms have arisen in the month when the forces of the North are in retreat, but not yet completely defeated.

The storm tracks of winter still prevail. There is less cyclogenesis over the Gulf of Mexico and more over the land in Texas, whence disturbances move northeast to the Carolinas to another storm-breeding region found to the lee of the Appalachians. Anticyclonic blocking in the North Atlantic Ocean becomes a growing influence as spring progresses, and this increasingly affects the March storm tracks.

"April is the month with the greatest number of storms," declares a recent National Weather Service survey. This conclusion applies especially to New England, which is vulnerable to cyclonic attack from two directions. First, the winter storm track which stretches from the Gulf of Mexico northeast along the Atlantic seaboard remains active, while a cyclogenetic area develops off the Middle Atlantic coast. Warm and cold airstreams clash in this area; new storm centers are created and others regenerate. Some of the great North Atlantic storms of history have occurred in March and April when easterly gales, with a long fetch of a thousand miles and more across ocean waters, raise massive waves and winds to drive mighty storm tides onto New England shores.

Meanwhile, the primary winter storm track down the St. Lawrence Valley continues to attract storm centers from the Great Lakes and Midwest. Though the disturbances now travel at a slightly more northerly latitude, their trailing frontal systems regularly swing across New England, bringing alternating wind shifts and weather variations.

The principal atmospheric changes that take place in May lie in the thermal sphere. The increasing solar radiation heats interior land surfaces so that they become warmer than bodies of inland water. The relatively cool Great Lakes, instead of harboring winter cyclonic activity, become a seat of anticyclonic formation, as do James Bay and Hudson Bay. Thus, two associated blocking areas form to the west of New England. As a result, the winter cyclone track across the Great Lakes shifts northward into Ontario. Storm passages through the region become less frequent and the pace of movement slows, sometimes becoming almost stationary under the blocking influence of the slow-moving anticyclones over the Northeast. The storm track along the Atlantic coastal plain decreases greatly in importance during May, since dry westerlies now dominate the former storm-breeding area in the Gulf of Mexico and the South Atlantic region. It is still too early for tropical storm formation.

Easter Sunday Storm, March 1823

A great storm lashed the Atlantic seaboard on Easter Sunday, March 30, 1823. The disturbance appeared to exert its greatest force in New Jersey and on Long Island while, according to the *Inquirer*, Nantucket experienced "a severe gale of wind from the S.E. which toward night increased in violence, accompanied by snow, hail, rain, heavy thunder and vivid lightning." This meteorological melange continued for more than 36 hours, causing damage to wharves and trees. Walter Folger's barometer dropped from a 7:00 a.m. reading of 29.69 inches to 28.90 inches at midnight of March 30, and next morning was down to 28.83 inches. The temperature dropped from near 40° to 34°F on the morning of the 31st, which accounted for the mixture of precipitation types. At New Bedford, it was mostly snow and said to have fallen deeper than any spring storm since the big April snows in 1785.

Storm of March, 1830

A cold northeast storm of wind, rain and snow raged along the coast of New England during the latter part of March, 1830, producing a great tide, which is some parts exceeded the highest tide remembered there. The storm began on the morning of Friday, the twenty-sixth, and continued till one o'clock in the afternoon, the tide being at its height at noon of that day.

Perley, *Historic Storms of New England*, 1891.

Walter Folger's barometer fell from 30.17 inches at noon on March 25 to 28.52 inches at 10:00 p.m. on March 26. He stated, "It was probably lower before 10:00 o'clock as it was then rising." This extremely low reading gave an indication of the intensity of the storm. Winds backed from south-southwest at noon of the 25th, to south-southeast at 10:00 p.m. to east-southeast at 7:00 a.m. on the 26th, to south-southwest at noon and finally to northwest by 10:00 p.m. on the 26th. Rain fell at the morning and evening observations on the 26th. The temperature throughout the storm ranged from near 35° at night to as high as 48°F around noon. No freezing temperatures were reported.

March Storm, 1843

In both the meteorological and spiritual history of our country, 1843 proved an uncommon year. It had been predicted for some years by the Adventist followers of Reverend William Miller of upstate New York that the second coming of Christ and the commencement of the millennium predicted in the Bible would occur in this year, possibly as early as the vernal equinox in 1843. The progress of events in a winter of unprecedented duration and abnormal severity did much to foster a spirit of gloomy uncertainty and foreboding among the susceptible. Then the appearance of a brilliant comet with an unusually long tail in early

March seemed to many to foretell unusual events in the heavenly realm.

The month of March produced the greatest winter temperature anomaly in all American history. Never has a month evinced such a disregard for the annual temperature trend, and never has a month evinced such a wide geographic homogeneity in running against the seasonal normal. On Nantucket, March 1843 with a mean of 30.2° was 5.8 degrees below normal, and ran 7.4 degrees F colder than the previous January. At locations in the Midwest, March 1843 ran as much as 25 degrees F below normal.

Two great storms marked the month: one at midmonth and the second two weeks later. Each dropped heavy snowfall over interior New England and gave the coast a severe wind and wave lashing.

Coming from the Gulf of Mexico, the first laid down a thick blanket of snow from Mississippi to Maine. The Nantucket barometer began to fall after noon of the 16th. After 9:00 p.m. it fell rapidly to a reading of 29.00 inches by 7:00 a.m. on the 17th. The lowest recorded reading was 28.96 inches at noon on the 17th. Winds shifted from north-northeast on the afternoon and evening of the 16th into the south-southwest and southwest on the morning of the 17th, indicating a passage of the storm center to the west. Professor Caswell at Providence reported: "Heavy snow and rain fell last night. Bar. fell to 28.74 [uncorrected] at 11 a.m. Wind W'ly; very blustering. Cleared in evening. Comet very bright." The combination of the very backward spring, winter-like storms, and the brilliance of the comet heightened the spiritual tension of those who were awaiting the Second Coming of Christ on March 21.

Lighthouse Storm, April 1851

The Late Storm—One of the heaviest and long continued gales, which has ever passed over our island commenced from the northwest on Tuesday last [Apr. 15]; and raged until Wednesday night, when it somewhat abated, though it still continued to blow hard during the day on Thursday from the eastward. The tides during the prevalence of the storm rose higher than they have done for the last twelve years [since 1839], though we have not heard of any damage therefrom. The steamer *Massachusetts*, from New Bedford for Nantucket, arrived here on Tuesday afternoon, and was in port when this paragraph was written, Thursday noon. We shall undoubtedly hear of many disasters on the coast.

Nantucket Inquirer,
April 18, 1851.

The fears of the editor of the *Inquirer* were well founded because the storm on April 15 and 16, 1851, achieved greater fame than any other of the mid-century. It became known as the Lighthouse Storm since its principal event was the destruction of Minot's Ledge lighthouse off Cohasset, a marker for Boston Harbor located about 15 miles southeast of the present Logan International Airport.

Sidney Perley described the last moments of the lighthouse and its crew of two:

The lighthouse was last seen standing at about half-past three o'clock on Wednesday afternoon [Apr. 16]. Amid the horrors of the storm, the young men were compelled to remain in their fatal rooms. There was no escaping to the shore through the hell of waters. As soon as darkness came on, probably about five o'clock on that stormy evening, they lighted the lamp as usual, and its warning rays beamed over the raging ocean. But that which saved others was powerless to save itself. The light was last seen burning at ten o'clock that evening by several persons, and about the same time the lighthouse bell rang with great violence, alarming the dwellers on the shore for the safety of the youthful custodians of the light. The bravery and faithfulness of these young men, who were careful to perform their full duty, even while they knew the certainty of their fate, and felt the pillars snapping asunder beneath them, and while the emotions of anguish that can neither be described nor imagined, were surging like billows through their souls, constitute them heroes of the highest order. The entire structure was endoubtedly carried over at once, and the men went down to death and a tomb beneath the surges, their bodies never being found.

Disastrous End-of-March Storm, 1879

During a violent storm of wind and rain on March 31, 1879, the following marine disaster occurred in this vicinity as related in Arthur Gardner's, *Wrecks Around Nantucket:*

Three-masted schooner, *Emma G. Edwards*, of Camden, N.J., from Philadelphia to Boston, with a cargo of coal, dragged her anchorage near Chatham to Tuckernuck Shoal, where she struck and rolled over on her beam ends, and but one of her crew survived to tell the story. The others were either washed overboard or perished from exposure lashed in the rigging.

Schooner, *J.W. Hall*, bound from New York to Lynn, with 339 tons of coal, anchored in sound, parted both chains and drove ashore on Muskeget. Her crew, six in number, were taken off and landed on Tuckernuck.

Schooner, *Jefferson Borden*, 561 tons burthen, from Cuba to Boston, with a cargo of 700 hogsheads of sugar, dragged from her anchorage in the sound and went ashore on Muskeget.

Schooner, *Convoy*, from Rockland, Me., to New York, with a cargo of lime, went ashore near the *Jefferson Borden*. The crews were taken off by Isaac P. Dunham and a boat's crew of four and landed on Tuckernuck. She was stripped of sails, rigging and effects, but the lime took fire and the vessel burned to the water's edge.

Schooner, *American Chief*, from Rockland, Me., to New York, with a cargo of lime, lost anchors and chains and went ashore on Muskeget.

Schooner *Emma*, of and for St. John, N.B.,

with a cargo of coal, lost anchors and chains and went ashore on Muskeget.

Schooner *Daniel Brittain*, of Somers Point, N.J., bound from Boston to Philadelphia, light, and Schooner *Alice Oaks*, from South Amboy to Boston, with a cargo of coal, went ashore on Great Point about 8:00 a.m. Both had dragged their anchorage, the former from the Cape, the latter from inside Great Point.

Schooner *Andrew H. Edwards*, loaded with gas coal, went ashore near Muskeget and rolled over on her beam ends, the sea making a clean breach over her. The crew took to the rigging and were rescued in an exhausted condition and with great difficulty by a boat's crew from Tuckernuck.

Brig *Manzanilla*, of Calais, Me., bound to New York with a cargo of lumber, anchored off Low Beach, sprang a leak and was run ashore. A bluefish line was thrown over the vessel and by this means a rope was drawn off and secured to one of the masts. When the first man attempted to come ashore, the rope parted between him and the vessel. He clung to the line, however, and was drawn ashore through the breakers. A hatchet head was then made fast to another small line, thrown over the vessel and another rope hauled off by means of which the remainder of the crew came ashore. The vessel soon after broke in two and went to pieces.

Schooner *William D. Cargill* of Providence, R.I., was also anchored off Low Beach, having lost main boom and all her sails. Her masts were cut away to keep her afloat. She rode out the storm safely and was towed to Vineyard Haven by steamer *Island Home*.

"Down to the sea in ships!" Gardner concluded.

Great March Storm, 1931

A great Atlantic storm developed during the first week of March 1931. The circulation originated over the Rio Grande Valley on February 28, then crossed the Gulf of Mexico from the area of Brownsville, Texas, to near Naples, Forida. A turn to the north-northeast carried it to the vicinity of Cape Lookout, North Carolina, with the central pressure down to 28.66 inches. Another 24 hours brought the center to the latitude of Nantucket, and about 135 miles to the east. Central pressure now read 28.38 inches, but the Nantucket barometer sank only to 29.12 inches at 8 a.m., the lowest for this storm period on the island.

Gale-force winds, starting at 2:55 p.m. on March 3, reached 60 miles per hour at 11:26 p.m. from the northeast. They continued above 50 miles per hour for the next three hours until 3:00 a.m. and above 40 miles per hour until 9:00 a.m. From 6:00 p.m. to 6:00 a.m. on March 3, winds averaged 46 miles per hour, one of the highest sustained wind periods in Nantucket history.

Rain began at 7:00 p.m. on the 3d, but amounted to only 0.05 inch by midnight. Snow began to fall at 4:00 a.m. on the 4th and continued through the day until midnight. A total of 8 inches fell over a twenty-hour period as the temperature hovered at 32 °F. The melted precipitation totaled 1.03 inches.

Low Pressure Storm, March 6–7, 1932

"A storm of wide extent and marked intensity, but did little damage here," declared the *Inquirer and Mirror* of the blow on March 6–7, 1932, which set low barometric records along the coastal plain from South Carolina to Maine. The disturbance reached its greatest development when near Block Island, Rhode Island, where the barometer descended to 28.20 inches, to equal the lowest ever reached at any land station in the United States in a non-hurricane situation.

On Nantucket, the lowest pressure of 28.35 inches occurred at 5:45 a.m. on March 7. At this time the wind, which had been at south, veered to southwest, and was blowing a steady 32 miles per hour. Later it peaked at 44 miles per hour at 11:14 a.m. and the wind direction veered west. These wind shifts indicated that the center of lowest pressure passed to the west and north of Nantucket. The wind on the 7th averaged 32.2 miles per hour for the full 24 hours of the 7th.

Only light precipitation fell: 0.10 inch from 4:00 to 10:00 a.m., and another 0.05 inch in the later afternoon and evening until it stopped at 9:20 p.m. The latter was a combination of snow and rain that amounted to 0.5 inch of snow. The temperature had fallen from 41° at midnight on the 6th to 32°F at midnight on the 7th.

May Storm in 1938

An outstanding feature of the month's weather was the northeast storm which reached the Section on the night of the 14th, and continued generally through the 15th. The storm was particularly severe along the coast, causing several marine disasters with loss of life, and being responsible for much damage on land. Early crops were severely injured by gales and heavy rain.
New England climatologist.

The wind on Nantucket reached gale force at 11:52 p.m. on the 14th. Rain had been falling since 5:20 p.m., amounting to 0.48 inch by midnight. The wind during the afternoon and evening backed from west through south to east by 9:00 p.m. The storm reached its peak at 2:03 a.m. on the 15th when a one-minute sustained wind speed of 47 miles per hour raged. After a relative lull from 5:00 to 11:00 a.m., the gales returned, but now from the southwest. Rain ended at 5:00 a.m. with an additional 0.41 inch having fallen since midnight. The barometer read 29.20 inches in early morning and remained below 29.30 inches until late evening.

It rained hard and it blew hard early last Sunday morning [the 15th] and bushes and trees which were in blossom suffered severely from the force of the elements.

Inquirer and Mirror,
May 21, 1938.

Windstorm, April 28–29, 1967

Long-sustained high wind hit especially hard at Nantucket, where the average speed for the entire day of April 28 was 43 m.p.h. There, 1 mile of wind passed at an average rate of 63 m.p.h. Momentary gust speeds reached well into the hurricane range. Heavy rain accompanied the storm on Nantucket and some rain fell on Cape Cod, but generally in the affected area this was a dry northeaster. The slowly moving storm center which caused the wind passed far at sea, its rain shield barely touching the land. Most concentrated structural damage was on Nantucket, but loss was also widespread over southeastern Massachusetts and Rhode Island.

The New England climatologist went on to describe the disasters which overtook shipping and fishing interests as a result of the late-season storm.

The high winds over coastal New England were caused by a very tight barometric gradient which developed between a high pressure over Labrador and the waters off southeast Greenland and a low pressure system stalled southeast of Nantucket. A disturbance developed over eastern Georgia and moved rapidly northeast on April 26. But upon reaching a location east of southern New Jersey and directly south of Nantucket on the 27th, it veered to the east, coming to a halt at 39°N, 68°W, about 275 miles east-southeast of Nantucket. There it performed a counterclockwise loop during the 28th, 29th, and 30th. The lowest central pressure reached about 28.94 inches. Meantime, the high pressure to the north greatly increased to 30.86 inches. A gradient of almost two inches existed between the two pressure entities.

The *Inquirer and Mirror* summarized the damage on the Island as: "ripping and tearing of roof tops, demolishing fences, dismembering some new structures partially erected, and even moving another newly constructed dwelling from its foundation."

Nantucket Meteorological Data

	Temp. (F°)	Dew Point (F°)	Precip. (inches)	Steady (miles per hour)	Wind Gusts (miles per hour)
April 27	44	34	0.51	18.6ENE	45NE
April 28	41	35	1.22	45.0NNE	63N
April 29	48	38	0.00	30.1N	42N
April 30	50	35	0.00	18.1N	30N

The highest wind reported was a gust at 71 miles per hour.

Storm of May 1967— Nantucket's Greatest Rain

A northeaster or coastal storm of unusual severity and especially unusual for so late in the season, began its effects on southern coastal areas on May 24. It continued into May 26, with the major effect generally on May 25, except on the 26th in northern areas. The storm was especially devastating along coastal areas from Rhode Island to southwestern Maine. It was comparable to the nearby passage of a full hurricane. Due to its very slow movement, the damaging action continued longer than that of the usual hurricane.

The New England climatologist continued to describe the vast damage such as downed power lines, thousands of trees toppled, and vehicles swept from highways by the high winds. Harbor barges and vessels were torn from their moorings, and shore installations were severely damaged.

The storm center slowed to a halt on the 25th when directly south of Nantucket, then moved off to the northeast very slowly. Lowest pressure over the ocean reached approximately 29.30 inches. During the next four days the center progressed only to a point south of Cape Race, Newfoundland, while continuing the strong circulation over New England and eastern Canada.

Rain began to fall on Nantucket soon after 6:00 p.m. on the 24th, became moderate on the morning of the 25th as the storm center approached from the south, and increased to heavy that afternoon when the center of the disturbance stalled about 100 miles offshore. Amounts in excess of 0.50 inch per hour fell from 12:00 midnight to 1:00 p.m., from 3:00 to 4:00 p.m., and in each hour from 6:00 to 9:00 p.m. A total of 2.03 inches came down during the last three hours. Very little was recorded on the 26th. In all, 7.08 inches fell during the storm to set an all-time record, and 6.53 inches falling within 24 hours established a new intensity mark.

Heavy amounts also fell over Cape Cod: Falmouth 5.19 inches; in Rhode Island: Providence 4.43 inches; and in eastern Massachusetts: Boston 3.99 inches and Worcester 3.55 inches.

The *Inquirer and Mirror* took notice of the torrents of water and the high tides:

Coupled with high tides and the wind direction, the torrents of water inundated areas of Brant Point and flooded cellars in other parts of town, causing damage to furnaces, foundation walls and house lots in general in the low sections of the island as well as Brant Point.

The harbor resembled the open sea with white crested waves smashing against the wharves and, as the tide came up, drove across the bulkheads and over the south harbor beaches. At Great Point the seas were breaking across the Galls, thus making an island out of the point itself. As the wind backed into the north northeast, the north shore of the island resembled the ocean beach, with the waves breaking up against the bluffs. The wrecked barge section near the old golf links frontage was washed from its bed and carried for some distance up the shore to the westward.

The editor summarized storm conditions: No Coast Guard calls. No boat Thursday to

Saturday. $25,000 damages. North Beach St.—water to Al Silva's garage. Easton Street afloat curb to curb. Gusts to 49 mi/h on 26th from north.

Northeast Storm, March 1973

Another no'theast gale of wind struck this area Thursday and Friday [March 22 and 23] last week, keeping *S.S. Nantucket* in for those two days. This was the worst breeze of the winter, the writer watching Mitch Havemeyer's wind gauge hitting up to 70 miles per hour Thursday morning. John Mendonca recorded 75 out at Pocomo and another party mentioned hearing of 85 at one time. Anyway, there was plenty of wind Thursday and Friday with 4 or 5 inches of wet snow. The worst of the breeze was during Thursday and Thursday night easing back to 35 to 50 miles all day Friday and most of the night. This breeze was the usual thing for weather reports calling for 20 to 25 the day before. Always wise to prepare one's boat for double to triple the amount of wind first expected when these easterlies come up the coast.

Inquirer and Mirror,
March 29, 1973.

The Great Point Lighthouse Storm, March 29, 1984

"One of Nantucket's familiar landmarks, Great Point Lighthouse, met with disaster on the night of March 29, 1984, the victim of a northeast gale," wrote historian Edouard Stackpole in *Historic Nantucket*. "A pounding surf, driven by the storm, smashed the tall stone tower, perched virtually on the beach edge, and the old walls could not withstand the elements. On the following morning, with the storm's ending, only a portion of the tower's base remained to stand as a mute monument."

Great Point Light, circa 1955.
Photograph by Louis Davidson;
collection of the Nantucket
Historical Association.

The northeaster causing the destruction was born over the Great Plains of Texas on March 23. Its normal progress northeastward toward the Great Lakes was blocked by a high pressure area over the Hudson Bay region of Canada, so it was shunted on an east-northeast path across Arkansas and Tennessee to the Atlantic coast near Cape Hatteras where rapid deepening of the storm's central barometric pressure took place. Record low pressures in the vicinity of 28.50 inches were registered along the coast from Virginia to Long Island, and winds mounted up to 65 miles per hour. High tides accompanied the gales along the southern New England coast.

The nearest meteorological installation of the National Weather Service to Great Point was located about nineteen miles to the north-northeast across the Monomoy channel at Chatham on Cape Cod. The wind there reached storm force by 9:00 a.m. on the 29th, blowing from east-northeast at 44 miles per hour. It attained a peak of 60 miles per hour at 6:00 p.m., having blown from the east-northeast all day. The storm center passed about 120 miles southeast of the island late in the evening. The barometer then reached

The rubble of Great Point Light on March 31, 1984, after the waves of the Great March Storm had undermined and demolished the structure. Photograph courtesy of H. Flint Ranney.

its lowest point of 28.84 inches at Chatham and the wind backed into the north-northeast. It was blowing at 46 miles per hour at midnight. The temperature during the day of the 26th ranged from 39° at midnight to 33° at 6:00 a.m. and then rose to 38°F by 6:00 p.m. Heavy rain was reported at all observations with the exception of 3:00 p.m. when a brief bit of freezing rain fell. A total of 2.24 inches of rain descended on the 29th and another .68 inches on the 30th, for a storm total of 2.92 inches.

On Nantucket at the FAA tower, located about nine miles south of Great Point, the barometer dropped to 28.82 inches between 8:00 and 9:00 p.m. The highest wind speed was clocked at 63 miles per hour from the north-northwest.

SUMMER STORMS

"The Greatest Summer Storm," July 4–5, 1933

Northeast winds blew at a rate of 37.0 miles per hour all day on July 4, 1933. They reached gale force about 1:00 a.m. and were still blowing at that rate at midnight. The peak wind speed of 59 miles per hour was recorded at 4:50 p.m. on the 4th. The high winds ended at 11:08 a.m. on the 5th.

It was unusually cold for early July with a reading of 52°F, only one degree above the longtime record low for July 4. Rain began at 8:02 a.m. on the 4th and continued, sometimes intermittently, through the 4th and 5th, completely washing out the holiday. Heavy amounts fell between 1:00 and 4:00 p.m. on the 4th, when the storm was at its height. A total of 0.59 inch fell on the 4th, and a 0.19 inch on the 5th.

Coming on a summer holiday, the storm did "untold damage to small boats and also to crops," according to the *Inquirer and Mirror*. All foliage was blighted by the wind blasts. It was judged the severest summer storm, excluding hurricanes, since the weather bureau station was established in 1886.

Thunderstorms

Thunderstorms provide an important portion of the water supply during the warm months of the year when precipitation from cyclonic storm activity is at a minimum.

A thunderstorm is a local storm cell invariably produced by a cumulonimbus cloud. It is always accompanied by lightning and thunder aloft and usually by strong gusts of wind, rain showers, and sometimes hail at the surface of the earth. In extreme cases, a funnel cloud or even a tornado may generate within the thunderstorm cloud. The activity of these weather elements in a single storm cell is usually of limited duration, often from ten to fifteen minutes, seldom over two hours.

The fundamental requirement for the development of a thunderstorm is an atmosphere that is unstable or potentially unstable if heat is added. Instability means that once a bubble of warm air is given an upward lift, it will become buoyant and continue to rise without additional impulse. The air bubble constantly finds itself in a colder environment, and, like a hot air balloon, is forced upward by the pressure of cooler, denser air surrounding it. This is the process of convection.

To quote Sir Napier Shaw, an eminent British meteorologist: "A thunderstorm is a gigantic, if comparatively slow, explosion of moist air, the latent heat of the moist air acting as fuel." Conditions favorable for convection arise from several circumstances. Daytime heating over flat land may result in rising thermal currents whose further ascent is stimulated by the unstable condition of the lower atmosphere. Air resting over rough or hilly terrain may receive unequal heating and cause vertical circulations. Airstreams passing over rising high ground may be forced upward, orographically, to an unstable level and continue the bubble-like ascent to higher levels. Convergence of airstreams in a frontal zone during cyclonic activity may create vertical currents and increase instability. Sometimes thunderstorm cells form in a line along a squall or instability line many miles ahead of a cold front and along the front itself.

Nantucket is not a thunderstorm prone area. Its size is not large enough to provide a broad surface of massive radiational heating, while cooling ocean breezes tend to inhibit island-wide heating. Many thunderstorms which form over the mainland find the updrafts of hot air necessary to sustain the convective process absent over the waters of Nantucket Sound and Buzzards Bay, and thus diminish in intensity or completely dissipate before completing the thirty to fifty miles of overwater passage. The main source of Nantucket thunderstorms comes from cold front passages. These supply the uplift of air that may create a line of thunderstorms several hundred miles long. If the cold front should stall in the vicinity of Cape Cod and the Islands, the thunderstorms may continue for several hours with their dangerous strokes of lightning, mighty rumbling in the sky, and often heavy deluges of rain.

Fog

Fog, of course, is not a storm; in fact, it forms generally under light wind conditions, yet its presence may be just as dangerous to navigation as storm winds. Since fogginess reaches a maximum frequency in late spring and early summer, it is discussed here in the summer section of this work.

Fog consists of minute, visible droplets of water suspended in the atmosphere, usually near the earth's surface. By technical definition, fog exists when horizontal visibility is reduced below one kilometer. Fog originates when the temperature and dew point of the air become identical or nearly so. This may occur either when the air is cooled to its dew point (producing advective fog, radiation fog, or up-slope fog), or when moisture is added to the air, thereby elevating the dew point (producing steam fog or frontal fog). Fog seldom forms when the difference between temperature and dew point is greater than four degrees.

Sea fog frequently occurs along the New England coast, making it the foggiest area of the eastern United States; the frequency along the coast generally decreases from northeast to southwest. The Labrador Current plays a major role in fog making. In the warm season, its cool waters stream southwest along the New England coast, while the Gulf Stream flows northeast well offshore. Warm air from the latter in moving across the cool water inshore has its temperature lowered to the dew point, causing condensation of its moisture into fog. This occurs particularly over the shallows of Brown and Georges banks.

Situations favorable for the formation of fog over Cape Cod and the Islands almost always

The Gloucester fishing schooner Evelyn & Ralph *came ashore in dense fog on the south shore of Nantucket on December 6, 1924. A fo'csle stove tipped over and the fire consumed the vessel on the beach.* Photograph courtesy of Charles F. Sayle.

Extremes of Fog Frequency
Number of days with dense fog

	Town 1893–1945		Airport 1946–1969	
	Greatest	Least	Greatest	Least
Jan.	12 1937	0 1942	10 1947	0 1968
Feb.	12 1922	0 1912	8 1946	2 1952
			1955	1956
			1959	
Mar.	14 1913	0 1915	11 1948	2 1958
Apr.	13 1908	1 1924	12 1955	2 1968
		1942		
		1943		
May	17 1911	3 1903	17 1946	2 1964
June	20 1928	4 1908	19 1968	6 1949
July	23 1906	7 1942	27 1959	5 1953
			1967	
Aug.	18 1915	2 1942	19 1967	7 1957
Sept.	15 1934	2 1924	21 1946	3 1952
Oct.	11 1919	0 1924	11 1959	3 1946
		1940		1955
Nov.	9 1908	0 1939	10 1960	1 1949
		1940		1965
Dec.	9 1929	0 1915	11 1964	0 1963
Annual	111 1919	62 1930	129 1961	77 1952

are cyclonic in pattern, involving convergence of airstreams at the surface. These may occur in the warm sector of a cyclone, ahead of an approaching cold front, or in association with a semistationary trough of low pressure along the coast. These conditions develop southwest winds that carry warm, moist air over the cold offshore waters, causing condensation of their moisture, and bring fog over the land. Over the sea there is little variation in fogginess during a 24-hour period, but over land fog tends to dissipate as the day progresses and solar heating warms the atmosphere.

The seasonal variation of fog is marked. At Nantucket, the late autumn and early winter have the minimum of three days with fog per month. The number increases to ten in May and to a midsummer peak of 14 in July. It decreases in August to ten and continues steadily downward to the minimum in November and December.

AUTUMN STORMS

Northeasters

John Winthrop, the first governor of the Massachusetts Bay Colony, early recognized the importance of northeast storms in the weather mix of New England. A journal entry declared: "It is a general rule, that when the wind blows 12 hours in any part of the east, it brings rain or snow in great abundance."

With the fading of the tropical storm menace and the revival of storm generation off the South Atlantic seaboard in early autumn, the coastal storm, with its combination of driving northeast winds and gales, surging tides and surf, and often heavy precipitation, increases in frequency. One may appear in October, and two or three generate in an active November. Occasionally, one develops great stature, such as in 1873, 1888, 1898, 1904, 1938, 1945, 1953, 1961, and 1984. On these occasions, seemingly innocuous coastal disturbances have intensified into major storms during their journey northeast and taken huge tolls of life and property along the New England shore.

Temperature contrasts between the rapidly cooling northern landmass and the still warm waters covered by the sub-tropical Atlantic Ocean and Gulf of Mexico constitute the principal factor in generating the autumn storminess of the coastal region. The Gulf Stream continues transporting huge volumes of tepid water northward, while Canadian anticyclones are sending increasingly frigid airstreams southeast all the way to the seaboard of the Carolinas and Georgia. Here the airsteams of opposing thermal content clash along the meeting line or front. This stimulates a cyclonic circulation which may lead to the formation of a full-fledged storm system.

According to the configurations of the atmospheric ridges and troughs of high and low barometric pressure areas on the weather map at the time, the nascent storm center may move northeast along the seaboard and threaten the urban complexes of the Northeast and their adjacent ports and coastal resorts. Alternatively, the growing disturbance may be forced by a blocking anticyclone spread across northern New England and southeast Canada to head east-northeast over the open Atlantic and expend its energies south of New England over the ocean waters between Bermuda and Nova Scotia.

The path followed by the storm center is all-important in determining what areas of New England will receive precipitation. Each storm is an individual product, differing from its predecessor and its follower. The canopy of falling rain or snow may cover only the Islands and outer Cape Cod, or it may reach well into the interior and bring wet weather to all of southeastern New England. Coastal storms can deviate considerably from an average path. If they track north-northeast from the Carolina coast, the center may pass inside or to the west of the Cape and Islands area, in which case a good part of western and northern New England would lie in the precipitation zone with heavy rains or snow possible for the elevated parts of the interior. The Cape and Islands, located east of the path of the storm center, would receive mild airstreams from the southeast with only light rain prevailing.

The speed of the storm center's movement is significant in determining the amount of precipitation that may fall. A storm moving at 40 miles per hour may yield only six hours of precipitation, while one progressing at half that rate will keep the precipitation process in action for a dozen hours or more, resulting in a much greater precipitation total.

In some cases, the normal path of the storm center to the northeast may be challenged by a high pressure ridge of great magnitude standing over Quebec and the Atlantic Provinces; occasionally a ridge extends south over the ocean toward Bermuda. Then the advancing storm center is entrapped between high pressure both to the east and the west, often resulting in a deepening of the barometric center, an increase in the strength of the circulatory winds, and a prolongation of the precipitation. Severe storm conditions develop around the center and the coast of southeastern New England might receive a strong lashing for many hours. Such were the storm situations in the Blizzard of '88, the Portland Storm in 1898, and Boston's Big Snow of February 1978.

The place of origin of northeasters long remained a mystery until Benjamin Franklin found a key. In observing a lunar eclipse in 1743 at Philadelphia, he was disappointed because clouds and rain from a northeast storm prevented his viewing it; later, he learned that his brother at Boston had seen the eclipse, but soon afterwards it began to rain with a northeast wind rising. Franklin concluded that the storm was moving northeast along the coast despite the contrary wind observed at both places. This comprised the first morsel of information about the movement of storms along the Atlantic seaboard. And Nantucket shared in this important discovery since Benjamin Franklin's mother came from the island.

November Storms

Anglo-Saxons called November in Old England the "winde-monath" and their descendants found the designation equally appropriate to New England after experiencing the late autumn's atmospheric behavior here.

The face of November weather maps takes on a wintry aspect as the month progresses. The principal storm track across Canada slips southward from its high latitude position in summer to about 50°N. Low pressure centers generating in Alberta or Colorado track eastward on converging paths toward the Great Lakes and then move eastward down the St. Lawrence Stormway and on toward Newfoundland over the Atlantic Provinces of Canada. Another storm track takes on new energy along the Atlantic seaboard as cyclogenesis makes a seasonal revival over the Gulf of Mexico. Barometric depressions move across the neck of northern Florida and

Georgia, pass close to Cape Hatteras, and then head for Cape Cod and the Islands. They may pass inside or outside of Nantucket, but, whether as northeasters or southeasters, they can raise considerable wind on the Island. Though true tropical storms and hurricanes are a rarity in November, one of the mightiest smote Nantucket as late as the 27th in 1888.

During the month of November areas of maximum storm frequency lie off Georgia and the Carolinas and southeast of Cape Cod.

The Great November Gale And Snowstorm, 1898: The Portland Storm

The terrible gale and heavy snowstorm that developed along the New England coast and offshore waters late on Saturday evening and raged all day Sunday, November 26th and 27th, 1898, caught the attention of the contemporary public more than any other news event of the time. A morbid fascination has always clung to the mystery attached to its distinguishing event—the foundering in complete silence to the outside world of the passenger ship *S.S. Portland* off the northern tip of Cape Cod, a loss as complete and unexplained as many modern airline crashes when all aboard are victims. The entire population of the region remained in suspense for many hours, knowing the ship had not made port on schedule, and anxiously awaited word from some source that would establish her fate.

There were no survivors among the 192 persons on the sailing list that Saturday of the Thanksgiving weekend when the popular ship left Boston Harbor for the short overnight run to Portland, Maine. Instead of arriving at their destinations for a relaxing Sunday among friends or families, this unfortunate group spent a night and day of terror in a desperate struggle for survival against unrelenting northeast gales of immense force. Finally, on Sunday evening

after twenty-four hours at sea, their weary ship, either out of fuel or so badly damaged by the constant battering of the seas that she was unable to keep her heading into the wind, broached and was overwhelmed by the huge crests and troughs of the waves, and went to a watery grave with all hands.

The hapless hulk went to the bottom about seven miles east of the northern tip of the Cape. Ever since, their great meteorological event has been known as the "Portland Storm." Even without such a tragedy it would deserve to be chronicled in any book about American storms, so great were the combination of adverse weather elements concentrated over the coastal area and offshore islands on that sad weekend.

The absence of radio communications, still ten years away for practical shipboard use, long sealed the exact fate of the *Portland* in eternal silence. Though the scene of the wreck was located in 1945 by the efforts of Edward Rowe Snow, the indefatigable historian of the coastal scene of New England, the exact circumstances surrounding her last agony will never be known. The possibility of a collision with another ship in the blinding snowstorm was investigated thoroughly by Snow in his *Storms and Shipwrecks of New England* (1943), but discarded. Snow's evidence, painstakingly assembled and logically analyzed, clearly pointed to the end of the *Portland* on Sunday evening about 9:15 p.m. off the North Truro Beach.

The genesis of the famous northeaster lay in a trough of low barometric pressure which moved southeast across the lower Great Lakes early on Saturday morning, the 26th. Its normal eastward progress had been blocked by a large anticyclone overlying northern New England and the Atlantic Provinces of Canada. As often happens in similar situations, a secondary disturbance developed in the southern part of the low pressure trough over the coastal areas of the Carolinas. By noon of the 26th, the new cyclonic center, having deepened considerably when in the vicinity of Cape Hatteras, became the main power point of the storm system. By evening,

the ever-widening circulatory whirl, developing greater and greater strength, advanced to a position directly east of southern New Jersey and south of the eastern tip of Long Island.

The key to its future course now lay over southern Quebec and the Atlantic Provinces where the strong anticyclone still persisted. A very tight barometric gradient developed between the two atmospheric forces as darkness descended on New England's offshore waters on this cold Saturday evening in November.

By dawn of Sunday, the 27th, as indicated by the barometer at Father Point on the northern shore of the Gulf of St. Lawrence, the pressure reading had increased to 30.20 inches while the central pressure of the coastal disturbance had lowered to 28.90 inches while moving to the vicinity of Chatham on the southwest tip of Cape Cod. Since the centers of the high and low pressure areas were separated by about only 700 miles, the increasingly tight pressure gradient resulted in raising the winds to whole-gale force, the rating just below full hurricane. These raked the coast of New England through all Saturday night and Sunday, reaching peaks in the morning of 55 miles per hour, according to anemometers at Block Island, Nantucket, Woods Hole, and Blue Hill Observatory near Boston. Gales prevailed west to New Haven and northeast to Eastport, Maine.

Weather data from the area definitely indicated the passage of the center inside of Nantucket, where the winds were squally and fitful in the unsteady air flow as the storm center drew abreast on Sunday morning. A slow traverse over Martha's Vineyard and across southeast Cape Cod seemed probable with the now-expanded center stalling over the area until noontime. A period of light winds, partial clearing overhead, and improved visibility continued for an hour or more inside the center of action around which strong winds were whirling on the outside at a distance of 20 to 30 miles. These conditions are characteristic of many great winter storms when a vigorous coastal storm confronts a strong high pressure area over Atlantic Canada. Both the famous Cold Storm of 1857 and the Blizzard of 1888 exhibited the same behavior.

The editor of the *Inquirer and Mirror* considered it "one of the most violent storms of wind and rain which ever visited this place." The local official of the Weather Bureau, W.W. Neifert, supplied the meteorological details:

Saturday, November 26: Pressure continued about stationary until 10 a.m., then began falling rapidly, continuing at midnight [to fall]. Partly cloudy weather in morning, but cloudiness increased in afternoon and light rain began at 7:30 p.m. Temperature rising slowly all day. Northwest winds continued during the night, with decreasing force, and by 6 a.m. was nearly calm, winds were variable to noon, then became easterly which continued for rest of day with increasing force, and by 11:55 p.m. a maximum velocity of 57, E, occurred.

Sunday, November 27: The most severe storm in the history of this station occurred this day. The barometer continued falling rapidly from midnight to 2 a.m., the barograph shows a fall of .28 [inch], while at 5 a.m., it shows 28.80 [inches], remained about 28.95 [inches] until noon, when it began rising and continued rapidly at midnight. Several decided temperature changes during morning, but in afternoon it fell rapidly. Rain ended at 7:10 a.m., about .57 [inch], then squally from 9:10 a.m. to 4 p.m., with .08 [inch]. Light snow set in at 5:30 p.m., ended at midnight, with about 1.5 [inches] dry snow on ground. East winds, varying to northeast continued during night with violence, maximum velocity of 72 miles per hour [corrected 56] during the day wind was about northeast but at 3:45 p.m. it backed to north, finally decreased in night. No signals were sent, wires being prostrate. Signal lantern flagstaff was blown from roof at 1:40 p.m. during a 65 mile [corrected 50] wind. Ruined pole and lanterns and broke some

guys to instrument shelter. About a dozen large size fishing catboats in harbor were capsized, sunk or otherwise damaged. Two masted schooner *Luther Eldridge* sunk at wharf. Considerable damage was sustained in town, in way of unroofing barns etc., demolishing chimneys and fences. The damage will aggregate $5000.00.

Monday, November 28: Day opened cloudy which continued until 2 p.m, when began to clear, much colder weather, with slowly rising pressure. High northwest winds continued during the night, and day becoming northerly in afternoon and decreasing. Maximum velocity 36, NW, at 12:10 a.m. . . . steamer did not make her usual trip to the mainland. Signals sent by mail.

The *Inquirer and Mirror* reported the local scene:

When the weather bureau gave warning Saturday of a "heavy northeaster," it was little thought that it would develop such force and be of so long duration, and it found people wholly unprepared. It was fully as severe as the storm of January 31st last, and the amount of damage done was much greater, one carpenter estimating it at $5,000. The storm center must have been very near Nantucket, the wind at times attaining a velocity of 90 miles per hour [corrected 69 to current three-cup anemometer standards].

Early Saturday evening rain began to fall, the wind gradually increasing from the southeast. By eleven o'clock it was blowing a gale, shifting to the northeast, accompanied by a mixture of rain, sleet, and snow. The sleep of many was broken by the shrieking of the wind through the wires and tree-tops, the creaking of fences, windows and blinds rattling, scuttles banging, twigs and branches falling, which all told of the fierce disturbance of the elements outside.

Between one and two o'clock Sunday morning the storm was at its height, snow and hail falling continuously. The wind gradually lessened in force at daylight, and the weather gave every prospect of clearing; but, Nature

deemed it otherwise, and by three o'clock Sunday afternoon, the storm came on again with great force. At 7 o'clock the wind was blowing fifty miles per hour [corrected 40], accompanied by blinding snow, which continued to fall until about midnight, when the storm gradually lessened in force. At 7 a.m., it was still blowing too hard for the steamer to make her trip, and she remained tied up at the wharf.

It was a weird spectacle that presented itself Sunday morning. Everything that was movable had moved. Fences were blown down, windows blown in, trees uprooted, shingles torn off, and electric wires and poles broken. Brant Point roads and meadows were completely submerged, the water rising as high as the cottage of Dr. Williams.

The principal damage was done about the wharves and water-front, although the out-of-town farms suffered considerably . . . The tide was so high as to submerge the wharves, and as it rose rats were seen in large numbers trying to escape drowning. Many were killed by dogs as they came out from under the wharves, and large numbers were drowned.

Inquirer and Mirror,
December 3, 1898.

The havoc created by the storm was widespread. Edward Rowe Snow estimated that 141 different ships were wrecked. Around 25 of these occurred in Boston Harbor, and 20 were damaged or wrecked on Martha's Vineyard. The loss of life was estimated at "over 456 persons."

As did the survivors of the Blizzard of '88 in New York City, a group of nautical people and historians met in Boston each year on the anniversary of the Portland Storm to commemorate the event. The meeting began in 1908, ten years after the tragedy, and continued through 1948 on the 50th anniversary when their number had dwindled to only a few.

Surf undermined and destroyed a wing of the Surfside Hotel during a series of severe storms in the fall of 1902. Collection of the Nantucket Historical Association.

Marconi Storm, November 1901

A northeast storm of considerable energy developed Sunday morning [Nov. 24], as forecast by the Weather Bureau on Saturday. The wind blew with terrible force at times, some of the gusts gaining a maximum velocity of 52 miles. Rain fell in copious showers during the entire day, but the gale abated early in the afternoon. The wharves were at times completely submerged. The partially completed cottage of Miss Baxter's, Beachside, was entirely wrecked, even the foundation piers being prostrated. Fences, window blinds, etc. succumbed to the blasts, and windows in the North Congregational Church were blown in. The temperature was fortunately moderate.

The barometer, despite the fact that the gale had abated to a calm, indicated that there was more to follow. Little by little it kept receding until it touched the rather alarming point of 29.12 at 8 o'clock Monday morning. Then the wind hauled from the southwest to N.N.W. and breezed gradually. By 10 o'clock it was blowing at a 47 mile clip. The tide was abnormally high, and two hours before the time of high water, the wharves were submerged, as well as the low lands of Brant Point and along the harbor front. Spectators sought lee places from which to view the turbulent scene, and an anxious group of boatmen worked hard to protect their boats from battering against the wharves.

Inquirer and Mirror,
November 30, 1901.

The new Marconi Company radio towers for trans-Atlantic communications at Wellfleet on Cape Cod were demolished by the wind. It was thought that a single stay snapped and brought on the collapse of the others.

Great November Storm, 1904

The chief feature of the November weather was the severe and general storm of the 13–14th, during which the major portion of the precipitation of the month in all sections occurred, falling in the form of heavy snow and sleet in interior and northern, and snow and rain in southern portions. The disturbance was also accompanied by high winds and gales, which attained hurricane force along the southern coast of New England. There was some loss of life, and damage by high winds to shipping, and also to telephone, telegraph, and trolley wires. The maximum velocity of the wind, as far as officially reported, was 76 miles per hour [corrected 59], at Block Island, R.I. The depression of the barometer during this storm was very marked, and a new minimum record was made at a number of stations. At Boston the pressure fell to 28.63 inches, which is the lowest of record, except February 1895, when it was 28.61 inches, reduced to sea level . . . The lowest barometer in New England was 28.50 inches at Fall River, Mass. on the 13th.

New England climatologist.

During the 12 hours from 8:00 a.m. to 8:00 p.m., the Nantucket barometer fell almost an inch, from 29.63 inches to 28.69 inches, the latter being the low point of the storm. The wind was also at its peak of 47 miles per hour from the northeast. During the day the rainfall measured 0.86 inch. Thunderstorms occurred, so the rain must have been of the shower type. The temperature read 48°, but next morning it was down to 39°F with the wind blowing a gale out of the northwest at 38 miles per hour. Another 0.23 inch of rain fell to bring the storm total to 1.09 inches. By 8:00 p.m. on the 14th, the barometer had recovered to 29.77 inches and the wind was down to northwest at 17 miles per hour with the highest gust at 30 miles per hour.

The Gale of '45

Since the Minot's Light Gale of 1851 there have been only a few easterly storms in New England severe enough to deserve special mention. Most of these have taken place in November. The Gale of 1888 is still considered by many as greater than the 1898 storm which caused the Portland disaster just ten years later.

The storm of November 1945, which will go down in history as the Gale of '45, caused more damage and suffering along the entire New England Coast than any easterly since the *Portland* foundered.

Edgar Rowe Snow,
Storms and Shipwrecks of New England. 3d edition 1946.

The New England climatologist agreed and added the details:

The storm first appeared as a small low-pressure area 70 miles northwest of Cape Hatteras early on Wednesday morning [28th]. It moved rapidly northward during the day, causing precipitation to spread northward through New England to northern Maine, and winds to increase over southern New England. From 7:30 p.m. Wednesday to 7:30 a.m. Thursday, the storm's center remained nearly stationary off the southern New Jersey coast, then changed its course to east-northeast, reaching a point about 60 miles south of central Long Island at 7:30 p.m. Thursday [29th]. During this period, winds became strong and precipitation heavy over southern New England. From then on the course of the storm was almost due east, its rate of progress slow, and rain changed to

snow in most sections except in the Cape Cod area.

. . . Although several small and medium sized craft were destroyed in the gale, shipping in general, aided by timely warnings, managed to ride out the storm without great casualties. Press reports stated that 33 deaths were ascribed to the storm.

Gale-force winds on Nantucket began at 11:21 a.m. on Friday, November 30, and continued until 9:04 p.m. on December 1. Winds came out of the north throughout the storm except for five hours at the outset when they were from the northeast. A maximum sustained wind of 42 miles per hour was reached at 3:25 a.m. on the 1st and an extreme speed of 56 miles at 5:08 a.m. The average hourly speed on the 1st was 30.8 miles per hour.

Rainfall proved heavy in the storm area. Nantucket received the following amounts: 1.24 inches on the 29th, 2.62 inches on the 30th, and a final 0.49 inch on the 1st, for a storm total of 4.35 inches. Chatham reported 3.88 inches and New Bedford 4.34 inches.

The *Inquirer and Mirror* took notice of the storm's visit:

The waterfront took a severe beating, the waves breaking right over the bulkhead on Easy Street, flooding the road for quite a distance. Commercial Wharf was also submerged. The water was high enough so that the Commercial Wharf Restaurant looked as if it were afloat—no wharf or piles beneath it. Waves broke across Washington Street and invaded the ballroom floor of the White Elephant. There was no boat service for three days. Little damage occurred except that by high water.

Great Easterly Gale, November 1950

The greatest combination of contrasting weather elements ever brought together over the Eastern States developed an atmospheric

disturbance of unprecedented severity along the length and breadth of the Appalachian Mountains from the Gulf of Mexico to Canada from the afternoon of November 24 to the morning of November 26, over the Thanksgiving holiday weekend. The storm has been called the Great Appalachian Storm from its expansive influence from Alabama to Maine on each slope of the mountains of that name; but for the Cape Cod and Islands area it has been known as the Great Easterly Gale of November 1950 for its tremendous and sustained wind flow from that direction.

The weather record books for November required a complete rewriting as a result of the meteorological events unfolding on this storm-filled weekend. More people were delayed, discomforted, or just inconvenienced over a wide area of the most heavily populated section of the country than in any other historic storm.

The New England climatologist described aspects of the storm's impact on the region:

Although New England was spared the heavy snow and extremely low temperatures that so paralyzed other sections in the eastern third of the country, the gale and flood toll was tremendous. Hurricane velocities in gusts were attained at many points, both coastal and inland. The inflowing marine air was relatively warm and very moist, and as it overrode the advancing cold air from the west, rapid condensation produced heavy general rainfall, exceeding two inches during the night of the 25–26th in the Southern Division, and as much as four to six inches over much of the Section in the following three days.

The path of the center of the storm lay over central Pennsylvania, some 400 miles west of Nantucket. Nevertheless, so great were the contrasting weather elements that day it raised a mighty wind on Cape Cod and the Islands. Nantucket's average wind speed for the day was the high figure of 37.7 miles per hour. A steady flow at 47 miles per hour was registered at 6:30 p.m., when one gust hit 65 miles per hour. At this time the warm front of the storm, sweeping northward, arrived on the southern New England shore. Soon, the cold front of the storm, having swept around the southern side of the storm center, also reached the southern New England shore. Heavy rain fell; the Nantucket gauge measured 2.33 inches, which came within the seven hours from 9:00 p.m. on the 25th to 4:00 a.m. on the 26th. A deluge of 0.82 inch descended in the single hour after midnight.

The *Inquirer and Mirror* made a familiar comment: "Once again a severe storm has bypassed Nantucket, bringing only a lot of rain and high winds."

Storm of November 29-30, 1963

An intense extratropical cyclone moved rapidly northward near the western border of New England during the a.m. of the 30th. New record-low barometric readings for November were noted at many stations . . . Southerly winds of damaging force affected most of the area east of the storm center's path. Inland damages were mostly confined to trees, utility lines, signs, windows, chimneys, and aerials, but much major devastation occurred in south coast areas. Coastal damages were like those of a hurricane. Especially hard hit were the coasts of eastern Connecticut, Rhode Island, Cape Cod in Massachusetts, and Maine. Some peak gust velocities noted were 85 m.p.h. at Block Island, 80 m.p.h. at Woods Hole and Chatham on Cape Cod, and 76 m.p.h. at Portland, Maine.

The New England climatologist cited erosion as the principal damage with tide in some places eight feet above normal.

This was a sou'wester on Nantucket with the wind averaging 31.6 miles an hour on the 30th. The wind began to pick up at 4:00 a.m. and at 6:00 a.m. was blowing at 25 miles per hour with gusts to 30 miles. By 10:30 a.m. the peak was reached with a steady 50 miles per hour and gusts to 69 miles. The high winds

continued until 10:00 p.m. The lowest barometer reading was 29.04 inches since Nantucket lay well to the east of the storm track over western New England. Burlington, VT reported the lowest reading at 28.62 inches.

The *Inquirer and Mirror* commented on the storm's presence:

The southwest storm that brought gusts that reached 69 miles per hour hit Nantucket on Friday and Saturday [Nov. 29 and 30] disrupted boat and phone service and caused minor damage. Intermittent rain squalls accompanied the storm. The precipitation was light and totaled 1.02 inches for the two days.

Nantucket escaped the full force of the storm which caused a great deal of damage in southeastern Massachusetts, particularly at New Bedford, Fairhaven, and towns on Cape Cod.

WINTER STORMS

By December, both the jet stream and the Canadian storm track have slipped southward, now passing over the Great Lakes and continuing eastward slightly north of the St. Lawrence Valley. Warm fronts from these systems move northward and cold fronts southward over New England in endless succession.

Mean pressure charts place a center of maximum anticyclonic activity over Quebec and an area of minimum pressure southeast of Nantucket, setting up a strong pressure gradient across all New England. Storms moving into this zone from any direction tend to slow down or stall, all the while intensifying with heightened winds and increased precipitation.

The winter circulation pattern across North America reaches fullest development in January. The westerly jet stream is found at its most southerly location by the month's end, often dipping into the Southern states before trending northeast toward the Middle Atlantic coast. Storminess is usually at a maximum just north of the path of the jet stream.

The main January storm tracks from the West converge on the Great Lakes from Alberta, Colorado, and Texas, then head east-northeast down the St. Lawrence Valley. The storm track along the Atlantic seaboard becomes well travelled, leading either from the western Gulf of Mexico or the warm Gulf Stream waters off Florida and Georgia to a meeting place near Cape Hatteras. The path of most storms then heads northeast, 100 to 150 miles off the New England shore, but their canopy of precipitation usually extends to Nantucket.

Most New England locations have more snowy days, average more inches of snowfall per day, and have a snow cover of greater depth in February than in any other month. The reason for the preponderance of frozen precipitation is directly attributable to the increased activity of coastal storms and northeasters.

The typical northeaster is a product of the Gulf of Mexico or the waters off the Atlantic seaboard of the Southeast, and February is the time of greatest activity in these areas. When an old front lies across the Gulf of Mexico and northern Florida and an upper-air trough of low pressure moves eastward across central United States, cyclogenesis frequently occurs in the southern end of the trough. If the newly formed center follows a storm track west of the Appalachians, it often commences to fade over Kentucky or Ohio and a new secondary center forms in the vicinity of Cape Hatteras. This soon becomes the principal disturbance. Sometimes a new center develops independently off the north Florida or Georgia coasts and moves rapidly northeastward to the Cape Hatteras area. Both types exhibit the same characteristics and often develop great energy in a few hours when nearing Nantucket.

Gale of Early December, 1830

The Gale—During Monday and Monday night [Dec. 6] last, a most violent gale was experienced at this place. On the afternoon and evening of Sunday the wind was at N.W. in the night for a short time at S.E. and in the morning of Monday sprang up from the N.E.—it blew with increasing violence, accompanied with copious showers during the day and night—and in the latter part of the night its course changed to N.W. The fury of the invisible element was unexampled; and its power was abundantly tested by the exhibition of its effects to our citizens Tuesday morning.

The long prevalence of easterly winds during the last week has frequently raised the tides to an unusual height. But during the gale, the tide was at an elevation only equalled here by the great tide of 1786 in which the sea broke into the harbor over the isthmus that connects Great Point with the body of the island. The water in the evening of Monday [Dec. 6] was over the wharves, sticks of heavy yellow pine timber, 18 inches in diameter were carried from the docks and floated about

the New North wharf . . . Much damage to North Wharf.

On the 5th instant the mercury in the Barometer at noon stood at 29.85 inches, it was nearly calm until the 6th at 5 a.m. when it began to blow from E.N.E. and rain—at noon of the 6th the mercury in the Barometer had fallen to 29 inches—at 7 p.m. it had fallen to 28.95—at 2 p.m. it stood at 28.85, when it became stationary; the wind blew tremendously, the rain fell in torrents—much damage was done to fences and old buildings; although the moon was not in a position for us to expect a great swell of the tide, it rose higher than it had been since December 5, 1786—the strong wind from the E.N.E. obstructed the flood tide in passing through the sound, and probably the sudden fall of the mercury in the Barometer contributed to swell the tide. In twenty-six hours it fell one inch, which removed a pressure of about half a pound from each square inch of surface, which if it extended to no great distance would have raised the sea about thirteen inches.

Nantucket Inquirer,
December 11, 1830.

Triple Storms, December 1839

December 1839 stood preeminent in the annals of coastal New England as a month with more destructive gales and severe snowstorms than any other in the nineteenth century. No less than eight distinct cyclonic disturbances crossed eastern Massachusetts during the month, each attended by shifting gales and by a mixture of rain, sleet, and heavy snow.

A unique pamphlet was issued early in 1840 chronicling the destruction wrought by the storms, entitled: *Awful Calamities: The Shipwrecks of December 1839, being a full account of the Dreadful Hurricanes of Dec. 15, 21 &* 27, *on the coast of Massachusetts; in which were lost more than 90 vessels, and nearly 200 dismasted, driven ashore or otherwise damaged, and More Than 150 Lives Destroyed, of which full statistics are given ...* The frontispiece comprised a good abstract of the pamphlet's contents. Like modern storm souvenirs, *Awful Calamities* proved popular with New England audiences and went through at least five editions during 1840.

The first and the last of the storms developed hurricane force winds along the southern New England coast and appeared to cause greater havoc in the harbors and along the beaches than any other single storm with perhaps the exception of the Great September Gale of 1815. It is interesting to note that the three principal storms in December 1839 struck at intervals of six days.

The storm on the 15th caused very heavy snow, up to two feet, across northwest Connecticut, central Massachusetts, and southern Vermont and New Hampshire. The center of the storm tracked across eastern Connecticut and eastern Massachusetts. This placed Nantucket in the southern sector of the storm system with easterly winds shifting to southwest. William Mitchell sent a full description of the storm at Nantucket to William C. Redfield, the investigator of hurricanes and severe storms in New York. The latter employed the Nantucket observations in his study of the December storms which appeared in the *American Journal of Science*, published by Professor Benjamin Silliman of Yale College, in New Haven.

Walter Folger's meteorological reports in the *Nantucket Inquirer* indicated a barometer reading of 28.96 inches at 7:00 a.m. on the 16th, though this may not have been the actual minimum. William Mitchell added the information that the wind on the morning of the 15th was quite heavy, a violent squall accompanied by hail hit about 2:00 p.m., and an hour later the wind abated.

The editor of the *Inquirer* commented on the stormy first part of the month:

Weather. With the exception of three or four days, the month of December has thus far been distinguished, meteorologically considered, for nothing but a series of humid storms from the eastward, exhibiting every variety of phenomena pertaining to the dismal class of tempests. The entire assortment of elemental disagreeables, seems to have been brought into action; and we have had rain, hail, sleet, snow, thunder, lightning, wind, northern rainbows, high tides, and as many other variations of atmospherical, terrestrial, and oceanic misery as could possibly be desired by the most accomplished troglodyte in all Mud-fog. Sunday last was a day particularly full of all sorts of weather, including a very palpable whirlwind, which may have caused much damage along our coast.

Nantucket Inquirer,
December 18, 1839.

The final storm of the December series was more severe from a meteorological point of view and of much greater areal scope than either of the gales of the 15–16th or 22–23d. Certainly the barometer descended lower and the precipitation shield covered a greater territory than any other storm occurrence in this boisterous season.

Though we do not have the benefit of daily weather maps to track the storm, William Redfield constructed charts of the barometric pressures and wind directions gathered from correspondents by mail and was able to present a picture that confirmed his theory that the winds circulated around a storm center in a circular manner, counterclockwise, and did not rush straightline to the center of lowest pressure as postulated by James Espy of Philadelphia. The barometer at Providence fell to 28.81 inches and at Boston to 28.77 inches on the evening of the 28th. Both lay in the eastern sector of the storm system which tracked northeast through central Connecticut, central Massachusetts, and into southern New Hampshire.

The coastal section of southeastern New England suffered severely as it always does when a strong southeaster prevails. The *Inquirer* declaring the storm on the night of the 27th, "one of the most violent within the recollection of the oldest inhabitant."

Winter Gale, January 1867

The storm on January 17th in 1867 deserved front ranking in the history of great New England weather events. No other tempest of the nineteenth century caused such a disruption in railroad traffic and such delays on highways in eastern New England to the inconvenience of so many travellers. The famous Blizzard of '88 skipped the populated centers of the region, buffeting them with slushy snow, sleet, and rain instead of heavy snow and deep drifts. Not until the out-of-season Portland Storm of November 1898 would eastern New Englanders see a similar paralysis of communications such as occurred in January 1867.

The Old Colony Line, running from Boston to New Bedford and Fall River, became so blocked by huge drifts that no traffic moved for a full week, an even longer stoppage than had occurred in the Great Cold Storm in January 1857. Mountainous drifts completely closed the inland rail route between New Haven and Worcester, and the shore line through Providence, too, experienced similar difficulties. The backlash of the deep coastal depression came in the form of gusty northwest gales continuing over 48 hours after the snow had ceased to fall.

At New Bedford the barometer dropped from 29.40 inches at 7:00 a.m. to 28.85 inches at 2:00 p.m., indicative of the rapid development of the storm and the deepening of its barometric depth. Unfortunately, we do not have any barometric reading for Nantucket. We can surmise that the center of the storm may have been directly over Nantucket from the wind behavior described by the *Inquirer and Mirror:*

The weather on Thursday last [17th] ... might be called changeable. In the morning the wind was E, and the snow was falling fast. By 10 o'clock the snow had changed to rain, and the wind increased to a gale. At 11:30 the wind had changed to west, and we had a severe hail squall. At 12 the sun shone out bright and warm. . . . In the afternoon the wind hauled to the NW, and by 8 was blowing a tremendous gale, whirling the snow with blinding fury. . . . The gale continued very violent during the whole day [Friday]. . . . There are those, who so reverence the past that they seem even to regret the "old-fashioned snow storms" which if we are not mistaken by tradition, come not so often in these later years, as when our grandfathers walked the stage of life. Such must be abundantly satisfied with the late storm."

No meteorological observations were known to have been taken on Nantucket at this time, so the exact local intensity and behavior of the storm cannot be related. We do know that the steamer made no trips to the mainland on the 17th and 18th.

The editor of the *New Bedford Mercury*, under the title "Local Intelligence," expressed his feelings about the isolating storm:

The storm—The snow-storm, the most severe we have had since 1859, commenced about five o'clock, yesterday morning, [17th] increasing in fierceness during the day. No mails have reached this city, after the arrival of that from New York, via Newport, early in the morning, and at 4½ o'clock p.m. the telegraph wires ceased working. We are as completely isolated for the time, as if we resided at Nantucket. We cannot tell our readers what the Legislature has been doing; our Congress reports break off abruptly; there are no news of moving accidents by flood or field; no arrivals by sea, and no departures by land. There is nothing but a driving, blinding, and howling snow-storm; which has no compensation, but in the lighter cheer it gives to home, and the excuse it affords the night editor for an earlier return to it.

Big Storm Over New England, January 31, 1898

The storm will take its place in the history of New England weather by the side of other terrific storms which occur only at rare intervals. It recalls the memorable storm of March 1888, and some state that not since January 1867 has one of like intensity reached this section. Scenes of havoc and damage rarely equalled in the annals of winter history were left in its wake.

The opinion of the New England regional climatologist was substantiated by the meteorological statistics of the storm and by extensive news coverage of the disruptions in public and private life occasioned by the vast atmospheric disturbance.

The storm system came from the Canadian border area of the West. It progressed to the vicinity of Lake Huron by the morning of the 31st when definite evidence of a secondary storm development on the coast near Cape Hatteras was charted. During the day the coastal depression became the main disturbance, gathering tremendous energy while moving northeast off the Delmarva peninsula and south of Long Island. A barometer fall of 1.40 inches in about 12 hours to an uncorrected reading of 28.43 inches at 2:00 a.m. on February 1 was indicative of the mighty energy of the cyclonic center. Heavy snow fell inland over New England on the 31st and 1st to a depth of 25 inches. Maximum wind blasts of 59 miles per hour were registered at Blue Hill Observatory, 55 miles at Nantucket, 43 miles at Vineyard Haven, and 40 miles at Boston.

The *Nantucket Journal* described "the severest storm which has raged for years," and the *Inquirer and Mirror* thought it "one of the most severe storms for many years but Nantucket received rain rather than snow."

The wind came from the southeast with light snow on the morning of the 31st. This soon turned to rain as the temperature mounted rapidly from a midnight low of 14°F. Rain fell the rest of the day, but amounted to only 0.37 inch since the island lay to the east of the storm center, an area in which precipitation is generally light in this type of coastal storm. Around midnight the wind veered into the northeast when the center of the storm passed a short distance to the southeast and the barometer reached its lowest point of 28.63 inches.

The wind blew hardest between 10:00 and 11:00 p.m., reaching a peak of 56 miles per hour. The average wind speed was 49 miles per hour. After shifting into the northwest, the wind continued, though with diminishing force, until 10:00 a.m. on the 1st. Precipitation on the second day added only 0.17 inch to the storm total of 0.54 inch.

The thermometer went through some interesting gyrations. From a low of 15° early on the morning of the 30th, it zoomed to 43°F by midnight with the arrival of the warm sector of the storm. It remained in that vicinity after midnight until the arrival of the cold front. By midnight of the 1st the mercury had dropped to a low of 14°F, just about where it had been 36 hours before.

The *Inquirer and Mirror* reported only "minor damage, but considerable in the aggregate." The electric works were shut down, and two chimneys on the Town Hall blown over. The article continued:

But as a storm it was the most severe known here for many years, and came so suddenly as to find people wholly unprepared.

By night a strong gale was blowing, and rain fell in torrents. Little by little the storm gained in energy and between 10 & 11 o'clock p.m. the hurricane had attained its full fury. The wind fairly shrieked among the telephone and electric wires, and moaned between the buildings, and roared about the roof tops with no unmistakable sound. . .

While, as noted before, the damage around the island was of a minor nature, yet in the aggregate it amounted to thousands of dollars.

Storm of January 24, 1908—Erosion

There was a heavy storm the previous week which made heavy inroads along the south shore from Surfside Life-saving Station down to Nobadeer. The configuration of the shoreline was greatly changed. For 20 hours the surf raged heavier than at any time in the last quarter century, eating as much as 25 feet into the bank in some places. The rutted road was entirely cut away. Bath houses on the bank were torn from the bluff and deposited on the beach as kindling wood a mile or two to the east. The life-savers said that only once—in the 1880's—had there been such a storm within their memories. By a strange freak of nature the shore in front of the station was not damaged. The beach was flattened along the entire shore and the sand was like quicksand, so much that a heavy stone could not be made to stay on top.

Thus the *Inquirer and Mirror*, on February 1, 1908, described the major erosion attending the northeaster. Other details of the storm followed:

The storm mentioned in this column last week was the most severe since the establishment of the Weather Bureau in Nantucket, in October 1886. A gust of 71 mph was registered at 7:31 a.m. on the 24th and a steady 50 mph was clocked for a 5-minute period at 7:36. The barometer went to 29.45.

"The fishing fleet suffered tremendous damage. Old North Wharf was washed out, as was the roadbed of the Nantucket Central Railroad between Old North and Steamboat Wharves. A large section of Swain's Wharf was swept away. The bulkhead at Beachside was demolished, as was the tool house of the Railroad. A section of the roof of the railroad station on steamboat wharf was torn off and several small buildings were razed. The 3-masted schooner *J.S. Lamprey* was carried about 30 feet from her anchorage. The hull of the schooner *Progress* was broken in two and was carried ashore. Catboats were wrecked. The fire alarm system was put out of order for three days. The flagstaff at Poets Corner was blown over into Prospect Hill Cemetery.

Inquirer and Mirror,
January 30, 1908.

Easterly Storm & High Tide, Christmas Night in 1909

The severe storm of Christmas, 1909, which takes rank among the notably severe and destructive winter storms that have visited the North Atlantic States during the last half century was first noted on the morning of December 23, as a rather weak cyclonic disturbance, central in southern Arizona. . . .

The advancement of the storm from Indiana eastward to the Atlantic coast, where it appeared on the morning of the 26th, was marked by the same rapid progress that had characterized its previous movement, and by a further increase of intensity that gave a barometric reading at Cape May, N.J., which was probably near the center at that time, of 28.57 inches, the lowest ever recorded at that station. On reaching the coast off New Jersey, the storm made an abrupt turn, passing up the New England coast during the 26th and disappearing from range of observation over the North Atlantic Ocean on the 27th.

Aside from the wrecking of a steamship, near Toms River, N.J., and several smaller vessels that were driven ashore on the New England coast, the damage on the water was comparatively light. On land the greatest property loss occurred with the tidal wave that swept the New England coast; the wrecking of electric lighting, trolley, telegraph, and telephone systems and the general interruption that resulted to transportation and traffic at nearly all points from the Potomac River to Maine.

New England climatologist.

"Escaped the blizzard . . . but experienced a phenomenal high tide which submerged the wharves, flooded the streets and property near the waterfront. . . . The tide rose to a height not known for many years," announced the *Inquirer and Mirror* to the outside world.

An easterly storm of severe dimensions began at Nantucket at 10:34 p.m. on December 25, 1909, with gale force winds rising to 38 miles per hour before midnight. The storm system came east on a transcontinental journey from Arizona that had started on the 23d. It tracked east to western Oklahoma and then north-northeast to central Indiana where the center was located on Christmas morning. A fast pace carried it to the Delaware coast by 8:00 p.m. Very heavy snow broke out in the Philadelphia and South Jersey area where a record 21 inches were reported on the 25–26th. The center deepened in barometric depth very rapidly as Atlantic Ocean moisture was drawn into the circulation, down to 28.63 inches at 4:00 p.m. on the 26th when off Cape Cod.

The Nantucket weather observer commented on December 26: "Easterly storm continued from midnight. At 3:07 a.m. the anemometer wire parted and the velocity interpolated from then until 7:00 a.m. when the break was repaired. Storm was severe, the building shook as if it were leaving its foundations. Tide was unusually high, all wharves submerged. Storm ended at 9:57 p.m."

The temperature remained above freezing on the island during the storm which deposited a total of 1.08 inches of rain. The maximum on the 26th reached 41°F. Only during the latter stages of the storm did snow fall and then only enough to cover the ground. The wind rose to a peak speed of 48 miles per hour.

The *Inquirer and Mirror* supplied details of the extraordinary tide accompanying the storm:

The tide rose to a height not known for many years, and shortly before noon on

Sunday the sight witnessed along the waterfront called many of our citizens from their homes to view the unusual conditions. Practically the only damage done anywhere was by the tide, the water strewing all sorts of material about the docks and adjacent streets, and when it subsided things were in a mess thereabouts. Numerous small craft were landed on top of the docks, others broke adrift and were driven a long distance from their berths, while several of the smaller catboats were sunk at their moorings."

Inquirer and Mirror,
January 1, 1910.

Brant Point was completely submerged, the meadows being flooded with several feet of water from the shore to the bluff. The cottages on the Beachside were surrounded with water and the road was inundated to within a few feet of the Point Breeze Hotel. Near Wauwinet the seas washed across the Haulover and also created "an entire change in the eastern shoreline of the island. Another opening threatened, but a shift of the wind to west apparently prevented this," observed the editor.

The local fishing fleet suffered "badly," and a three-masted schooner *Belle Halladay* was stranded on Coatue flats on Christmas Day.

Great First-of-March Storm, 1914

This island was swept by one of the worst gales in years Sunday afternoon and evening [Mar. 1], the high wind velocity created considerable damage all over the island and caused the destruction of much farm property. At one time the "extreme" recorded at the local weather bureau station was 120 miles [91 corrected]—shortly after six o'clock in the evening—when everything movable moved and many things not considered movable moved.

Inquirer and Mirror, March 7, 1914.

Wind at		
2:49 p.m. (corrected) -	48	mi/h
3:59	49	
4:04	60	
5:50	72	
6:23	86	SE
7:04	54	

The extreme wind speed of 91 miles per hour from the east occurred at 6:21 p.m. and another peak of 89 miles struck at 7:36 p.m. Thereafter the wind diminished rapidly.

The barometer reached an extreme depth of 28.50 inches, the second lowest reading in Weather Bureau history on the Island, and exceeded only by 28.38 inches on January 14, 1904. But Nantucket was not at the center of the disturbance; New Haven registered the lowest pressure of 28.27 inches, a record there until the New England Hurricane came along in 1938.

This was a warm storm with the center moving inside of Nantucket, probably over Nantucket Sound and the westerly part of the Cape. Thus the temperature remained well above freezing, ranging from 38° to 49°F on the 1st. On the island 1.05 inches of precipitation was all rain, unlike in some New Jersey, New York, and Connecticut localities where up to two feet of snow fell.

The End-of-January Long Storm, 1933

After a "weather breeder" morning with clear skies and light winds on January 25, 1933, the wind went into the east after noontime and gradually increased to a steady 29 miles per hour by midnight with gusts to 33 miles per hour. During the day a southern disturbance, moving from Tennessee to central Virginia, began to affect the Nantucket area with a steadily falling barometer and rising easterly winds.

By next morning, Thursday, the 26th, the storm center advanced to a position about 200 miles east-southeast of Atlantic City, still headed northeast. The wind at Nantucket,

after backing from east to northeast at 5:00 a.m., raged at gale force all day and evening. The average hourly speed was 40.8 miles per hour, and the peak one-minute blow reached 56 miles at 1:50 p.m. Though some rain was measured every hour, the total amounted to only 1.31 inches.

"Unusually high tides did considerable damage to wharves and small boats. All shipping remained in port, and no boat came or went," the *Inquirer and Mirror* reported.

On Friday morning, the 27th, another coastal disturbance developed east of the Carolina capes and bore northeast. A northerly gale in the early morning veered to northeast and continued at a high speed. The average for 24 hours was 33 miles per hour and the maximum registered 54 miles per hour in a gust at 7:47 p.m. The barometer fell off during the day from 29.51 to 29.28 inches. Rain fell intermittently all day, amounting to only 0.18 inch.

The morning of the third day, Saturday, the 28th, found the second storm center now about 300 miles south of Halifax, Nova Scotia. Gales were registered on Nantucket at every hourly observation, at an average of 35.8 miles per hour; the peak gust attained 56 miles at 6:50 a.m. Light rain fell at times, but totalled only 0.03 inch. Wind remained steady in the north all day, causing the temperature to decline gradually from 37° to 33°F at midnight. The barometer dropped to 29.12 at 8:00 a.m. and rose slightly to 29.18 inches at 8:00 p.m. Snow flurries occurred in mid-afternoon.

"The northerly gales caused unusually high tides which did considerable damage. No boats on this day. All Brant Point was submerged, water reaching to the middle of Easton street near the Point Breeze Hotel," according to the weather bureau log.

The gale-force winds finally relented at 4:18 a.m. on the 29th after a steady blow of 79 hours' duration, probably Nantucket's longest sustained storm. They dropped from an average of 31 miles per hour in the early morning to 19 miles per hour at midnight. While the deep storm center stalled and

High tide at Old South Wharf on January 13, 1915. Photograph courtesy of Charles F. Sayle.

intensified southeast of Halifax, the Nantucket barometer continued very low, rising to only 29.21 at 8:00 a.m. and to 29.30 inches at 8:00 p.m. on the 29th. The wind shifted from north to northwest at about 5:00 a.m. and diminished gradually to below gale force. Light snow, 0.7 inch, fell during the day with the thermometer hovering close to 30°F.

On Thursday, the 26th, Nantucket Lightship No. 117 broke loose from its mooring 43 miles southeast of the island. It took until Saturday night for her to fight the huge waves from the northwest and return to her original station.

The *Inquirer and Mirror* told of the long storm's impact:

One of the worst storms that have swept the New England coast in years developed from the "easterly" which broke on Thursday of last week [Jan. 26] and kept the steamer *Nantucket* in port for the day. It proved to be a "four-day storm" and continued until well into Sunday night [Jan. 29], when the condition moderated and the breeze gradually subsided. While it lasted, however, the disturbance was quite general all along the coast, bringing a phenomenally high tide and

causing damage estimated at around $2,000,000 [for all New England].

Nantucket got its full share of the disturbance, with no steamboat connections on Thursday and again on Saturday.

Two-Tanker Gale, February 1952

On the 17th, three low pressure areas moved from the Gulf and South Atlantic States northeastward to the vicinity of Nantucket, merging into a single center of great violence. All components productive of heavy precipitation existed—the strong inflow of moist, relatively warm air from the sea, and the cold Canadian air under-running from the northwest. Northeast gales and extremely heavy seas split two tankers, one, the *Pendleton*, just off Chatham, and the other, the *Fort Mercer*, 32 miles east. The crew of the *Pendleton* were rescued by a launch of the Coast Guard, operated by 4 men, enacting the latest saga of the sea. One man was fatally injured in the transfer, another was lost overboard from the bow section, and two others were sent to the hospital. The *Fort Mercer* was less fortunate as 4 were swept away in the raging sea during the rescue operation.

New England climatologist.

Gale-force winds raged on Nantucket for two days. The anemometer spun at an average of 33.0 miles per hour on the 17th and at 32.9 miles per hour on the 18th. Peak one-minute winds were 51 miles per hour from the east on the 16th and 52 miles per hour from the north on the 17th.

The barometer sank to a low of 28.79 inches early on the 18th when the storm center to the east was nearest.

Heavy rain in the amount of 1.83 inches fell on the 17th with the temperature above the freezing mark, but when the wind shifted to north on the 18th the rain changed to snow and 4.9 inches lay on the ground by the end of the storm. The melted precipitation on the 18th amounted to 0.65 inch, for a storm total of 2.58 inches, a goodly amount for a winter storm.

Great Atlantic Storm, March 6–7, 1962

This was one of the most severe Atlantic storms of the present century. Fortunately, for New England, the storm center remained well south of New England as it moved eastward in the Atlantic. Its effects were therefore not

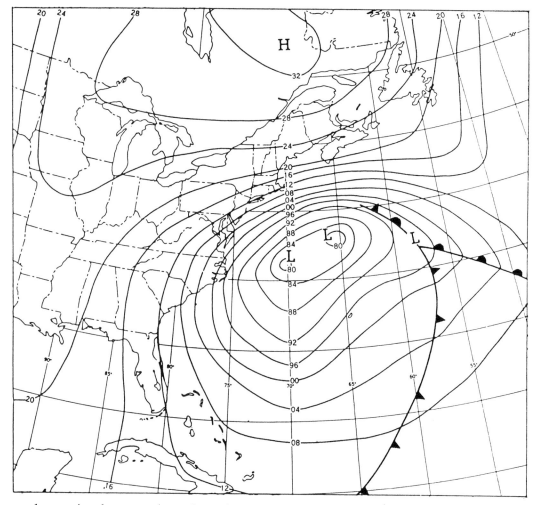

The Great Atlantic Storm of March 1962 at its height. The weather map for March 7 depicts the very deep barometric centers south and southeast of Nantucket. The long ocean fetch of northeast winds raised mighty waves at five successive high tides on Cape Cod and Nantucket.

so devastating here as along the Atlantic seaboard farther south. Nevertheless, spring tides and gale force winds combined to raise the water level and create great waves which pounded offshore islands and coastal areas for two days. This extremely long siege, lasting through four successive high tides, was the outstanding feature of the storm. The high storm-surge tides were generally only 2 to 4 feet above normal even along the more severely affected southern New England coast. Though these heights have been greatly exceeded during previous storms, most past storms have created only one or two, rather than four, damaging storm surges. Great

damage was caused by tidal flooding of beach installations and sand erosion of beaches.

New England climatologist.

Nantucket sustained gales for a period of nearly 48 hours on March 6 and 7. The midnight-to-midnight average wind speed on the 6th was 36.9 miles per hour and on the 7th, 34.3 miles from the northeast and east-northeast. Highest wind speeds were 50 miles per hour on the 6th and 47 miles on the 7th. Only traces of rain fell on these two windy days.

Boat service was suspended for two days,

and there was some interruption in airline schedules. Flooding was confined to Washington Street, Commercial Wharf, Easy Street, and parts of Easton Street. The swells in the harbor reached six feet and more in height. The tide at noon on Wednesday, the 7th, did not reach as high as anticipated as the storm diminished. The moon was new at 5:30 a.m. on March 6, the peak day of the storm.

The Great Atlantic Storm of March 1962 covered all of the western North Atlantic Ocean from the Maritime Provinces of Canada to the West Indies. The center of lowest pressure extended for five degrees of longitude with the lowest barometer at 28.90 inches. The tightly-packed isobars north of the storm center and the long easterly fetch of the winds produced strong gales, high tides, and massive waves for three days.

"Nantucket Battered by Hurricane Force Winds," February 2, 1976

Nantucket was battered with a southwest gale Monday that carried winds of hurricane force that raised havoc with the scallop boats in Madaket and Nantucket Harbors and caused the 325-foot Federal Aviation Administration Consolan tower at Madaket to crumble to the ground.

The strong winds that started to blow with force at 3:00 a.m. swept across the island at 80–90 miles per hour in gusts and by daybreak was uprooting trees, causing power and telephone lines to come down, created 20-foot waves along the south shore that resulted in extensive shore erosion and did a great deal of property damage in all parts of the island. It was apparent that Nantucket was hit harder than any other section of southeastern Massachusetts.

Thus the *Inquirer and Mirror* summarized the worst southwester to hit the island in many years. Tom Giffin in the "Flight Deck" column in the same issue described the effect of the storm at the airport:

Nantucket, and all of us who share its daily destiny, enjoyed a generally good weekend, but it all came to a bad end as the island got a real pasting Monday morning from hurricane-force winds. It came from one of those deep Canadian lows that trail cold fronts southwestward across the northeastern U.S. as they move from the St. Lawrence valley, bringing strong southerly winds which haul westerly as the fronts pass. They tend to be windy, but this one went a little overboard. . . .

"Sunday began VFR [visual flight rules], with indermediate ceilings and a lower scattered deck, but the trend was down as a cold front approached from the west, trailing from a Quebec low. Temperature was in the 30s and climbed another ten degrees during the day, but the wind was southeast, raw and penetrating. Around three p.m. light rain began and the weather soon went IFR [instrument flight rules], seven hundred and three [seven hundred foot ceiling and three miles visibility]. Shortly before nine that night we closed [the airport], going down to a hundred and a quarter [one hundred foot ceiling and a quarter mile visibility] as the wind crept farther around to the south and began to pick up.

Through the rest of the night the wind strengthened fitfully, reaching a peak at 3:20 a.m. from due south, 45 knots with gusts to 60 knots [52 miles per hour with gusts to 69 miles per hour]. Then it eased off noticeably until seven o'clock, at which time it began to pick up rapidly. It not only picked up—it forgot to stop. At 7:35 the tower noted a gust to 62 and trees in town began to shed limbs.

At half past nine the storm, for such it had become, reached a peak of fury with a recorded gust of 80 knots, or 92 m.p.h., from due sou'west, and the wind then hauled another 20 or 30 degrees without abating all that much.

The barometer dropped to 28.57 inches, a rare low outside of a hurricane, and I suspected that when the glass started climbing with the northwest wind things would get even worse, but happily I was wrong.

Tom Giffin, "Flight Deck,"
Inquirer and Mirror,
February 5, 1976.

The meteorological data from the daily record sheet of the Federal Aviation Agency related the following details:

Between 8:50 and 9:50 a.m. observation times, the wind shifted from 210° (southwest) to 240° (west-southwest); the steady wind increased from 35 to 46 miles per hour, and the gusts from 52 to 69 miles; the barometer rose from 28.57 inches to 28.65 inches; the temperature dropped from 46° to 28°F; the rain changed to snow. During the day the temperature ranged from a high of 54° about 3:00 a.m. to a low of 15°F about 4:00 p.m. A total of 1.10 inches of precipitation fell.

HIGH TIDES AND GREAT SURFS

Old North Wharf under water during the northeast gale and record high tide on January 13, 1915. Winds were clocked at 60 miles per hour (corrected to modern scale) at the Weather Bureau on Orange Street. Photograph courtesy of Charles F. Sayle.

"On the seashore at Nantucket," wrote Ralph Waldo Emerson in 1847, "I saw the play of the Atlantic with the coast. Here was wealth; every wave reached a quarter of a mile along shore as it broke . . . Ah, what freedom and grace and beauty with all this might! . . . Place of winds, bleak, shelterless, and when it blows, a large part of the island is suspended in the air and comes into your face and eyes as if it was glad to see you."

Nantucket Island has always been on the move. Wind and wave have transported sand and soil through the centuries, taking away in some places and depositing in other places. But the overall result has been a gradual diminution in the extent of land surface. The sea, aided by a rising level over the past century, is winning the battle. Geologic evidence has shown that the south shore once extended more than a mile seaward where now dangerous shoals exist. Two islands have disappeared off the western extremity, and Smith's Point, once a long promontory, is now occasionally an island. The most dramatic evidence of the losses to the sea occurred in the destruction of Great Point Light in the storm of March 29, 1984.

The following reports of high tides and great surfs are from the *Nantucket Inquirer*, *Nantucket Mirror*, or *Nantucket Inquirer and Mirror* unless otherwise stated. Full and New Moon times are Eastern Standard Time.

1786, December 5. A dreadful high tide and storm Dec. 5th 1786 swept the wharves, washed away shops, vessels, tryhouses, wood, etc. On Dec. 7 a town meeting was convened and a committee appointed to salvage the wreck and return property to owners. Records of the Town Clerk.

1786, December 5th. Smith's Point runs to the south of Tuckernuck. The sea made a breach through the point; and the strait is now half a mile wide; but the breadth is continually varying. Twelve or fourteen years ago, the irruptions of the sea converted it into three islands.
"Notes on Nantucket," *Collections of the Massachusetts Historical Society,* Second Series, Volume III.
Moon was full on December 5 at 7:25 a.m.

1829, October 31. During the forenoon of the 31st [Oct.] the wind blew with great force, which occasioned a higher tide than has been known here for many years; but the damage sustained by vessels or other exposed property was not great.
Moon was new on October 27 at 2:29 p.m.

1830, December 6. . . . although the moon was not in a position for us to expect a great swell in the tide, it rose higher than it had been since December 5, 1786 . . . The water in the evening of Monday was over the wharves . . . much damage to North wharf.
Moon was full on November 29 at 9:58 p.m.

1839, December. During the past month Boreas has raged so horribly around us that the tides have been higher than at any time within the period of fifty years . . . A passage has been cut through Brant Point and Smith's Point, where the stump of a very large tree was laid bare, having probably been imbedded there for many years.
Moon was full on December 20 at 7:44 a.m.

1840, November 5–11. Tides rose to an unusual height . . . the quays were frequently submerged, most of the lower streets overflowed, and many cellars completely filled with water. At Siasconset the waves broke against the cliff tearing away large pieces of the bank, and endangering many dwelling places.
Moon was full on November 9 at 12:53 p.m.

1841, October 3–4. The October Gale of '41—The tide rose to a height almost unprecedented—reaching from two to three feet above the surface of the wharves and extending into most of the lower streets, strewing in various directions quantities of lumber, cord-wood, and other buoyant articles.
Moon was full on September 30 at 11:19 a.m.

1851, April 16. The Lighthouse Storm—The tide rose to an unusual height doing some damage to the wharves as well as the shipping . . . Tide rose higher than for 12 years past.
Moon was full on April 15 at 5:36 p.m.

1853, December 30. The sea broke over all the wharves, tide flowed up Main Street as far as the store of Edward W. Gardner . . . Tide very high.
Mitchell Mss.
Moon was new on December 30 at 1:05 a.m.

1856, January 5–6. The tide rose to a great height, flooding the wharves, sweeping off lumber, wood &c.; some of the wharves were injured . . . Tide within four inches of last February.
New Moon on January 7 at 6:18 p.m.

1867, August 2. Hurricane—The sea on the south side of the island broke over the banks, raising Hummock Pond to such a height that it cut a channel through the beach 100 yards wide.
New Moon on July 30 at 11:43 p.m.

1870, March 17. The heavy southerly blows of the past week, have washed away the end of Smith's Point to such a degree that the house of the Humane Society floated away during the night of Thursday [March 17]. The boat and the property of the Society in the house was saved. Efforts were made to save the house, but the heavy sea washing over the beach, rendered them unavailing.
The moon was full on March 17 at 8:52 a.m.

1873, November 18. Heavy Surf—There has been a severe storm somewhere to the southward of the island was evident from the tremendous surf which came tumbling in at the south shore on Tuesday [Nov. 18]. The heavy surf could be heard in town during the entire day, and many persons to whom the sight was a novelty, procured teams and drove to the shore to look upon Old Ocean in one of his angry moods.
New Moon on November 19 at 10:36 p.m.

1875, November 16. The tide was so very high on Tuesday [Nov. 16] afternoon last as to overflow various parts of the wharves . . . The water at the Creek overflowed the banks and adjoining meadows Wednesday . . . The unusually heavy surf was rolling upon the south shore of the island on Wednesday morning last.
Full Moon on November 13 at 4:31 a.m.

1876, November 20–21. Extremely high tides prevailed during the easterly storm of Monday and Tuesday, and the wharves in several places were submerged. Several spots on the steamboat wharf were undermined, but have been repaired.
Full Moon on November 16 at 7:45 p.m.

1878, October 12. Hurricane—During the height of the gale, the tide rose until it covered the steamboat wharf to a depth of one foot.
Full Moon on October 11 at 3:54 a.m.

1878, November 28. Surf on Thursday broke across beaches on south side into coves . . . At Siasconset surf spray went over first row of houses.
Moon new on November 24 at 4:11 a.m.

1879, August 18–19. Hurricane—The surf

at Surfside was terrific. *Moon was full on August 17 at 3:09 p.m.*

1879, October 29. Surf "heavier than they remember ever to have seen it before."
Moon full on October 29 at 9:10 p.m.

1883, January 9–10. Flood tide completely submerged the lower sections of the wharves, flowing over them to a depth of at least 18 inches . . . Water encircled Brant Point Lighthouse . . . Railroad across Goose Pond terribly wrecked.
Highest tide since 1855.
New moon on January 9 at 12:59 a.m.

1883, August 29. A Scene of Wild Grandeur. Such a sight . . . has not been seen from these shores within our memory, and even gray-bearded fishermen, who have haunted the beach for years, and witnessed the ocean during the progress of many storms in all stages of tumult, were as completely fascinated as the most enthusiastic islander on the spot, agreeing that it was the "biggest yet."
Capt. George Veeder of the life-saving station [said], "This very far eclipsed anything previously presented to his vision, expressing his belief that there was no one (not even the oldest inhabitant) who could remember a surf so magnificently grand."
New Moon on September 1 at 9:14 a.m.

1884, January 9. Heavy surf—The surf of Wednesday at the south side of the island is reported to have been terrific, even surpassing that at the time of the wreck of the *Newton* and producing more serious results than any rage for years.
Full Moon on January 12 at 10:27 a.m.

1885, November 23–24. Tides washed over Great Point at the 'Galls' and also at the 'Glades' and haulover. Water came up to floor of lighthouse stable.
Full Moon on November 22 at 4:40 a.m.

1885, December 25. A dry northeaster caused tide that undermined tracks near harbor where [the locomotive] Dionis and car were parked. Tracks along South Beach and over marshes inundated.
Full Moon on December 21 at 3:59 p.m.

1887, August 25–26. Hurricane—There has been no such exhibit of the rude freaks of Boreas since . . . these ten years. As the sea rolled up around the summer tents the scenes were exciting.
Moon was new on August 19 at 12:38 a.m.

1888, July 11–12. Heavy surf at Surfside in summer gale drew many people to see the show.
New Moon on July 9 at 1:17 a.m.

1888, November 25–27. Those who witnessed the great waves off Surfside during the 29th day of August, 1883, well remember their grand and formidable appearance as they swept onward to the beach, which even they suffered seriously from the inroads of the raging waters; but that grand spectacle and attendant damage were fairly eclipsed last Sunday; at least, those who saw both so state and there is every reason to think that the statement is correct. During the storm of 1883 huge masses of the bluff were washed away along the shore of Surfside and to the eastward, and the great billows dashed against the bluff, sending their clouds of spray high in the air over the bank; but on Sunday the billows went even farther breaking on top of the bluff, and in one or two instances sending the water to the gates of Surfside Hotel.
There were certain remarkable features attendant upon that great disturbance of the elements that were apparent in the storm on Sunday; viz., that the wind was blowing a gale from the northeast, and the waves all came from the southeast, which has always been explained by the direct result of the tidal waves in the Straits of Sunda which occurred but a short time previous to it. With Sunday's storm, as stated, these same peculiarities were noticed, and the fishermen also remarked a few days prior to it, while launching their dories, the sea being quiet on the beach, that an occasional wall of water would come tumbling in and go rolling way up the back and quiet would immediately follow.
New Moon on December 3 at 5:07 a.m.

1889, September 10. Three-day blow. Sea broke into Hummock and Miacomet ponds, but railroad tracks not seriously damaged.
Full Moon on September 9 at 8:53 a.m.

1892, August 20. Waves broke over rails at Nobadeer and caused washout at Toupchue.
New Moon on August 22 at 5:59 a.m.

1893, August 21. Tropical Storm. Tracks of railroad overturned and stood on end. Dionis and cars isolated at Siasconset. Portended end of railroads.
Full Moon on August 27 at 3:43 a.m.

1896, September 10. High surf on south side of island broke across beach into ponds. Second tropical storm of active season.
New Moon on September 7 at 8:43 a.m.

1896, October 12. The tide in many localities rose higher during the recent storm than heretofore experienced, and damage to property was immense . . . At flood tide waves were breaking savagely against wharves, Brant Point flooded. Third tropical storm of season.
New Moon on October 6 at 5:18 p.m.

1896, December 16. The Haulover Storm— Sea swept across the Haulover cutting a channel from the ocean to harbor at the northward of Wauwinet, creating an island of Great Point, Coskata, and Coatue. "The tide higher at Madaket than since 1854."
Full Moon on December 19 at 11:05 p.m.

1900, December 4. . . . an extreme tide, which lifted the vessel from the beach and carried her off near the channel.
Full Moon on December 6 at 5:37 a.m.

1905, January 25. Tide rose 7.4 feet above

Steamboat Wharf inundated by the record high tide on January 13, 1915.

Photograph courtesy of Charles F. Sayle.

Brant Point was completely submerged, the meadows being flooded with several feet of water from the shore to the bluff. The cottages on the Beachside were surrounded with water and the road was inundated to within a few feet of the Point Breeze Hotel. Near Wauwinet the seas washed across the Haulover and created "an entire change in the eastern shoreline of the island. Another opening threatened, but a shift of the wind to the west apparently prevented this."
Full Moon on December 26 at 4:29 p.m.

1915, January 13. Tide reached Springfield House dining room and came up to Point Breeze Hotel on Easton Street. One foot deep in front of Smith's stable on Steamboat Wharf where much damage done ... Isle of Muskeget under water.
Full Moon on January 15 at 9:41 a.m.

1921, November 28-29. Unusually high tides prevailed Monday and Tuesday, the water rising close to the top of the wharves.
New Moon on November 29 at 8:25 a.m.

low water and inundated every wharf around the harbor. On the south side of the island, "the topography was considerably changed ... Have seen nobody who recalls a time when the tide reached such an extreme height."
Full Moon on January 21 at 3:15 a.m.

1908, January 24. There was a heavy storm the previous week which made heavy inroads along the south shore from Surfside Life-saving Station down to Nobadeer. The configuration of the shoreline was greatly changed. For 20 hours the surf raged heavier than at any time in the last quarter century, eating as much as 25 feet into the bank in some places. The rutted road was entirely cut away. Bath houses on the bank were torn from the bluff and deposited on the beach as kindling wood a mile or two to the east. The life-savers said that only once—in the 1880's—had there been such a storm within

their memories. By a strange freak of nature the shore in front of the station was not damaged. The beach was flattened along the entire shore and the sand was like quicksand, so much that a heavy stone could not be made to stay on top.
Full Moon on January 18 at 8:37 a.m.

1909, December 26. The tide rose to a height not known for many years, and shortly before noon on Sunday the sight witnessed along the waterfront called many of our citizens from their homes to view the unusual conditions. Practically the only damage done anywhere was by the tide, the water strewing all sorts of material about the docks and adjacent streets, and when it subsided things were in a mess thereabouts. Numerous small craft were landed on top of the docks, others broke adrift and were driven a long distance from their berths, while several of the smaller catboats were sunk at their moorings.

1924, August 26. A tremendous surf was heaving on the south shore of the islands and hundreds of persons braved the elements and went out to see the unusual sight. The direction of the wind was such, however, that at Surfside it had the tendency to sweep the top off the waves before they broke, which prevented the heavy rollers that sometimes accompany a storm like this. The surf was very pretty, however, and the breakers showing up far off-shore and the seas surging up into the bank, cutting it away considerably in several sections ...

Unquestionably the worst part of the storm was felt at Great Neck on the west end of the Island near the Maddaquet Coast Guard station where the stretch of beach below the bluff is much narrower than at Surfside. This section has been eating away steadily for the last twenty years, each successive storm making great inroads into the bluff. Twice the government has found it necessary to move the station and now another move will be necessary.

Between 1:00 and 2:00 o'clock Tuesday afternoon the surf was at its worst at Madaket, breaking upon the beach continuously, and the heavy seas surging around the station building and across the roadway several hundred feet. Captain Norcross and his men at one time thought they would have to abandon the station, as the surf was pounding its way through the bluff and the surging water sweeping under and around the building.
New Moon on August 30 at 3:37 a.m.

1931, March 4. Tides unusually high and did considerable damage.
Full Moon on March 4 at 5:35 a.m.

1933, January 26–29. A heavy storm and high tide damaged shore property. It was the longest easterly in the Weather Bureau records. The Nantucket Yacht Club tennis courts were a lake, Easy Street was covered with two feet of water, and the water was up Washington Street into the meadows on the other side of the street.
New Moon on January 25 at 6:19 p.m.

1938, September 21. Only those who braved the elements and went out to the south and west shores of the island Wednesday night realized the full force of the storm. From Tom Nevers head to Surfside and Point-o'-Breakers, the bluff was pounded by the great seas, which cut into the land from ten to fifteen feet. A number of indentations at Nobadeer were even more deeply cut back. What was once the dried-up Nobadeer pond became filled with water again.
New Moon on September 23 at 3:34 p.m.

1944, September 14–15. Hummock Pond was opened to the sea, the surf pounding its way through the beach and letting the pond run out to a low level. Other ponds were invaded by the sea along the south shore and in places the water came up through the low places a quarter of a mile or more.
New Moon on September 17 at 7:37 a.m.

1945, November 29–30. The waterfront took a severe beating, the waves breaking right over the bulkhead on Easy Street, flooding the road for quite a distance. Commercial wharf was also submerged. The water was high enough so that Commercial Wharf Restaurant looked as if it were afloat—no wharf or piles beneath it.
New Moon on December 4 at 1:06 p.m.

1947, November 8. On the western end of Nantucket a residence and six bath houses were swept into the sea by heavy surf and high tide.
New Moon on November 12 at 12:24 p.m.

1950, September 11–12. Hurricane—There was practically no 'low tide' and as darkness fell the boats at the wharf were riding nearly as high as they would during a normal high tide . . . Tide reached Washington and Easton streets . . . Commercial wharf submerged for most of its length.
New Moon on September 11 at 10:28 p.m.

1950, November 26. The pounding surf along the south shore attracted many spectators Sunday afternoon, and the sight was well worth the trip.
Full Moon on November 24 at 10:14 a.m.

1956, March 17. Extreme high tide at 1:00 a.m. on Saturday morning, flooded Brant Point and Washington street areas—almost unprecedented evacuation of families. Water two feet deep on Washington street. Tide rose quickly. Water higher than for 25 years, even compares with 1915 according to old timers.
New Moon on March 12 at 8:36 a.m.

1958, April 1. Considerable flooding and property damage in Nantucket harbor on April 1 with tides 3 to 4 feet above normal . . . families evacuated from Brant Point.
Full Moon on April 3 at 10:44 p.m.

1959, December 29. While Nantucket had a flooding of a few streets along the waterfront, caused mainly by the high tide sending sea water backing through the surface drains, the islands escaped the serious damage that was caused by the water to other communities along the New England sea coast.

With the rise in the tide, tons of salt water started pouring out of the catch basins along Easton Street, South Beach Street, and at the Easy Street bulkhead. These streets, in places, were filled with water from curb to curb. At full tide the water was lapping at the floors of the cottages on Old North Wharf and had surrounded the cottages on the harbor side of Washington Street near Francis Street. The water came just to the edge of the roadbed on Washington Street but did not overflow it. Water also overflowed at the Jetties Bathing Beach and flooded the parking area and a portion of the road leading to it.

At the Steamboat Wharf, Straight Wharf, Island Services Wharf, and Commercial Wharf, the water reached the caplogs and caused fishing boats and other craft to ride at a level with the wharf but there was no danger reported.

Predicted high winds did not materialize because storm center moved almost overhead.
New Moon on December 29 at 2:09 p.m.

1961, January 19–20. The four foot high flood tide swept over Children's Bathing Beach and sent waves of water along North Beach, Easton, Walsh, and Willard Streets, as well as along Hulbert Avenue. Houses and hotels in the area were flooded and the water also covered most of the wharves in the harbor.
Full Moon on January 17 at 8:37 a.m.

1983, March 3. Last week saw very high tides here, with the nearly continuous easterly gales offshore and the full moon Sunday, Feb. 27th. Water was up over Easy St. nearly every high tide last week. A seventy-five or more mile easterly at this time could have covered

the parking lot and seen water up to the Whaling Museum. I will dig out some photos of the February 1915 breeze showing the tide at high water and two of the wharves.
Charles Sayle, "Waterfront News," *Inquirer and Mirror*, March 3, 1983.
Full Moon on February 27 at 3:58 a.m.

1984, March 29. Nantucket had its own disaster, winds from 60 to 70 mph, extreme high tides, the creeks turned into a lake at high tide, Easy Street covered with vicious waves breaking over the bulkhead, parts of Steamboat Wharf under water, the Washington Street Extension area flooded to include the cellars and first floors (in some instances), trees blown over etc.—and then came the disaster! Great Point Lighthouse was gone, undermined by fierce waves and left mainly in one huge pile of rubble washed by the ocean.
Merle Orleans, *Inquirer and Mirror*, April 5, 1984.
New Moon, April 1 at 7:11 a.m.

"The Honorable Walter Folger, Jr., 1765–1849. Scientist and Philosopher. The Islanders said: 'He's as odd as huckleberry chowder.'" From The *Clock That Talks*, by Will Gardner, Whaling Museum Publications.

Part Three:
Observing the Weather on Nantucket

THE WEATHERMEN

The first human observers of the weather on Nantucket were the native Indian population who arrived on the island at an undetermined date, perhaps many centuries before the white settlers in 1659. Unfortunately, these first Americans had no means of transmitting their knowledge of local weather behavior except by oral tradition. Even the European settlers on the island left no written record of weather events for more than one hundred years after their arrival. The first statements about atmospheric conditions that are extant today appeared in diaries and newspapers in the 1770s. No doubt, prior diaries with weather entries were composed, but they have been lost.

The first reference to the presence of a thermometer on Nantucket was found in a February 1788 diary entry by Mrs. Kezia Coffin Fanning to the effect that the temperature on February 2 was several degrees colder than during the Hard Winter of 1780. Obed Macy in his *History of Nantucket* (1835) stated that the thermometer read −11°F in that famous winter, but gave no details as to the location or owner of the instrument.

No other records of thermometer readings on the island survived until the appearance of "Notes on Nantucket" in the *Collections of the Massachusetts Historical Society*, wherein Walter Folger, jun., presented the thermometer readings of Robert Barker taken at the Marine Insurance Office. They contained the means and the extremes for the months from January 1806 through July 1807.

The first set of local meteorological observations appeared in the *Nantucket Inquirer* in January 1823. They contained thrice daily readings of thermometer, barometer, wind direction, and sky conditions. The editor noted: "We are indebted to a scientific and observant friend for the following table. We propose, by his assistance, to continue it monthly." The series of observations appeared anonymously and in the same format for several years with no identification of the contributor until a reference was made in January 1835 to "Mr.

Folger's meteorological journal."

In 1827, observer Folger (b. Nantucket, June 12, 1765; d. Nantucket, Sept. 8, 1849) revised his presentation and the column thereafter made a regular appearance each week. In the 1830s, a cumulative summary of all previous months back to 1827 was included at the end of each month, so that comparisons with the past could be made.

Folger's last contribution appeared in October 1843. Since the issues of the *Inquirer* for 1844, 1845, and part of 1846 are missing from the Atheneum file, it is not known whether the column continued in those years. The missing issues were probably consumed in the Great Fire in July 1846. The weather reports did not appear in the later issues of 1846, nor were they carried in the *Nantucket Mirror*, which began publication in 1845. No manuscripts of his meteorological records have been found among the Folger papers. Perhaps they were consumed in the fire, as well.

The most avid watcher of the Nantucket skies, both by day and by night, was William Mitchell (b. Nantucket, Dec. 20, 1791; d. Poughkeepsie, New York, Apr. 19, 1869). Primarily interested in astronomical phenomena, Mitchell first appeared in a meteorological role in the early 1830s with an occasional reference to current weather conditions in his workbooks, now preserved in the Maria Mitchell Science Library. The first strictly meteorological logbook, running from 1835 to 1840, contained a record of temperature, barometric pressure, wind, and sky conditions. Entries were made nearly every day, though sometimes only one entry per day appeared. Designated Book No. 1, it runs from November 29, 1835, to February 16, 1840.

A second book containing records from 1840 to 1844 is missing from the library. Whether it was irretrievably lost, we do not know, but Mitchell continued to make his observations as indicated by brief extracts contributed to the *Inquirer*. He also included local data in his correspondence with William C. Redfield of New York, the pioneer student

of hurricanes. Redfield employed some of Mitchell's data in his frequent articles in the *American Journal of Science*, especially those concerning the Triple Storms of December 1839 and the Great October Gale of October 1841. Mitchell's letters are included in the Redfield Manuscripts in the Beinecke Library of Yale University.

The logbook designated No. 2 in the library, extended from June 20, 1844, to June 30, 1849, and presented much the same form of entry as No. 1. A record of daily precipitation was added. Unbound tear sheets contain monthly temperature means for 1847 through June 1853.

Book No. 3 carried the record from July 1, 1849, to December 31, 1856, and No. 4 from January 1, 1857, to September 4, 1861. Readings in the latter two are based generally on the monthly forms put out by the Smithsonian Institution, which instituted a nationwide climatological observing system in 1849. Observations were made three times daily at 7:00 a.m., 2:00 and 10:00 p.m. Mitchell appears to have first participated in the Smithsonian system in January 1852 and thereafter mailed his observation sheets to Washington at the end of each month; they were summarized and published periodically.

All the Smithsonian records from 1849 to 1873 were preserved in Washington until the late 1930s and early 1940s when they were microfilmed. They are now available at the National Climatic Data Center at Asheville, North Carolina, with copies in the National Archives at Washington, D.C. Prints can be purchased at either institution. The Nantucket records of Mitchell on microfilm include scattered reports from July 1852 to February 1854 and an almost complete file from January 1855 to March 1861, with the exception of the missing year 1860. Mitchell frequently contributed astronomical and meteorological observations and comments in letters to newspapers and periodicals. These reveal many details about special events which the routine log books do not contain.

William Mitchell's daughter, Maria, won international fame for her discovery of a

FAA weather tower at Nantucket Memorial Airport. Photograph courtesy of Lucy Bixby.

comet in October 1847, the first woman to do so. An enthusiastic comet-seeker, she was the first in America to sight several comets discovered elsewhere. She served as librarian of the Atheneum for several years and kept a meteorological record there. Two notebooks covering the observations from 1850 to 1856 are in the Maria Mitchell Science Library and microfilm copies are in the Atheneum.

The Mitchells, father and daughter, moved to Lynn, Massachusetts, in September 1861, to be near relatives. Soon after, Maria accepted a position as professor of astronomy at the recently founded Vassar College for Women in Poughkeepsie, New York. Her brother, Henry, moved to New York City and became a leading authority on hydrography while associated with the U.S. Coast Survey from 1849 to 1888. Among his many published studies was one on the Nantucket shoreline made in 1871 and published in the U.S. Coast Guard Survey *Report* in 1872.

Nantucket's "Dark Ages" of Meteorology: 1861–86

The twenty-five years from the beginning of the Civil War to 1886 may be considered the "Dark Ages" of meteorology on the island. No one came along to fill the observational shoes of Walter Folger, Jr., and William Mitchell. We do not have any reliable guide to the many interesting weather events that took place during this quarter century. Two individuals did keep precipitation records, however. They were Captain Charles Coleman (1799–1881), and Henry Paddack (1838–1919), both members of distinguished Nantucket families.

Charles Coleman served from 1848 to 1861 as chief officer of the Cross Rip lightship. Upon his retirement, he took up local weather observing and often supplied precipitation figures to the *Inquirer and Mirror*. No manuscript or printed summary of Coleman's records has been located. There exists a lamentable hiatus in the island's weather records from 1861 to 1885.

Henry Paddack also kept a precipitation record in the 1880s, which was published occasionally in the columns of the *Inquirer and Mirror*. In February 1886, his record appeared in the bulletin of the newly-organized New England Meteorological Society, originally composed of a group of Boston and Providence professors and government officials. Paddack's observations from August 1885 to February 1889 are now in the National Climatic Data Center at Asheville, North Carolina.

Another meteorological enterprise at this time was located in the Citizens' News Room. The *Inquirer and Mirror* mentioned the three-per-day thermometer and barometer readings early in 1876, and a manuscript covering this year is in the library of the Nantucket Historical Association.

A very valuable record that sheds much light on the regional conditions prevailing on Cape Cod and the Islands was maintained during most of the nineteenth century by the Rodman family of New Bedford. Samuel Rodman, a prominent businessman and a leading Quaker in the community, started a meteorological record in October 1812 and made three observations per day until his death on August 1, 1876. His son, Thomas R., took up the daily task and kept the record until his own death on December 18, 1905. For a period of 93 years, we have an account of the daily weather and the climatic trends for the region. In addition, the *Diary of Samuel Rodman, 1812 to 1859*, affords a valuable record of affairs in that seafaring community whose activities were often interconnected with those of Nantucket.

In addition to these detailed weather records, several personal diaries kept on Nantucket during the late nineteenth century contain occasional weather mention. Located in the Nantucket Historical Association Library, they include the journal of Samuel Swain, 1876–88 and 1870–76; the logbook of Engine Company No. 4, 1871–99; and William Starbuck's diary, 1890–94.

The Federal Role in Meteorology on Nantucket

On February 9, 1870, President Ulysses S. Grant signed an order establishing a Storm Warning Service at the behest of Congress which heeded the urgent suggestions of many agricultural, commercial, and shipping interests. After the usual bureaucratic struggle between several Washington agencies, the task of establishing and administrating the service was awarded to the United States Signal Service because it possessed the communication capabilities necessary for the venture. Stations were quickly established along many seacoasts and on the Great Lakes, but none at Nantucket since the island lacked any means of immediate communication with the mainland.

With the laying of a cable in November 1885 to the Vineyard, where a relay to the mainland existed, the establishment of a Signal Service weather station on Nantucket became possible. Congressman R.T. Davis and General W.B. Hazen of the Signal Service were influential in Washington in securing the desired facility.

From Madaket, the cable was brought into town by means of 560 specially fabricated 21-foot iron poles. The line to the Pacific Club building on lower Main Street was completed in April 1886, and other lines were strung to Sankaty and Surfside where auxiliary observation posts were set up.

The station went into operation on October 18, 1886, and thrice daily observations were cabled to the mainland to be included in a national summary. Weather maps were constructed twice a day at Washington with Nantucket's report occupying a prominent place on the East Coast reports. In return, forecasts and storm advisories were transmitted to Nantucket.

Those who served as Official in Charge or Meteorologist in Charge while the Weather Bureau was located in town were:

Sergeant B.A. Blundon, Oct. 18, 1886 to Sept. 1, 1893.

Max Wagner, Sept. 1, 1893 to Feb. 2, 1897.

William W. Niefert, Feb. 2, 1897 to Aug. 1, 1900.

George E. Grimes, Aug. 1, 1900 to 1938.

In view of the greatly increased demands of aviation and the increase in military preparedness, the Weather Bureau was transferred to the Department of Commerce on June 30, 1940. Following this trend, the site of weather observations on the island was moved from Orange Street to Memorial Airport on April 16, 1946, where they have been carried on since.

In the 1960s, it became increasingly difficult for the government to interest its personnel in residing on Nantucket due to the island's isolated location, high rental costs, and long winter seasons. Despite great efforts by local interests to retain the station and the temporary intervention of senators and congressmen, the weather station was removed in December 1970. Its upper-air facility was relocated at Chatham at the southwest tip of Cape Cod, only 20 miles from Great Point.

The basic duties of reporting local aviation weather conditions became the responsibility of the Federal Aviation Administration, which operated the airport tower. Only daylight observations were made, and soon the publication of Nantucket daily and monthly climatological data ceased. The continuity of the fine record of some 85 years was lost to the world of meteorology and to the general public.

The former site of the United States Weather Bureau at 46 Orange Street from 1906 to 1946. Building has since been demolished. A tower, not shown, exposed wind instruments at an elevation of 90 feet above the ground. Operations were moved to the Memorial Airport on April 16, 1946. Collection of the Nantucket Historical Association.

THEIR OBSERVATIONAL DATA

Record Date Temperature Extremes
°F/year

Maximum

	January	Febuary	March	April	May	June	July	August	September	October	November	December
1	54/45	53/51	53/76+	57/45+	71/74	77/1895	92/64	88/75	82/74+	77/50	71/71	61/27 *
2	56/1890	54/76	54/72	69/67	73/1894	89/1895	87/13	100/75 *	85/1898	83/71 *	74/71 *	58/70+
3	56/37	54/68	50/72+	64/67+	69/13	83/43	87/75	97/75	87/21	81/22	69/71	58/32
4	55/33	51/70+	54/06	56/74+	75/05	78/19	92/19 *	87/26	82/00	77/67	67/75	58/32
5	57/50	55/1890	55/74	66/21	67/06+	83/25+	92/19	90/30	85/75	75/71	70/75	60/14
6	58/29	52/1896	56/25	66/42	77/30	87/25	88/03	88/18	82/80+	82/41	67/38	58/53
7	55/35	54/53	53/21+	62/28+	76/30	82/25	89/08	86/31	81/34	80/46	68/71+	59/71+
8	56/30	55/25	56/42	68/29	73/64	79/22	86/37	89/09	83/71+	76/41	67/38	59/27
9	57/30	59/25	55/21	66/22	71/63	84/59	87/03	84/32	86/71	76/20	72/75	58/66
10	54/35	54/25	57/36	65/1887	75/1896	80/49	88/11	92/49	83/31	76/09	65/50	58/46
11	57/24	52/25+	53/1898+	69/55	72/1887+	82/14	85/11	88/49	88/31 *	77/19	66/70	59/71+
12	55/75	53/66	56/08	67/45	84/70	81/64	88/11	87/75	82/71	77/38	66/09	60/11
13	56/1890	54/00	62/29	62/45+	76/56	79/1892+	88/08	85/65	82/21+	72/68	62/31+	58/11
14	64/32 *	54/46	54/79+	71/45	74/33	82/64	89/52	86/28	82/16	76/71	63/20+	58/80+
15	55/47	54/39	58/21+	70/1896	75/76+	80/25	83/31	87/28	80/44	75/71	62/02+	55/1897
16	53/1890	52/54	58/76	65/41	80/74	87/56	86/79+	85/28	85/71	74/08	63/32	56/1893
17	51/1889+	54/21	57/27+	77/76	71/20	84/29+	85/53	82/11+	80/42	73/08	63/20+	55/36
18	53/30	51/81+	59/45	67/64	76/06	87/29	90/69	86/35	78/21	73/08+	65/78	58/29
19	55/00	52/1887	59/27	65/15+	79/06	85/29	89/05	84/14	85/06	70/10+	64/21	57/12
20	57/00	54/39	62/48	74/15	77/1887	87/1893	88/52	84/37	80/46	72/06	63/34+	57/1895
21	53/79+	60/30 *	63/38	68/23+	73/03+	90/23 * +	89/23	86/76+	86/14	73/63	65/31	59/1895
22	56/06	55/25	62/38	68/32+	70/03+	84/49	87/75	92/76	86/1895	72/20	63/31	55/31
23	56/06+	51/43	67/07	70/26	82/41	82/1894	89/52	85/76	81/41	71/71	63/31	58/07
24	52/06	52/81	56/13+	68/57	75/57	84/21	88/52	82/36+	77/70	71/08	66/31	54/57
25	52/75+	53/16	58/13+	73/61	76/36	85/63	84/79	82/80	81/20	74/71	62/79	53/79+
26	55/50	54/57	65/21	72/25	79/33	88/43+	84/42+	92/48	82/20+	68/18+	61/79+	54/69+
27	53/67	58/76	63/46	73/15	76/14+	87/63	88/40	91/48	85/72	73/46	61/1896	55/69+
28	53/74	53/76	60/46	68/79	79/44	90/78	89/31	95/48	76/08	71/24	61/1896	55/36+
29	53/50	52/76	68/07 * +	73/03	81/31	89/69	90/49	87/73	78/71	70/35	60/16+	55/01
30	53/47		62/07+	79/42 *	78/78	88/59	88/29	87/73	78/71	72/46	61/27	55/1895
31	55/13+		60/68		86/1895 *		90/17	83/53		70/42+		57/1895

* = maximum for month
+ Also on earlier dates

Minimum

	January	Febuary	March	April	May	June	July	August	September	October	November	December
1	7/18	3/61	6/1887 *	15/23	33/67	44/07+	49/1893	50/47	49/75	40/73+	28/75	17/65
2	5/18	0/61	15/50	22/19	32/67	43/07	48/1891	49/47	51/75	38/72	27/65	16/1890
3	7/04	5/71	10/50	22/1894+	32/46	35/76 *	52/1893	52/53	49/49+	39/1888+	25/76	9/76
4	1/81	1/18	7/50	20/54	31/46	39/76	51/14	52/47	47/65	36/72	32/1891+	8/76
5	2/81	-6/18 *	8/1893	26/08	35/74+	39/47	53/78+	45/72	45/72	36/65	27/65	14/35
6	3/1896	1/1895	14/01	23/43	33/67	41/71	50/68	43/72	46/65	31/65	28/67	13/35
7	7/12	3/10	13/01	23/43	32/67	44/08	50/72	53/13+	47/52+	33/65	31/30	11/06
8	3/68	-1/34	13/13	25/72	34/81	42/75+	47/72 * +	54/55	45/52	34/67	25/73	7/06
9	2/68	-4/34	18/72+	23/67	34/74+	41/75	50/49	52/55	43/52	37/73	25/76	-2/02
10	7/1899	2/04	7/72	25/17	35/75	45/49	54/1894+	50/64	48/79+	31/72	26/54	8/76
11	4/82+	2/79+	12/72	26/72	36/67	43/66	52/1888	54/68	44/18	29/72	18/73	13/58
12	2/81	-4/14	14/00	24/76	36/07+	45/07+	48/73	53/50	44/18	32/76	22/73	14/43+
13	-1/14	2/54	16/74	22/73	36/62	38/76	53/73+	50/71	46/54	30/76	27/20	11/1898
14	-1/14	0/79	16/1892	26/59	35/69+	41/67	52/33	50/71	46/11	33/72	25/05+	6/76+
15	6/57	-5/43	15/32	27/59	34/57	43/71+	49/46	46/72	46/11+	38/46+	21/76+	14/60
16	5/20	-1/1888	10/1893	29/26+	34/47+	40/71	47/46	45/72	41/66	34/61	22/33+	9/10
17	2/82	-1/1896	12/16	29/71	30/57 *	45/73	48/46	51/23+	40/66	30/65	17/24	3/42
18	2/82	3/79	9/16	29/71	34/56	43/1891	52/46	47/68	43/50	29/65	18/36	3/19
19	3/01	7/36	10/67	30/1887	36/56	44/32	56/57	46/68	44/56	30/70	18/36	6/19
20	2/01	5/50	15/23	26/1897	36/50	44/47	51/72	51/72	42/69+	24/72	20/73	-3/42
21	2/70	4/50	18/67	26/73	35/50	44/47	49/72	49/72	35/73	23/72	19/73	3/55
22	2/70	6/18	20/59	32/72	36/50	43/47	54/39	46/69	34/73 * +	29/74+	23/69	8/21
23	-1/70	2/07	13/34	31/48	38/72	45/47	52/67	50/56+	41/72	32/69+	20/49	10/43+
24	5/25	2/1894	15/1888	31/71	37/72	49/28	54/62	50/67+	38/76	30/74+	21/1897+	6/1892
25	2/21+	4/1894	15/74	30/48	37/56	48/58	55/53+	45/71	37/76	33/47	22/70	1/80
26	6/24+	10/00+	10/74	28/72	34/72	50/65	51/81	50/69	34/13	32/72	18/70	1/80
27	5/1892+	0/00	17/75	28/72	28/72	48/74	53/46	53/14+	38/66	30/79+	18/17	3/50
28	1/1888	10/34	12/23	29/48	40/74	46/71	55/35	52/82+	36/65	24/74	16/01	8/50
29	-4/1888 *	13/1888	8/23	30/75	37/70	47/67	54/81	50/57	35/47	32/76	15/01 *	-3/33
30	5/48		24/15	30/75	35/70	49/19	53/72	42/65	38/78	28/66	19/05	0/62
31	5/73+		20/23		38/74		51/72	39/65 *		22/66 *		-3/62 * +

* = minimum for month

+ Also on earlier dates

Monthly Climate Data

	January Year:Date	February Year:Date	March Year:Date	April Year:Date	May Year:Date
Temperature: °F					
Mean maximum	38.2	37.8	43	51.0	59.9
Mean minimum	24.7	24.7	30.3	37.3	45.4
Mean	31.5	31.2	36.7	44.2	52.7
Record maximum	64.0 1932:14	60.0 1930:21	68.0 1907:29	79 1942:30	86.0 1895:31
Record minimum	-3.5 1888:29	-6.2 1918:5	6.0 1887:6	15 1923:1	28.0 1972:27
Precipitation: inches					
Average for month	4.04	3.71	3.93	3.57	3.31
Wettest month	8.24 1953	8.07 1952	8.88 1959	8.41 1953	10.38 1967
Driest month	1.21 1955	.75 1980	0.25 1915	0.62 1896	0.37 1923
Greatest in 24 hours	2.82 1953:9	2.77 1920	3.22 1889	4.48 1953	6.53 1967
Mean days with 0.01"	13	7	12	12	11
Snowfall: inches					
Average for month	9.1	9.8	7.7	0.7	0.1
Snowiest month	39.5 1904	28.6 1967	40.2 1960	9.5 1955	2.8 1917:9
Least snowy month	T 1973 +	T 1925	T 1971 +	0.0	0
Greatest in 24 hours	21.4 1905:25-26	20.1 1952	16.1 1960	8.0 1955	2.8 1917:9
Maximum depth	21.4 1905:26	20.0 1952	20.0 1952	4.0 1955	2.8 1917:9
Barometer: inches					
Average for month	30.02	30.01	29.96	29.96	29.96
Highest ever in month	30.99 1890	30.97 1920	30.98 1943	30.76 1895	30.59 1943 +
Lowest ever in month	28.35 1958	28.66 1940	28.36 1932	28.82 1907	29.19 1945
Wind: miles per hour					
Average for month	14.7	15.2	15.2	14.6	13
Extreme speed	69NE 1932	66	73 1956	63N 1967	52 NE 1939
Prevailing direction	NW	WNW	N	WSW	SW
Dense Fog Frequency: Number of days					
Mean	5	5	6	8	10
Greatest of record	12 1937	12 1922	14 1913	13 1908	17 1946 +
Least of record	0 1968 +	0 1912	0 1915	1 1924	2 1964
Relative Humidity: percent					
Mean at 7:00 a.m.	80	78	82	80	82
Mean at 1:00 p.m.	67	65	69	66	71
Cloudiness: Number of days					
Clear	7	6	8	7	7
Partly cloudy	6	6	8	8	8
Cloudy	18	16	15	15	16
With thunderstorms -			1	2	3
Sunshine					
Percent of possible in month	42	49	56	56	59
Average langleys per day	352	473	648	825	914
Home Heating					
Degree days for month	1039	946	877	624	381
Percent of season concluded by:					
15th of month	42	59	73	86	95
31st of month	51	66	81	92	98

	June Year:Date	July Year:Date	August Year:Date	September Year:Date	October Year:Date	November Year:Date	December Year:Date	Year Year:Date
	68.5	74.9	74.9	69.5	61.2	52.1	42.9	56.2
	54.5	61.3	61.5	55.5	47.0	39.0	29.1	42.5
	61.5	68.1	68.2	62.5	54.1	45.6	36.0	49.4
	90.0 1978:28	92.0 1964:1	100.0 1972:2	88.0 1931:11	82.0 1971:2	74.0 1971:2	61.0 1927:1	100.0 1975:8,2
	35.0 1976:3	47.0 1972:7	39.0 1965:31	34.0 1973:26 +	22.0 1966:31	15.0 1901:29	−3.0 1962:31	−6.2 1918:2,5
	2.27	2.77	3.43	3.38	3.41	4.03	4.36	42.41
	7.69 1917	7.45 1958	12.92 1946	9.55 1938	10.05 1894	8.76 1944	9.74 1969	60.69 1958
	0.01 1949	0.07 1974	0.27 1902	0.07 1971	0.10 1924	0.62 1917	1.08 1899	25.31 1965
	4.60 1945	4.37 1978	5.73 1889	5.05 1969	4.25 1932	4.95 1966:2-3	4.26 1969	5.73 1889:8,14
	8	8	9	8	9	12	12	125
	0	0	0	0	T	0.3	6.9	35.3
	0	0	0	0	0.2 1925	8.1 1904	24.7 1963	82.0 1903-04
	0	0	0	0	0	0	T 1953 +	3.8 1952-53
	0	0	0	0	0.2 1925	8.1 1904	15.5 1960:11-12	20.1 1952:2,27-28
	0	0	0	0	0.2 1925	8.1 1904	16.0 1960	23.0 1952:2,28
	29.95	29.96	30.00	30.05	30.03	30.02	30.01	29.99
	30.54 1902	30.52 1892	30.45 1918	30.65 1947	30.65 1901	30.81 1889	31.02 1949:25	31.02 1949:12,25
	29.31 1923	29.25 1932	28.71 1924	28.18 1954	29.05 1927	28.32 1904	28.50 1956:29	28.11 1954:9,11
	12.0	11.0	10.9	11.8	12.9	13.4	14.1	13.2
	68NE 1945	62 NE 1933	72SE 1954	79 SW 1944	69 E 1947	70NW 1947	62 NE 1930	79SW 1944:9,15
	SW	SW	SW	SW	SW	NW	WNW	SW
	12	15	13	7	7	5	4	98
	20 1928	27 1967 +	19 1967	21 1946	11 1959 +	10 1960	11 1964	129 1961
	4 1908	5 1953	2 1942	2 1924	0 1940	0 1940	0 1963	62 1930
	90	88	91	89	85	81	79	84
	78	76	77	72	68	72	69	71
	7	6	8	9	10	6	6	87
	8	9	8	8	8	7	8	92
	15	16	15	13	13	17	17	186
	3	4	3	2	1	1		20
	62	61	60	60	58	42	42	55
	1003	975	870	707	524	378	315	644
	122	17	21	111	341	582	899	5960
	99	.002	.005	2	5	13	26	
	100	.003	.006	3	8	18	33	

Monthly Solar Data

	January 5th	15th	25th	February 5th	15th	25th	March 5th	15th	25th	April 5th	15th	25th	May 5th	15th	25th	June 5th	15th	25th
Twilight Astronomical begins	5:28	5:27	5:22	5:13	5:03	4:49	4:38	4:20	4:02	3:41	3:29	3:03	3:45	3:28	3:13	3:03	3:00	3:01
Civil begins	6:35	6:34	6:28	6:18	6:07	5:53	5:41	5:25	5:07	4:49	4:32	4:17	5:03	4:51	4:42	4:35	4:33	4:34
Sunrise Time	7:06	7:04	6:58	6:47	6:35	6:21	6:09	5:52	5:35	5:17	5:01	4:46	5:33	5:22	5:14	5:08	5:07	5:08
Sunrise horizon point (degrees from equator)	29.9S	27.8S	24.7S	20.5S	16.1S	11.3S	7.2S	2.0S	3.2N	8.9N	13.9N	18.5N	22.7N	26.3N	29.3N	31.6N	32.7N	32.8N
Noontime, local by sun	11:46	11:50	11:53	11:55	11:55	11:54	11:52	11:50	11:47	11:43	11:41	11:39	12:37	12:37	12:37	12:39	12:41	12:43
Noon altitude of sun (degrees above south horizon)	26.2	27.7	29.9	33.0	36.2	39.8	42.9	46.8	50.7	55.0	58.6	62.1	65.1	67.7	69.7	71.3	72.0	72.1
Solar intensity at noon (average langleys)*	340	352	392	433	473	531	590	648	708	765	825	867	909	951	968	986	1003	994
Sunset Time	16:26	16:36	16:48	17:02	17:14	17:27	17:36	17:47	17:58	18:10	18:21	18:31	19:42	19:52	20:02	20:10	20:15	20:18
Sunset horizon point (degrees from equator)	29.8S	27.7S	24.6S	20.4S	15.9S	11.1S	7.0S	1.8S	3.5N	9.2N	14.1N	18.8N	22.9N	26.5N	29.4N	31.7N	32.7N	32.8N
Twilight Civil ends	16:56	17:06	17:18	17:33	17:42	17:55	18:04	18:14	18:26	18:38	18:50	19:00	20:14	20:23	20:34	20:43	20:49	20:52
Astronomical ends	18:00	18:09	18:21	18:36	18:46	18:59	19:07	19:19	19:31	19:46	20:00	20:14	21:30	21:46	22:01	22:15	22:22	22:25
Duration of Direct Sunlight (hours from sunrise to sunset)	9:20	10:02	10:20	10:15	10:39	11:05	11:26	11:54	12:21	12:52	13:18	13:43	14:08	14:28	14:46	14:59	15:07	15:07

	July 5th	15th	25th	August 5th	15th	25th	September 5th	15th	25th	October 5th	15th	25th	November 5th	15th	25th	December 5th	15th	25th
Twilight Astronomical begins	3:08	3:19	3:34	3:45	4:06	4:20	4:35	4:48	4:59	5:10	5:21	5:33	4:43	4:54	5:03	5:13	5:20	5:26
Civil begins	4:40	4:48	4:57	5:10	5:20	5:31	5:43	5:53	6:04	6:14	6:24	6:36	5:48	5:59	6:10	6:20	6:28	6:34
Sunrise Time	5:13	5:20	5:29	5:40	5:50	6:00	6:11	6:21	6:31	6:41	6:52	7:04	6:17	6:29	6:40	6:51	6:59	7:05
Sunrise horizon point (degrees from equator)	31.9N	30.0N	27.4N	23.6N	19.6N	15.1N	9.7N	4.7N	0.5S	5.7S	10.7S	15.5S	20.4S	24.2S	27.4S	29.6S	30.9S	31.0S
Noontime, local by sun	12:45	12:46	12:47	12:46	12:44	12:42	12:39	12:35	12:32	12:28	12:26	12:24	11:24	11:25	11:27	11:31	11:36	11:41
Noon altitude of sun (degrees above south horizon)	71.5	70.2	68.3	65.6	62.6	59.3	55.4	51.6	47.7	43.8	40.1	36.5	32.9	30.2	27.9	26.3	25.5	25.4
Solar intensity at noon (average langleys)*	984	975	940	905	870	816	761	707	646	585	524	476	426	378	357	336	315	327
Sunset Time	20:16	20:12	20:04	19:53	19:39	19:24	19:07	18:50	18:32	18:16	18:00	17:45	16:31	16:21	16:14	16:11	16:12	16:17
Sunset horizon point (degrees from equator)	31.8N	29.9N	27.2N	23.4N	19.3N	14.8N	9.5N	4.4N	0.8S	5.9S	9.9S	15.7S	20.6S	24.4S	27.5S	29.6S	30.9S	31.0S
Twilight Civil ends	20:49	20:44	20:36	20:26	20:09	19:53	19:35	19:18	18:59	18:43	18:28	18:13	17:00	16:51	16:44	16:42	16:43	16:48
Astronomical ends	22:21	22:13	21:59	21:42	21:19	21:04	20:43	20:23	20:00	19:45	19:31	19:17	18:05	17:56	17:51	17:49	17:51	17:56
Duration of Direct Sunlight (hours from sunrise to sunset)	15:02	14:51	14:34	14:13	13:50	13:25	12:57	12:30	12:03	11:36	11:09	10:43	10:17	9:55	9:36	9:23	9:15	9:14

Snowfall Data

(inches, T = trace, not measurable)

	Nov.	Dec.	Jan.	Feb.	Mar.	Apr.	Annual	5-year mean
-87	0	5.6	1.8	3.4	4.4	6.8	22.0	
-88	T	2.3	4.2	1.8	2.9	0	11.2	
-89	.2	.3	T	11.8	T	0	12.3	
-90	0	6.5	1.0	T	14.0	0	21.5	16.8
-91	.7	3.5	5.0	3.5	2.0	0	14.7	
-92	.5	T	2.0	1.5	11.5	0	15.5	
-93	T	4.0	13.2	13.0	3.3	T	33.5	
-94	T	T	2.3	17.5	T	0	19.8	
-95	.5	5.5	7.3	7.1	8.4	0	28.8	22.5
-96	T	2.4	6.7	6.5	16.4	.1	32.1	
-97	.4	9.5	3.5	12.8	.3	T	26.5	
-98	2.5	6.6	3.1	1.7	1.0	T	14.9	
-99	1.5	1.7	7.7	30.1	3.7	T	44.7	
-00	0	1.7	5.2	19.8	1.4	0	28.1	29.3
1900-01	0	4.1	11.6	11.5	0.8	0	28.0	
-02	1.3	20.0	12.7	10.6	8.0	1.7	54.3	
-03	0	20.1	10.9	7.0	0	0.2	38.2	
-04	7.2	7.8	39.5	19.1	8.4	T	82.0	
-05	8.1	24.1	32.4	7.6	T	T	72.2	55.0
-06	T	0.5	7.7	3.8	10.4	T	22.4	
-07	T	4.3	8.9	17.0	18.0	1.0	49.2	
-08	T	6.1	12.6	3.6	0.4	T	22.7	
-09	0	3.0	5.9	T	T	T	8.9	
-10	T	0.8	21.5	3.3	2.8	0	28.4	26.4
1910-11	T	7.3	4.3	19.7	6.8	2.9	41.0	
-12	T	4.4	14.6	2.5	6.9	T	28.4	
-13	T	8.7	T	1.8	T	0.9	11.4	
-14	T	T	0.5	19.2	13.6	T	33.3	
-15	T	2.2	6.6	5.1	1.0	T	14.9	25.8
-16	T	3.2	0.5	13.2	22.9	0.2	40.0	
-17	T	5.4	6.6	7.1	13.6	5.0	37.7	
-18	1.0	6.8	15.0	3.1	7.5	T	33.4	
-19	0	0.6	3.2	7.4	4.9	T	16.1	
-20	0	4.0	12.5	8.2	3.6	0.1	28.4	31.2
-21	0	2.2	0.9	3.4	T	T	6.5	
-22	T	3.9	0.5	18.2	6.5	1.8	30.9	
-23	T	6.3	9.9	12.7	7.0	0	35.9	
-24	0	5.8	0.3	3.6	7.6	0	17.3	
-25	0	4.5	11.7	T	0	0.4	16.6	21.5
-26	0	3.4	5.6	6.1	0.8	T	16.1	
-27	0	9.5	6.2	2.0	T	T	17.7	
-28	T	T	5.4	2.6	9.1	0	17.1	
-29	0.6	T	1.9	12.0	1.9	T	16.4	
-30	T	1.6	10.1	11.8	1.9	T	25.4	18.5

	Nov.	Dec.	Jan.	Feb.	Mar.	Apr.	Annual	5-year mean
1930-31	1.6	0.4	5.9	5.7	12.3	0	25.9	
-32	0	T	T	0.7	4.5	0.2	5.4	
-33	T	4.5	0.7	8.6	9.0	0	22.8	
-34	T	9.7	0.8	10.2	13.5	0	34.2	
-35	T	0.4	7.0	7.3	T	1.8	16.5	21.0
-36	0	13.8	0.7	4.1	T	0	18.6	
-37	0.2	T	1.5	3.1	1.0	T	5.8	
-38	T	0.4	11.3	3.8	0.2	2.3	18.0	
-39	0.2	1.1	7.9	1.5	8.8	0.7	20.2	
-40	T	4.5	13.4	5.4	0.6	0.2	24.1	17.4
-41	1.2	1.0	1.0	3.9	11.2	2.8	21.1	
-42	0	0.2	18.7	3.6	T	1.8	24.1	
-43	T	13.0	9.4	12.5	7.2	0	42.1	
-44	T	2.6	4.6	11.6	8.1	T	26.9	
-45	T	2.6	3.8	13.8	1.6	0	21.8	27.2
-46	T	s13.9	0.8	13.1	0.4	T	28.2	
-47	0	2.0	8.7	17.6	0.3	0.6	29.2	
-48	T	1.0	15.3	14.2	1.8	0	32.3	
-49	0	3.1	6.6	4.5	1.6	0	15.3	
-50	T	T	0.2	5.5	1.6	4.0	11.3	23.3
1950-51	T	6.5	1.0	21.3	1.7	0	30.5	
-52	T	2.9	6.5	36.4	8.3	0	54.1	
-53	T	T	1.2	2.3	.3	T	3.8	
-54	T	T	11.0	.5	.5	T	12.0	
-55	0	19.9	3.0	6.0	3.2	9.5	41.	28.4
-56	1.2	5.2	9.5	.4	24.5	T	40.8	
-57	2.2	6.0	8.9	5.1	12.4	.1	34.7	
-58	.2	4.0	.4	17.2	4.6	1.3	27.7	
-59	T	9.9	5.6	2.9	19.0	1.5	38.9	
-60	T	7.9	9.7	1.5	40.2	T	59.4	40.3
-61	T	21.9	21.9	15.4	2.8	.1	62.1	
-62	T	3.6	10.4	13.1	1.2	.7	29.0	
-63	T	17.0	3.9	2.1	4.5	.5	28.0	
-64	0	24.7	21.3	24.9	2.2	0	73.1	
-65	T	3.2	38.9	3.1	7.4	.5	53.1	49.1
-66	.2	.3	10.9	1.9	1.7	0	15.0	
-67	0	6.4	.7	28.6	20.7	1.2	57.6	
-68	2.7	4.6	4.3	13.5	.8	0	25.9	
-69	T	2.9	.4	4.9	12.1	T	20.3	
-70	T	4.8	10.7	8.2	T	T	23.7	28.5
-71	T	4.2	7.0	1.0	T	T	12.2	
-72	T	2.9	2.0	5.1	.7	T	10.7	
-73	T	1.3	T	10.1	6.2	2.0	19.6	

Earliest trace:	October 10, 1925
Earliest measurable:	October 30, 1925, 0.2
Earliest 4.0 or more:	November 27, 1904, 8.1
Earliest 8.0 or more:	November 27, 1904, 8.1
Earliest 12.0 or more:	December 11-12, 1960, 15.7
Latest 12.0 or more:	March 15-17, 1967, 13.6
Latest 8.0 or more:	April 3-4, 1955, 8.3
Latest 4.0 or more:	April 9, 1917, 5.0
Latest measurable:	May 9, 1917, trace official; 2.8 inches by Inquirer
Latest trace:	May 19, 1917, trace official; 2.8 inches by Inquirer

Legedary snows in early period preceding the official record, 1886-1984: Trace on October 5, 1881; "ground white" on October 9 and 15, 1876; 1.0 inch on October 27, 1859; 18 inches April 14-15, 1854.

Maximum and Minimum Snowfall Seasons, 1886-87 to 1972-73 (inches)

Snowiest seasons:	82.0	1903-04
	73.1	1963-64
	72.2	1904-05
	62.1	1960-61
	59.4	1959-60
	57.6	1966-67
	54.1	1951-52
	53.1	1964-65
Least snowy seasons:	3.8	1952-53
	5.4	1931-32
	5.8	1936-37
	6.5	1920-21
	8.9	1908-09

Nantucket Average Temperature, 1827-1843—Walter Folger, Jr.
1847-1861—William Mitchell
1886-1982—Federal Weather Service

	Jan.	Feb.	Mar.	Apr.	May	June	July	Aug.	Sept.	Oct.	Nov.	Dec.	Annual	5-Year Average
1827	27.9	32.5	37.6	49.2	52.8	62.3	69.7	68.9	63.8	56.1	38.6	37.6	49.9	
1828	35.7	38.6	38.7	43.8	53.9	64.2	70.8	71.6	65.1	54.6	46.8	40.0	52.0	
1829	31.3	26.5	32.2	44.3	54.2	62.7	66.4	68.1	59.8	53.0	45.0	41.7	48.8	
1830	32.0	29.9	38.5	45.8	55.3	62.9	69.6	67.7	61.8	55.7	50.0	40.1	50.8	
1831	28.5	28.4	38.3	46.6	56.8	67.0	69.7	71.1	65.1	57.5	44.1	26.1	50.0	
1832	32.3	32.1	36.0	40.1	50.0	57.1	65.1	67.7	61.3	55.0	45.9	37.1	48.3	
1833	34.7	29.2	33.7	46.1	55.0	61.3	67.4	67.0	62.5	54.4	43.0	37.6	49.4	
1834	29.7	35.0	38.5	46.4	52.3	60.7	57.8	67.6	64.7	52.8	42.8	35.0	48.6	
1835	33.8	29.2	34.0	42.6	51.4	61.1	67.4	65.8	60.1	55.9	44.7	29.5	48.1	
1836	31.9	24.7	33.6	41.8	51.6	57.3	64.7	64.4	m	48.9	39.4	33.8	m	
1837	25.3	29.6	33.3	42.9	50.7	58.6	65.7	64.3	59.5	51.7	43.0	34.1	46.6	
1838	36.3	24.6	35.9	41.0	50.0	62.5	70.8	67.3	62.3	51.9	40.8	32.9	48.0	
1839	31.7	31.9	36.7	44.4	53.1	59.8	68.3	63.1	62.4	53.8	42.0	36.7	48.7	
1840	26.0	35.4	37.7	47.5	52.8	62.2	67.7	67.8	61.9	56.0	43.2	33.7	45.9	
1841	35.3	30.1	37.7	43.4	51.0	62.9	67.6	66.5	62.4	49.4	41.8	m	m	
1842	33.9	35.8	39.7	44.4	52.4	59.4	67.9	67.9	60.8	53.0	41.7	m	m	
1843	37.6	28.4	30.2	43.6	51.0	m	67.8	68.0	62.2	52.8	m	m	m	
Mean	32.0	30.6	36.0	44.3	52.6	61.4	67.3	67.3	62.2	53.7	43.3	35.4	48.6	
1847	31.9	31.5	34.0	41.9	51.5	64.6	71.1	70.5	64.2	54.6	47.5	40.6	50.3	
1848	34.6	31.9	35.9	46.8	57.4	64.5	70.9	71.2	63.4	54.6	44.0	42.0	51.4	
1849	28.8	28.1	39.0	46.8	54.5	69.0	72.1	73.5	66.9	55.3	50.4	36.9	52.6	
1850	35.9	36.0	37.0	44.8	54.6	64.6	73.7	71.1	66.0	57.5	47.4	36.9	52.1	
1851	34.8	36.6	40.4	47.4	56.3	64.8	73.7	69.9	64.8	59.6	43.3	32.1	52.0	
1852	30.7	33.4	37.5	43.7	55.2	66.5	m	70.8	57.6	50.4	m	39.9	m	
1853m	m	m	m	m	m	70.6	68.6	m	m	46.2	35.6	m		
1854	32.6	30.6	37.1	44.0	53.1	63.5	71.9	69.3	62.7	56.8	47.2	35.1	50.2	
1855	36.6	29.2	36.7	44.8	50.3	63.7	m	m	64.1	57.3	46.8	39.3	m	
1856	28.0	28.1	32.8	45.9	52.2	63.9	72.4	m	66.0	55.9	45.1	32.6	m	
1857	23.8	35.8	35.7	43.0	53.5	61.9	68.7	68.4	64.3	54.7	47.0	40.2	49.8	
1858	37.7	29.8	35.3	46.6	50.7	63.2	68.5	69.3	63.4	56.3	41.7	37.2	50.0	
1859	33.9	36.0	41.4	44.9	54.8	63.2	68.5	69.3	63.4	51.9	46.3	35.0	50.7	
1860	33.7	30.4	39.1	44.1	52.1	60.1	64.4	69.9	61.6	54.1	44.6	33.7	49.0	
1861	30.4	34.7	37.0	45.5	52.2	m	m	m	m	m	m	m	m	
Mean	32.4	32.3	37.1	45.0	57.3	64.2	70.4	70.1	63.6	55.3	45.9	33.9	50.9	
1886										52.5	46.8	36.3		
1887	32.5	33.2	33.3	42.6	55.0	60.8	70.2	67.4	60.5	53.5	44.7	36.8	49.2	
1888	25.3	30.8	32.4	41.8	50.5	61.2	63.9	66.3	59.6	48.8	46.2	36.2	46.9	
1889	37.7	27.9	36.4	44.4	54.2	65.8	67.1	67.4	63.0	52.0	46.1	39.0	49.9	
1890	34.6	35.6	35.7	43.6	51.9	60.4	67.2	67.7	63.8	52.5	44.0	31.1	49.0	48.75
1891	33.9	33.8	34.9	44.2	51.4	59.8	64.6	68.8	65.4	52.4	43.7	41.4	49.5	
1892	33.1	31.4	34.0	46.2	51.8	61.8	68.9	68.7	62.6	53.0	43.1	32.2	48.9	
1893	23.8	29.0	33.3	41.7	51.9	59.7	66.9	68.2	60.0	54.2	43.6	36.0	47.4	
1894	33.2	29.6	39.3	42.3	52.6	61.3	68.7	66.4	65.0	54.9	41.6	36.2	49.3	
1895	31.4	25.8	34.6	43.0	53.8	62.4	66.4	68.8	64.4	51.6	47.2	39.6	49.1	48.84
1896	29.4	31.1	32.8	42.8	54.2	61.2	68.1	68.2	61.8	51.5	48.5	35.1	48.7	
1897	30.8	32.5	38.0	44.2	53.6	60.0	68.7	62.4	54.7	45.0	37.5	49.6		
1898	32.8	34.0	40.6	42.4	51.4	59.6	67.3	70.6	65.2	55.3	44.8	35.7	50.0	
1899	32.7	28.6	36.6	43.4	52.7	64.4	68.6	67.0	62.2	54.5	45.3	37.4	49.4	
1900	34.4	31.2	34.3	45.2	52.4	61.6	69.4	69.2	64.6	57.4	48.0	37.2	50.4	49.62
1901	31.5	25.4	36.4	42.8	51.1	61.8	68.8	68.3	65.0	54.8	40.0	37.2	48.6	
1902	29.8	30.0	40.4	46.0	51.9	60.6	64.9	66.7	63.1	54.4	48.9	33.6	49.2	
1903	31.6	32.7	42.2	45.7	53.8	57.6	67.6	64.2	62.8	54.4	42.8	32.7	49.0	
1904	28.1	25.4	33.8	42.8	55.2	59.2	67.9	65.9	61.9	52.2	40.6	30.0	46.9	
1905	29.0	24.5	36.0	43.9	53.1	59.8	69.0	66.9	62.0	55.2	44.0	38.4	48.5	48.44
1906	36.9	33.0	34.0	44.2	54.2	62.4	66.6	69.5	63.8	55.2	43.8	33.2	49.7	
1907	32.6	25.4	37.1	42.0	48.3	57.1	67.6	64.0	62.2	50.5	44.8	38.5	47.9	
1908	32.8	28.4	37.3	43.7	54.0	63.2	71.0	67.0	63.2	57.0	45.5	33.7	50.0	
1909	34.8	35.4	36.7	44.2	52.7	61.4	66.9	67.0	63.2	51.8	47.2	33.2	49.7	
1910	34.5	32.2	39.2	47.8	53.2	61.3	69.4	66.8	62.2	55.8	43.0	30.8	49.7	49.4
1911	33.9	30.3	34.8	41.8	54.4	62.4	71.0	67.4	61.2	53.6	43.8	40.0	49.6	
1912	26.3	27.9	35.2	44.5	53.6	62.4	68.5	67.0	62.2	56.5	47.2	40.4	49.3	
1913	40.0	30.5	40.8	46.4	52.8	60.7	69.8	67.8	61.6	56.8	46.6	39.3	51.1	
1914	31.9	28.2	35.2	42.6	53.6	60.7	64.6	67.6	63.5	56.2	44.4	34.7	48.6	
1915	35.6	35.0	35.0	45.5	52.6	61.0	66.8	67.0	65.0	54.8	45.8	35.6	50.0	49.72

	Jan.	Feb.	Mar.	Apr.	May	June	July	Aug.	Sept.	Oct.	Nov.	Dec.	Annual	5-Year Average
1916	33.9	29.8	30.4	42.8	52.0	59.6	65.4	67.3	63.5	54.6	44.5	34.5	48.2	
1917	31.4	27.6	35.2	41.6	48.1	60.6	67.5	69.2	59.7	52.6	40.2	29.4	46.9	
1918	24.0	27.7	34.2	43.4	55.5	60.6	67.0	67.6	62.2	55.0	46.0	38.2	48.4	
1919	35.4	33.1	38.6	43.2	53.4	60.8	68.8	67.0	62.6	55.0	44.6	32.0	49.5	
1920	26.4	30.1	36.6	43.1	49.2	59.2	67.2	69.6	64.4	58.5	45.0	37.8	48.8	48.36
1921	32.6	33.6	43.4	48.4	51.0	62.7	68.6	67.2	66.7	57.0	46.0	34.2	51.0	
1922	30.0	32.1	38.6	45.5	55.6	64.4	65.8	68.2	63.8	55.9	44.5	35.6	50.0	
1923	31.4	25.8	32.9	43.0	52.0	62.4	66.5	65.4	62.8	55.0	45.0	41.6	48.6	
1924	34.0	29.8	35.8	44.1	51.8	59.8	67.4	68.2	60.8	53.6	44.9	33.8	48.7	
1925	31.3	37.2	40.3	45.8	52.8	64.4	67.8	68.4	62.8	49.9	43.7	34.8	49.9	49.64
1926	32.2	30.2	33.5	42.3	52.0	59.9	67.2	67.6	61.1	53.9	45.0	33.0	48.2	
1927	32.0	34.8	39.2	43.8	52.2	60.2	67.0	66.3	62.9	57.4	49.2	38.7	50.3	
1928	34.2	31.2	36.2	43.7	52.1	60.6	67.6	70.6	62.6	55.2	45.4	39.2	49.9	
1929	31.6	33.2	39.9	45.2	54.5	64.1	68.7	67.3	64.8	53.6	46.2	37.3	50.5	
1930	35.0	33.3	37.8	43.8	54.6	65.7	69.6	68.4	67.6	54.6	46.4	36.4	51.1	50.00
1931	33.0	33.2	37.8	47.0	54.6	62.0	69.4	70.6	65.6	57.7	49.3	39.4	51.6	
1932	40.3	33.1	35.2	44.6	53.0	62.1	69.4	71.6	64.2	57.2	46.4	40.8	51.5	
1933	39.3	35.0	36.8	45.5	55.6	62.8	65.9	69.4	66.0	55.2	41.4	33.6	50.5	
1934	32.8	22.6	34.6	44.8	55.4	63.2	70.2	67.2	66.8	52.6	47.7	33.6	49.3	
1935	29.6	30.6	37.8	43.8	51.8	61.4	68.4	69.6	63.0	55.7	50.0	32.1	49.5	50.48
1936	31.4	26.8	43.2	44.6	55.0	62.4	67.4	67.6	62.8	55.0	43.4	39.8	50.0	
1937	40.0	35.6	36.2	43.9	54.7	61.8	68.6	71.8	63.4	53.7	46.2	36.4	51.0	
1938	33.0	33.4	39.4	46.1	53.2	62.4	69.4	71.0	63.0	56.0	48.8	38.1	51.2	
1939	32.6	36.2	35.8	44.0	52.4	61.5	68.2	70.6	63.0	55.2	42.9	36.2	49.9	
1940	25.8	32.0	33.8	42.3	53.7	61.1	67.6	66.4	62.7	51.0	45.0	38.7	48.3	50.08
1941	30.8	31.5	34.2	46.6	55.2	61.8	66.8	68.0	63.7	55.8	48.6	38.0	50.0	
1942	31.4	28.6	39.7	45.8	56.1	63.2	68.6	68.6	63.8	55.8	45.6	32.3	50.0	
1943	29.4	31.2	36.4	41.8	53.6	64.8	69.4	68.8	62.8	55.4	45.8	33.1	49.4	
1944	32.8	31.0	35.8	44.0	57.2	62.8	70.2	71.0	65.6	54.6	44.9	35.2	50.4	
1945	28.4	31.9	42.8	49.3	53.9	62.0	68.7	68.0	65.9	54.6	47.4	32.4	50.4	50.04
1946	32.9	30.4	42.6	43.4	52.3	59.8	65.7	64.9	63.2	56.2	48.3	37.8	49.8	
1947	35.2	30.8	36.2	43.4	52.0	58.4	69.8	68.0	63.6	56.9	42.6	32.8	49.1	
1948	27.8	29.2	37.3	43.6	51.4	58.2	67.8	69.3	62.4	53.1	48.8	37.8	48.9	
1949	36.6	35.4	37.7	46.2	52.8	65.0	71.0	70.0	62.6	55.8	45.1	38.4	51.4	
1950	38.9	31.5	33.5	42.1	50.5	61.3	67.8	66.9	59.9	54.4	48.2	37.1	49.3	49.70
1951	35.8	35.2	38.6	47.1	54.2	60.7	69.4	68.1	64.7	55.5	44.6	37.7	51.0	
1952	34.7	33.4	36.1	46.4	53.9	63.3	71.6	69.3	62.2	53.5	45.7	37.1	50.6	
1953	36.4	35.6	37.9	45.8	53.6	62.8	67.8	66.1	63.7	55.1	47.9	41.3	51.2	
1954	31.8	35.2	37.4	44.8	52.0	61.1	67.0	66.8	60.9	56.6	45.8	36.7	49.7	
1955	30.0	32.5	36.9	43.7	53.2	59.7	68.8	69.5	61.2	55.1	43.7	28.6	48.6	50.22
1956	32.9	33.6	34.8	42.4	48.7	60.8	66.3	66.8	60.8	53.3	46.1	39.9	48.9	
1957	27.2	34.1	37.8	45.3	53.0	64.4	68.8	66.6	64.1	53.5	47.2	40.6	50.2	
1958	34.1	26.7	37.1	44.8	51.0	58.0	66.5	67.3	61.5	52.0	46.6	30.0	48.0	
1959	30.0	29.1	35.9	44.0	54.0	59.9	66.6	67.9	64.5	54.9	46.2	38.1	49.2	
1960	33.0	35.5	31.8	44.1	53.5	61.5	67.1	66.4	62.0	53.4	47.4	31.8	49.0	49.05
1961	27.6	31.0	36.5	43.0	50.6	60.2	66.5	67.9	65.7	56.0	45.4	36.3	48.9	
1962	31.9	31.0	36.9	45.5	52.4	61.9	65.9	66.0	61.5	53.6	43.4	33.5	48.6	
1963	31.8	28.5	37.8	44.4	52.7	63.3	67.8	67.7	59.3	55.8	48.8	30.8	49.0	
1964	33.4	30.6	36.6	42.7	54.1	62.7	67.3	65.7	60.9	53.4	45.1	37.9	49.2	
1965	29.0	29.7	35.5	41.2	53.0	60.4	67.4	68.6	59.5	50.8	42.0	35.4	47.7	48.68
1966	29.6	30.5	36.4	40.6	49.5	60.6	67.4	67.6	59.2	51.3	45.9	36.1	47.9	
1967	35.2	29.0	32.5	40.8	47.5	58.7	66.2	65.7	60.6	54.5	42.6	37.7	47.6	
1968	28.9	27.5	38.3	45.2	53.0	60.5	67.8	66.9	62.8	57.0	45.1	33.6	48.9	
1969	32.8	34.4	37.5	46.3	53.7	63.8	67.7	66.2	63.2	53.2	46.1	36.1	50.3	
1970	24.8	32.6m	36.9	44.9	54.5	62.7	69.2	69.6	63.6	54.9m	47.2m	35.6	49.7m	48.88
1971	28.3	32.5	36.2	42.3	52.7	61.8	70.6	69.3	69.5	62.5	47.2	38.9	51.0	
1972	29.7	29.5	39.7	44.7	51.3	62.8	67.1	68.8	60.5	53.2	42.7	37.1	48.9	
1973	33.7	29.8	34.8	40.7	50.8	59.5	65.6	66.1	62.2	49.1	42.1	38.4	47.7	
1974	32.3	28.6	36.8	45.5	51.0m	58.1	68.6	71.1m	64.4	50.6	44.7	37.5	49.1m	
1975	36.8m	33.1m	34.2m	41.7m	54.1	61.1	72.0	71.9	64.6	57.4	50.7	37.4	51.3m	49.60
1976	30.2	36.0m	37.9m	46.5m	54.5	62.6	68.1	67.9	62.5	52.3	40.5	31.1	49.2m	
1977	24.6	30.4	41.7	46.6m	54.1m	61.4	69.1	70.5	63.6m	53.7	46.8	34.8	49.8m	
1978	29.7	25.9	34.0	43.3	53.1	66.0	68.7	72.3	m	55.0	47.7	39.1	m	
1979	35.9	24.5	39.5	44.8	57.1m	m	70.6	68.4	62.6	53.7	49.2	39.5	m	
1980	32.5	28.6	36.3	46.6	54.4	62.4m	70.0	70.9	64.0	52.9	42.7	32.4	49.5m	
1981	22.6	36.3	35.4	46.5	52.8	63.3	69.4	67.8	62.7	50.8	44.9	35.3	49.0	
1982	25.7	31.1	37.4	m	52.5	58.4	m	65.6	61.2	m	m	m	m	
Mean*	31.5	31.2	36.7	44.2	52.7	61.5	68.1	68.2	62.5	54.1	45.6	36.0	49.4	1951-80

* The standard period for temperature averages is thirty years. The normals for 1951-80 will be employed through 1990.

Figures followed by m, as 49.1m, indicate that several days were missing from the record for that month.

Nantucket Monthly Precipitation, 1847–1861—William Mitchell
1886–1982—Federal Weather Service

	Jan.	Feb.	Mar.	Apr.	May	June	July	Aug.	Sept.	Oct.	Nov.	Dec.	Annual	5-Year Average
1847	0.90	m	3.00	0.45	1.25	4.79	2.31	1.55	4.41	0.91	3.91	6.15	m	
1848	2.58	3.74	1.60	0.45	4.43	1.67	1.70	0.72	3.79	6.54	3.25	4.13	34.60	
1849	0.08	0.50	2.67	1.36	2.03	2.69	2.74	0.21	1.55	6.87	3.60	2.78	27.08	
1850	6.69	2.99	8.87	2.85	5.17	2.42	1.01	2.27	2.57	1.96	1.79	4.26	42.85	
1851	1.58	3.70	2.00	4.64	6.22	2.05	2.12	2.67	2.42	6.15	3.90	4.37	41.82	
1852	5.59	0.75	0.83	7.52	3.17	1.08	1.78	4.46	2.93	2.06	2.89	6.71	39.77	
1853	2.38	5.75	3.94	4.25	3.78	5.01	1.72	3.85	0.94	2.64	4.77	2.97	42.00	
1854	2.10	4.89	1.16	5.95	2.48	2.02	4.83	2.19	7.80	3.11	5.84	5.06	47.43	
1855	4.50	3.04	3.84	8.49	5.87	4.77	2.16	1.51	1.21	4.13	3.11	6.30	48.93	
1856	3.75	2.03	1.35	3.00	2.90	5.39	1.47	1.16	5.20	2.03	3.61	3.81	35.70	
1857	6.75	2.21	3.97	5.96	4.87	2.90	3.07	7.03	2.51	3.25	2.22	5.14	49.88	
1858	4.41	1.63	2.80	4.33	2.43	1.98	4.56	4.26	2.46	3.58	3.71	5.78	41.93	
1859	7.96	4.27	4.63	3.01	4.15	5.68	2.77	3.45	3.30	3.16	1.37	4.60	48.35	
1860	m	m	m	m	m	m	m	m	m	m	m	m	m	
1861	5.57	2.04	4.80	m	m	m	m	m	m	m	m	m	m	
Mean	3.91	2.96	3.13	4.02	3.75	3.27	2.48	2.72	3.16	3.56	3.38	4.77	41.70	
1886											2.25	4.93		
1887	2.97	3.97	2.84	6.23	1.75	2.12	2.10	4.35	1.99	1.81	2.54	4.60	37.27	
1888	3.48	1.50	3.14	1.43	7.87	1.51	3.68	0.87	7.30	4.99	6.49	3.45	45.71	
1889	5.03	4.23	5.46	4.02	2.26	3.45	2.92	11.05	3.12	6.58	7.80	2.07	57.99	
1890	3.52	2.72	6.07	1.17	2.48	3.49	2.90	2.81	8.33	6.72	0.89	2.70	43.80	46.19
1891	4.51	3.30	1.86	1.47	2.05	2.83	3.16	3.41	3.12	4.96	1.02	3.14	34.83	
1892	2.23	1.46	5.88	2.76	2.57	1.81	0.91	1.79	2.01	1.66	7.63	1.67	32.38	
1893	2.06	3.90	4.35	4.73	2.68	2.26	1.45	4.40	2.24	2.17	1.31	4.21	35.76	
1894	3.14	3.11	1.89	2.24	1.88	0.81	0.29	1.20	1.90	10.05	2.80	5.83	35.14	
1895	3.91	1.56	4.41	2.52	4.92	1.29	4.06	4.46	1.69	1.91	4.86	2.73	38.32	35.29
1896	1.57	2.67	5.97	0.62	2.35	2.43	4.12	1.38	2.06	5.03	2.29	2.68	33.17	
1897	2.59	2.69	3.05	4.47	2.30	1.64	5.32	2.66	1.31	1.63	3.90	3.17	34.73	
1898	2.76	1.87	2.56	2.97	3.53	0.63	2.93	2.20	0.83	3.69	5.15	2.22	31.34	
1899	2.74	4.53	5.66	1.52	0.77	2.08	1.99	2.08	1.88	3.06	1.54	1.08	28.93	
1900	3.20	4.86	2.95	2.61	1.65	1.50	1.89	1.56	2.59	2.57	3.96	1.88	31.22	31.88
1901	3.03	1.33	4.74	3.71	4.92	1.43	1.16	2.60	2.11	0.44	0.89	6.52	32.88	
1902	2.75	2.87	4.55	2.23	0.74	6.34	1.76	0.27	2.35	4.25	1.96	5.90	35.97	
1903	3.02	3.32	3.53	3.04	0.93	1.10	1.81	2.09	1.37	3.33	3.82	2.97	30.33	
1904	5.98	3.86	2.11	4.08	2.39	2.38	2.09	2.25	0.78	1.01	3.29	4.67	34.89	
1905	5.70	2.16	3.12	1.57	2.62	6.50	4.02	4.93	4.07	2.06	2.82	3.73	43.30	35.47
1906	4.93	3.94	7.41	2.17	2.36	1.21	4.50	6.93	2.72	2.33	1.84	4.58	44.92	
1907	5.33	3.12	4.62	2.90	4.23	2.17	3.32	1.76	4.35	1.99	6.69	5.49	45.97	
1908	3.78	3.71	2.74	3.55	1.27	1.66	1.00	4.28	2.98	4.97	0.95	4.89	35.78	
1909	4.54	4.88	3.34	4.40	4.32	2.30	0.98	1.72	3.71	6.39	1.85	4.23	42.83	
1910	6.90	3.41	2.74	2.95	3.36	6.06	4.18	2.67	0.61	4.72	3.46	4.33	45.39	42.97
1911	3.77	3.88	3.35	5.17	0.82	2.56	3.20	8.03	3.34	2.57	6.30	3.76	46.75	
1912	4.13	2.77	5.85	2.91	4.19	0.14	4.89	2.87	2.25	1.41	2.94	6.25	40.60	
1913	5.57	4.44	3.17	2.19	1.71	1.59	0.58	3.26	7.76	6.49	1.91	3.21	41.88	
1914	2.68	4.00	4.63	3.30	3.38	2.58	3.25	4.42	1.61	2.15	2.32	6.73	41.05	
1915	6.34	3.32	0.25	1.72	4.01	1.31	1.32	4.93	0.85	3.18	2.13	3.87	33.23	40.70
1916	2.03	4.04	3.60	2.90	4.35	4.89	5.02	1.05	1.44	1.92	2.55	3.24	37.03	
1917	2.68	2.96	5.85	4.21	4.22	7.69	3.32	1.56	2.37	4.59	0.62	2.13	42.20	
1918	2.71	2.22	2.42	3.84	1.44	3.19	1.47	1.62	2.06	2.12	1.53	3.65	28.27	
1919	4.83	1.86	3.81	2.46	4.67	2.82	4.76	7.17	3.45	4.25	4.20	3.67	47.95	
1920	3.84	7.00	3.46	3.86	4.15	3.58	1.98	4.43	1.18	3.96	3.32	4.24	45.00	40.09
1921	2.23	2.89	2.37	2.49	4.43	2.79	3.41	1.33	1.22	2.13	5.25	2.45	32.99	
1922	3.68	4.91	6.24	2.90	3.44	2.61	5.05	8.40	0.83	5.34	0.67	4.87	48.94	
1923	4.75	2.25	6.46	4.27	0.37	1.27	3.48	1.90	1.01	2.82	2.38	5.19	36.15	
1924	3.28	1.92	4.43	4.30	4.07	4.51	1.78	4.74	2.89	0.10	2.76	2.61	37.39	
1925	3.64	1.02	2.18	2.37	2.22	4.06	2.29	2.49	2.05	4.60	3.18	2.73	32.83	37.66

	Jan.	Feb.	Mar.	Apr.	May	June	July	Aug.	Sept.	Oct.	Nov.	Dec.	Annual	5-Year Average
1926	2.84	3.99	2.23	2.11	3.93	2.53	3.53	2.56	0.83	6.86	3.05	3.22	37.68	
1927	3.03	3.52	2.14	1.27	1.64	2.76	6.55	7.79	2.58	1.91	3.11	5.49	41.79	
1928	3.22	4.81	3.22	3.44	3.13	4.34	3.50	0.57	6.98	0.61	4.24	3.61	41.67	
1929	3.02	5.76	4.66	6.28	4.10	0.41	1.18	3.18	5.88	2.22	3.86	4.13	44.68	
1930	4.42	3.41	3.05	1.01	2.03	0.49	2.16	1.79	0.15	3.28	7.01	5.14	33.94	39.95
1931	3.23	3.30	6.30	3.69	4.24	6.55	5.88	3.49	2.84	5.57	1.68	4.05	50.82	
1932	6.30	1.60	4.52	1.27	2.66	3.56	0.66	1.54	3.51	7.66	4.72	3.06	41.06	
1933	2.73	4.72	7.34	4.78	1.62	4.78	1.01	3.99	7.54	8.31	2.80	5.05	54.67	
1934	3.30	4.22	3.22	2.73	2.23	2.33	0.86	2.21	3.37	4.89	2.54	3.48	35.38	
1935	5.19	2.99	2.71	3.83	2.41	6.09	5.73	2.15	5.21	2.76	5.40	2.97	47.44	45.87
1936	4.92	2.71	4.27	2.21	0.87	3.59	1.58	2.84	4.15	4.28	1.81	7.04	40.27	
1937	4.09	1.30	3.03	5.29	2.16	4.74	1.26	3.39	4.27	4.37	3.36	2.76	40.02	
1938	4.39	3.01	3.53	5.72	2.91	6.24	2.00	3.02	9.55	3.79	3.84	5.60	53.60	
1939	5.89	5.38	7.27	3.52	1.36	2.94	2.29	4.41	1.08	4.56	1.19	2.05	41.94	
1940	2.37	5.22	2.39	4.97	1.52	1.90	2.35	2.17	5.23	2.06	5.22	3.29	38.69	42.90
1941	3.45	1.81	3.83	4.79	1.92	5.90	5.46	4.17	0.49	3.80	2.02	2.58	40.22	
1942	4.24	2.74	7.42	0.90	2.11	1.63	2.18	7.12	2.46	3.70	3.40	4.56	42.46	
1943	4.48	3.76	4.57	2.82	4.00	1.33	4.10	4.03	3.54	3.72	3.50	1.10	40.95	
1944	3.58	2.38	6.46	4.23	1.26	2.62	1.04	0.57	2.67	2.39	8.76	3.39	39.35	
1945	4.38	5.07	1.84	1.80	3.44	5.65	3.97	1.72	0.69	2.97	6.38	6.59	44.50	41.50
1946	3.06	3.78	2.17	4.65	6.79	2.89	3.66	12.92	4.16	0.37	1.06	3.85	49.36	
1947	2.32	2.88	2.06	6.07	5.52	2.95	2.63	0.28	3.02	1.13	3.28	2.87	35.01	
1948	7.15	3.79	4.08	2.71	8.24	3.39	1.28	3.12	3.62	7.22	4.72	2.46	51.78	
1949	3.70	4.17	3.34	4.45	1.78	0.01	0.87	1.95	3.53	3.23	4.13	2.59	33.75	
1950	3.18	3.25	4.20	2.69	0.86	2.20	3.25	2.99	5.74	1.26	6.23	5.27	41.12	42.21
1951	3.48	4.36	3.69	2.17	4.12	0.96	1.45	3.82	1.98	5.06	3.77	5.27	40.13	
1952	6.29	8.07	4.58	2.59	3.22	0.66	0.15	5.87	0.73	2.01	2.04	4.74	40.95	
1953	8.24	5.37	6.22	8.41	1.86	0.21	5.86	3.15	4.53	4.35	7.83	3.92	59.95	
1954	5.10	2.36	2.62	3.84	3.61	0.72	1.12	4.80	5.00	1.29	4.48	6.39	41.33	
1955	1.21	2.77	3.92	4.69	1.33	1.90	1.52	4.66	2.58	5.44	5.09	1.31	36.42	43.76
1956	4.95	6.03	6.53	2.26	3.46	2.29	2.75	6.61	1.30	2.10	2.29	4.67	45.24	
1957	2.97	2.30	6.08	2.67	1.46	0.26	2.84	4.19	2.37	2.41	4.84	5.36	37.75	
1958	5.25	3.97	4.24	6.79	6.57	2.42	7.45	6.50	7.20	2.95	5.06	1.99	60.39	
1959	2.78	4.75	8.88	3.66	1.02	4.92	4.16	1.86	0.42	4.19	6.51	3.43	46.48	
1960	4.32	4.80	4.85	2.55	1.76	2.09	1.91	0.96	2.57	3.08	3.61	6.07	38.57	45.69
1961	4.06	4.50	4.30	5.88	5.69	2.16	6.16	1.91	3.25	6.15	2.41	3.35	49.82	
1962	4.86	5.14	0.97	3.81	0.59	5.01	3.60	3.85	3.95	7.45	7.44	4.06	50.73	
1963	4.39	4.46	5.45	2.52	4.68	1.80	2.58	4.80	6.59	3.92	3.49	4.56	49.24	
1964	5.32	5.60	2.06	5.34	1.08	0.59	2.78	2.04	6.26	3.92	1.20	6.40	42.59	
1965	5.17	2.41	2.02	3.21	0.71	1.10	1.85	0.68	3.01	0.88	2.63	1.64	25.31	43.58
1966	4.27	1.77	1.71	1.51	8.19	1.91	0.49	4.22	3.33	3.51	6.95	3.02	40.88	
1967	2.36	4.70	4.85	5.06	10.38	3.37	6.58	6.74	2.30	2.77	3.86	4.23	57.20	
1968	2.46	2.73	4.35	1.55	3.40	4.96	0.15	3.41	2.63	2.99	4.51	5.97	39.11	
1969	1.83	3.89	4.41	3.53	1.96	0.63	2.31	1.62	7.80	1.65	4.16	9.74	43.53	
1970	1.68	4.32	3.32	2.06	1.35	3.04	1.86	6.12	2.37	1.88	4.48	3.39	35.87	43.32
1971	3.05	4.91	2.35	2.44	5.43	0.25	2.62	2.30	0.07	1.60	3.84	2.28	31.14	
1972	2.84	2.89	6.34	4.34	3.96	2.79	1.56	2.36	9.49	4.27	5.80	6.88	53.52	
1973	1.19	3.40	3.40	7.24	4.35	2.90	9.12	3.51	2.59	5.37	2.14	5.90	50.89	
1974	4.32	3.06	1.58	3.65	3.35	4.48	0.07	2.08	3.44	2.26	3.31	3.28	34.88	
1975	4.98	3.51	4.20	3.81	2.92	2.42	1.08	3.82	1.79	2.70	5.79	3.93	40.95	36.05
1976	4.33	2.16	2.56	1.35	2.40	0.60	2.29	0.85	2.53	5.12	2.24	5.12	31.55	
1977	4.55	1.41	4.98	2.20	1.35	6.83	2.27	2.26	4.53	6.46	2.86	6.23	45.93	
1978	7.37	0.90	1.50	1.93	5.48	0.91	6.35	3.49	1.93	2.37	2.38	3.91	38.52	
1979	4.00	4.08	2.18	2.99	2.65	1.27	1.01	3.93	2.10	3.46	2.65	1.89	32.21	
1980	3.44	0.75	3.85	3.14	1.67	2.08	2.18	0.33	1.23	2.39	3.00	2.08	26.14	34.87
1981	2.72	3.31	0.67	1.94	1.80	4.38	0.76	1.81	1.52	1.48	3.22	6.89	30.50	

Temperature Extremes

Precipitation Data

Town Oct. 18, 1886 to Apr. 16, 1946

	Highest reading	Year	Warmest month	Year	Coldest reading	Year	Coldest month	Year	Normal	Maximum monthly	Year	Minimum monthly	Year	Maximum in 24 hours	Year
Jan.	64	1932	40.3	1932	-3.5	1888	23.8	1893	3.78	6.90	1910	1.57	1896	2.54	1939
Feb.	60	1930	37.2	1925	-6.2	1918	22.55	1934	3.39	6.99	1920	1.02	1925	2.77	1920
Mar.	68	1907	43.5	1921	6	1887	30.4	1916	3.88	7.42	1942	0.25	1915	3.22	1889
Apr.	79	1942	49.3	1945	15	1923	41.6	1917	2.95	6.28	1929	0.62	1896	2.81	1938
May	86	1895	57.2	1944	34	1917	48.1	1917	2.84	7.87	1888	0.37	1923	2.78	1888
June	90	1923	65.7	1930	42	1944	57.6	1903	2.68	7.69	1917	0.14	1912	4.60	1945
July	92	1919	71.0	1944 +	48	1891	63.9	1888	2.87	6.55	1927	0.29	1894	3.69	1935
Aug.	90	1930	71.8	1937	51	1910	64.2	1903	3.40	11.05	1889	0.27	1902	5.73	1889
Sept.	88	1931	67.6	1930	41	1888	59.6	1888	2.44	9.55	1938	0.15	1930	4.05	1938
Oct.	82	1941	58.5	1920	30	1928	48.8	1888	3.38	10.05	1894	0.10	1924	4.25	1932
Nov.	68	1935	50.0	1935	15	1901	40.0	1901	3.39	8.76	1944	0.62	1917	3.58	1930
Dec.	61	1927	41.6	1923	-3	1942 +	29.4	1917	3.75	7.04	1936	1.08	1899	2.62	1894
Year	92	1919	71.8	1937	-6.2	1918	22.55	1934	38.75	11.05	1889 Aug.	0.10	1924 Oct.	5.73	1889 Aug.

Airport 1946–1982

	Highest reading	Year	Warmest month	Year	Coldest reading	Year	Coldest month	Year	Normal	Maximum monthly	Year	Minimum monthly	Year	Maximum in 24 hours	Year
Jan.	63	1967	38.9	1950	-1	1970	22.6	1981	4.04	8.24	1953	1.21	1955	2.82	1953
Feb.	58	1976	36.3	1981	0	1979 +	24.5	1979	3.71	8.07	1952	.75	1980	2.32	1953
Mar.	62	1948	41.7	1977	7	1972 +	31.8	1960	4.06	8.88	1959	.97	1962	2.92	1968
Apr.	77	1976	47.1	1951	20	1954	40.6	1966	3.45	8.41	1953	1.51	1966	4.48	1953
May	84	1970	57.1 +	1979	28	1972	47.5	1967	3.30	10.38	1967	.59	1962	6.53	1967
June	90	1978	66.0	1978	35	1976	58.0	1958	2.16	6.83	1977	.01	1949	3.02	1967
July	92	1964	72.0	1975	47	1972 +	65.6	1973	2.66	7.45	1958	.07	1974	4.37	1978
Aug.	100	1975	72.3	1978	39	1973 +	64.9	1946	3.42	12.92	1946	.28	1947	3.67	1946
Sept.	86	1971	69.5	1971	34	1947	59.2	1966	3.35	9.49	1972	.07	1971	5.05	1969
Oct.	82	1971	62.5	1971	22	1966	49.1	1973	3.40	7.45	1962	.37	1946	3.21	1948
Nov.	74	1971	50.7	1975	18	1973 +	40.5	1976	4.03	7.83	1953	1.06	1946	4.95	1966
Dec.	59	1978 +	41.3	1953	-3	1962	28.6	1955	4.36	9.74	1969	1.31	1955	4.26	1969
Year	100	1975	72.3	1978	-3	1962	22.6	1981	41.94	12.92	1946 Aug.	.01	1949 May	6.53	1967 June

Pressure Data

Ten Lowest Barometric Pressures

Highest			Lowest			Ten Lowest	
Jan.	30.99	1890	28.35	1958		28.18	1954, September 11
Feb.	30.97	1920	28.57	1976		28.35	1958, January 8
Mar.	30.98	1943	28.36	1932		28.36	1932, March 7
Apr.	30.76	1895	28.82	1907		28.47	1923, March 7
May	30.59	1936	29.19	1945		28.50	1956, December 29
		1943				28.57	1976, February 2
June	30.54	1902	29.31	1923		28.58	1968, March 1
July	30.52	1892	29.25	1932		28.61	1914, March 1
Aug.	30.45	1918	28.71	1924		28.66	1940, February 16
Sept.	30.65	1947	28.18	1954*		28.67	1942, December 2
Oct.	30.65	1901	29.05	1927			
Nov.	30.81	1889	28.69	1904			
Dec.	31.02	1949	28.05	1956			

* 28.18 on September 11, 1954 during Hurricane Edna.

In the pre-Weather Bureau records on Nantucket, the highest reading noted was 31.03 inches on February 13, 1851, and the lowest was 28.30 inches on November 11, 1873.

Wind Data

Snowfall Data

Town Oct. 18, 1886 to Apr. 16, 1946

	Mean Speed Dir. mi/h	Extreme Speed Dir. mi/h			Max.			Max.	
Jan.	14.9 NW	69 NE 1932		7.3	39.5	1904	19.1	1905	
Feb.	14.9 NW	60 NE 1926		8.2	30.1	1899	12.1	1944	
Mar.	15.1 SW	66 SE 1914		5.1	22.9	1916	11.9	1916	
Apr.	14.6 SW	61 NE 1915		0.5	6.8	1887	4.8	1887	
May	13.3 SW	52 NE 1939		0.0	T	1917	T	1917	
June	12.5 SW	68 NE 1945		0.0	0.0		0.0		
July	11.8 SW	62 NE 1933		0.0	0.0		0.0		
Aug.	11.4 SW	59 NE 1931		0.0	0.0		0.0		
Sept.	12.3 SW	79 SW 1944		0.0	0.0		0.0		
Oct.	13.8 SW	53 N 1927+		0.0	0.2	1925	0.2	1925	
Nov.	14.3 NW	62 NE 1935		0.4	8.1	1904	8.1	1904	
Dec.	14.4 NW	62 NE 1930		4.6	24.1	1904	11.6	1904	
Year	13.6 SW	79 SW 1944		26.1	39.5	1904 Jan.	19.1	1905 Jan.	

Airport Apr. 17, 1946 to Mar. 31, 1982

	Mean Speed Dir. mi/h	Extreme Speed Dir. mi/h			Max.			Max.	
Jan.	14.7 NE	59 NW 1958		9.1	38.9	1965	17.8	1964	
Feb.	15.2 WNW	66 NW 1964		10.8	36.4	1952	20.1	1952	
Mar.	15.2 NW	73 N 1956		7.3	40.2	1960	16.1	1960	
Apr.	14.6 WSW	63 N 1967		0.9	9.5	1955	8.0	1955	
May	13.0 SW	49 N 1967+		0.0	0.0		0.0		
June	12.0 SW	39 NE 1947		0.0	0.0		0.0		
July	11.0 SW	42 S 1960		0.0	0.0		0.0		
Aug.	10.9 SW	72 SE 1954		0.0	0.0		0.0		
Sept.	11.8 SW	73 SE 1954		0.0	0.0		0.0		
Oct.	12.9 NW	69 E 1947		T	T	1977+	T	1977+	
Nov.	13.4 NW	70 NW 1947		0.3	2.7	1967	2.5	1967	
Dec.	14.1 WNW	57 W 1956		6.9	24.7	1963	15.5	1960	
	13.2 SW	73 N 1956+		35.3	40.2	1960 Mar.	20.1	1952 Feb.	

+ = Also occurred in earlier years
Wind speed data prior to 1928 were measured on 4-cup anemometers; these were found to overestimate true speed by about 20 percent; thus corrections have been applied since 1928 to all records.

T = trace, not measurable